Walt Disney's
NINE OLD MEN
& THE ART OF ANIMATION

other books by **JOHN CANEMAKER:**

The Animated Raggedy Ann & Andy (1977)

Winsor McCay: His Life and Art (1987)

Felix: The Twisted Tale of the World's Most Famous Cat (1991)

Tex Avery: The MGM Years (1997)

Before the Animation Begins: The Art and Lives of Disney Inspirational Sketch Artists (1997)

Paper Dreams: The Art and Artists of Disney Storyboards (1999)

by John Canemaker and Robert E. Abrams: *Treasures of Disney Animation Art* (1982)

by John Canemaker and Joseph Kennedy: *Lucy Goes to the Country* (1998)

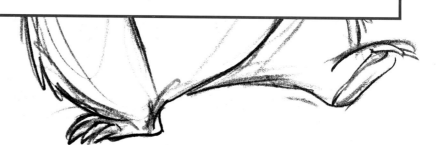

Walt Disney's
NINE OLD MEN
& THE ART OF ANIMATION

by JOHN CANEMAKER

EDITIONS

NEW YORK

For information address
Disney Editions, 114 Fifth Avenue, New York, New York 10011-5690.

Printed in the United States of America

Library of Congress Cataloging-in-Publication Data
Canemaker, John.
Walt Disney's nine old men and the art of animation / by John Canemaker
p. cm.
Includes bibliographical references and index.
ISBN: 0-7868-6496-6
1. Animators—United States—Biography.
2. Walt Disney Company. I. Title: Nine old men and the art of animation. II. Title.
NC975.C28 2001
778.5'347'092273—dc21
[B]

FIRST EDITION
10 9 8 7 6 5 4 3 2

Unless otherwise indicated, all artwork and photographs are from the Walt Disney Archives, Walt Disney Animation Research Library, Walt Disney Photo Library, and Walt Disney Imagineering Photo Library.

Book design by Holly McNeely

Visit www.disneyeditions.com

CONTENTS

Preface

first became aware of Walt Disney's Nine Old Men when, as a teenager in 1958, I read Bob Thomas's book *The Art of Animation*. In a black-and-white photograph spread over two pages, there they were: Les Clark, Wolfgang Reitherman, Eric Larson, Ward Kimball, Milt Kahl, Frank Thomas, Ollie Johnston, John Lounsbery, and Marc Davis. Nine great animators, described as "the group Walt has called 'the nine old men.'"

They looked middle-aged, not old, and the text did not explain that Walt Disney's sobriquet was a joking reference to President Roosevelt's description of his hostile Supreme Court as "nine old men, all too aged to recognize a new idea." But the book introduced to the public a filmmaking team whose ironic appellation has come to represent some of the highest achievements in character (or personality) animation. The Nine Old Men were, wrote Thomas, "the creators who add the touch of genius to the Disney features."

Think of your favorite moments and characters in Disney films from the 1930s through the 1970s—pathos, comedy, or action performed by heroes, heroines, villains, or clowns—and chances are most were animated by one of the Nine Old Men. Although the principles and techniques of character animation were forged by an earlier group at Disney, the Nine Old Men developed and refined those methods to a high degree of expressiveness and subtlety over a forty-year period. In films

OPPOSITE, *the two official group portraits of the Nine Old Men: the original black-and-white setup from 1958 and a subsequent color sitting in 1972.*

such as *Snow White and the Seven Dwarfs, Pinocchio, Fantasia, Bambi, Song of the South, Cinderella, Alice in Wonderland, Peter Pan, Lady and the Tramp, Sleeping Beauty, 101 Dalmatians,* and *The Rescuers*, among others, their virtuosity remains a benchmark against which all other character animation continues to be measured.

After Walt Disney's death in 1966, the studio publicity department perpetuated and built the legend of the Nine Old Men with a second and final group photograph, this time in color; magazines and books touted the group's accomplishments. It was an attempt to personalize the continuation of the art form that Walt developed by shining a spotlight on his closest, most loyal, and gifted collaborators.

But the term obscured the individual achievements of nine unique talents and temperaments, even as it purportedly illuminated them. One got the impression that the Nine Old Men were similar, interlocking, and equal parts of a smoothly running machine. Nothing could have been further from the truth, which makes them and their achievements all the more remarkable.

I saw how different they were from each other during my first visit to the Disney Studio in Burbank, California, in the summer of 1973. Researching an academic paper on the development of Disney animation, it was my good fortune to meet and interview several of the Nine. I found them to be individualists with widely differing artistic gifts, viewpoints, personalities, and degrees of ambition and competitiveness. That they had worked together so well for so long seems, upon reflection, miraculous. Of course, the attributes and liabilities of one man complemented another's, and they had much in common.

An example of their commonality is the fact that each man came to Disney merely seeking a job. All were affected by the Depression, a period of rampant unemployment in America; Disney was one of the few places offering paying jobs to artists. The studio's 1933 short *Three Little Pigs*, with its theme song "Who's Afraid of the Big Bad Wolf?," became a national symbol of the spunk and optimism of the American people. It also held a special relevance for the future Nine Old Men, who arrived at the studio with the wolf literally at their door. But the film also demonstrated a powerful new kind of animation that could communicate with vast audiences by inspiring as well as amusing them. The Nine Old Men stayed at the Disney studio for decades not merely out of loyalty; they became fascinated with character animation and excited by the opportunity to expand the art form's potential.

At the time of my first visit, the Nine were no longer working as a complete team. Wolfgang Reitherman was directing and producing the features; Les Clark was directing television shows; Eric Larson was in charge of training new animators; Marc Davis was designing Disney theme park attractions; Ward Kimball was less than a month from officially retiring. (In fact, I interviewed him at his home where I had the pleasure of riding the cars of his life-size train collection.) Only Milt Kahl, John Lounsbery, Frank Thomas, and Ollie Johnston were still animating. (I was privileged to observe the latter two gentlemen at their drawing boards animating scenes for 1977's *The Rescuers*.)

Over the years, during subsequent visits to research articles or books, I learned more about the Nine Old Men: their individual relationships with Walt and with each other; their predecessors and mentors at the studio upon whose inspirations and innovations the Nine built; their artistic breakthroughs and failures; their rivalries and their involvement in studio politics.

My closest friendships have been with Frank Thomas and Ollie Johnston, who have shared a unique and long-lived loyalty to each other as well as a deep dedication to their art. For over a quarter century we have shared phone calls, letters, and meals in different parts of the world, from Chicago, Illinois, to Cakovec, Yugoslavia. I have interviewed them countless times privately and in front of audiences large and small. I have been privileged to receive their warm encouragement and bracing "tough-love" critiques of my films and writings.

My books on animation history include biographies of Winsor McCay, Tex Avery, and even Felix the Cat; two recent books concentrated on aspects of preanimation processes at the Walt Disney Studio, namely the conceptual artwork and the storyboards. When I was finally offered the opportunity to write about the art of Disney animation itself—through the prism of the Nine Old Men, in a candid assessment of their lives and contributions to a special form of cinema—I leaped at the chance.

Both Frank and Ollie were, as always, enthusiastic. They encouraged me to tell the truth as I see it about the remarkable Disney animated films, how they were made, and who made them. Here, for example, is an excerpt from a September 28, 1998, letter to me from Frank Thomas:

> So have fun and choose a heart-wrenching philosophy that will make your audience cheer while wiping a tear from their eye. The subject is BIG, from the casual way it all started, to the resentments, the unhappiness that went hand in hand with the glow of success, the failures, the continuous changes in the studio and in Walt, down to his death and the degeneration of the whole idea surrounding the 9 Old Men.
>
> Don't give it that sugary Disney treatment, these are real people leading real lives. And what's more, they are real artists, extremely talented artists, and few talented writers, historians, teachers, critics, and animators themselves, ever get a chance to do a book with this much importance and potential. Go to it!

I have always wanted to write a book on animators modeled after Giorgio Vasari's *Lives of the Artists,* the famous sixteenth-century biographical work about the greatest artists of the Italian Renaissance. This project attempts to fulfill that wish.

My purpose is the same as Vasari's: "to revive the memory of those who adorned these professions, who do not merit that their names and works should remain the prey of death and oblivion."

WALT DISNEY'S
NINE OLD MEN
& THE ART OF ANIMATION

Snow White and the Nine Young Men

The old Disney studio on Hyperion Avenue in Hollywood had no air-conditioning and, in the summer of 1937, it was a very hot house indeed. "The animation lightboards had ordinary incandescent lightbulbs," remembered Marc Davis, "and they got so hot, especially in summer, you could burn your hands and arms on the glass."[1]

The "in-betweeners"—men on the lowest rung of the animation industry hierarchy who made the drawings between the animators' main sketches—sat bent over lightboards in the basement of the central building; on especially humid days, when the sweating 'tweeners stripped to the waist, it resembled nothing so much as a slave-ship galley.

Space was at a premium everywhere in the odd-looking studio, where makeshift buildings were cobbled together around a former organ factory, and an art-deco Mickey Mouse flashed a neon hello from the rooftop. Some artists were crammed four to a small room. It is said that the closeness at the Hyperion studio was an important factor in the development of Disney animation. Certainly information was readily shared and breakthroughs instantly communicated; but there could be no secrets of any kind in that close space and it was a combustible arrangement when artistic tempers flared.

The studio's psychological temperature was high at the time not from friction, but from excitement and energy. For the heat was on to finish (by the end of December) Walt Disney's first feature-length cartoon, *Snow White and the Seven Dwarfs*. After three years, the story was finally set, the characters defined and designed, and major sections of the animation

nearly done. The Bank of America loaned the necessary finishing funds (the final budget would be an unprecedented 1.5 million dollars), but there was still much to do.

During that long-ago hot summer, a good portion of the nearly six hundred employees toiled furiously from early morning till late at night. Twenty-four-hour alternating shifts were in place for the camera crew and the all-female Ink and Paint Department; and in those pre-union days everyone was expected to put in a half day on Saturday. Some dedicated top animators took on extra assignments, to assure they would be done properly, not perfunctorily.

In cubicles throughout the studio, animators and their assistants viewed test scenes over and over again on stand-up Moviolas. The machine's reels clattered loudly as film sped through their mechanical guts, and the noise reverberated through the halls mingled with snatches of dialogue ("I'm Snow White!"

A preliminary (or "rough") drawing of Grumpy by Vladimir Tytla. OPPOSITE, *a frame from* Snow White and the Seven Dwarfs *(1937), produced at Disney's Hyperion Avenue studio in Hollywood (*INSET*).*

All of the Nine Old Men were involved in the making of Snow White and the Seven Dwarfs *in varying degrees of responsibility.* AT LEFT, *a frame from the finished film;* ABOVE, *a rough animation drawing by Vladimir Tytla of Dopey blowing bubbles out of his ears.*

"The Princess?!") and bits of song ("Heigh-ho heigh-ho, it's off to work we go!").

The fever at the studio came from the thrill of doing something new. Walt Disney (henceforth known as Walt, to distinguish the man from the studio and the corporate entity) had "bet the farm" on a belief that he could bring character animation to unprecedented artistic and emotional heights. He believed that moviegoers would sit still for almost an hour and a half watching an animated cartoon; and he believed they would so deeply relate to the characters' personalities that they would laugh *with* them (not *at* them), fear for their safety, and weep at their demise. Such a major suspension of disbelief required storytelling and animation skills (or a magic) never seen before in moving cartoons. Hollywood cynics sneered, of course, calling *Snow White* "Disney's Folly."

But confident, stubborn thirty-five-year-old Walt—who was involved in every detail of the production—had chosen his creative staff well in all departments from story to layout, direction to animation. During the 1930s, several of the *Snow White* animators innovated a new kind of believable, expressive animation. Chief among them were Vladimir Tytla, who explored powerful inner emotions in animated characters for the first time; Grim Natwick, a specialist in animating the female form; Norman Ferguson, whose characters appeared to think and reason before acting; Hamilton Luske, a keen analyzer who codified real motions and actions; and Fred Moore, a natural-born animator whose graphic lines exuded visual appeal and life. More will be said in the chapters that follow about the important influence these mentors had on the future Nine Old Men.

These nine—Les Clark, Wolfgang Reitherman, Eric Larson, Ward Kimball, Milt Kahl, Frank Thomas, Ollie Johnston, John Lounsbery, and Marc Davis—were all involved in the making of *Snow White* in varying capacities and degrees of responsibility; most were at the beginning of their long careers. "These were exciting times," wrote Ward Kimball years later. "Walt was constantly upgrading the quality of the pictures and likewise demanding more and more from his artists. I was fortunate to be part of these halcyon days."[2]

In fact, that summer of 1937 found Kimball ready to quit. At age twenty-three the studio's youngest animator, he had advanced rapidly to that exalted status within two years of arriving in 1934. But now two of his *Snow White* sequences of the Dwarfs—comic songs about building a bed and eating soup—were cut from the film after he had spent months working on them. It wasn't because they lacked entertainment value; the sequences were as funny and charming as any that remained. But Walt, after much deliberation, had decided that both slowed the story; so they were out. Period. His decision was not lightly made; tossing aside nearly finished animation is always expensive because of the waste of time and talent, as well as the psychological effect on everyone involved.

At least Walt was aware of Kimball. That was not the case for several of the other young animators who later became the Nine Old Men, for they participated in *Snow White* in subordinate positions. Milt Kahl and Eric Larson, for example, toiled in a large room with two other animators on the myriad animals in

OPPOSITE, TOP, *two frames from* Snow White; SECOND ROW, LEFT, *roughhousing at a Disney studio sandlot baseball game, c. 1932 (Roy Disney in dark suit, Walt at far right);* CENTER, *Norman Ferguson;* RIGHT, *Ward Kimball and feline friend.* THIRD ROW, LEFT, *Vladimir Tytla picks up a* Snow White *assignment from director Wilfred Jackson and composer Frank Churchill;* CENTER, *Milt Kahl, c. 1939;* RIGHT, AND BOTTOM ROW, *expressive animation roughs by Fred Moore.*

2

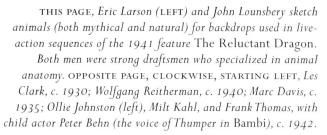

THIS PAGE, *Eric Larson* (LEFT) *and John Lounsbery sketch animals (both mythical and natural) for backdrops used in live-action sequences of the 1941 feature* The Reluctant Dragon. *Both men were strong draftsmen who specialized in animal anatomy.* OPPOSITE PAGE, CLOCKWISE, STARTING LEFT, *Les Clark, c. 1930; Wolfgang Reitherman, c. 1940; Marc Davis, c. 1935; Ollie Johnston (left), Milt Kahl, and Frank Thomas, with child actor Peter Behn (the voice of Thumper in* Bambi), *c. 1942.*

Snow White, including deer, squirrels, chipmunks, raccoons, mice, birds, and a turtle.

Some future Nine Old Men were assistants to older, more experienced animators who laid the groundwork of Disney animation principles and techniques. John Lounsbery was an assistant animator to Norman Ferguson, a master of broad comedy and an early experimenter with "thinking" characters; in *Playful Pluto* (1934), his famous extended sequence of the pup Pluto trying to remove flypaper from himself is considered a classic example of reinforcing a cartoon character's personality via thought processes. In *Snow White*, Ferguson and Lounsbery worked together on the wicked Queen after she turned herself into a crone.

Marc Davis assisted Grim Natwick, a specialist in the animation of females (he created Betty Boop for Max Fleischer) and one of Snow White's three main animators. Among Davis's duties was keeping the peace between Natwick and *Snow White* animation supervisor Hamilton Luske, an innovative action ana-

lyzer, who clashed with Natwick over Snow White's personality, design, and animation.

Ollie Johnston was an assistant animator to Fred Moore, who, although only one year older than Johnston, had joined the studio as a teenager and quickly became one of the studio's top animator-designers; Moore's appealing drawing style improved Mickey Mouse's design and established the look of the Seven Dwarfs.

Poor Wolfgang (Woolie) Reitherman animated the face in the wicked Queen's magic mirror nine times before it passed muster; then he saw his efforts practically obliterated by "special effects," such as smoke and distortion glass.

Les Clark, who had joined Disney in 1927, was a reliable and loyal workhorse who filled in wherever he was needed, including the animation of technically difficult scenes, such as Snow White's dance with the dwarfs.

Of all the future Nine Old Men, Frank Thomas was given a crucial assignment in the picture. It was young Thomas's task to

animate scenes in which the dwarfs grieve and weep over the body of Snow White after she has eaten the witch's poisoned apple. The groundbreaking sequence hints at the sensitive acting and emotions, subtle draftsmanship, and characterizations that were to come regularly in the near future from the group of nine.

By the early 1940s, Thomas, Clark, Reitherman, Johnston, Davis, Lounsbery, Larson, Kahl, and Kimball had begun their ascendancy. Several made significant contributions to *Pinocchio* and *Bambi* and all became part of the Animation Board, established in 1940, to help manage the animation department. "Its members advised on hiring, firing, assignments, moves, promotions, and training," wrote Frank Thomas and Ollie Johnston in their book *Disney Animation: The Illusion of Life.* "But, bit by bit, they were also determining what an animator should be and how he should be used more effectively." By 1950 "the board

5

ABOVE, *a scene from* Snow White and the Seven Dwarfs; OPPOSITE, *a self-caricature by animator Frank Thomas made in 1972 for the author, referring to two of the major creators of Dopey, the most popular character in* Snow White.

had settled down to a permanent group of nine supervising animators." It was then that Walt jokingly called them his Nine Old Men, after FDR's nickname for the Supreme Court justices whose alleged "lowered mental and physical vigor" threatened his New Deal programs.[3]

Some of the Nine Old Men's mentors left the Disney Studio—because of the 1941 employees' strike and World War II—or were moved into managerial positions; a few, who found it difficult to cope with the changes in the animation department, left of their own accord or were dismissed. Because of economic factors during and after the war, said Thomas and Johnston, the staff was reduced in all areas of production, "team effort was stressed to an even greater degree, and Walt began to rely more and more on animation to carry the films."[4]

And carry them it did, often gloriously. The continuing explorations of the Nine Old Men brought characters to the screen who exhibited a rainbow of emotions in situations ranging from broad comedy to action to pathos. Individually and as a group, the Nine gradually made significant changes in the Disney animation system. Formerly, two (or more) characters in a scene would be animated by separate animators; under the Nine Old Men, a single animator became responsible for animating all the characters in his scene. "The new casting overcame many problems," wrote Thomas and Johnston, "and, more important, produced a major advancement in cartoon entertainment: the character relationship. With one man now animating every character in his scene, he could feel all the vibrations and subtle nuances between his characters."

The "supervising" or "directing" animators, as they were called, assumed unprecedented power at the studio, not only in deciding whom to hire and fire, but in determining a film's content and direction. They could (and eagerly did) make changes in story development, layout, and direction. The process continued even up to the moments before they began to animate: several made thumbnail sketches planning out the action of their scenes "changing footages, shifting scenes, calling for long shots, close-ups, expressions, actions—anything that makes a stronger statement and richer characterization."[5]

They called it "sincere" animation, this rich, magical communication between moving drawings and audiences. "Sincerity is not having an openhearted approach to cartoon characters and situations," noted Stephen Holden in the *New York Times*, "but the ability to enter so completely into the world you are imagining that you inhabit the bodies and minds of the creations that spring from your pencil."[6]

The Nine Old Men made us believe in the most fantastic things because *they* believed in them: Bambi ice skating, Mickey Mouse giving a broom its marching orders, Sleeping Beauty's prince slaying a dragon, a hippo and an alligator in a pas de deux, two dogs having a romantic pasta dinner. The Nine became a dazzling repertory company of "actors with a pencil" (as the bromide goes), who, for all their differences, fit remarkably well together and changed roles nimbly with each new film; at various times they were lovesick squirrels, grandfatherly cats, princes and princesses, befuddled wizards, treacherous pirates, sexy pixies, kidnapping and dognapping harridans, the Mad Hatter and the March Hare, centaurs, and Pegasus, among other fabulous creatures.

Neither sex nor species (nor reality, for that matter) proved barriers to their performances, which were consistently real, genuine, honest, and true. The Nine Old Men are among the world's greatest tragedians and comedians, mimes, and clowns, charged with a power to make audiences laugh and weep, sometimes (as did Chaplin) in the same scene.

There was also a "Tenth Old Man," and that was Walt Disney himself. He was the lodestar and inspiration for the Nine, even as his interest in animation waned in the last decade of his life. He allowed them their power, confident that they shared his philosophy of entertainment and would make animated films the way he wanted them made.

There were also dangers and traps inherent in the new systems and in Walt's very idea of the "Nine Old Men." Among artists and animators who were not part of the charmed circle, it bred jealousy and discontent; one such animator regarded the Nine Old Men as "a group jealously guarding its prerogatives."[7] Who knows how much enriched the films might have been had other studio artists been allowed comparable creative power? Alongside their teamwork and dedication, there existed between some of the Nine Old Men a competitiveness that intensified over the years and ultimately affected the films adversely. And, with such a strong emphasis on animation, there was the pitfall of skewing productions too far toward performance to the detriment of story structure and development. These problems became all too evident after Walt died in 1966.

"We vowed that if we ever had a chance to run things ourselves," said Frank Thomas in 1974, "every sequence would be an animatable sequence, where we could conceive it in terms of what works good in animation, what will relate to the audience,

what a guy can have fun doing!" The films after Walt (such as *The Aristocats, Robin Hood, The Rescuers, The Fox and the Hound*) are certainly rich in personality animation and character relationships, the forte of the remaining Nine Old Men who were still animating in the 1970s (Thomas, Johnston, Kahl, and Reitherman). Many sequences sparkle, but generally the stories are weak in detail, structure, and development; one wag remarked that watching the 1970s Disney cartoon features was like watching great chefs cook hot dogs. It was not until a new generation—mentored by some of the Nine Old Men—took over in the mid-1980s that Disney animation once again received critical acclaim reminiscent of the *Snow White* and *Pinocchio* days of glory.

Both the values and faults in the concept and systems of the Nine Old Men are debatable; but it is important to note that for the current generation of animators and directors, who have spearheaded the recent resurgence of animation in all its variety, the Nine Old Men have had a considerable influence. Years from now, when animation morphs into new art forms as yet unknown, the work of the Nine Old Men will continue to be a significant, essential source for study and inspiration.

Future artists and researchers will want to know who the makers of these remarkable images were, much as we would love to know details about the lives and work of the creative teams in Renaissance art guilds. The lives and art-making methods of the Nine Old Men shed light on a certain period in film history at a particular Hollywood fantasy factory whose creations "represent America to more people than the bald eagle."[8]

"The most important aim of any of the fine arts," Walt Disney once said, "is to get a purely emotional response from the beholder."[9] This each of the Nine Old Men surely did, and they did it with pencils "charged with intelligence and humanity, tons of paper, and the persistence of vision."[10]

It is time to meet the Nine Old Men, in the order in which they arrived at the Disney Studio.

John—
Walt + Freddie Moore
created this guy — I just
animated him along with a
bunch of other guys

Frank Thomas →

INSET TOP, *eighteen-year-old Leslie James Clark in 1925, the year he met Walt Disney; film frame from "The Sorcerer's Apprentice" section of* Fantasia *(1940);* INSET BOTTOM, *a 1947 King Features Syndicate newspaper column "Seein' Stars by Feg Murray" featured Les Clark.*

CHAPTER one

Les Clark

In the summer of 1925, Leslie James Clark served Walt Disney ice cream at a confectionery located on Vermont Avenue at the eastern edge of Hollywood. Disney's small animation studio was across the street and Walt, his brother Roy, and their employees often ate lunch at the candy store.[1]

Clark, a shy high school student who waited tables part-time, "was always interested in art" and "loved cartoons and animation." His favorites were Felix the Cat and Paul Terry's Aesop's Fables. "I used to sit through two or three features to see the cartoon run over again," he once said. "I guess I was destined to become an animator, even though I didn't know it at the time."[2]

Clark's meeting Disney was fortuitous, for twenty-three-year-old Walt was at the beginning of his extraordinary career. The Disney brothers' company was less than two years old, founded in 1923 soon after Walt arrived in Los Angeles. In Kansas City, his first cartoon studio went bankrupt; in the movie capital, with business-minded Roy and a contract for a series of short silent films, he started over.

Disney's Alice Comedies starred a real little girl in a cartoon world. Live action of Alice and her pals was filmed in an empty lot on Hollywood Boulevard three blocks away from the candy store where Clark worked. The cartoons were made even nearer: at 4649 Kingswell Avenue, a tiny rented storefront was crammed with a dozen artists and staff—including former Kansas City associates and friends, such as Ub Iwerks, Hugh and Walker Harman, and Rudolf Ising.

That summer of 1925, with money steadily coming in from the Alice series, the Disney brothers decided to expand their operation. They bought a vacant lot a mile away near Griffith Park Boulevard, where they would build their own studio and move into it in the spring of 1926.

Over the next thirteen years, 2719 Hyperion Avenue, the new studio's address, became a beehive of mismatched buildings and bungalows constructed haphazardly as the Disney company steadily grew. Today the site is a supermarket; the original buildings, abandoned when the Disney studio moved to larger quarters in Burbank in 1939, are long gone. To animators around the world, however, 2719 Hyperion remains a magical location: the birthplace of Mickey Mouse and other cartoon immortals, the spot where many of the greatest animated films were made, and where the new American art form of character animation was defined and perfected.

Walt complimented Les Clark on the lettering he made for the menus on the mirrors at the candy store. Two years later in 1927, about to graduate from Venice High School, Clark got up the nerve to ask Walt for a job. "Bring some of your drawings in and let's see what they look like," he recalled Walt saying. At the Hyperion studio, Clark showed his samples, which he admitted were freehand copies of cartoons in *College Humor*.[3] But Walt admired his "swift, deft" graphic line and hired him.[4]

Clark graduated from high school on a Thursday and jubilantly reported to work the following Monday (February 23, 1927), though Walt warned him "it might just be a temporary job."[5] The "temporary" job lasted nearly half a century. By the

At the Walt Disney Studio on Hyperion Avenue, circa 1930: standing left to right: Jack King, Dick Lundy, Burt Gillett, Ub Iwerks, Walt Disney, Carl Stalling, Wilfred Jackson; kneeling left to right: Johnny Cannon, Norman Ferguson, Merle Gibson, Ben Sharpsteen, Les Clark.

time he retired in 1975, Les Clark was a senior animator and director, and the "longest continuously employed member of Walt Disney Productions."[6]

Dependability and a quiet determination to succeed were Clark's outstanding traits. The eldest of twelve children, he was unusually self-contained and mature. In fact, he was his family's main breadwinner. His father, James Elliot Clark, had made a modest living as a carpenter until the day he fell off a roof; his injured back incapacitated him from the late 1920s through the Depression. "I can always remember looking up to Les," recalls his brother Mickey Clark, "the supreme person as far as all us kids were concerned."[7]

At the turn of the century, James, a large man of English and Irish extraction, married "spunky" Welsh-English Lute Wadsworth in or near Salt Lake City, Utah. Both were Mormons, but "religion didn't play a strong role in our family," says Mickey Clark.[8]

Les, the Clarks' first child, was born on November 17, 1907, in Ogden, Utah, and attended grade school there.[9] Their fifth child, Marceil, who was born in 1914 in Idaho, remembers that her father owned a motion-picture theater in Utah or Idaho before getting into house construction.[10] According to Mickey (their seventh child), it was two years after *he* was born in 1918 in Twin Falls, Idaho, that his parents moved their growing family to California. First they settled in the Santa Monica–Venice–Ocean Park area, then in Glendale in the 1930s. Until his accident, James Clark did meticulous carpentry work and built houses mostly for other contractors.

Five more children were born in Los Angeles. "My mother was rather harassed from all the children," recalls Marceil Clark Ferguson, but "my dad loved babies."[11] After James's accident, the

family's finances went from precarious to penurious. Mother Lute was a proud woman who refused outside assistance. Instead, she made the family a self-sufficient unit in which each child performed household duties.[12] "Mother had us all working," recalls Mickey. "Saturdays I had to scrub floors and did the washing, ironing. We all had our chores to do." In addition to Les, several children had part-time jobs. For example, after school and on weekends Mickey, at age eleven, worked at the Venice pier pulling younger children on a pony ride. "Money I made there helped put food on the table," he says.

"There were trying times," admits Mickey. How tough were things for the Clark family? Sometimes a free meal was supplied by corn the kids stole from a field on Walnut Street above Ocean Park. When the gas was shut off because a bill went unpaid, the family built a fire in the backyard to cook food and boil water. As for clothes, "it was mostly the younger ones getting the older ones, what they outgrew," says Mickey, who wore hand-me-downs until his middle teens. "I remember becoming quite a sewer because I would take a pair of pants and recut them to fit me from one of my bigger brothers."[13] Les disrupted his high school schedule and delayed graduating because he skipped a semester to work, in order to afford school clothes for the next semester.[14]

Yet, for all their difficulties, the family was a loving one, according to surviving members. Sometimes Father, who had a temper, gave swift back-of-the-hand discipline "if you got out of line." More often, he was "despondent" because he was unable to support his family. It was his energetic wife who held them together. "She was the matriarch," says Mickey. "You give birth to twelve children and raise them through the good times and the bad, it has its imprint."[15]

Their mother's imprint can be seen in the independent, self-contained personalities all the Clark kids developed. "We all helped each other," says Mickey, "but we had to be able to take care of ourselves."

Les's job at Disney became the financial mainstay of his family throughout the Depression; eventually he found a job for his father as a guard at the Disney studio gate, and one for sister Marceil in the Ink and Paint Department. "He was an angel," says Marceil of Les. "He was our God. He looked after us, gave us money when he had it, and expected a certain amount of discipline from us. He was just so great."[16]

Of the Clark siblings, only Les and Marceil showed a talent for drawing. Mickey recently recalled a "fantastic charcoal drawing" of a police dog his brother made in high school. Les's father wanted him to be a doctor and warned against a career in art "'cause you can't make money at it." Les dutifully passed the

TOP: The Clark brothers in Hollywood in the 1940s, left to right, Lewis, Bill, Mickey, Les, and Jim; MIDDLE:*Walt checks in with Disney studio guard James Clark, Les's father;* BOTTOM: Frolicking Fish, *a 1930 Silly Symphony full of the rhythmic patterns of movement Les Clark excelled in.*

entrance exam to the University of Southern California and seriously considered the medical profession. His mother's father was, in fact, a doctor who had crossed the country to Salt Lake City on a wagon train in the 1800s. Les fondly remembered sitting with his maternal grandfather on clear Utah nights, looking at and discussing the stars.[17]

Disney's job offer changed Clark's life. Throughout his lengthy career he repaid Walt with loyalty and a dogged striving to improve his work. In return, he gained a knowledge of the animation business from the ground up.[18] During Clark's first year at the studio, he happily toiled in the industry's lowest entry-level positions: for his first six months he operated the animation camera, then spent a subsequent six months as an inker-painter. That is, he traced hundreds of animation drawings onto sheets of clear celluloid acetate ("cels") in ink with a crow-quill pen and painted them on the reverse side with opaque colors (black, white, and gray only, in those pre-Technicolor days).

Clark entered animation at a pivotal time and participated in events that shaped not only Disney's future but the history of the art form itself. When he arrived, the Alice series was winding down and a series starring a new character named Oswald the Lucky Rabbit was beginning. Ub Iwerks, who became Clark's mentor, was the studio's top animator, capable of turning out large numbers of cleverly animated drawings each day.

Ub and Walt, both born in 1901, had been business associates as teenagers in 1919 in Kansas City. They were a great team, whose contrasting personalities and artistic abilities complemented each other. Quiet, shy Iwerks communicated primarily through his impressive, facile draftsmanship; Walt was an outgoing salesman with limited drawing ability. His greatest creative talent lay in constructing entertaining stories around believable cartoon personalities, an ability that Ub lacked and had little interest in.

Walt dominated the studio and controlled every aspect of the filmmaking process. At impromptu story meetings, he shaped gags into a narrative, timed the animation after it had been drawn, and filled out the exposure sheets, which cameramen

used to shoot the scenes. Sometimes he ordered a special "pencil test" (a film shot from roughly drawn preliminary animation) in order to study the action's effectiveness before committing the drawings to ink and paint; often he sent scenes back for revisions.

Walt was groping toward a new type of animation that incorporated the "stylistic conventions of live-action films" with emotions derived from the characters' personalities. "I want characters to be somebody," he said in 1927. "I don't want them just to be a drawing!"[19]

Clark couldn't help but notice quiet dissension among the animators due to Walt's strong personality. The boss's demeanor at work was different from what it was over a lunchtime confectionery counter. He behaved, well, like a boss. He clashed often with some artists about their work, and in turn they grumbled about Walt's impatience, verbal abuse, and staff firings. Several of the Kansas City animators had ambitions to open their own studios and were biding their time until opportunity beckoned.[20]

Even Iwerks was not immune to Walt's demands. They had ongoing differences regarding the timing of characters' actions and Iwerks's method of animating "straight ahead." That is, Iwerks preferred to make every drawing one after the other, from, say, drawing A through drawing Z. Walt preferred the "key-pose" method, in which a head animator makes main (or "extreme") poses of an action and an assistant fills in the "in-between" drawings. The key-pose method would allow the already speedy Iwerks to turn out even more animation, a saving of time and money. Eventually Walt pressured Iwerks into seeing things his way.

Oswald the Lucky Rabbit was a moderate success and in March of 1928 Walt went to New York to renegotiate his contract. But, to his shock, the distributor to the series asked him to accept inferior terms. If he did not, Oswald would be taken from him, for the character's copyright belonged to Universal Pictures, not Disney. In addition, the distributor said he had secretly signed up Walt's animators—with the exception of Iwerks—and they were prepared to leave him to work on Oswald at a new studio. Les Clark was not approached;

although he had risen to "in-betweener," he was still considered a greenhorn.

Walt refused the distributor's offer and returned to Los Angeles. There, Iwerks thought up a new character to replace the stolen rabbit. It was, of course, the mouse that Walt's wife, Lillian, named Mickey.

Back at the studio, the soon-to-depart animation crew finished the remaining Oswalds on Disney's contract. (One can only imagine the stressful working environment.) In a backroom Walt secretly worked with Ub designing the new mouse character and creating his first film, *Plane Crazy* (1928). Mickey's circular face and torso, tubelike appendages, and white mask on a black head were a generic formula used by all the studios. Ear shapes mainly distinguished one character from another: Felix the Cat's sharp points, Oswald's oblong lozenges, and Mickey's rigid globes. "The reason that Mickey was drawn in circles," explained Clark to Michael Barrier years later, "was that it was easier and faster to draw: the round head, the round body, the round fanny, and so forth."[21] Iwerks, facile master of loopy, eccentric patterns of rubbery action, once made six hundred animation drawings in a single day. Small wonder he completed *Plane Crazy* by himself in only two months.[22]

Clark admired Walt's determination and strong ego. "I think that is what enabled him to surmount the difficulties on Mickey and get it going," he told Frank Thomas and Ollie Johnston. "I mean, he was fighting real odds."[23] A new young man, Wilfred Jackson, talked his way into a job during this difficult period. "I needed to learn how to make cartoons," Jackson said years later. "[Walt] said he didn't know if there was going to be a studio here in a week anyway. I thought that's a funny way for a guy to be talking. In a week everybody walked out except two or three of them."[24]

In general, there would always be a difference in attitude toward Walt between novices trained on the job (including all of the Nine Old Men), and animators who came to Disney's with prior experience. With exceptions, most of the former were more loyal to and fond of Walt and his ways than the latter. Jackson (who became one of Walt's best, most meticulous directors) was, like Les Clark, devoted to the man who gave

OPPOSITE PAGE, *two caricatures by Ub Iwerks, Les Clark's mentor, of himself* (RIGHT) *and Clark animating in a padded cell, circa 1927.* THIS PAGE, *original animation drawings by Ub Iwerks for* Steamboat Willie *(1928), the first Mickey Mouse cartoon with a soundtrack.*

him his start. "It wasn't just because he was the boss," Jackson once said. "It wasn't just bread-and-butter. Somehow it was the most important thing in the world to me to get what Walt wanted in the picture." [25]

Plane Crazy found no distributor. Nevertheless, Walt optimistically (or bullheadedly) went ahead in May with a second Mickey Mouse short called *The Gallopin' Gaucho*. Iwerks again animated the entire film quickly, with Clark assisting with in-betweens. As this short was being completed, however, Walt decided to distinguish his product by building a third Mickey short (*Steamboat Willie*) with a sound track.

The previous year, Al Jolson had spoken and sung in his inimitable style in Warner Brothers' *The Jazz Singer* (1927). Audiences were thrilled and Hollywood at last saw the potential of movies with synchronized sound tracks. "Walt was always trying something new," said Clark years later. "Sound had just come in and hadn't been proven. There were still distributors and picture makers wondering whether they should convert the cameras to twenty-four frames per second." [26]

Clark once explained how *Steamboat Willie*'s basic technical problems were surmounted:

Wilfred Jackson worked closely with Walt. His mother was a musician and he brought a metronome to the studio and they'd work out these various speeds we'd animate to. We worked with an exposure sheet on which every line was a frame of action. We could break down the sound effects so every eight frames we'd have an accent, or sixteen frames, or twelve frames. And on that twelfth drawing, say, we'd accent whatever was happening. A hit on the head or a footstep or whatever it would be to synchronize to the sound effect or the music. [27]

Iwerks animated the film at his usual breakneck speed (it was completed in two months), Clark assisted by in-betweening drawings, and Jackson animated a brief scene of Minnie Mouse running along a riverbank. Following is Walt Disney Archives director David R. Smith's account of the exciting evening in 1928 the film was tested with sound:

Then came the big night. The opening scenes, animated by Ub, had been put on a loop of film. Roy stationed himself outside a window of the studio on Hyperion Avenue with a projector (so the projector noise would not be heard). Ub had rigged up a microphone and a speaker, and the speaker was placed behind the bedsheet that was being used as a screen. [Animator] Johnny Cannon was there—he could make funny sounds with his

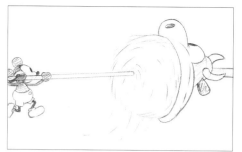

voice; Ub and Les Clark were there with sound effects, and Walt did Mickey's voice. In the audience were Ub's wife, Roy's wife, Walt's wife, Hazel Sewell, and Jackson's sweetheart, Jane Ames. Walt and the boys ran the film over and over, trying to perfect the timing of the sound effects with the action on the screen. The animators, if not the captive audience, were fascinated with the results. Each of the men took turns going out in front of the screen to watch. Ub recalled: "It was wonderful; there was no precedent of any kind. I've never been so thrilled in my life. Nothing since has ever equaled it. That evening proved that an idea could be made to work."[28]

"It was quite a time," Clark once recalled in his understated way. "The illusion of sound with the action was what was so pleasing and so convincing to people."[29] Although it was not the first cartoon with sound (there had been earlier attempts by the Fleischer and Terry studios), *Steamboat Willie* was the first to imaginatively integrate music, voice, and effects into an entertaining and believable whole.

Walt dashed to New York with a silent print of the film to record the soundtrack on rented equipment. After some technical difficulties, *Steamboat Willie* opened at the Colony Theater on Broadway on Sunday, November 18, 1928, and proved a hit with moviegoers and film reviewers. The trade paper *Variety* said: "It's a peach of a synchronization job all the way, bright, snappy and fitting the situation perfectly. . . . With most of the animated cartoons qualifying as a pain in the neck, it's a signal tribute to this particular one. . . . Recommended unreservedly for all wired houses."[30]

The little Disney studio plunged into the production of a series of Mickey Mouse shorts in which music and other sounds were built around the character's actions. A second series called Silly Symphonies, started in 1929, subordinated action to music. Now that sound tracks controlled the majority of the timing of the pictures, Walt, according to Clark "spent his time on gags, stories, and getting pictures out."[31]

To handle the increased production load, he began recruiting experienced New York animators; Ben Sharpsteen, Burt Gillett, Jack King, and Norman ("Fergie") Ferguson arrived at the studio between March and August 1929.

Ferguson's work truly came alive on the screen. His roughly drawn but eloquent, pantomimic acting implied a thought process in cartoon characters, particularly the dumb but lovable pup Pluto. Fergie's "acting animation" (in contrast to

Iwerks's action animation) involved audiences more fully in the characters' predicaments by making their personalities believable. It was the direction Walt wanted animation to go in and Fergie's star rose rapidly at the studio, as did his influence on the other animators.

Iwerks animated most of the first Silly Symphony, *The Skeleton Dance* (delivered on May 10, 1929), which also marks Les Clark's debut as an animator: a scene of a skeleton playing the ribs of a bony buddy like a xylophone. In January 1930, Iwerks, fed up with continuing disagreements with Walt, resigned to start his own studio. For about a decade, he produced shorts starring unappealing characters, such as Flip the Frog and Willie Whopper, who wandered through plotless, meandering stories filled with comic visual non sequiturs. When his studio failed, Iwerks returned to Disney in 1940, not as an animator but as an inventor of special-effects equipment, for which he eventually won two Academy Awards. To this writer, Clark fondly remembered Iwerks, the best and most respected animator of his day, as a "very patient" teacher and "very gifted man."[32]

Clark emulated his master well. Early in his career he was known for animating smoothly rhythmic ("ripple") actions that repeat in pleasing cycles and patterns of motion. "That came out

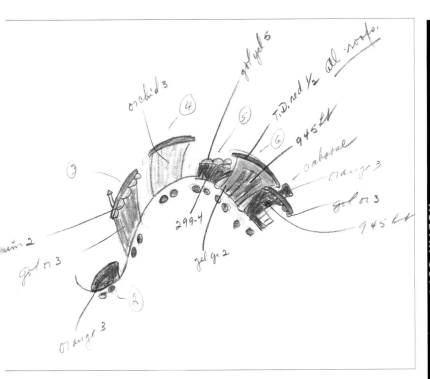

OPPOSITE PAGE, the wild cartoon-y style of Ub Iwerks as seen in Steamboat Willie; THIS PAGE, *Les Clark's animation of the train to Baia from* The Three Caballeros *(1945) shows Iwerks's influence*

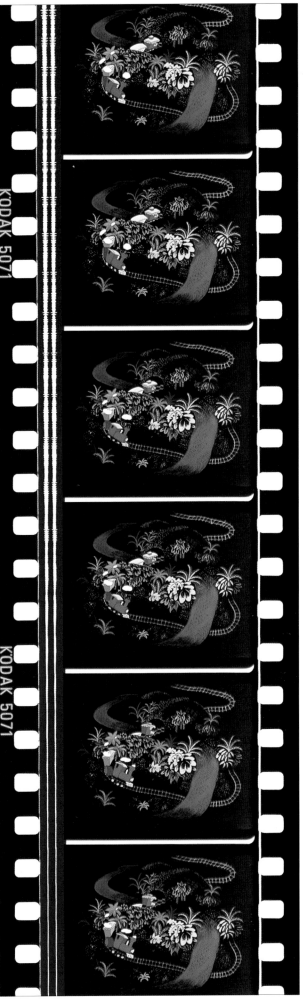

of working on the Silly Symphonies," explained Clark in a late interview, "which was rhythmic to music and to a musical beat for most of it. Walt gave me an awful lot of rhythm animation to do, so I guess he liked it."[33]

Over the years, the pupil surpassed his teacher. Clark's draftsmanship skills and versatility as a personality animator developed way beyond what Ub Iwerks was capable of. But echoes of the magical, cartoony Iwerks always remained in Clark's work. A charming example is the little train to Baia in *The Three Caballeros* (released in 1945), chugging and puffing on crayon rails to a bouncy samba beat through stylized jungle landscapes. The childlike choo-choo moves like a sentient toy: a Slinky, stretching as it climbs over small hoops representing mountains, catching up with itself at the peak, then unbunching cabin-to-caboose to descend nonchalantly into a blue lake, and emerge on the other side. "He carries on [from Ub] what is essentially choreography," says animation historian and author John Culhane.[34]

Clark learned his craft, he claimed, "from working with the fellas and from Walt," who was "so far ahead of us even then [in knowing] what he wanted to do. We couldn't understand some-times why he was giving us hell for something we thought was acceptable. Then later on we knew what he was talking about."[35]

WALT DISNEY'S NINE OLD MEN

In 1929 Walt paid for some animators to attend figure-drawing classes at the Chouinard Art Institute in downtown Los Angeles.[36] Through the classes, Clark (who lacked formal art training) was able to improve his draftsmanship and bolster his fragile confidence as an artist. When an after-hours art school started on the studio lot (from 1932 to 1941), he attended as many classes as possible.

"He tried awfully hard," says Frank Thomas. "He's the only guy I know at the studio who continued going to art school the whole time that he worked there. Other guys could say, well, I'm too good to go to art school. I don't need to sit in on life drawing classes with a bunch of beginners. Les wouldn't care. He needed to keep working to learn more and he studied what the other guys were doing. He'd talk to you about it."[37]

Under Walt's driving leadership, basic principles of animation and communication were discovered (or rediscovered) and codified. "Walt said, 'Work in silhouettes so that everything can be seen clearly,'" according to Clark. "'Don't have a hand come over a face so that you can't see what's happening. Put it away from the face and make it clear.'" Techniques that gave vitality and life to animation, such as "squash-and-stretch," were particularly important, Clark once remarked. "From one picture to another, we found out that if we pulled something out and brought it back to its normal volume, why, it would look good," he said. "And I remember one time we were very excited with 'follow-through,' where one line would follow through to the next. It was a wagon coming down a hill or something turning, and one drawing flowed into the other."[38]

Clark used plenty of squash-and-stretch and follow-through on Clara Cluck, a minor character in several Mickey shorts, who was sort of a barnyard Florence Foster Jenkins. Clark's Cluck is an operatic hen suffering from delusions of talent. Reaching for (and unfortunately hitting) a high, excruciating squawk, her ample bosoms heave dangerously and the silly feather in her hat takes on a life of its own. "Walt liked what I did on her because I kept everything moving," Clark once said, whose affectionate animation of the buxom bird made her touching as well as funny.[39] "You had a lot to work with on her," he once deadpanned.[40]

Walt insisted that all the animators share their creative discoveries and technical information. A photograph taken at the Hyperion studio in May 1931 shows how physically easy it was to comply with his request. Clark—then twenty-three years old, thin, and earnest looking—sits in a small room with Norman Ferguson and two other animators, each young man elbow-to-elbow at animation drawing tables. The proximity to helpful advice ("Hey, Fergie, what's wrong with this drawing?") and an open exchange of ideas ("I think the character needs more squash here.") was remembered by Hyperion studio veterans as a crucial factor in the development of Disney animation.

The acting that Ferguson got into his characters came from spontaneously putting lines down on the paper quickly, almost improvisationally, without concern about details. "Fergie roughs," they were called. Walt approved and "felt that if you roughed out an action," Clark once said, "you could see much faster whether it would turn out the way Walt wanted it to. If it didn't, discard it and make changes. You didn't have to throw away a lot of cleaned-up work." Assistants and "breakdown" artists were hired to clean up the roughs which, according to Clark, "helped us exaggerate more and to use more freedom in our drawing. Psychologically, it had a better effect on animators" by encouraging experimentation.[41]

Walt was not an articulate man, according to Clark. "He talked a lot, and sometimes you didn't understand what he wanted, what he was after. Maybe he didn't either, until he saw something he liked."[42]

By 1930, Clark was a full-fledged animator with numerous Mickey Mouse and Silly Symphony films under his belt. "In order to become an animator of any stature," said Clark in 1976, "it took some time. In that time, you learned to get along with [Walt] or not. You would have gotten over any personal differences. It may be that in the beginning, before the animator had a chance to show what he could do, Walt would let individual personality [differences] color his opinion of him; but not when an animator did a good job."[43]

In 1930, Clark acquired a new assistant named Fred Moore, age nineteen. Moore, like Ferguson, rose rapidly to the top ranks of animators and made important contributions to the Disney animation style. His drawings held enormous charm and he had a natural flair for animation. "Like some Renaissance artist filling his canvas with centaurs," writes animation historian Michael Barrier, "Moore drew fabulous animals that seemed to be made of flesh and blood."[44]

Moore blossomed as a major design and animation talent in 1933 on *Three Little Pigs*; and with Walt's blessing, he redesigned Mickey Mouse. "He streamlined the character, made the proportions a little more graceful than the circle upon a circle upon a circle," said Clark.[45] Moore's magic pencil sculpted the mouse's rigid circular body into an expressive pear shape, enlarged his head, and gave him cute, childlike poses that increased his visual appeal and expressiveness. But "animation came too easily to him," Clark once observed, perhaps with a bit of envy. "He didn't have to exert any real effort."[46]

Moore and Ferguson soared to great heights; however, by the early 1950s, both were gone from the studio. Promoted to director, then demoted back to animator, Fergie had his share of run-ins with Walt; Moore was a self-destructive alcoholic. Their professional demise also occurred because both were untrained, intuitive artists. They did not (or could not) adapt to the sophisticated changes in drawing style and subtle acting that developed with the rise of the Nine Old Men. "It was tragic," Clark once said of Moore and Ferguson. "They had not followed what the studio had progressed in."[47]

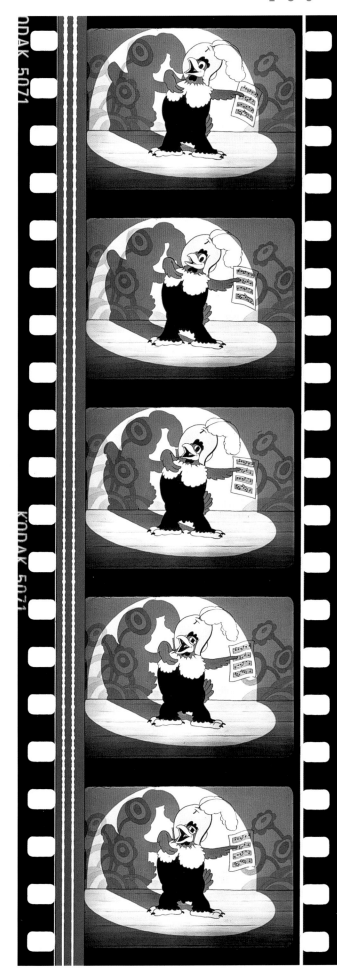

Clara Cluck, a barnyard Maria Callas, animated by Les Clark; animating in close quarters at the Disney studio are, left to right, David Hand, Dick Lundy, Norman Ferguson, and Les Clark.

Les Clark, on the other hand, was a slow and steady tortoise to Moore and Ferguson's swift hares. He won the long race by diligently keeping up—immersing himself in art classes and painstakingly expanding his talents as a superbly versatile personality animator. "Les was amazing," according to Ken Peterson, one of his assistants. "He had the quality of pleasing Walt that [Wilfred] Jackson had. That was the only thing that mattered to Les. He would do a thing over and over again. [I] always respected Les because he would get you quality. He would get you all the quality that was within him to get you. And he was very sensitive."[48]

When Clark and two other animators attempted to animate

Deems Taylor watches Fred Moore draw Mickey Mouse for
Fantasia *in 1940; Moore redesigned the character by
making Ub Iwerks's rigid circular shapes,
top left, more supple and pleasing.*

human figures in *The Goddess of Spring* (1934), he used his sister Marceil as a model. But the design was an uncomfortable clash of old Iwerks-style graphics and art-school figure drawings. "I had a hard time with the figure," Clark once noted. "Not that I didn't know how to draw it, but to animate it." The goddess is tightly drawn, but her appendages lack joints or angular lines, and her rubbery opening dance is ludicrous. Clark apologized to Walt, something no one ever did ("I'm sorry it's such a poor effort."). Perhaps startled by Clark's sincere expression of distress, Walt "sloughed it off, saying, 'I guess we could do better next time.'"[49]

"I never felt [from] Walt as a boss, that if I didn't do something right, I'd be canned," Clark once said.[50] "Walt and I got along very well. [There were] very few times that he chewed me out. But he was just unmerciful on some of the animators."[51] Although in general Walt did not give out compliments ("I don't think he thought it was good psychology to flatter," said Clark),[52] he singled out Clark's animation of Mickey Mouse in *The Band Concert* and *The Sorcerer's Apprentice* for praise.

Clark, along with a few other animators through the years (including Fred Moore, Frank Thomas, Ward Kimball, Ollie Johnston, and Andreas Deja), was a Mickey Mouse expert; that is, he developed a special affinity for the character and animated him in films that expanded his acting range. He was the only animator to work on Mickey in four decades of his long screen career, from 1928's *The Barn Dance* through *The Mickey Mouse Anniversary Show*, a 1968 television program.

After Iwerks left the studio, Clark was assigned to animate Mickey Mouse in numerous films.[53] On August 17, 1936, as a specialist on the character, he spoke at a studio training course for new animators, dwelling on how the Mouse's personality affects his movements.

The character of Mickey's walk depends on his personality and action. He is usually carried as a very spry, lively, snappy person, full of life. He is generally considered and handled as a little boy. . . . He doesn't bring his feet up too high off the ground. His walk is

The Disney animators excelled in animating animal characters, such as Mickey Mouse in The Band Concert *(1935); but the human figure, such as* The Goddess of Spring *(1934) proved daunting.*

natural. . . . It all depends on what character he is given in the story. If he is happy, he may have a cute spring in his walk. If he is dejected, his walk will be different.[54]

In *The Band Concert* (1935) Mickey is a stalwart music conductor of a motley group of barnyard musicians whose eccentric performance of the William Tell Overture is interrupted by two natural disasters: a cyclone and Donald Duck. In Clark's scenes, Mickey registers a change of attitude. In scene 33, for example, dressed in an oversized coat with epaulets and a feathered hat, Mickey finishes the first movement of the

In The Band Concert, *the first Technicolor Mickey Mouse short, Les Clark (a Mickey expert) animated the close-up personality scenes of the star.*

music with a serene expression of accomplishment. Wetting his thumb to flip the sheet music to the "Storm" section, he registers surprise. A close-up (scene 34) shows a score so complicated that extra notes are pasted onto the side and bottom of the pages. In the next scene, Mickey cocks his hat as a sign of his determination and control of the situation, and begins to conduct again.

One can spot several influences in Clark's *Band Concert* animation. There is a bit of Ub Iwerks in the exaggerated, cartoony length of Mickey's tongue as he licks his thumb, and the way his hat flies off his head to mirror his surprise. There is Fred Moore's malleable stretch-and-squash in the way Mickey's head does "takes." Walt's advice to keep action clearly staged in the open is also evident—if Mickey's main poses were blackened in, the silhouetted image would still describe the gist of the action. Fergie influenced the way Mickey thinks before he acts. But Clark wove all of these inspirational sources together into a seamless whole and made the scenes his own.

A droll sense of humor and comic timing are evident in Clark's *Band Concert* animation when Mickey rids himself of a dollop of ice cream (thrown by the disruptive duck) that slides down his back. As the cold dessert makes its way from head to heel, the mouse performs an epaulet-tossing hootchy-kootch to rival Little Egypt in her heyday. Mickey's elaborate squirm is viewed from the back, and Clark staged the action carefully in order for it to be read and savored by the audience.

Three years later Clark's animation of Mickey Mouse as *The Sorcerer's Apprentice* showed how masterly he had become. Animated in 1938 and released in 1940 as part of *Fantasia*, *Sorcerer* is one of the Mouse's finest, most nuanced screen performances. Clark's sequences include a stern Mickey bringing a broom to life and, after he trains it to draw water from a well, a jubilant Mickey cakewalking down cavern stairs and jumping into the Sorcerer's chair. Clark's poses are strong and (as always) clearly staged. His animation of the drapery of Mickey's oversized robe contains beautiful figurations (surely a result of Clark's constant attendance at drawing classes). Mickey's robe's weighty texture, its long sleeves falling over the mouse's conjuring fingers as he brings the broom to life, threatens to break his concentration as well as the magic spell.

Mickey's manipulation of his overlong sleeves in both *The Band Concert* and *The Sorcerer's Apprentice* is similar to the use of "water sleeves," a traditional part of Peking opera costuming. Water sleeves are silk extensions of the singers' costumes that they toss in graceful, billowing arcs to punctuate scenes of sung dialogue or instrumental music.[55]

Clark's imaginative versatility is further showcased in *Fantasia* in the "Nutcracker Suite" sequence featuring the Sugarplum Fairies. The tiny, nude apparitions, who fly about moonlit gardens moistening flowers and leaves, puzzled the animators. Exactly how should the slender sprites navigate? Clark

adapted the concept of a hummingbird darting back and forth, and he eased the fairies into and out of hovering poses like hummingbirds or dragonflies.[56] His solution lent the fairies a special charm and a grounding in reality that made them plausible. John Culhane believes Clark had a "reverence for movement, different kinds of movement."[57] Again, his animation won special praise from Walt.

"[Walt] would evaluate what a man could do," Clark once said. "He'd give someone an assignment and they'd be frightened of it. But he finally pulled out what he wanted from them because he recognized [their] ability to do so."[58] Walt often provided inspiration for Clark's animation of Mickey. "Walt was Mickey, and Mickey was Walt. Especially in story meetings, or even recordings, when you'd watch Walt record Mickey's voice. He'd go through gestures or facial [expressions] or intonations of voice that would give you an idea what Mickey was like."[59]

Clark was well liked and helpful to his coworkers. He warned new animators about the modus operandi of David Hand (1900–1986), one of Disney's top directors in the 1930s. Hand, it seems, could not get his points across unless he got mad. The first time he entered Clark's room while Clark was animating, he gingerly made suggestions. "Oh, Les, you've got to get more of this or that in it," he said gently, then added with concern, "You seem to be troubled about something." Relaxing under Hand's sympathetic inquiry, Clark began to discuss problems with his scene. All of a sudden, Hand, red-faced and trembling, grabbed Clark's drawing board, threw it in the air, and yelled, "Goddamn it! We gotta get the picture out!" Hand admitted that it wasn't until he got good and angry that he could "really make points"[60] forcefully enough that the animators would get something done.

Clark's kindness extended beyond his coworkers. Storyman Otto Englander's wife Erna came to Hollywood from Yugoslavia knowing little English. At Disney studio social gatherings, "Nobody paid any attention to me except Les Clark," she says. "He would tell my husband, tell her this and that, and I would tell my husband what to tell Les in French. He was a wonderful human being."[61]

Clark enjoyed participating in the occasional practical joke. Once he and animator Gerry Geronimi (later a director) played a trick on a nervous new assistant named Eddie Strickland, with whom they shared an office. Geronimi warned Strickland that Clark occasionally "went off his rocker" when imaginary pigeons bothered him. So Strickland began to watch Clark closely all the time. Occasionally, Clark would look about his desk and make shooing gestures, then return to drawing. Over a period of three days the shooing gradually became more vigorous. On the third day, Clark suddenly screamed, "Get these goddamn pigeons out of here!" Poor Strickland was out of the office and at the end of the hall "before his feet touched the

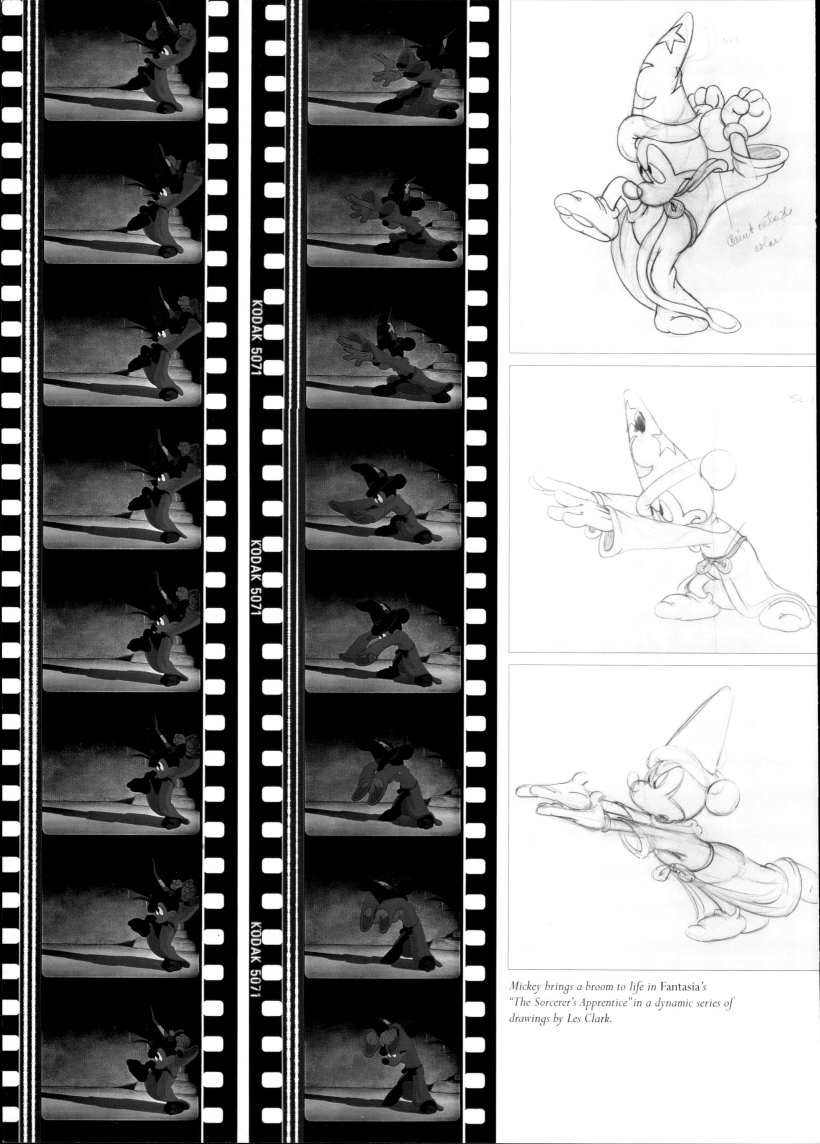

Mickey brings a broom to life in Fantasia's *"The Sorcerer's Apprentice" in a dynamic series of drawings by Les Clark.*

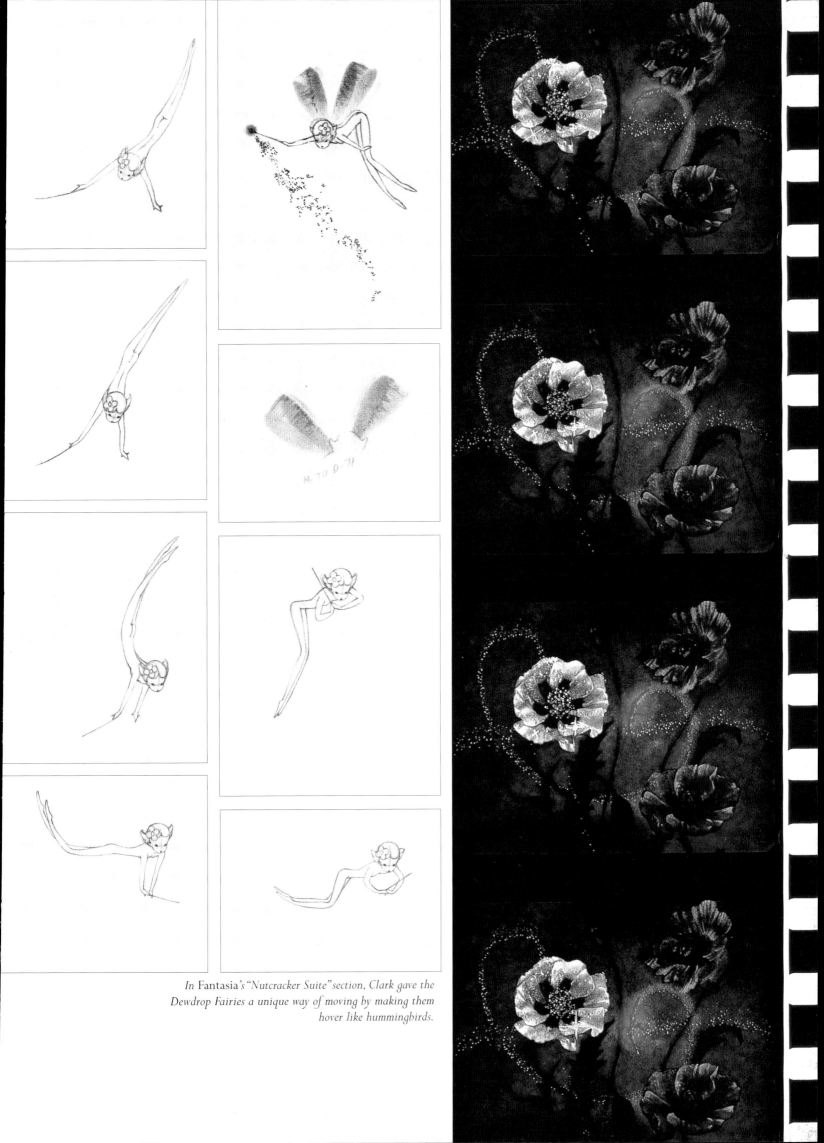

In Fantasia's *"Nutcracker Suite" section, Clark gave the Dewdrop Fairies a unique way of moving by making them hover like hummingbirds.*

TOP, *The Disney studio polo team, left to right, unknown, Les Clark, Norman Ferguson, Walt, Roy Disney, William Cottrell, Dick Lundy, Gunther Lessing.* ABOVE, LEFT, *a portrait of Clark's first wife Miriam Lauritzen in 1934;* RIGHT, *Les Clark posing in 1946 with infant daughter Miriam Leslie.*

ground," according to Frank Thomas, "and he wouldn't come back in the room."[62]

Les Clark's wavy black hair, thin mustache, and handsome, classic profile gave him a debonair resemblance to John Barrymore (minus the famous actor's massive ego and flair).[63] In the early 1930s he was part of Walt's eight-man polo team, which included Walt and Roy, Norman Ferguson, and the studio lawyer Gunther Lessing, among others. A photo shows the amateur horsemen dressed in full riding gear atop rented horses, grinning in the sun in a Burbank sandlot, ready to take on all comers.

Les Clark animated a complex scene of Snow White dancing with the dwarfs in their cottage.

In the late 1930s, at a Los Angeles stage production of the musical *Anything Goes*, Clark met beautiful, blond Miriam Lauritzen, a decorator and model. "She was not a typical show-girl," says her daughter Miri Clark Weible. "She was always reading on the set[s of movies she appeared in] and wrote three [unpublished] novels." Two years older than Clark, she was a divorcee with a son, Richard, born in 1926.[64] Clark adopted him when he married Miriam, and their daughter Miri was born in 1945.[65] A stunning couple, they were happy for a time, but the marriage ended in divorce in 1952. A contributing factor to the split was Miriam's alcoholism. However, they remained close friends who, according to Miri, "treated each other so beautifully." A year after the divorce, Miriam recovered and "spent the rest of her life" helping other alcoholics. Although they never got back together, Les "was always the love of her life."[66]

In a 1973 interview, Clark articulated how he felt about his work. "It's all animation," he said simply. "Whether it's a feature or short, it didn't matter."[67] His bland comment has a dutiful-son passivity that belies the effort he put into his work. "I never saw him being enthusiastic about his assignment, what he was working on," observes Frank Thomas. "I never heard him object to it or say, 'Gee, I wish they wouldn't put me on this.' He was always accepting. This is the thing we want you to do [he would be told]. Then he'd do the best he could."[68] For the feature-length cartoons, he was considered a dependable workhorse who would see any scene through satisfactorily, from the mundane to the complex. "Les never settled for anything that wasn't top quality," said Ollie Johnston one time. "His work always had that fine finish."[69]

In *Snow White and the Seven Dwarfs*, for the party in the dwarfs' cottage, Clark animated various small scenes involving nearly all of the dwarfs: Dopey smashing his face with a cymbal, Doc playing a horn, Doc and Happy running from Sneezy's nasal explosion as he carries Dopey on his shoulders, and their cautious peering around after.

Clark also had the thankless task of co-animating (with Ham Luske and Marc Davis) a complex scene of Snow White dancing with Doc and Happy. The full figures—moving toward and away from the viewer across the floor to a musical beat, each dancing in a way that expressed their character—were extremely difficult to organize and animate. There were problems in matching tight, traced-over live-action ("rotoscoped") footage of Snow White with the freehand caricatures of the dwarfs. Clark accepted the thankless high-wire act without a qualm and worked like hell to complete it successfully. "Animating the decrease in the girl's size as she moved away from the camera was controlled by working from the live-action film," write Frank Thomas and Ollie Johnston, "but the

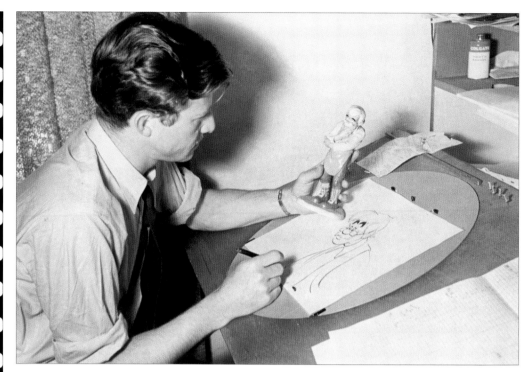

ABOVE, *Art Babbitt prepares to animate Geppetto in* Pinocchio *(1940);* LEFT, *a scene of Pinocchio turning around animated by Clark.*

matching perspectives of the dwarfs that Les animated from imagination made the scene amazingly convincing and added to the whole sequence."[70]

In *Pinocchio*, several animators were aligned with certain characters. Frank Thomas, Milt Kahl, and Ollie Johnston had heartrending sequences with Pinocchio; Ward Kimball animated Jiminy Cricket; Woolie Reitherman animated Monstro the whale; Vladimir Tytla took on the flamboyant puppeteer Stromboli; Norman Ferguson was assigned the sly fox and cat; Eric Larson got cute Figaro the kitten; Art Babbitt worked on Geppetto; and Fred Moore had the show-off Lampwick. Clark recalled being given "a couple of dance scenes" and filling in with "personality scenes" of various characters, most often Pinocchio, including the scene in which Geppetto asks to inspect the wooden boy, who is about to go to school for the first time; Pinocchio's body does a 360-degree turn while his smiling head remains in place.

Clark was also responsible for medium and long shots of Pinocchio under the sea calling out for his father. Scenes inside the whale—the reunion of Geppetto and Pinocchio, the boy's embarrassment when his donkey ears are discovered, the frantic building of a fire to aid their escape—demonstrate that Clark could have handled more of the emotional sequences.

In *Song of the South* (1946), directing animators Kahl, Davis, Johnston, Larson, and Lounsbery devoured with gusto large chunks of the three cartoon sequences starring Brer Rabbit, Brer Bear, and Brer Fox, as if they were thick steaks. Clark, also a directing animator, handled the opening with a live-action Uncle Remus and animated animals, singing "Zip-a-Dee-Doo-Dah." It was another technically difficult assignment with little personality animation. Clark, as usual, brought to it a deceptively easy charm and verve.

Some of the Nine Old Men fought for juicy acting roles throughout their careers, or were assigned bravura sequences that matched their strong personalities, styles, and egos. Clark's less forceful personality and versatility resulted in his being assigned what was left. In *Lady and the Tramp* (1955) he animated the opening sequences when the pup is being trained to stay in the kitchen and howls through the night. "That was all Les's, 'cause it had that nice feeling he was always able to get," recalls Frank Thomas, who, in the same film, animated the unforgettably romantic spaghetti-eating sequence.

Clark's reticent, compliant personality blinded even peers to his power as a personality animator. Clark's animation, says Ollie Johnston, "wasn't what I'd call spectacular. But he did good stuff, [it] worked, [and was] good entertainment."[71] Clark consistently gave life and charm to many a minor character,

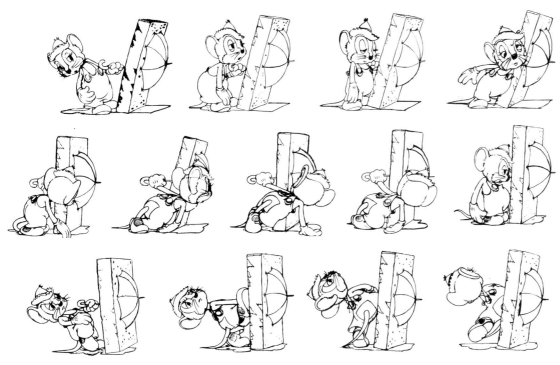

Animation was shared in The Country Cousin *(1936) by Art Babbitt (*LINE DRAWINGS ABOVE*) and Les Clark (*COLOR FILM FRAMES*).*

such as the girl bear in *Bongo* from *Fun and Fancy Free* (1947) or a confused bee trapped in a surreal world in *Bumble Boogie* from *Melody Time* (1948).

The shorts showcased Clark better. A fine example is *The Country Cousin* (1936), an assignment he shared with Art Babbitt (1907–1992), a great animator and a strong personality. Babbitt was a New Yorker who arrived at Disney in 1932; his self-described "firebrand" personality grated against Walt's from the beginning. In 1941, Babbitt played a leading role in the infamous Disney strike, which alienated him from studio loyalists, including the Nine Old Men. Politics aside, Babbitt was gifted at Chaplinesque pantomime and comic timing—Goofy's personality and the balletic mushrooms in *Fantasia* are two of his masterpieces.[72]

He has often been solely credited for *Country Cousin*'s depiction of a city mouse demonstrating big-city culinary delights to a rube relative from the sticks. But production scene drafts reveal that the film's main scenes were almost evenly divided between Babbitt and Clark.

Clark's fourteen scenes, in fact, precede Babbitt's and establish the personalities of the two mice. The table manners of the urban mouse—suavely dabbing his whiskers with a handkerchief after delicately savoring a tiny bit of cheese—are contrasted with the rural rodent, who grabs a hunk of cheddar, gulps it down, wipes his entire face with a red polka-dotted bandanna and vulgarly blows his nose in it.

Indeed, scene for scene Clark equals Babbitt. The performances are seamless, to all appearances the work of one hand. Years later, according to animator-director Richard Williams, Babbitt (a tough critic) always spoke admiringly of Clark, who

"never received the recognition the others did. And he should have," said Babbitt, "because he was marvelous! Terrific animator, very inventive. But taken for granted."[73]

In his diligent pursuit of quality, Clark often subjected his drawings to critiques by Milt Kahl, whose character designs keyed the features from *Pinocchio* on. Kahl, a brilliant draftsman, was notorious for being honest "to the point of insulting people" and possessing "absolutely no finesse whatever" in his blunt assessments of the drawing ability of coworkers. "He actually broke the heart of guys like Les Clark," said one.[74]

Like a hapless ant walking into a spider's web, Clark sacrificed his self-esteem to Kahl's verbal abuse for the greater good. "Milt developed the character of Alice," said Clark about the heroine of *Alice in Wonderland* (1951). "In that case, Milt was the man that I'd go to for suggestions [as to] whether the drawing was right or not."[75] "He was no match for Milt on anything," recalls Ken Peterson sadly. "He was awfully mean to Les Clark," says Frank Thomas, who remembers one of Kahl's cantankerous art lessons as follows: "'Well, you haven't spent any time working on this yet! I'm not gonna waste my time going over it till you've done the best you can! You can do better than this! Christ's sake! Here, take it back!'"[76]

Clark animated scenes in the White Rabbit's house in which Alice grows and shrinks, and he requested Ken Southworth, one of Kahl's assistants, to work with him. "He'd say, does this look like the way Milt would draw it?" says Southworth. "He didn't say, how would [Milt] animate it, but how he would draw it. I'd say, well, you've got the eyes too far apart, blah blah blah. It was very flattering to be asked."[77]

In the 1940s, at meetings of the Disney Animation Board (the studio organization from which the Nine Old Men emerged), Clark was a respected colleague. "We liked Les because he was unemotional and he was compassionate," says Thomas. "You could get mad at some guy and say he ought to get his ass clear out of here. Les would laugh, chuckle, and say, 'Well, you ought to use him for whatever it is.'" Clark was "more the oldest brother," according to Thomas, who would "calm you down and had a practical way of going at things."[78]

Clark avoided becoming a director, even though Walt personally asked him to when the studio moved over to Burbank in 1939. Asked again in the mid-1950s, he knew it would be unwise to refuse again. Over the next twenty years Clark directed numerous informational shorts, as well as inserts in the Mickey Mouse Club television shows; for example, the 1955–56 series *You—The Human Animal*, featuring Jiminy Cricket. "Info-tainment" inserts and theatrical shorts he directed, such as *Paul Bunyan* (1958), are simply staged, brightly paced, and well-animated—even subsidiary characters are entertaining.

Of happy memory for baby boomers are the opening titles for the original Disneyland TV series featuring Tinker Bell from *Peter Pan* (1953). Clark directed and animated them in 1954 (with John Hench handling fairy dust and other effects). Clark's animation of the girlish sprite is a nuclear-age version of the Nutcracker Suite "hummingbird" fairies. In less than thirty seconds Tinker Bell pantomimes rhythmic dancing and stealthful prowling in Frontierland, gracefully changes backgrounds to reveal Fantasyland, and so on. She illustrates the wonders of Tomorrowland (in about four seconds) by conjuring dazzling abstract circles and spirals of atoms in space; finally, Tink plunges into the whirling molecules and is transformed into a rocket whose fiery blasts become a curtain that smoothly segues into the next section.

For *Sleeping Beauty* (1959), Clark was a sequence director, which necessitated staging scenes to guide other animators, a task he found daunting. His self-contained direction of shorts and inserts was of little help with this large, overproduced, and expensive project. Frank Thomas recalls Clark's coming to him

for help with a sequence in which the three good fairies invade the wicked fairy's castle and sneak past her guards. Clark had staged the scenes in a "very matter-of-fact, very unimaginative" way with little suspense, says Thomas, placing characters in the middle of the screen "the way you'd do Pluto chewing a bone. . . . I didn't want to hurt his feelings and yet I wanted him to do better," says Thomas who, with Clark's tacit agreement, restaged the scenes. "No," concludes Thomas, Clark was not features-director material, "not in our terms."[79]

Walt Disney's death in 1966 was, to each of the Nine Old Men, equivalent to losing their father. Les Clark, whose closeness with both Disney brothers went back to the earliest days, was "devastated."[80] He continued to direct educational films and to animate into the mid-1970s.[81] By that time, the studio was in a state of flux, with the future of Disney animation in doubt. When Clark overheard a young executive say "he wanted to get rid of everyone over thirty-five years" of age in the animation department, the remark angered him and hastened his decision to leave. He retired on September 30, 1975.[82]

In preparation for retirement, Clark had begun to paint portraits and landscapes, and at a local art exhibit he met artist Georgia Vester. "I thought he was a very genuine person, a gentleman," she says. "And interesting." The couple was married in 1967 and spent their honeymoon on a freighter to Japan, where, says Vester, "Roy Disney had the red carpet spread out for us."

The Clarks enjoyed traveling, especially to Mexico, for extended periods of painting and sculpting. When Georgia was recently asked how long they had been together, she replied "not long enough." Their twelve years of marriage ended when Les died on September 11, 1979, just six months after learning he had cancer.[83]

Les Clark had an extraordinary capacity to reinvent himself. His mild manner (like Clark Kent's) hid a superior discipline and determination to keep up with his colleagues and to improve. As his brother Mickey notes, Les "was very determined to be as good as he could be."[84]

He was the only one of the Nine Old Men whose career spanned the silent-movie era and the age of television; arguably, he was the one most comfortable in blending abstraction and rhythmic choreography with personality animation. Clark participated in major developments in the art of animation: from the Mickey Mouse and Silly Symphony series, to the expansion of animation acting and design in the features, to TV's simplified graphics and staging.

He evolved from emulating Ub Iwerks's rubber-hose-and-circle patterns into a mastery of personality animation. His work matches the best of his peers in charm, timing, sincere emotion, visual appeal, and pure entertainment.

The difficult family circumstances he endured while growing up did not harden him; nearly everyone remembers

Les Clark as gentle, kind, and empathetic. He was always the dutiful son, the responsible big brother, the loyal employee. His familial feelings were transferred to Walt and Roy. For their faith in him, there was nothing he would not do to please them, help them, and do them proud.

Clark's quietness and versatility led him and his contributions to the films to be taken for granted, and he was often passed over for choice assignments. Among cartoon fans, he is the least known and appreciated of the Nine Old Men.

To Les Clark himself, his near anonymity mattered little. He was the ultimate team player, one who placed duty to the studio above his personal needs and desires. His ambitions were not for himself but for a job well done.

"This may sound facetious," he once said, "but I enjoy doing everything that is given me."[85]

Georgia and Les Clark in 1971

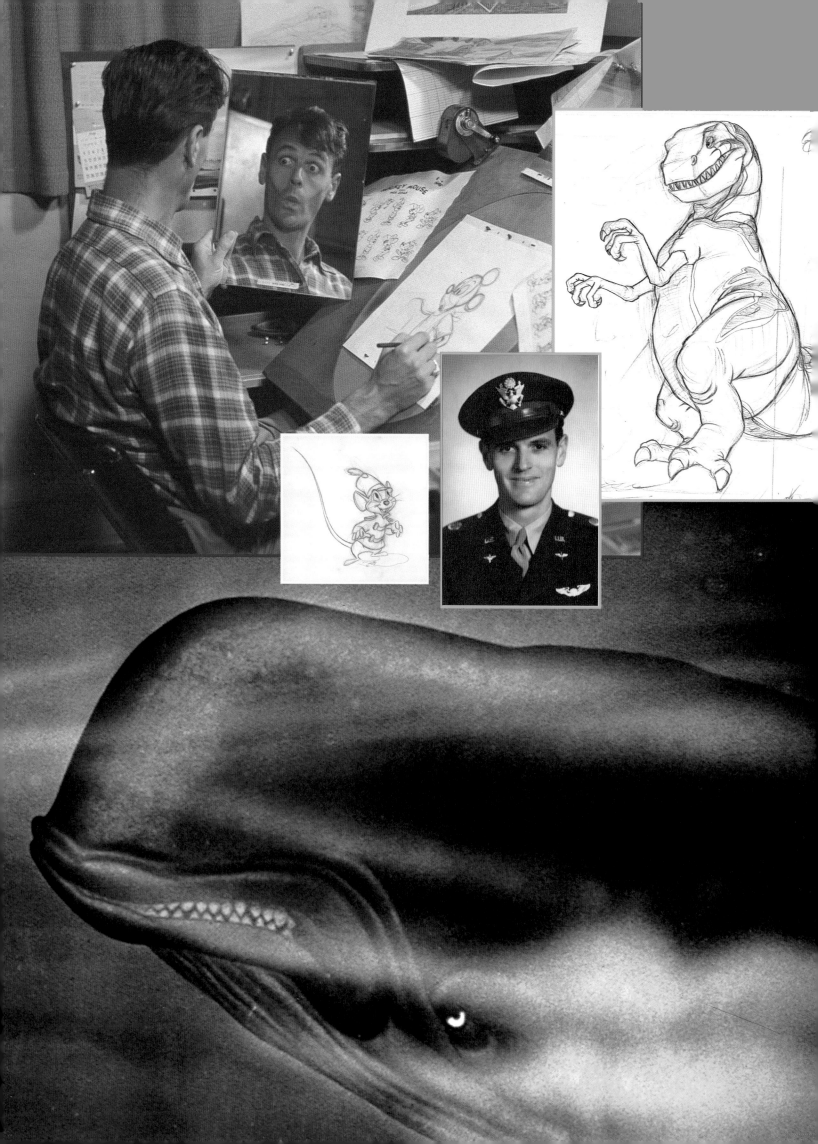

CHAPTER two
Wolfgang Reitherman

Wolfgang Reitherman's nickname "Woolie" was, in one sense, a misnomer. There was nothing fuzzy, unfocused, or sheepish about the man. If, however, "Woolie" is associated with the phrase "wild and woolly"—as in resembling the roughness and excitement of the American West—it aptly described his vibrant personality, decisiveness, and abundant macho energy.

"My work had vitality and an 'I don't give a damn—try it!' quality," he once said of his animation.[1] Early on at Disney, Reitherman was pegged for action-oriented assignments: a whale chase in *Pinocchio*, dinosaurs doing battle in *Fantasia*, Captain Hook fighting off a hungry crocodile in *Peter Pan*, and ten rounds between a prince and a dragon in *Sleeping Beauty* ("We took the approach that we were going to kill that damn prince!").[2] He also gave Goofy, the dim-witted humanoid dog, some of his funniest slapstick moments.

A lover of flying and airplanes since his teen years,

OPPOSITE, *Wolfgang Reitherman at the drawing board circa 1950, and Major Wolfgang Reitherman in uniform during World War II surrounded by Timothy Mouse from* Dumbo *(1941), T. rex from* Fantasia *(1940) and Monstro the whale from* Pinocchio *(1940);* THIS PAGE, *"Woolie" Reitherman studies a dinosaur model for the "Rite of Spring."*

Reitherman was a World War II pilot, a deputy commander who ferried planes with the Army Air Transport Command on dangerous missions "over the hump" in China, Burma, and India. In 1946, after three years of service, he was awarded the Distinguished Flying Cross and the Air Medal with one bronze Oak Leaf Cluster. He continued to fly for pleasure up to and including the day he died in 1985.[3] Reitherman was a born leader with an air of derring-do, qualities that led Walt Disney to choose him as his director heir apparent.

There was something of the movie star about Reitherman—think John Wayne or Robert Taylor during their World War II career phase. Physically, he was impressive: six-foot-two, wide-shouldered, bowlegged, his lanky frame topped by a strikingly handsome face crowned with wavy brown hair. "He was a man's man, as well as a lady's man," says his wife Janie.[4]

Reitherman was fond of wearing loud Hawaiian shirts and smoking cigars. Reviewing an animator's work at the Moviola projector, he would be surrounded by a cloud of cigar smoke. "Everybody'd take about two steps back," according to John Pomeroy. "I pictured him in the cockpit of his B-17 flying missions over the Philippines."[5]

Reitherman was respected and obeyed by both the Nine

Old Men and a younger generation of animators. "He was a very strong individual," comments Frank Thomas, adding that he also "had a strong streak of decency in him."[6] For example, when actress Barbara Luddy (the voice of Lady in *Lady and the Tramp*) was in the hospital, it was Reitherman who sent her flowers "from the animation crew."

"Woolie's strength was [that] he was the dauntless captain of the ship," says Don Bluth, who worked on Reitherman-directed features in the early 1970s. "He took over after Walt died. He knew where he wanted to go. Just damn the torpedoes and full steam ahead! He was always saying that."[7] John Pomeroy recalls: "He had this persona like *Twelve O'clock High*. Blood and guts! And that's the way he did his movies. He was not always the most eloquent guy, not the most sensitive guy, but damn it! He knew how to command."[8]

"I enjoy life," he once told an interviewer with a wide smile.[9]

The exuberant life of Wolfgang "Woolie" Reitherman began on June 26, 1909, in Munich, Germany, where he was (as he put it) the "tail end" of seven children.[10] Father Philip and mother Marie eloped and married in London; after living briefly in France, they returned to Munich to settle in a beautiful three-story house. Philip was Catholic, but all of the children were raised in their mother's Episcopal religion and were "very active in church activities."[11] Also, "Woolie had an enthusiastic appreciation of music that he got from his parents"; Philip owned five elegant opera hats.[12]

As proprietor of a bottled water company, Philip made deliveries from a horse and wagon to local hotels and resorts. In 1911, owing to "political unrest," the whole family moved from Germany to America, joining one of Philip's brothers in Kansas City. Years later in a conversation with Roy Disney's wife, Edna, Woolie discovered they had lived two blocks from each other, and discussed sliding down the same snow slopes on sleds.[13]

In the United States, English became the preferred language in the Reitherman home; as a result of his parents' assimilative urge, Wolfgang understood little German.[14] Philip worked for an accounting company for a couple of years before a doctor advised a move westward to cure his daughter Emily's tuberculosis. The family moved to an acre in Sierra Madre, California, a sleepy town of about 2,000 residents east of Pasadena at the foot of Mount Wilson.

Woolie fondly remembered Sierra Madre as "a beautiful little town" with wooden sidewalks and a bandstand in its center. Wolfgang and his favorite brother, Alfred, who was older by two years, hiked constantly in the hills, rode horses, and raised

German shepherds.[15] He once recalled the numerous weekend hikers who arrived on the famous big Red Car trolleys, their raucous camps with "a lot of girls," and how "some of those camps were pretty sexy."

As kids, Wolfgang and Alfred were more interested in the beauty of the mountains, the crystal-clear streams, and how fast they could run up and down the slopes. After a long hike up the side of the mountain to a little cave "hideout," the brothers often

Alfred (left) and Wolfgang Reitherman, circa 1930.

were late for supper. As the sun set, church bells from the town below began to peal and distant dogs barked. "It had such a peaceful quality," Reitherman remembered, "and you'd enjoy that for about a minute and a half, and then you'd tear back down the hill."[16]

Wolfgang and Alfred attended an old wooden country schoolhouse near an orange grove, where students arrived on horseback. Woolie recalled the school's cloak room on rainy days where wet coats and sweaters hung and lunch bags were stored. "I can still remember that smell," he said over six decades later. "It was mostly a scrambled-egg sandwich and stuff like that. And kids always had this smelly old stuff."[17]

Wolfgang described himself as a tagalong to his tenacious brother. Even hobbies, like butterfly collecting, Alfred pursued with a determined purposefulness. The boys liked to chop wood, and when Woolie was about ten, he accidentally broke a long-handled ax. "I said, 'Well, so much for that,' and walked off," said Reitherman. But Alfred, who was nearly twelve, "finished it off with a hand ax. That, to me, is real determination."

It was Alfred who started flying first while in high school. Wolfgang tagged along again when Alfred got a part-time job cleaning airplane parts from old World War I Jennys, SE-5s, and a de Havilland; a mechanic named Harry Boer overhauled Liberty engines for speedboats that were running booze back and forth off the coast. The Reitherman brothers hung around Western Avenue in Los Angeles, which had dirt fields in the 1920s, where for a buck they could joyride with an unlicensed pilot.

"In those days you didn't need a license," said Reitherman, who learned to fly by observing his brother and other pilots. "I didn't know what I was doing, but if I watched something I could follow." Years later he would learn how to direct films the same way, by observing Walt and others. In order to fly, he learned that the wires of an airplane vibrated if it was going too slowly, and that if you got the nose right you could make a proper landing. The brothers built their own airplane, which they flew out of Monrovia airport a few miles east of their hometown. "Flying gets in your blood," said Woolie in 1983, "and that ability to soar up over everything and everybody."[18]

Reitherman attended Pasadena Junior College for two years. A history teacher was so impressed by his "smirky" drawings on exam papers that she kept them for years and encouraged him to go into art. In an elective "snap" course in freehand drawing, he garnered more encouragement from the same teacher. "He said he owed a lot to her," according to Janie Reitherman.

Alfred got a job in the engineering department at Douglas Aircraft and also secured one for his nineteen-year-old brother Woolie in the experimental department. "They had a crazy observation airplane there with a gull wing," he once recalled in a television interview. "I guess I had a sense of geometry because I could measure things accurately, [could use] plumb bobs, and did a lot of work on jigs and things like that." He helped install the first automatic pilot in engines.

Woolie continued to fly in his spare time as a hobby ("There wasn't any money in it in those days"), and worked from December 1927 through June 1933 at Douglas earning $50 a week. Then, in the middle of the Depression, "I was kind of silly," he said. "I decided I'd go to art school." "His goal was to become an outstanding watercolorist," says Janie Reitherman. Douglas allowed him to work part-time while attending Chouinard Art Institute for a year. "I didn't really go to art school too well because I was away most of the time sketching on my own and painting," he said. "I was just fascinated with life and people, and once color grabs hold of you, it becomes a thing!"[19]

Surviving paintings testify to Reitherman's promise as a watercolorist; his loose brushstrokes and transparent washes depicting horsemen and polo players are in the California regionalist style. His work attracted the attention of a leading practitioner of the style: Philip L. Dyke, a twenty-seven-year-old Chouinard drawing and painting instructor and respected member of the California Water Color Society. Dyke suggested that Reitherman apply for a job at Disney, which was in a period of expansion and one of the few places hiring artists during the Depression. Reitherman, having heard that the process of animation was exceedingly tedious, replied "no dice." But Dyke, who would himself soon be employed by Disney as an instructor and color coordinator (from 1935 to 1945), prevailed.[20]

"In those days they gave you about a week's tryout, and I remember after about the first day I was fascinated," Reitherman says of his virgin flight into animation.

> Because you could move those things! You can't move a painting. And all of a sudden, on a white sheet of paper, you could make something move. The other thing that grabbed me was that it was about people and situations. My paintings weren't very good, but all of them had people in them, doing something. Here was a way of developing that.
>
> Then I'd get the feeling, gee, even if I get to be a pretty good painter, galleries and things, I'd be in somebody's home. Maybe a tenth of the people will see my stuff as compared to one night with this wonderful mass medium for the public. So my ego came through there. I just felt this was a new twentieth-century art form, probably the most unique of anything that had appeared on the art horizon for centuries, since perspective. So that got me hooked.[21]

Reitherman, age twenty-three, was hired at Disney on May 21, 1933, and started at the studio in June. He claims to have advanced into animation without going through the assistant process. "Had I gone through all that I would have been long gone," he said. "Maybe they knew that." Apparently he was assigned to simple repetitive animation cycles in Silly Symphonies, such as *Funny Little Bunnies* (released in March 1934) in which rabbits mechanically prepare Easter eggs on

Funny Little Bunnies (1934), one of the first films Reitherman worked on.

assembly lines. He also animated small bits in Mickey Mouse shorts, such as *Two-Gun Mickey* (December 1934) and was helped by Ham Luske and other experienced animators.

Reitherman loved the atmosphere of discovery that existed at the Hyperion Avenue studio and Walt's quest to improve animation's communicativeness. "How in the hell do you look at something that's moving and capture that," wondered Reitherman. "We learned some great things. Walt was in on them, too. We used to watch pictures in slow motion at night after work—sports, race horses in slow motion. And all you could do was talk about it, you never could grab hold of any fixed formula, but finally things came to pass. You knew that weight had to be supported all the time because from birth to death gravity is working on you. That was lacking in a lot of animation up to this time. As soon as you could make something feel it had weight, it had more credibility on the screen.

"Generally, fantasy becomes stronger if you have reality to counter it or to spring off of. Of course, this whole action analysis had to be tied to personality or characterization because it's the personality up there that comes back to the audiences [who say] subconsciously, I've experienced that, or, it feels like something I could do. This to me was one of the great things Walt knew before the rest of us did: that personality was the most important communicator we had."[22]

Reitherman rose quickly, working on many classic shorts, such as *The Wise Little Hen* (1934), *The Band Concert* (1935), *Elmer Elephant* (1935), *Music Land* (1935), *Cock o' the Walk* (1935), and *Broken Toys* (1935), among others. Art Babbitt, who came to Disney a year before Reitherman, defined the personality of Goofy. But Reitherman also became associated with the character after his imaginative and energetic animation in *Clock Cleaners* (1937) and *Hawaiian Holiday* (1937).

The hyper-active Goofy

Once, at a Chouinard lecture in April 1937, Reitherman articulated his approach to animation:

If we make a slapstick picture, we go all the way. If we make a subtler picture like *[The] Flying Mouse* and *[The] Country Cousin*, which won the Academy Award this year, it gets slightly different handling. . . . But the real charm in handling cartoon slapstick is to go broad in them and still retain a high level of quality. . . . Lots of times I think we run our pictures too fast; but there is a certain speed of tempo people expect in a cartoon. . . . You must keep the picture going along at a sparkling pace to keep it alive and interesting. . . .

I don't want you to forget that creativeness, imagination, fantasy have to stay with you. You must stay pepped up on your work*—you can't get along on a system alone. The first thing we come up against is sincerity and honesty, by which I mean if a thing looks

sincere on the screen, it looks as though it would really work, as though it really existed . . . as though gravity held it down. It looks plausible, feasible, logical. . . . [C]aricature or exaggeration in drawing . . . is very important. The public never pays for a good drawing. It pays for an exaggerated effect. . . . By caricature, I don't always mean funny drawing. If you are going to make a fellow lean over, make him lean over plenty. Go twice as far as you think you can in the drawing and you will be just about right. Make the character do everything he does in a decisive, definite way so . . . that the audience will know what he is doing. . . .

The drawing should be very direct, definite, and simple. That means again you must have a very clear idea of what you are after, because it is hard to make a simple drawing. Harder than to make a jumbled-up drawing with all the details on it.[23]

He also spoke of self-doubts when the director hands out a sequence:

You don't know where to start. You are enthusiastic about your sequence. You have a whole bunch of [exposure] sheets [i.e., timing charts] that describe the action in a very rough way, but it's up to you to draw your characters and present them in such a way that you will get entertainment for your audience. That's a pretty rough stage because you don't know exactly where to begin. And that's where organization comes in.[24]

Reitherman usually began by going over story points because "the idea you are trying to put over must be very clear in your mind." He outlined the business involved to see how the action could be done in a funny, interesting way. "I try to use my creative imagination to build what I am trying to put over, rather than go off on a tangent by myself and coming back with a version the director never dreamed of."

Next, he reviewed the layouts—drawings of the scene's basic composition, or what Reitherman called "staging." "I see [that] my characters have plenty of room to work [in]. I plan my action as though the paper actually were a stage." He drew key poses and considered "almost every verb in an action: the character walks or sits down or gets up." He considered those actions as story points at that stage and tried "to make a story of each one, visualizing how I would work in and out of those poses." In planning a scene using key (or extreme) poses, he felt "you must caricature each pose, go further with it each time, and also try to put as much of the mood and the feeling of the character itself into that pose as you possibly can." Otherwise, "the work will suffer," he warned.

Reitherman showed key poses to his assistant for advice, or put them away for a later look. Often he and his assistant acted out the business. If both thought he had not been as clear and direct as possible, he started over. Like a good soup, the scene became more flavorful as it boiled down. "Then I begin to get satisfied," he said. "When the work begins to get simpler, it is good. When it is complicated, it is not." Finally, he began to animate "straight ahead"; that is, using extreme poses as goal posts "to get a flow and feeling in the animation."

After viewing black-and-white tests of a scene's rough animation, his first reaction was usually, "My God! What did I do that for?" The pencil tests, checked for "sincerity, definite impression, or the ideas you had at first," were redone, if necessary. Then the scene was cut into a rough reel of the whole film and viewed by the director, other animators, and Walt in the "sweatbox" (projection room). "That is where the work is criticized in terms of how the whole story works," he said. "At that time the animator takes a pretty good beating! Sometimes the criticism is awful. Sometimes it isn't. You have to be able to take it. You must be able to enter into the session and criticism of your work with the idea of getting a better picture."[25]

In *Snow White and the Seven Dwarfs*, Reitherman animated the slave in the Magic Mirror, a reflective apparition who tells the truth to power: the wicked Queen. The ghostly disembodied mask, appears in only two sequences, but casts a memorably spooky spell. Speaking in a deep voice, the floating phantasm—a face in space—twice dishes out bad news to the Queen: Snow White is "far more fair" than she, and her plot to murder the girl has flopped ("'Tis the heart of a pig you hold in your hand.")

After Goofy's slapstick fun, the Mirror was a difficult assignment. "It was tough because it didn't move. It was just there all the time," he once said. Animating dialogue with only lips and eyes shapes (not even pupils) and no body movements

is extremely difficult, and Reitherman redid his scenes several times. "I worked and worked on that," he said.

Studying the original animation drawings, one notices how closely spaced the in-between drawings are. For each extreme pose, the paper was folded in half down the middle of the Mirror's face. This allowed Reitherman to animate one side of the face, fold the paper, and (over a light table) trace the other side, so the two halves were perfectly matched in size and movement. Ironically, in the final film, special effects were added for an ethereal effect: smoke and a distortion glass ripple the mask's features. "So that all of my work," he said, "was sort of for nothing."[26]

A churning sea plays a major part in Reitherman's scenes

Reitherman animated the slave in the Magic Mirror nine times before it pleased Walt Disney.

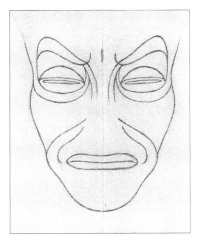 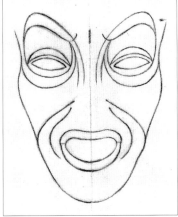 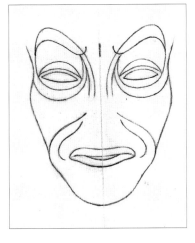 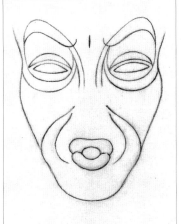

of Monstro, the gigantic whale in *Pinocchio*. Again, Reitherman thought his animation was obscured by the effects animators. "Damn it, they covered it with splashes," he told John Lasseter. "Couldn't see anything I did."[27] But his animation of the huge animal more than holds its own against ocean waves, foam, spray, and bubbles. "It was exciting," said Reitherman, "because it was the largest thing we'd ever done on the screen. And to get the weight and the timing of all those things was a challenge."[28]

Originally, the assignment went to Vladimir Tytla, animator of the overbearing puppeteer Stromboli. "Walt wasn't satisfied," according to Ollie Johnston. "I think Walt trusted Woolie not to run away with something," speculates Johnston. "Not to hide something the way some directors would. They wanted to hide the stuff and not let anybody see it till they got it ready. Walt didn't like that. Woolie didn't do that." Indeed, Reitherman shared the creative process with the men in his unit. "Each guy would get a crack at the scene," said Johnston. "So it'd be passed around a lot. Lot of erasing."[29]

Monstro is one-third mouth, an enormous eating machine so gigantic that the *Titanic*, *Queen Mary*, and *QE 2* could conceivably fit inside with room to spare. Pinocchio and Geppetto escape from the beast's belly by setting a smoky fire that makes the whale sneeze. Furious and vengeful, Monstro chases the escapees through the ocean, trying to destroy them.

Reitherman's animation has a frightening power, not just because of the behemoth's nightmarish appearance—all huge teeth, gums, blubbery lips, and warehouse body; but also because of its cunning and relentless pursuit of Pinocchio and Geppetto.

Monstro has a brain, and, like Moby Dick, is a sea monster whose sentience makes him doubly dangerous. Surely, Pinocchio's aquatic nemesis lurked in Steven Spielberg's mind when he directed *Jaws* (1973) more than three decades later. Reitherman's staging of scenes might today be tagged "Spielbergian": the quick cuts (including a dynamic shot only twenty frames in length of Monstro barreling through the air toward us), the emotional intercutting between the pursued and the pursuer, the imagery of the very small coping with something supernaturally big. Likewise, Spielberg's fondness for fantasy, special effects, and manipulative, heart-tugging cinematic craft is thought to be "Disney-esque."

Listed as one of *Pinocchio*'s eight animation directors, Reitherman's talent for staging action and menace can be seen in idea sketches drawn for a discarded scene: how Monstro initially swallowed Geppetto's boat. In nine tiny sequential thumbnail drawings on a single sheet of animation paper, the budding director emerges.

The first, nearly abstract drawing shows a tiny sail (a white triangle) on a billowing wave; a few marks represent seagulls in the sky. All is placid and calm. A hint of the unusual comes in the second panel: a spray of foam shoots unexpectedly straight up out of the sea. In the next two panels, a bulky form rises, seemingly made of water. The watery shape grows larger and the boat (tiny by comparison) tries to move away. In the fifth and sixth drawings, a hideously large mouth with teeth opens and closes on the boat, then quickly submerges again (panels seven and eight) with a repeat of the spray plume. Finally, in the last panel, all appears as peaceful as in the first drawing, except now the sailboat is nowhere to be seen.

By way of contrast, Reitherman also animated tiny Jiminy Cricket—for example, excitedly hopping back and forth while reading a letter to Pinocchio about Geppetto's Monstro

THIS PAGE, *thumbnail sketches by Reitherman for an unused scene in* Pinocchio *reveal the budding director;* OPPOSITE PAGE, *Monstro the whale.*

encounter. Ward Kimball, five years Reitherman's junior and supervisor of the cricket's animation, admired Woolie's work, but thought the older man "suffered with a little inferiority complex. He didn't think [he was], even though he was, a very good artist." Kimball had detected the kernel of insecurity that always lay beneath Reitherman's swashbuckling, confident surface.

Reitherman compared himself to others, says Kimball, which "made him work harder. He was tenacious and didn't have the quick, facile way of working [of] Fred Moore or the flamboyant, spontaneous timing of Norm Ferguson. He had to work harder, but he ended up with good stuff." Kimball compares Reitherman to baseball player Pete Rose: "The drive he has playing baseball, the guy who is probably too old . . . wants to be better and he is. Consequently, the stuff in the 'Rite of Spring' in *Fantasia* has a great monumental weight to it, because Woolie in his own way just kept after it. He was always stuck with the chase

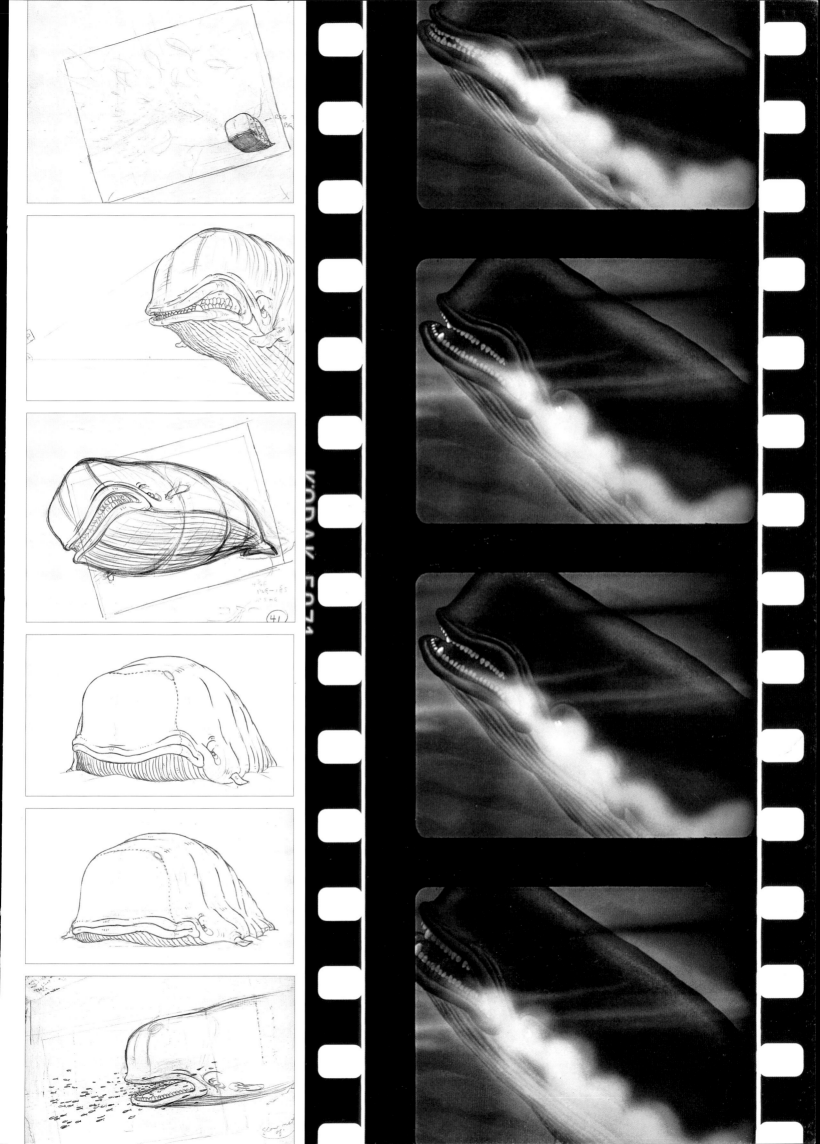

stuff because most people hated to do this, but Woolie got a big kick out of doing fast action and he did it well."[30]

Reitherman constructed the "Rite" dinosaurs out of boxy forms, just as he did with Monstro. Square and rectangular shapes allowed for a dramatic perspective; most of the battle between the tall T. rex and a squat stegosaurus was staged at ground level looking up. Animation supervisor Reitherman worked closely with Bill Roberts, one of "Rite"'s two sequence directors, who advised "just draw a twelve-story building in perspective, then convert it into a dinosaur and animate it."[31]

Walt Disney warned against anthropomorphism: "Don't make them cute animal personalities. They've got small brains, y'know; make them real!"[32] Reitherman recalled, "We went down to museums to look at the bone structure." Prehistoric skeletal remains gave clues to how the dinosaurs' anatomy might have worked. However, despite their search for accuracy, the Disney artists neglected pairing battling dinosaurs that existed in the same time period. Stegosaurus and tyrannosaurus never had the pleasure of tearing each other apart because they lived millions of years apart. They were chosen for *Fantasia* for the best of Hollywood reasons: they looked good on screen together and stegosaurus's spiked tail was a nice animatable weapon.

"When Woolie got the assignment on the dinosaurs in *Fantasia*, it absolutely drove him up the wall," according to Ken Peterson, a cleanup artist on the film. "You know how Woolie is: he's gonna lick this if it's the last thing he ever does in his life." Reitherman, said Peterson in 1979, had "been struggling on Goofy, struggling but getting a lot of entertainment. The way Woolie is, he'll fight for entertainment, y'know."[33] The drawing problems the dinosaurs presented were beyond Goofy, the Magic Mirror, Monstro, or anything he had yet encountered in his young career; starting with the feet of monstrous tyrannosaurus. "The bones had to absorb the weight. Then you moved up and here was this great, huge head. It was tough to draw it from the bottom [angle]. Then the Stegosaurus, which is a huge creature that he finally killed. That's the scene I did first."

Bulky stegosaurus's waddling walk was apparently particularly difficult to animate: the foot farthest away from camera often lags. But the weight of both creatures is right on, and their battle is full of dynamic stretch-and-squash; audiences really feel the wallop of the spiked tail and the breaking of the plated neck. When defeated stegosaurus rolls over to die, extra-large animation bond was required. "I had to paste paper on it because I couldn't draw it [on a single sheet of paper]," said Reitherman. "And finally when [T. rex] grabbed [stegosaurus] by the neck . . . I animated the whole big thing slowly going over and then the tail coming late. And then I just moved the camera along. It was very effective as I remember."[34]

The original animation drawings bear the scars of Reitherman's struggle. They are full of erasures, different colored pencils, smudges, sweat stains, doodles, and wrinkled cor-

ners where he flipped papers back and forth constantly, checking the movements. "Some of those papers," said Peterson, "you know, when you'd go to clean them up, there was practically nothing left of them. They were like crumpled dollar bills!"[35] The tortured animation papers speak to Reitherman's determination, perfectionism, and insecurity. "With Woolie," said Peterson, "nothing was ever [finished] unless it was going out of his hands. As long as he could flip it, there were going to be changes made. You never gave up on a thing. If some little thing bothered you and you thought you could make it better, why, he'd try to make it better."[36]

Regarding his way of animating, Reitherman used to say, "However it takes to get you there, get there!" Don Bluth once observed how Reitherman's "strange method" started with "scribbling the *power* of the drawing. You couldn't see a charac-

THIS PAGE AND OPPOSITE, *Reitherman fleshes out a memorable battle between prehistoric behemoths in* Fantasia.

ter in there. [Then he'd] put a piece of paper over that and finally get a character to represent those same powerful scribbles that were just pencil marks on a page. So it took him two or three generations to find the actual drawing."[37]

Reitherman's believable, exciting animation has inspired a fascination with dinosaurs in generations of children. Spielberg (again) must be counted among them; both the traditionally animated feature *The Land Before Time* (1988), which he produced, and the computer-generated *Jurassic Park* (1993), which he directed, owe a great deal to Woolie's battling thunder lizards.

The year 1941 proved a busy one for Reitherman, and also ushered in profound changes at Disney. The war raging in Europe had cut off a considerable portion of the studio's

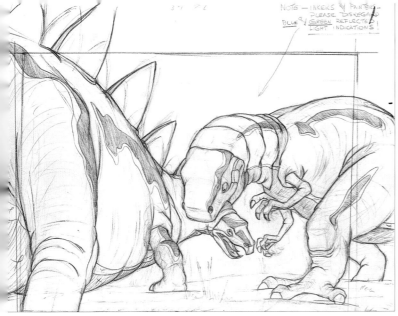

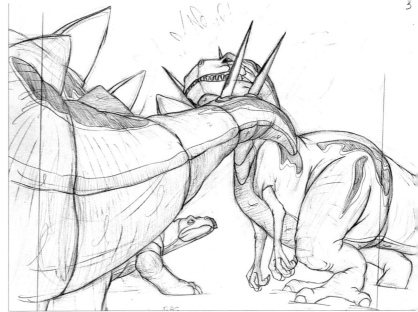

STEGOSAURUS

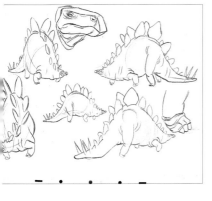

revenue; also, disappointing box-office returns for both *Pinocchio* and *Fantasia*, plus expensive construction of a new studio in Burbank, put the Disney brothers deeply in debt. In addition, in May an acrimonious strike of forty percent of the studio's workforce crippled Disney's output until the fall. Reitherman, like all of his colleagues who became the Nine Old Men, did not participate in the strike.

The Reluctant Dragon, released in June 1941 in the middle of the strike, was a cheaply produced, feature-length tour of the new studio using short cartoons interspersed with live action

(starring humorist Robert Benchley). The film's primary purpose was to generate much-needed income; it featured several animators as "actors" in cameo roles; Reitherman appears briefly in a drawing class. He also animated Goofy in *How to Ride a Horse*, a mock lesson in equestrianism that led to a popular how-to series starring the dull-witted character.

Little more than a month before the Japanese attacked Pearl Harbor, *Dumbo* was released. Reitherman, a directing animator on the film, was again cast against type. In several scenes featuring Timothy, the small, pugnacious mouse who is Dumbo's

best friend, he reveals a sensitive side—for example, in the scene in which the mouse sympathizes with the little elephant about his oversize ears and attempts to calm him, saying, "You're not really afraid of little me . . . are ya?"

Saludos Amigos, a feature-length compilation of four shorts, had its origin in a goodwill tour Walt and several artists made of South America in 1941. Arranged by the United States Office of the Co-ordinator of Inter-American Affairs (CIAA), the trip was part of our government's so-called "Good Neighbor" policy, a hedge against the spread of Nazi and Fascist sentiment in

Reitherman became a specialist in animating the slapstick actions of Goofy.

Latin America. Reitherman animated Goofy in a segment that compared the North American cowboy to the South American gaucho. Florencio Molina Campos (1891–1959), an Argentinean artist famed for paintings of gaucho life, was consulted and gave a lecture-demonstration at the studio in full gaucho costume. The final film, however, horrified Molina Campos because it spoofed everything he had taught and held sacred. "But horses don't play the piano," was his mildest complaint about the satiric film.[38]

By the time *Saludos* was released in February 1943, Reitherman had been gone from Disney for over a year. When America entered the war, he took a flight test; because he was an experienced civilian pilot, he easily got combat wings and a direct commission to ferry airplanes domestically, as well as to South America, North Africa, India, and the South Pacific. "I was more in love with flying than most of my contemporaries," he once said. "I would fly day and night, anytime. They used to call me 'iron fanny.' Interpret that any way you want."[39]

Reitherman flew into Burma to evacuate the wounded and makes it sound easy: "With any kind of luck, if you didn't have a fire and if you watched your navigation and didn't get lost, and you kinda knew where you were and how high the mountains were, it wasn't bad at all. And compared to the foot soldiers, what

those guys were going through, gee, it was a piece of cake, really."

Reitherman was Chief Pilot for the China wing. "Part of the Orient when I first got over there with the air corps, the living conditions, the squalor, all the pitiful human beings, the human condition, the dirt and the smell was, well, you had a deep sympathy for it, but also it was abhorrent." He flew from Shanghai to Bangkok to New Delhi and was again affected by "the human condition." Viewing people living in the streets of Shanghai or Calcutta, he said "some of it rubbed off on me in terms of the values of life and how transient it can be and what was really worthwhile. You can't watch that without wanting to do something about it."[40]

Reitherman was continually promoted and finally made Deputy Wing Commander, a desk job which he didn't enjoy. So he got himself demoted back to Chief Pilot because he "wanted to fly." When discharged in February 1946, his rank was that of major.

"I've often wondered why I did get promoted that fast because actually I was so satisfied just pushing throttles and flying as much and as hard as I could. It was fun for me." However, Reitherman was a careful, conservative pilot, not a daredevil. "There's a saying," says his wife Janie, "that there are old pilots and bold pilots, but no old, bold pilots." Reitherman still flew at age seventy-five. His bold, beloved brother Alfred was not so lucky: he died in a crash in 1944 after insisting on test-piloting a prototype of the Flying Wing.[41]

Flying, to Woolie, represented freedom. "You feel free of a whole lot of things you thought were responsibilities," he said.

Dashing and handsome and in his early thirties, he had no trouble attracting women. "I liked girls," he said, "and had some intimate things, relationships, certainly, but marriage kind of wasn't for me. I didn't want that sort of thing, at least not yet." But toward the end of the war, he began to wonder "when is 'not yet' going to end?"

The answer came when he met "the best thing that ever happened to me": twenty-two-year-old Janie McMillan, who was a perfect match for the thirty-seven-year-old, marriage-shy bachelor. Beautiful, intelligent, and as much in love with flying as he, Ms. McMillan was a former Latin teacher who "chucked it all and took off for the wild blue yonder" when she joined United Airlines as a stewardess in the fall of 1945. She met Woolie in 1946 when both were working for a new airline called Far Eastern Air Transport, Inc. F.E.A.T.I. initiated the first service in, out, and around Asia after World War II. Four DC-4s flew to Hong Kong, Shanghai, Bangkok, New Delhi, and back to Oakland, California, from Manila. Woolie was Chief Pilot International and Janie was Chief Stewardess in charge of a training school she set up in Manila.

Woolie and Janie met at Burbank Airport, briefly said "How do you do?", then flew a DC-4 to San Francisco, and four days later left for Manila.[42] There were six DC-4 pilots, but Janie tried to get on Woolie's flights because he was an excellent pilot with whom she "felt very safe." He was also "a real fun-loving guy" with "excellent good looks" who drew cartoons in the cockpit, then passed them out to the passengers. The couple quickly fell in love. "Once you'd flown internationally," says

OPPOSITE, *Janie McMillan and Woolie Reitherman met and married in 1946;* THIS PAGE, *the Reitherman family in the 1950s: (clockwise) Janie, Bruce, Robert, Woolie, and Richard.*

Janie, "with all the weather, radio, and maintenance problems you encounter in Hong Kong, Singapore, Bangkok, and later India, you knew a person better than you knew your own state-side friends." They sometimes flew one-hundred-eighty hours a month.

Three months after meeting, Janie and Woolie were married on November 26, 1946, at Ermita Presbyterian Church in Manila.

Outside the church, a typhoon was raging, an apt metaphor for their passionate, whirlwind courtship. Woolie called their relationship "a beautiful romance" and Janie felt "when you're twenty-two years old nothing is dangerous. Just all adventure."

The romantic adventurers had some near-death experiences. Once, coming back to Oakland from Manila—a forty-two-hour flight with three relief crews on board and about seventy passengers—four engines went out. Woolie managed to pull them out of that one when the DC-4 was only 800 feet above the water.

F.E.A.T.I. merged with Philippine Airlines and both Reithermans could have had jobs there, but they elected to return to the United States to start a family. When Janie became pregnant (she claims it was a "mile-high baby"), Woolie said "it kind of changed me"; that is, it altered his attitude toward international flying, its long hours and dangers. "I guess it's like building a nest or something. I wanted to stick around. I didn't want to be away. I wanted to see what the little guy looked like and be there when it was born, and it should be born in the USA and all those things. So you begin to have second thoughts. And surely flying was something I did love. There were two loves there, although there wasn't any real doubt in what I would give up. I wanted Janie and the kid and I think it was a natural urge."

In Oakland the newlyweds stayed for three months in a house Janie had earlier bought to rent rooms to stewardesses. Woolie looked for a job where he could "fly on a little feeder line" in the Bay Area. He also considered becoming a farmer or an outdoor worker at a nursery, ideas that to Janie, a self-described city girl, "sounded scary." Woolie went to an employment counselor who "couldn't understand why a man with his background wanted to do that." But like many men who came home from the war overseas, he felt it was "sort of heartbreaking to see how we were living at home [in America]"; our nation's comparative bounty and wastefulness compared to what he'd seen in the Far East. Janie said Woolie found the transition difficult because "he just didn't want to settle down and be a civilian."

It was at this vulnerable juncture that Walt Disney stepped back into Reitherman's life. While visiting Los Angeles to pack some furniture and books to take to Oakland, Woolie stopped to say hello and good-bye to friends at the Disney Studio in Burbank. Janie dropped him off at 9 A.M., drove up and down the street, read three or four books, and "didn't know where she was. Finally," she says, "about four o'clock, he and Walt walked out and Woolie introduced me." "We'd like to have Woolie come back," Walt said, disingenuously asking Janie if it was okay. "Whatever he wants," said she.

Walt, Woolie believed, had always been jealous of his free spirit and the fact that he "wasn't tied down too much." He admired Reitherman as a man and as an animator, and trusted him as a directing animator. Ollie Johnston noticed that "at parties Walt talked to him a lot and introduced people to him." When he learned that wild Woolie was married and expecting his first child, Walt thought (as Reitherman put it) "maybe now I gotcha."

For his part, Reitherman had always enjoyed working for Walt. But his decision to return *was* affected by his new status as husband and expectant father. "I came from a family of seven," he said. "It sure took me a long time to get my own. But that

feeling of family, I think, might subconsciously be part of what I enjoyed about the studio. I know I always thought Walt's values were so simple and all, as a human being. And his goals of doing family entertainment always attracted me."[43]

Reitherman rejoined the studio in late April 1947; he and Janie bought a house nearby in Burbank ("It had to be within five miles so he could come home for lunch."). Richard, the first of their three sons, was born in November.[44]

Reitherman was a directing animator (mostly of silly Goofy) in "Mickey and the Beanstalk" (part of *Fun and Fancy Free* [1947]); in *The Adventures of Ichabod and Mr. Toad* (1949), his Headless Horseman gave Ichabod Crane a hair-raising chase through the woods of Sleepy Hollow.

The postwar years at the Disney Studio were full of insecu-

rity, as Walt and Roy struggled to survive by diversifying their product. They made "package" features, such as *Make Mine Music* (1946) and *Melody Time* (1948), which strung together musical shorts, like a poor man's *Fantasia*. There were films that combined animation with live action, notably *Song of the South* (1946), and feature films that were completely live action, such as *Treasure Island* (1950). Some animated features, such as *Fun and Fancy Free* (1947) and *The Adventures of Ichabod and Mr. Toad* (1949), cobbled together projects that (before the war) were intended to be full-length features. None of these films had the impact of the prewar animated features. Walt wanted desperately to return to full-length cartoons, but the gamble was too expensive.

There were large staff layoffs and much belt tightening. Many animators and directors, prominent in the 1930s, had left the studio because of the strike or the war. "The day of the specialist was over," write animators Frank Thomas and Ollie Johnston in *The Illusion of Life*. Joe Grant's Character Model department, the studio's think tank for new ideas, characters and stories, was disbanded. Numerous writers, storyboard artists, and special effects animators were let go. Character animators, those who developed their art and craft during the 1930s under older masters, now began to gain unprecedented power.[45]

Walt's personal interest in animation waned after the strike and was further diminished by the war films the studio had to turn out to survive. Reitherman once said film cartoons "were a pain in the ass to Walt: the personnel problems, waiting around for animation to come in, changes, and all those things. I don't know any features that sailed through. Maybe *Dumbo*,

and that was below Walt's level of achievement. This is a tough damn medium, the way we do it."[46]

After his return to the studio, Reitherman participated in Animation Board meetings, which ruled on personnel changes, assignments, screen credits, etc. "When I came back, there was quite a lot of down feeling at the studio," he said. He observed Walt eating lunch at the Penthouse (the studio's private restaurant) and thought "he always seemed to be a little worried." Walt showed Reitherman his miniature train, a hobby his doctor had suggested to get his mind off the studio. He was always interested in Reitherman's opinion because he believed the

After animating monstrous dinosaurs and a whale, Reitherman showed a tender side with Timothy, the kind-hearted mouse who befriends Dumbo.

4 5

animator's separation from the studio during the war gave him a different perspective. Reitherman agreed and thought that "sabbatical leaves are very important for animation." His great escapes—first, through what he called a "respite" in Asia, then later as a director—gave him, he felt, "a power surge to a new altitude."[47]

Walt "used to be very much interested in what I thought of a property before it went into work," said Reitherman. "And I remember once, it embarrasses me, he'd say, 'Well, Woolie likes it.'" Reitherman also once claimed he "tipped Walt off dead center" in making his decision to produce *Cinderella*, a fairy tale that had bounced about the studio since the early thirties. By 1947 a treatment had been written and rough storyboards prepared. "I just went in his office, which I rarely did," said Reitherman, "and I said, 'Gee, that looks great. We ought to do it.' It might have been a little nudge to say, 'Hey, let's get going again and let's do a feature.'"[48]

Tightly budgeted, *Cinderella* relied heavily on live-action photography to guide the animators with the movements of the human characters (Cinderella, the Prince, the Stepmother, and others). The film was also pre-edited and assembled using live-action shots. "Economically, we could not experiment," write Thomas and Johnston, "we had to know, and it had to be good.[49] Only the animals (singing mice, a cat, dog, birds, and horses) were animated freely, that is, without live-action templates.

Reitherman animated a climactic sequence with two mice (Gus and Jaq), laboriously pushing and pulling a key up two flights of stairs to Cinderella, who has been locked in a garret by her evil stepmother. Reitherman believably communicates the plight of the little fellows who, given their small size, are faced with a formidable task. The mice struggling with the heavy object, their lack of coordination, and emotional stress made the sequence a comedy-drama gem.

Released in 1950, *Cinderella* was a success, the comeback of Disney feature cartoons and the fortunes of Walt Disney himself. Success in television and theme parks followed soon after. More animated features were produced, including *Alice in Wonderland* (1951) and *Peter Pan* (1953). In the former, Reitherman was the directing animator of the destruction of the White Rabbit's abode by a grossly enlarged Alice and an incompetent Lizard and Dodo; in the latter film, he was the directing animator of Captain Hook trying to escape a hungry crocodile.

Hook's personality had, at first, proved elusive for Frank Thomas, the lead animator on the character. After several tests, he incarnated him as a creature of varied moods and nuances. In Thomas's scenes, Hook is an elegant fop, vain about his appearance, and cultured; he is also paranoid, sly, and cunning: a control freak possessed of a hellish temper and a cruel streak. Since Thomas couldn't animate every scene of Hook in the feature (" 'Cause there was more stuff to be done than I could possibly do, and things still to be done that I should do, which were more important to the picture—ones they were trying to save

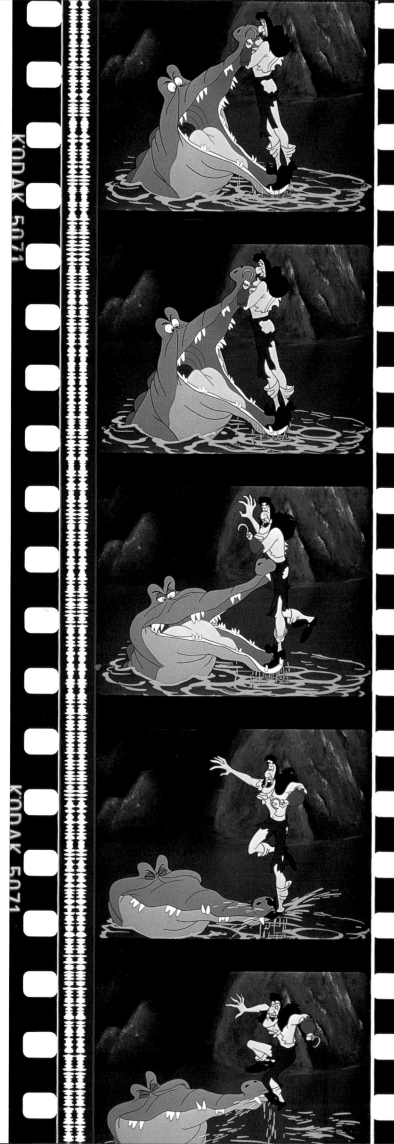

Reitherman animated Captain Hook as both a buffoon and a dangerous threat in Peter Pan *(1953);* THIS PAGE, *Woolie draws for Katherine Beaumont, the voice of Pan's Wendy.*

for me."), certain scenes were parceled out to Reitherman, "which they thought of as just action scenes," says Thomas.

Reitherman's over-the-top slapstick sequence, in which Hook attempts to flee a persistent crocodile, is hilarious despite (or perhaps because of) its unbelievability. The frantic sea captain is hit over the head with an oar, swallowed whole by the croc, and sent to the bottom of a lagoon in its belly; at one point he stands in the beast's jaws, forcing them open like a large mousetrap; finally, he smashes into the side of a cave, which the huge crocodile also crashes through. As if this were not cartoony enough, Reitherman also threw in animation's oldest gag: when Captain Hook steps off a precipice, he continues to walk on thin air until he realizes where he is, and then falls.

Throughout his ordeal, Hook remains unhurt and none the worse for wear. Reitherman was allowed to treat Hook as if he were Goofy. "The broadest sort of comedy intrudes suddenly in *Peter Pan* even when the threat of death is supposed to be taken seriously," writes Michael Barrier disapprovingly.[50] The broad approach was suggested by Walt himself. "Instead of killing anybody, we ought to get rid of them," he said at a story conference. "Maybe with the crocodile and Hook—the crocodile is waiting for him—then have a funny chase—the last thing you see is Hook going like hell. That's better than having him get caught. . . the audience will get to liking Hook and they won't want to see him killed."[51]

"That was so much fun," said Reitherman of his Captain Hook chase, "because I got that sequence with very little to go on." Left to his own devices, Reitherman dove in—damn the torpedoes, full steam ahead! "I think that's one of the things that Walt liked about what I was doing. I would usually build a sequence. Strengthen and enhance, make it funnier, make it more dramatic, whatever. I know some of the guys criticized me. There's no crocodile in the world that a man can stand up straight in and hold the jaws apart. I said, 'Nobody's gonna care about that if it's funny.'"

There are, however, other Hook scenes animated by Reitherman that show his versatility and ability to produce a more subtle characterization. "I'm a huge fan of Reitherman's animation," says animator Andreas Deja, who has brought his share of villains to the screen, including Jafar in *Aladdin* (1992), Gaston in *Beauty and the Beast* (1991), and Scar in *The Lion King* (1994). "He did fantastic Captain Hook scenes where he is climbing the mast, very distraught. Camera looking down," says Deja. "Great acting scene." Hook climbs the ship's rigging coming slowly toward the camera, his face dark, backlit by the sparkling sea. "Ha! You wouldn't dare fight old Hook man to man," he shouts at Peter in frustration. "You'd fly away like a cowardly sparrow!" "Woolie did a lot of action," says Deja, "but that scene showed me he was capable of great subtlety and insight into the character."[52]

The dog fight sequence in *Lady and the Tramp* is, according to Charles Solomon, "a textbook example of a Reitherman fight scene: Tramp defeats a pack of vicious mongrels to save Lady, helpless in her muzzle."[53] Originally, the sequence was lengthy, but Reitherman thought it should be shorter. "And what I wanted to do," he said, "was simply have a chase, corner, and then pow! And then a moment of pause. And don't fool around with it. A moment of pause. And then dive in and then go like everything! Then it had that one little great thing in it which was biting the rear hock of a dog and then they all fled."[54]

"Generally, you like to feel that the bad guy is going to win, and the good guy is going to come back," he explained years later. "And eventually the ebb and flow of that battle changes and then it ends up that the good guy wins. But I think it is so effective in action sequences if you can stop for a minute, because again, it is just too much to absorb. When it starts again, then it gives the audience a little jolt."[55]

The only sequence in *Sleeping Beauty* (1959) that gives audiences "a little jolt" is the one Reitherman directed: a battle between the prince and the dragon. He claimed he was on the serpent's side. "You bet! If you don't go at it that way, you'll tip our hand unconsciously and you'll start leading up to it in a slower way." Throughout the battle Prince Phillip is aided by three elderly fairies. "I could have done without the little fairy in there," grumbled Reitherman, "but I think Walt wanted it in there. It was a nice touch. It worked."

The sequence was propelled by Ken Anderson's storyboard, which was "choreographed" to Tchaikovsky's music. "The cutting was very contemporary in that it didn't have everything set up for the battle or anything. It just damn well happened," said Reitherman. "You didn't know how he got

Sleeping Beauty (1959) provided Reitherman with a classic fight sequence between a prince and a dragon.

Left to right, Ken Anderson, Bill Peet, Wolfgang Reitherman, and Hamilton Luske discuss a car accident for 101 Dalmatians *(1961).*

through the [forest of] thorns or how his horse ever got up there. We used to criticize that thing. But Walt liked it, thank goodness. You didn't need the logic. You didn't have time to think. That damn thing was driving at you all the time. That's what makes your adrenaline flow."[56]

In *101 Dalmatians* (1961), Reitherman directed the delightful "Twilight Bark" sequence: dogs from city to country-side spread a message about stolen puppies by their barking. The next feature, *The Sword in the Stone* (1963), based on a juvenile novel by T. H. White, marks the beginning of Reitherman's reign as a solo director of the features.

According to a 1963 studio press release, he "held the directorial reins alone on [*Sword*] . . . this marked the first time in the history of the studio that a full-length animated cartoon has been entrusted to the care and supervision of but one car-toon director." Historically, however, that is not accurate. David R. Smith and Robert Tieman, respectively the director and the manager of the Walt Disney Archives, point out that *Snow White* had one supervising director [David Hand], as did *Dumbo* [Ben Sharpsteen] and *Bambi* [Hand]. For *The Three Caballeros,* Norm Ferguson is listed as production supervisor–director. *Sleeping Beauty* had one supervising director [Geronimi]. There was a production supervisor [Ken Peterson] over Woolie on *The Sword in the Stone.* The *Sword* publicity release, which was sent out with Walt's approval, would seem to indicate, Smith surmises, "that Walt thought of Woolie's role as different on this film than he

had for those known as supervising directors on previous films. . . . Perhaps, and very likely, Walt gave Woolie more responsibilities on S*word* than he had given directors [or] super-vising directors on previous films."[57]

Why did Walt select Reitherman out of all of the Nine Old Men for this position? "Energy and experience," says Frank Thomas. "He'd done a lot more different types of scenes." Also, Walt shrewdly assessed the plusses and minuses of the leader-ship potential of his personnel at the time. Milt Kahl, Ollie Johnston, John Lounsbery, and Thomas were too valuable as personality animators. "Les [Clark] was off on his commercials," says Thomas. "Eric [Larson] was teaching the trainee animators. Kimball was out of the question. So who do you have? I would have picked Woolie."

"Ward Kimball suggested that Reitherman wound up in charge of the features because 'they picked out a guy who wouldn't give them much trouble,'" writes Michael Barrier in *The Hollywood Cartoon.* "Kimball was surely right," continues Barrier, for "as early as September 1939, Walt Disney had spo-ken approvingly of Reitherman's willingness to accept any assignment 'with a smile.'"[58]

Ollie Johnston says that when he and Frank Thomas first started working with Woolie as a director, "he didn't know enough about us. He was kind of doubtful of what we were try-ing to do. We were always talking about character relationships, humor that you got that way, rather than by gags. Woolie used a

"I became a director," Reitherman once said, "because Walt said, 'Be a director!' And also because I wanted to be a director."

lot of gags in his pictures. But Woolie gained confidence on *Sword*, did some wonderful stuff there, and he liked my stuff. I did the owl and Merlin and Wart [the boy who would be king], and Frank did the squirrel stuff." When the team started on *The Jungle Book*, Reitherman "was much more open" to what Thomas and Johnston wanted to do."

Bill Peet, arguably Disney's most creative story artist and writer, was an important figure in Walt's plan to pare down feature animation's top creatives to one director (Reitherman), one art director (Ken Anderson), and four master animators (Thomas, Johnston, Kahl, and Lounsbery). Peet did extraordinary work on *Dumbo* and *Song of the South*, among other films, and he was the only storyman to work solo on two features: *101 Dalmatians* and *The Sword in the Stone*. But in 1964, the volatile Peet quit abruptly after completing the first storyboards for *The Jungle Book*. "They wouldn't leave me alone on it," complained Peet of the animators; also he and Walt had an embarrassing public falling out. So story work fell to a committee (headed by Story Department veteran Larry Clemmons), with heavy input from the animators. The subsequent features of the 1970s contain often brilliant examples of personality animation, but lack Peet's strong sense of continuity and story structure.⁵⁹

Of his directorial method, Reitherman once said he attempted "to open up the communication so that the team was with you. There were maybe ten people who were very, very important to this. There were certain things in the story that you knew were going to happen, but you had to find out whether these animators could feel animation and situation possibilities to create good personalities. They had to get an enthusiasm.

"You had to respect and listen to everybody because we were all equals. The most important thing was the real cooperation of the four or five animators, and there were some story people that were tremendous, too."

Thomas recalls that Reitherman often "would have more faith in me than he should have had. 'Keep hangin' on,' [he'd say], 'you ought to be able to fix this. You ought to know what should be done.' Whatever. Once you showed him what it ought to be, he'd say, 'Hey, thanks. That's great. I now know what to do.' He'd change it all, but it'd still be good."

"There were a couple of times when he had a sequence that wasn't coming off," recalls Thomas. "He asked Ollie and me to rework it: 'Change the scenes, put in new scenes, you know what's supposed to happen.' So we'd take two or three weeks and reshoot some scenes and put it together. He'd say 'Yeah! yeah! That's it! That's it!' But he'd never go back and say, 'Well, let's see what did you do here? Like Ham [Luske] would have done; [try to] understand the whole thing." Reitherman thought that Luske "was just great," and said, "He taught me to analyze, [but] I'm not that kind of person, usually. I'm more impulsive about things."⁶⁰

To Thomas, Reitherman's problem as a director was that "he couldn't visualize. He didn't really know that. Ken Anderson and several people would say he can't visualize a thing. Somebody else shows how it should be, then he grabs hold of it. Now he knows and he can make it funny or whatever you want."

Reitherman directs voice talent: LEFT, *Maurice Chevalier, who sang the title song for* The Aristocats *(1970), and,* RIGHT, *Nancy Kulp and Sterling Holloway who (in the same film) played, respectively, a horse and a mouse.*

"I didn't stir conflict," claimed Reitherman. "I tried to cool it if I could." Nevertheless, he was capable of making decisions and sticking with them no matter what. "I guess I got this from the Air Force. Once you make up your mind, fly the flight plan out before you spook and go for a whole bunch of ideas. And that, I think, had a centralizing, a cohesive effect."

Another of Reitherman's weaknesses as a director, according to Thomas, "was that if he couldn't understand what was going on, his theory was to tip the boat over. So everybody's in the water. Time after time, I've seen him get just this close to a really good sequence and just by changing two little items—something the character did, something in the action, something in the arrangement of the scenes—you'd get it up to that point, you began to see this look on his face. 'What, what are they talkin' about? What, what?' Says, 'I don't think, I, I don't think the sequence belongs in the picture! Really. No, I don't think it belongs there at all.'" The sequence would be cut and that was that. "You couldn't [change his mind] when it had gone that far," says Thomas. "It's done."

One thing that made Thomas "the maddest about him" was his rough treatment of ideas. "If you have something tender," says Thomas, speaking allegorically, "like a flower growing up in a patch, and it's an unusual flower, and it hasn't got very far yet, but gee, it sure looks pretty and interesting, well, what he would do is pound it down to see if it grew back up! See if it was strong enough to take care of itself. He wouldn't nurture it, he wouldn't try to develop it. Just pound it down into the dirt." Reitherman "may have gotten mad at me several times," admits Thomas, but he never showed it, "except to stubbornly stick to something that he knew I didn't like."

On the other hand, Reitherman's openness to new ideas was one of his directorial attributes. "If something wasn't working," says Thomas, "his theory was take something new. Throw that out. Don't try to fix it." To Thomas, who said he spent his life "fixing things so they did work," this was an admirable trait.

Woolie learned directly from Walt, particularly on *The Jungle Book*, Walt's last film. Walt died during the production; Reitherman and his crew had to complete it by themselves. Reitherman followed Walt's dictates regarding the film's budget and his approach to entertainment. "Walt says you just gotta keep the costs down because [feature cartoons are] going to price themselves out of the business. So with that piece of advice, and with the way he pointed *Jungle Book* into entertainment and character development rather than into complicated stories that needed a lot of production qualities, he set the course for ten years after his death."

Jungle Book influenced Reitherman greatly in its approach to personalities, simple stories, and pure entertainment. "Instead of going the Rudyard Kipling way and trying to be authentic and complex with the story, [Walt] went straight for personality and entertainment. People reacted to those characters and the real earthy humor that was involved in that picture." In 1966 when Walt died (or, as Reitherman put it, "checked out") it became a matter of survival as far as he and the animators were concerned, "to keep this thing going, this thing called Walt Disney animation."[61]

The Jungle Book was a success. "The film earned a sensational thirteen million dollars on its initial release—a record for a Disney cartoon feature that stood for ten years," reports Charles Solomon.[62] *The Aristocats* (1970), the next feature, was remembered by Reitherman as "the picture that kept us [Disney's animation department] alive. There were some people at the studio," he said, "that really thought that maybe we had done enough of these feature cartoons, and maybe we just ought to capitalize on what we got and put the money into more live-action features, which you get your return on so much faster."

He recalled *Aristocats* was made for "a very reasonable" cost and "from then on things went well." In fact, the film was an enormous success at the box office, grossing $10.1 million domestically on its initial release (against production costs of $4 million). The film, which was also very popular in France, grossed an additional $16 million on its first release overseas.[63]

In 1971, Janie Reitherman started her own travel agency in Burbank, which lasted more than two decades and specialized in travel to Asia; Woolie occasionally helped out the office staff of five. The Reithermans—Woolie, Janie, Richard, Robert, and Bruce—were an active, busy family. "Woolie didn't have time to work on anything [from the studio] at home," says Janie. "Our weekends were hiking, horseback riding, flying trips." The family lived in a large house at the foot of the Verdugo Mountains filled with Far Eastern objets d'art and Woolie's early watercolors; panoramic windows offered a magnificent view of the San Fernando Valley. Seated there in a plush upholstered chair at sunset, before the twinkling lights of Burbank, was like being in a cockpit in a hovering aircraft perpetually poised between landing and taking off.

Reitherman continued to produce box office hits, such as *Robin Hood* (1973) and *The Rescuers* (1977), the latter described by Christopher Finch as "a transitional movie" in that "it was the first feature to display a significant influence from the next generation of Disney artists," including Ron Clements, Glen Keane, Andy Gaskill, and Don Bluth, among others.[64] Woolie looked at everybody's potential, says Dale Oliver, a top animation assistant whom Woolie decided should be an animator. The status change was, in Reitherman's mind, more important than mundane monetary considerations. When Ollie Johnston pointed out that Oliver's salary was already at the level of an animator's, Reitherman said, "What's your problem? Cut his pay and make him an animator!" Oliver laughs, remembering that "Ollie couldn't wait to come down and tell me."

Glen Keane remembers one of his "scariest times as a trainee" was presenting ideas to Reitherman for various animals—the Swamp Volunteers—in *The Rescuers*. "Woolie had this habit when he was thinking about something, he would suck on his cigar with his teeth gritted and his face scrunched as if what he was looking at was really painful. His face was this explosion of wrinkles. I thought I've never seen anyone hate

something as much as that." He didn't hate the drawings; he just looked as though he did. "He was a decision maker from his gut, not an intellectual one at all," says Keane. *The Rescuers* grossed nearly $45 million worldwide in gross box office receipts, outdrawing *Star Wars* in Europe. Reitherman was now one of the highest grossing directors of all time.

Keane noticed that among the older animators there was "a genuine respect" for Reitherman, even from Milt Kahl, who had loud differences of opinion with the director. "Everybody treated Woolie as the leader and as the decision maker. If Woolie made a decision, it went."

Reitherman's swashbuckling approach reminds John Culhane of James Thurber's implacable Commander in *The Secret Life of Walter Mitty*: he of the full-dress uniform with braided white cap rakishly tipped over one eye; he whose voice was like thin ice breaking; he who bolstered the confidence of the crew of an eight-engined Navy hydroplane. "The Old Man'll get us through," said the frightened sailors to one another. "The Old Man ain't afraid of Hell!"[65]

Besides Kahl, the only other one of the Nine Old Men to confront Reitherman about his directorial choices was Ward Kimball, then working on TV projects. "He made mistakes," says Kimball. "Like in *Robin Hood*: I said, 'Whatever happened to Maid Marian, who was in the tower? Don't you remember Errol Flynn saved her, [then] brought her in for the finish? What's this last sequence [where] she all of a sudden appears after being out of two sequences?' I told that to Frank and Ollie and they agreed with me. They were patsies 'cause all they said was, 'Oh, you know Woolie. He's stubborn.' But they let him go. If I had been on that picture, even though Walt wasn't there, I'd have raised hell!"[66]

With *The Fox and the Hound*, released in 1981, even more animation responsibilities fell to the younger artists. It was the last Disney feature Frank Thomas and Ollie Johnston worked on—they retired in 1978. After working on *The Rescuers*, Milt Kahl retired in a spectacular huff in 1976, and that same year John Lounsbery died. Eric Larson, a consultant deeply involved with the animator trainee program, was no longer animating.

Keane remembers that after Frank and Ollie retired "poor Woolie inherited this motley staff of neophyte animators to replace his big guns. He had worked with the best. Now, instead, he had me and a couple other guys. I remember him going over a *Fox and Hound* story reel on a Moviola in his office, looking through scenes. He said, "Let's see. We have this scene, a close-up kind of a romantic scene between Tod and Vixie, where they're face-to-face and supposed to be communicating a lot between them in their eyes. Well, I'm gonna have to cut this one out of the film. No one here can animate that.'"

Keane meekly protested. "I'd like to try," he said.

"Nope! No!" said Reitherman, moving on. "That one's okay," he said of the next scene. But the one after that? "No, this

Wolfgang Reitherman in his seventies.

one can't do. Nobody here can animate that one. Cut that out!"

"I would really like to try," said Keane.

"No!"

"He really felt," says Keane, "for him, there was nobody he had the confidence to give those kinds of scenes to. That was a very difficult time for him and for us, too. It takes a lot of faith in each other to do an animated film. At that time the deck had been shuffled a little bit too much for him."

"'Course, Woolie you must remember was a fighter pilot," says Don Bluth. "When you dive planes around and shoot at other airplanes, there's a certain something inside you that may not be able to access sympathy or softness without feeling threatened. When it came to the moment in the movie where you would expect a tender or sentimental moment, Woolie struggled with that, wasn't really able to let those emotions flow."

Personally, Bluth found Reitherman "very charitable. Many times he took me into his room and would say, I think you have the ability to be a director. You certainly have the ability to be a good animator. No doubts there. I'm going to help groom you and tell you what you should do." His first rule was "Do not change your mind a million times. Once you've made a decision, stick with it." "He did that himself," says Bluth.

In 1981, Reitherman decided it was time to retire. "There's a lot of world out there to see," he said.

In 1985, during a physical exam to renew his pilot's license, Reitherman's doctor told the seventy-five-year-old, "I wish I had a body like yours." On May 22, Reitherman played tennis in the morning and took his plane for a quick flight. After lunch with Janie, he stopped at the bank because the couple was leaving the next day for three weeks of fun in Maui. But, says Janie, "he died on the way home from the bank."[67]

At 2 P.M., two blocks from their house, Reitherman was driving at forty-five miles per hour when suddenly the car veered to the right, hit a stop sign, a fence, and a tree. Thrown against the steering wheel of his 1978 Lincoln Continental, he sustained head and chest injuries. Apparently, his heart had failed, but the shock of the accident brought him to consciousness again.

A friend driving past the scene saw Reitherman surrounded by an ambulance and police cars, "sitting outside and talking to people." He gave Janie's phone number and where to take the car for repairs. An hour and forty minutes later at nearby St. Joseph Medical Center, he was pronounced dead.[68]

Two years before, Reitherman had spoken with disarming candor to an interviewer about his directing career: "I became a director because Walt said, 'Be a director!' And also because I think I wanted to be a director. I grabbed hold real quick. Walt wanted to begin to get one director and one story man, which was Bill Peet in those days, and unify and solidify and keep the cream of the crop there. So, I guess I did all right. I think I always had enthusiasm about something or other. I couldn't do it, but I could generate it if I found the right kernel to get into.

"And, of course, when he died, it was more again a matter of, who else? and I think the animators always respected me up to a point. With the large talents there, it wasn't always easy to get respect. I always had little meetings so that those animators who were key to producing any picture were in on the decisions. It wasn't a fearless-leader type of thing by any means. They were part of the creative process, instead of dumping it out there and saying, 'Look, do it!'

"I think I had that facility to draw people out, to contribute, and keep . . . communication going."[69]

Eric Larson in 1905 and at his drawing board in 1970, surrounded by the owl in Bambi *(1942)*, Sasha, the bird from Peter and the Wolf *(1946)*, and Peg, a canine chanteuse from Lady and the Tramp *(1955)*.

CHAPTER three

Eric Larson

The young trainee animator was in a terrible fix. He had animated his test scene over and over again, five ways to Sunday, but it still didn't work. What's a novice to do?

"Usually it was at a point where you really thought your world had ended, nothing was ever going to be right again, the scene was completely unsavable," recalls Glen Keane, one of Disney's finest animators who, in the mid-1970s, often found himself in such a predicament. "That's when you would go in to see Eric."[1]

Eric was Eric Cleon Larson, the animator who gave Geppetto's kitten Figaro his feisty charm; made Peg, an aging canine chanteuse in *Lady and the Tramp*, strut her stuff; and was the method behind the madness of the zany Aracuan bird in *The Three Caballeros*. Larson flew Peter Pan and company spectacularly from London to Never Land, brought a prince and princess together for a song in the forest in *Sleeping Beauty*, directed the Brers Fox, Bear, and Rabbit to their Laughin' Place, gave centaurs their gallop and a Pegasus family their wings in *Fantasia*.

In 1970, the sixty-five-year-old master animator—considered as wise as the old owl he animated in *Bambi*—

Geppetto's kitten, Figaro, animated by Eric Larson.

was placed in charge of finding and training new animation talent. By that time, Larson more resembled a bear than an owl: a roly-poly hulk of a man with a belt line pulled up high across his ample belly. His voice was deep, his manner gentle, and a beautiful smile often lit up his large, florid face.

Larson's young charges adored him and constantly sought his calm and reasoned counsel. "Eric was very, very gentle," recalls Betsy Baytos, animator and dancer. "And he knew timing like nobody's business."[2] "He really cared for [cartoon] characters as human beings," says designer-animator Dan Haskett. "I was doing a pencil test on a baby boy, and Eric started pantomiming

patting this little kid on the head and got lost in what he was doing because he was thinking about the character so completely."[3] "He was someone you'd want to have as your grandfather," says top Disney animator Andreas Deja. "Very gentle, very deep. He was so much in line with Walt's philosophy on filmmaking."[4]

Larson's office was next to a large bullpen that at various times housed a dozen lively twenty-something novices learning their craft. Several of his former trainees have forged major careers in the areas of animation, design, and direction, including Tim Burton, Henry Selick, Brad Bird, John Pomeroy, Gary Goldman, Ron Clements, John Musker, Bill Kroyer, and Andy Gaskill, among others.

Back then, Larson was always available to provide encouragement and guidance in the difficult art of animation. "There was a ritual," says Glen Keane of the master's way of instructing. "He always did it the same way." It started with a knock on Larson's door and a mumbled "C'min!" The distressed trainee entered a tidy room where Larson sat at an orderly desk, a corner of which always held a selection of dog studies drawn for *101 Dalmatians* by Marc Davis, whose draftsmanship Larson respected highly. Larson would invariably be found writing a memoir begun in 1941, tentatively titled *Mouse House*.[5]

"Well, let's take a look at what you have here," he would say, referring to the stack of drawings clutched in the sweaty hands of the frustrated neophyte. Larson took the artwork and pounded the edges of the animation paper on the desk to straighten it (three times one way, three times the other); he cleared his throat, held the scene up and then began flipping the drawings very slowly, one after another.

"You'd be looking over his shoulder," says Keane. "It was so humbling and horrible to know Eric was looking at this chaotic mess of your animation."

"Well, this looks pretty good," Larson would calmly say. "I think maybe we can simplify it a bit."

He'd place the scene on his drawing board. Then, like a surgeon making the right incisions to save a patient's life, he'd select perhaps five out of, say, a hundred drawings that communicated the meaning of the scene. "And you may have done some travesty of confusing animation between them which he would ignore," says Keane. "But he'd find a couple of key poses that actually worked and that you had *actually* done. He'd flip those two and say, 'Now this! What we have here is a positive statement,'" a phrase Larson often used, meaning "Don't be ambiguous in what you're saying. Make it clear and strong."

Smoothing the papers with his large hands, he next laid a clean sheet of paper on top and drew a simple rough outline, an arc or action line, connecting the two poses. "I won't make drawings for them," he once said. "I make diagrams because if I made drawings they would be *my* drawings."[6]

"Now if you follow that action with the head here," he'd tell the kid, "you're going to get a nice, fluid movement and it's going to communicate. It's going to make a nice positive statement!" The relieved trainee left Larson's office feeling, "This is easy!" recalls Keane. "Why couldn't I have seen this? When you came in, it was the end of the world. When you left, the sun was shining, the clouds had parted and everything was possible. That's all a new animator is looking for—some hope, some reason to continue," says Keane. "Eric was really good at that."[7]

Eric Cleon Larson was born on September 3, 1905 in Cleveland, Utah (located about a hundred miles southeast of Salt Lake City), the eldest of five brothers and two sisters. His father, Lars Peter, born in 1877 in Spanish Fork, Utah, was the son of parents who arrived in Salt Lake City from Denmark in 1866. Eric's mother, Nora Oveson, was born in Ephraim, Utah in 1881; her father also left Denmark and landed in 1863 in Salt Lake City.

Both families were "part of the driving force that settled what is now Emery County, Utah, and the St. Johns area of Arizona on the Little Colorado River," according to Eric's brother Roald O. Larson.[8] The "driving force" was the Church of Jesus Christ of Latter Day Saints, commonly called the Mormon Church, which colonized numerous communities in sections of both states. Lars Larson wasn't necessarily a religious man, but he and his wife did go to church and raised their children as Mormons.[9]

Eric attended Mormon meetings throughout his life and was devout though not "extreme" in his faith, according to his brother Peter. None of Larson's coworkers or students at Disney recall him discussing his religious beliefs. "Eric was a collapsed Mormon," jokes Disney storyman Burny Mattinson, an assistant animator to Larson in the early 1960s. "'Cause he liked having a cup of coffee and they don't drink coffee. And then he had his sherry every day at lunch at Alphonse's," a Toluca Lake bar-restaurant frequented by Disney personnel.[10]

The first five Larson children were born in the small town of Cleveland, where Lars ran a general merchandising store. "I was born and raised on a ranch," said Eric in a 1985 interview, three years before his death. "And I always wanted to be a rancher up to the time of my second year in college. It's a life I still love, would still like to do."[11] It was not a life his father loved, however. "He had no desire to be a farmer, which his two brothers and father were. He didn't like that kind of work," says Peter Larson.

In late summer 1915, Lars and Nora moved their family to Salt Lake City, "prompted by their concern to provide educational opportunities for their children and a work market for their maturing family to move into."[12] "He figured he might be able to do better for the family [there] than in a little town," says Peter of his father.[13] In the big city, Lars became a buyer of men's apparel and manager of a clothing store. Peter describes both his parents as "very gentle," and his father as "a hard

LEFT, *Eric Larson with his sister, Clovis, and brother, Roald;* RIGHT, *Eric Larson in 1925.*

worker" who "spent most of his time coming to and from work" and who "loved every one of us." Nora was a homemaker who gave birth three times more in Salt Lake, but the youngest baby died only eight hours after her birth.

Economically, the family was "about medium class," says Peter Larson. "We had enough to get us along. We didn't have lots of money but we didn't seem to go without."[14]

In Salt Lake City, Eric completed his elementary education and attended Latter Day Saints University (a high school), where he developed his talent for art. He drew from about the age of ten, according to Peter, and once took a correspondence course.[15] In high school he worked on the yearbook for four years and in his final year became its art director; he also sold illustrations to *Westerner* magazine.[16]

In 1925, Eric entered the University of Utah, where he majored in journalism, "which at the time was his primary interest," according to Roald Larson. He wrote for the university newspaper *The Chronicle* and the yearbook *The Utonian.* Privately he studied drawing "with two men in Salt Lake" and drew cartoons for *Humoresque,* the university humor magazine,

which he also edited.[17] In addition, Larson drew illustrations for the Phoenix (Arizona) University yearbook, thanks to a recommendation from Commercial Arts & Engraving (familiarly known as Commercial A&E), a Los Angeles-based printer of yearbooks, which was impressed by his talent.

In order to help him juggle his writing, editing, and drawing assignments, Larson was allowed a private office with a skylight in one of the university's main buildings. Only two or three students were privileged to have keys to the office, which was off-limits to all others.

This busy, happy period of experimentation with literature and graphic arts ended in the spring quarter of 1927 when Larson abruptly left the university and Salt Lake City. A tragic accident and its aftermath changed the direction of his life; the incident so traumatized and embarrassed Larson that he never mentioned it to his colleagues at Disney, or in any interviews throughout his subsequent career.

It seems that one of the keepers of the keys to Larson's office broke the rules and brought friends there for "tomfoolery," as Roald Larson puts it. The highjinks ended when a school football

Eric Larson as a young man in Utah.

Commercial A&E heard about the young artist's predicament and offered him a job in Los Angeles, which he immediately accepted. "My whole attitude or my whole hope after getting out of school was to just travel and write," Larson told an interviewer in 1985, ignoring (as always) the sad event that had led to his leaving school before graduating and his desire to escape Salt Lake. "I had had a little success at school and I wanted to travel . . . just go around the United States and do nothing but sketches . . . of people and of the locales and write it up."[19] Instead, he worked at Commercial A&E as an art director for nearly six years, and on his own time made numerous oil and watercolor paintings and woodblock prints.[20]

While employed at Commercial A&E, he and an artist friend named Lewie Ryan traveled from Mexico to Canada making sketches for woodblock prints. At the eleventh annual Printmaker International Exhibit in Los Angeles, Larson's work was exhibited. Jurors accepted only works that "showed a definite purpose on the part of the artist to present his experiences in terms of art."[21]

Two Larson prints received an honorable mention, and a Salt Lake newspaper wrote a local-boy-makes-good article. The piece was illustrated with examples of his art and a photo of young Larson in a necktie and jacket, his hair parted in the middle, looking serious. The newspaper praised a print titled "Pursuit" as "a striking portrayal of a desert scene, showing a cowboy rider following a trail across the white sands," and noted that while Larson's "prints are a little heavily weighted with black . . . he shows a sharp incisive line."[22]

One day Larson looked out a window at work and saw a young woman. "He told the person he was sitting with that that's the girl he's going to marry," says Peter Larson. Gertrude Jannes, a Catholic whose parents had immigrated from Germany, worked in the building next door. Her third floor office was opposite Eric's across a small alley, and their romance began through the open windows of their two offices. Finally, Larson made a date and was "instantly attracted by her vivacious personality," while she, he said, "liked my Panama hat."[23] On February 17, 1933, they were, as he foretold, married. "Maybe he was a prophet, too," says his brother Peter, laughing.[24]

With marriage, Larson sought a new job with greater potential.[25] He thought that writing (his first love) might offer new opportunities, particularly in the popular medium of radio. At school he had written a western adventure serial titled *The Chill of the Viking,* and a friend suggested he bring it to Los Angeles radio station KHJ.[26] "They read it, and kind of liked the thought," Larson told Michael Barrier, "but they said that I didn't know anything about radio writing."[27]

KHJ sent Larson to seek advice from Richard Creedon, a writer who had recently left the radio station to work in the Disney studio story department. Creedon, whom Larson once

player fell through the office skylight and was killed. Although Larson was not even on campus at the time, several yearbook staffers and faculty members blamed him. He became a scapegoat for their rage and grief. "There were never any charges made, but they just kept hounding him about it," says Roald. The dean of the college defended Eric, but "they wouldn't let it die and [Eric] finally gave up on it."[18]

Walt Disney, left, views Pinocchio *test animation with Hamilton ("Ham") Luske, who became an important mentor to Eric Larson.*

likened to a koala bear because "he never smiled," agreed to work with him on the script, but some time in the future. "In the meantime," he suggested, "why don't you try something here?"—at Disney.

Larson replied that he had done a lot of cartooning, but had never taken it seriously. Besides, he felt the processes of animation were "mechanical as hell and all you do is sit on your butt and make a drawing between a drawing that somebody else made."[28] Also, Larson wasn't looking for that kind of job "'cause I could still sell stuff freelance. I wasn't suffering moneywise," a remarkable situation for an artist during the Depression and a testament to Larson's abilities.

Creedon shot back with a statement that stopped Larson's protestations cold, one that he never forgot: "The animated film will challenge any creative ability that you have or can develop." Creedon then explained what Walt was looking for, that he intended to produce animated features, and needed a creative staff.[29] Intrigued, Larson submitted some sample drawings ("A gal sweeping, a guy climbing a ladder, a guy tossing a lariat over a fence."), which Creedon gave to taciturn Ben Sharpsteen, a director and the Disney studio manager.[30]

To Larson, Sharpsteen was (like Creedon) "a father" figure who took studio newcomers under his wing and dispensed practical advice.[31] Impressed with Larson's drawings, Sharpsteen brought him to George Drake, head of the In-between Department, for a tryout. Drake, thought Larson, was "a strange person" who "meant well, but didn't have the capacity to work with people."[32] That's putting it mildly. By all accounts, Drake was a well-hated martinet who sat in a glass booth scowling at the pool of toiling in-betweeners. A former bricklayer, he arbitrarily destroyed many a newcomer's chances and held his position solely because he was married to Sharpsteen's sister.[33]

After two days Larson was ready to quit. "Drake would sit down and make a correction for you," he recalled. "And he couldn't draw worth a damn!" Drake's continual erasures of his own corrections made a drawing so black, it became indeci-pherable.[34] Creedon urged Larson to stick it out, and after a week he was hired at fifteen dollars per week on June 1, 1933. He spent five weeks in the in-betweener pool until animator Ham Luske saw his work and requested him for an assistant. His salary became eighteen dollars a week and soon it was twenty-five dollars. "I moved up with Ham," recalled Larson, "and less than a year later I was animating."[35]

Before coming to Disney in 1931, Hamilton S. Luske (1903–1968), a business major at the University of California at Berkeley, was an assistant cartoonist on the *Oakland Post-Enquirer* and a freelance cartoonist for *Collier's* and *The Saturday Evening Post*. At thirty years of age, he was two years older than Larson and poised to make important contributions to the development of personality animation through his keen analytical and organizational powers. Larson later described Luske as one of the most inspirational people he had ever met. As his assistant, Larson was in a unique position to learn from, and participate in, Luske's animation innovations.

"Ham was one of the first to really caricature action, to go way out in analyzing action," as Larson remarked to Michael Barrier in 1976.[36] Apparently, Luske never ceased studying motion, even on social occasions. Once, on a boat to Santa Catalina Island, for example, he took off his tie and pointed out the movement as the wind carried it. On the golf course, said Larson, "you'd go to putt and after you'd putted he'd act it out for you and talk about 'anticipation,'" an animation drawing principle in which each major action is preceded with a specific move that anticipates for the audience what is about to happen.[37]

What rescued Luske from being a boor who talked shop even at parties was his sincerity and an endearing sense of humor that leaned toward corny puns. There was also his personal struggle to make his hand achieve what he saw in his mind. Larson was impressed with Luske's unceasing efforts to get personality into his drawings. "He had to work like the dickens to draw. Freddy Moore just wrote it off, but Ham had to work his fool head off to make a drawing." Every action had to be "honest, and had to have character, and sincerity."[38]

Larson's start with Luske coincided with a new policy regarding the separation of tasks between an animator and his assistant. Up to that time, the animator functioned in two capacities: he was responsible for making the key poses of a character's action in rough form (and the assistant would make the in-between drawings also in rough); then the animator cleaned up those same key drawings as a guide for the assistant, who then in-betweened them in cleaned-up form as well. "I

moved in with Ham," said Larson, "and the first word I got was, we are now going to let the assistants be responsible for all the clean-up work. That was a heck of a thing to toss to me. I wasn't too sure what a clean-up drawing should be! Ham was very patient. He helped." It was a part of Walt's segmentation of labor into units of specialization, in order to foster quality and efficiency. In this case, the animators were freed to concentrate on the movement and expressiveness of what they were drawing. The tedious, time-consuming task of making the final lines neat and consistent ("clean") on all the drawings fell to their assistants. "To my knowledge," said Larson, "I'm the first guy who started that transition."[39]

Part of Larson's job was to act out actions for Luske. "I was everything from a rabbit with a tennis racket to Persephone."[40] The show-off rabbit who plays tennis with himself in *The Tortoise and the Hare* (1935) is one of Luske's triumphs, an example of his ability to observe real-life actions (he was himself a fine

athlete) and amplify them in animation. Another example is Jenny Wren in *Who Killed Cock Robin* (1935), a sophisticated parody of the mannerisms and movements of Mae West.

"You must exaggerate a character very much," Luske told new animators in a 1936 lecture:

Once you have picked up a character and are working on him, getting to know him better and better, you will find [that] moving pictures of other people will suggest attitudes, poses, characteristics you would like to get into your character. It's a matter of observation and trying to apply these observations to your work. . . . [It is] a cardinal sin not to put over each piece of business in our scene. In order to do that, we must do the action out in the clear where it can be seen. We must anticipate so the audience will know what will happen, and then show the result of the action.[41]

Persephone, the female lead in *The Goddess of Spring* (1934) represents a failed Luske experiment in animating the human form. Part of the problem was inappropriate models, such as bulky Eric Larson; part of it was poor design. But mostly, Luske had not yet figured how to adapt live-action humans into an animated "illusion of life" (a phrase he coined). That changed in time for *Snow White and the Seven Dwarfs*, thanks to Luske's insatiable explorations and analysis of motion.

"When they started on the heroine in *Snow White*," write Frank Thomas and Ollie Johnston, "Ham concentrated on her eyes and mouth and getting as much relative movement in her face as in her body. Crude as many scenes were, they began to live."[42]

"We want to make things more interesting than ordinary life," Luske theorized in a 1938 meeting with experienced animators on Character Handling:

Our actors are more rehearsed than everyday people— if somebody gets on a horse or opens a door or sits in a chair, we want to do it as simply and professionally as possible. Our actors must be more interesting and more unusual than you and [me]. Their thought process must be quicker than ours, and their uninteresting progressions from one situation to another must be skipped.[43]

During his year with Ham Luske, Larson learned much about animation theory and technique. He also observed how a master teacher communicates effectively; Larson spoke admiringly of Luske's ability to handle people and his understanding nature. Thirty years later Larson applied all that he had learned from Ham Luske, and how he learned it, to his own teaching.

He also got a lesson in dealing with the unpredictable Walt

Disney. Larson's first contact with the boss was in December 1933, shortly after Walt's daughter Diane was born. In the yard outside the Hyperion studio, Walt was talking to a director, when Larson passed by and said, "Congratulations, Mr. Disney," and kept going. "All of a sudden, I heard, 'Who the hell is that?' I told Ham about it, and he said, 'Don't say, Mr. Disney. You call him Walt, never Mr. Disney.' So that was my introduction to him."[44]

As a junior animator, Larson first worked with director Sharpsteen on *Two-Gun Mickey* (released in 1934) picking up odds and ends of other animator's scenes.[45] In subsequent, meatier assignments, such as *Cock o' the Walk* (1935) and *Three Little Wolves* (1936), Larson brought charm and personality to animals. For *Snow White*, he and three other novice animators (including Milt Kahl, a promising talent hired in 1934) animated about a thousand feet of film of the numerous animals that follow the princess throughout.

Some scenes of the critters—birds, squirrels, chipmunk, bunnies, deer, a faun, and a turtle—contain twenty-three animals, each moving differently and interacting with each other, Snow White, or the dwarfs. In animating this logistical nightmare, Larson did not separate the animals onto different levels; he animated every one on a single sheet of paper. "I've got to see everything down there," he explained. "It's the only way to keep things fluid—part of them moving, part of them coming to a stop." Larson used thumbnail sketches every two feet to "try and feel my composition. For example, when a whole bunch of them are creeping up to Snow White, how are you going to control them unless you take it about every foot and work out your drawings, and then just work straight ahead. With a little

THIS PAGE AND OPPOSITE, *Larson animated the forest creatures in* Snow White and the Seven Dwarfs *(1937), a multitude that was hard to keep track of.*

inspiration, a little luck, you come into your patterns. But you'd better kind of know where you're going."[46]

During the production, Larson and Luske (who supervised the animal sequences as well as Snow White's animation) gave a talk to trainees on the handling and construction of the animal characters. Among Larson's comments:

In action, it is necessary to consider characteristic poses of the animals. The animals are generally alert and inquisitive at times. . . .The turtle is on the Edward Evertt [sic] Horton type. More or less sleepy in his looks. He gets where he is going, but is always just a little bit late. He is the comedy relief in the picture, not a snappy little character like the chipmunk. . . .The deer are the closest to being natural of anything we have. It is hard to caricature them or make them look nice without drawing them like deer . . . .[47]

Years later, Larson criticized the design of the animals in *Snow White*, especially the deer. "You could hardly call them deer. They were sacks of wheat," he said. "When we got to *Bambi*, the idea was to be honest with them."[48]

Larson's salary at the beginning of *Snow White* was fifty dollars a week, but toward the end of production in October 1937 he was making $125.[49] He was now a full animator and his next assignments were . . . more animals! Mostly fowl of one kind or another in the Silly Symphonies *Farmyard Symphony* (1938) and *The Ugly Duckling* (1939).

He became an animation director for the feature

Pinocchio, and his affinity for animals brought him a role that he fashioned into a masterpiece of pantomimic personality animation. Figaro, Geppetto's delightfully childish kitten, established Eric Larson as a master animator, less than a decade after joining the Disney studio.

"Trying to come across on the screen with a character that people can relate to is your first challenge," Larson once explained. Figaro was based on a young nephew.

A four-year-old kid is quick to feel hurt if he doesn't get his way. He is probably going to put on a little show for us, a tantrum. . . .[T]ake an animal, like Figaro, move him around as a kitten would move. You don't take any liberties with that kind of action, but now

you inject into him a personality of this young kid who is used to having everything he wanted. . . .[T]his is where we would cross from realism to fantasy, in my opinion. . . .[50]

A magical crossover from reality to fantasy occurs in Larson's very first scene with Figaro, which lasts about five seconds. Descending a staircase ahead of Geppetto, the kitten's head is lowered as he bounds down a couple of steps to the wooden floor. The cute, believable action is that of any real kitten, nicely observed and animated. Figaro next turns his head away from us (we haven't clearly seen his face) to meow in answer to comments from Geppetto. Again, cat owners will recognize the reality within this action: how cats often "converse" in response to their owner's voice.

But then Figaro turns and, for the first time, we see him full-face, smiling, his paws tracing an elegant arc

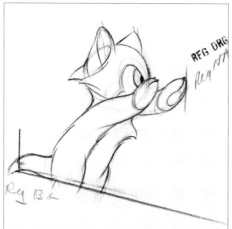

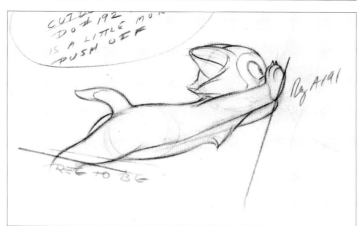

that leads to a proud and twinkling prance out of the scene screen-right. He is now an eager kid ready for adventure and leading the way with pleasure. Real cats, as we know, do not smile. But a Cheshire Cat can. In Larson's brief scene, Figaro's natural actions and anatomy have melded into something beyond the ordinary. He is a caricature of life, injected (Larson's word) with sentience and humanity. Before our eyes he became a sparkling personality: Figaro, a special kitten indeed.

Figaro's change from the real to the super-real reminds one of a similar scene in *Feline Follies*, a silent, black and white cartoon from 1919 marking the debut of the cat who became world famous as Felix. Like Figaro, Felix alternates between animal and human behavior in his very first scene:

Figaro opens a window in Pinocchio, *in magical pantomimic animation by Eric Larson.*

He first appears as a normal cat standing on all fours, but soon becomes an anthropomorphic "supercat"; not only can he, at will, change his prehensile tail into both functional objects and symbols of the human thought process [a question mark], but he is also able to stand upright to woo his ladylove, acting and looking like a little man in a cat suit.[51]

Larson's most memorable Figaro sequence occurs when Geppetto asks the sleepy kitten to open the window after they have retired to bed. As he petulantly kicks back the covers, a scowl sours Figaro's whiskered face, and he rolls out of his small

bed. Bounding across Geppetto's wide bed, he sinks into the thick blanket. Opening the window is formidable for the fur person. Cleverly using his hind legs, the kitten opens the heavy wooden frame a crack, then pushes it wider with his front paws as he runs along the sill. Misjudging the distance, he loses his balance and has to hold onto the sash with two front paws for dear life. Figuring it all out in his cartoon brain, Figaro swings his lower body so that his toes touch the wall; then he inches up backward to safety. Throughout, Larson maintains a delicate balance between reality and caricature in both drawing and performance. The sequence never spills over into pure cartoon exaggeration, yet neither is it slavish to natural motion either. Always believable and entertaining, the little character brims with personality. Figaro's window-opening sequence is "thrill" comedy reminiscent of Harold Lloyd hanging from a huge clock in the silent classic *Safety Last* (1923).

Larson enjoyed supervising animation of the majestic flying horses in *Fantasia*'s "Pastoral Symphony." "You warmed [to] the beauty of the movement that the horses were capable of doing," he once said, "of landing on the water as if they were as light as birds. No big heavy splashes or anything, but they would land with a quality of assurance. They were positive in what they were doing."[52] Centaurs carrying baskets of grapes to a bacchanal were another matter. Larson thought they were "lousy to animate," because their design was "completely wrong." For reference, he and a couple of other animators carried baskets on their shoulders and skipped before a live-action camera; but Larson felt they "did not analyze it sufficiently to get a horse action in there. If you watch the front legs of those centaurs," he said, speaking of the mythical beasts as if they were flesh and blood, "they have a certain human feeling, and it shouldn't have been that way."[53]

How seriously Larson took the challenge of animation (and how real were the characters to him) is indicated by the fact that he still complained about the centaurs forty years later. "If I had just thought about this then, it would have been so much better," Larson lamented to his young trainees in 1980. "He was honestly upset," recalls Dan Haskett.[54]

Walt Disney appreciated Larson's talent, although he rarely gave direct praise. For instance, when he saw *Pinocchio*'s pencil tests, according to Larson, Walt "fell in love with Figaro and made the point [to one of the film's directors]: 'Give Eric all the footage he wants.' And away we went."[55] Larson's perfectionism, reflecting Walt's own, was learned the hard way: through tough, face-to-face criticism from Walt in the cramped Hyperion studio projection room aptly named "the sweatbox."

"I had some demoralizing experiences with him right off the bat when I started animating," Larson recalled. In *On Ice* (1935), Mickey and Minnie skated through a long scene with big, open-mouthed smiles on their faces because, said Larson, "they were happy." Walt sat glumly watching, then abruptly said to Larson, "Can't they ever shut their damned mouths?" News

6 5

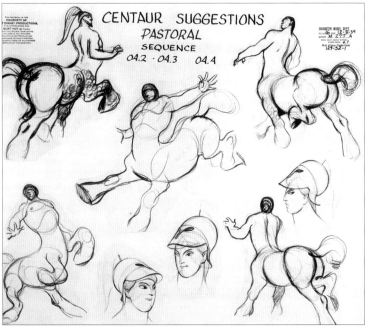

Larson at work on Pinocchio in 1939; for years he bemoaned his "poor" animation of Fantasia's centaurs. The old owl in Bambi was a happier assignment.

of the blunt critique flew through the studio, where Walt's sycophants made *Schadenfreude* a cottage industry. "I hadn't even gotten to my room," said Larson, "when somebody stopped me on the way and said, 'I hear Walt wants you to shut Mickey and Minnie's mouths.'"[56]

Larson perceived Walt's attitude toward animators as "You're only as good as your last scene." Although he claimed he was "never taken over the coals by him," Larson knew when the boss was displeased, even though Walt's statements were often Delphic in their oracular ambiguity. After watching *Bambi* test animation of an old owl that Larson had designed, Walt stood up, said "I'm disappointed," and walked out. Others might have required a Rosetta stone to decipher the meaning of that remark, but not Larson. "You bet your life I knew what he meant." Larson had gotten "too wound up in beautiful drawings" and Walt was suggesting that the owl's design be simplified to make it easier to read on the screen. "For still drawings they were nice," said Larson, "but they just would not animate worth a damn."[57]

As one of *Bambi*'s four supervising animators, Larson managed a staff of nearly thirty people including ten animators working on various scenes of the stags and birds. "He had the largest crews of any of the top men," write Frank Thomas and Ollie Johnston:

> and there was always someone in his room with a problem, often nothing to do with production. Eric was always patiently listening, occasionally counseling, but somehow in spite of this, he was one of the best footage men in the studio. When and how he did it no one ever figured out. And to top it all, he was able to get footage out of most of his crew.[58]

Larson's pedagogical bent was tested by two in his crew from the story department who had excellent drawing skills, but had never animated before. Retta Scott drew like no one else the powerful, vicious dogs that attack *Bambi*'s girlfriend,

Larson's sensitivity, draftsmanship skills, and affection toward animals led him to animate many a bird, deer, and mouse throughout his Disney career.

and Jack Hubbard drew birds proficiently. It was Larson who patiently helped each artist plan the patterns of action and timings of their scenes. In addition to his directing chores, at five P.M. each day for months, he went downstairs to animate the owl and various other characters until nine P.M.

On the morning of May 28, 1941, Larson arrived at work to find his wing of the studio empty and his crew missing. Nearly all of them were outside on a picket line, part of the 300-plus employees participating in a labor strike against the Disney studio which lasted till mid-September. The strikers, mostly from the so-called "lower echelons" of the animation hierarchy (assistant animators, in-betweeners, inkers, and painters), demanded union representation, higher wages, and job security. Only two top animators joined the line: Art Babbitt, a union organizer and a leader of the strike, and Vladimir Tytla, who struck out of loyalty to his good friend Babbitt.

None of the animators who became the Nine Old Men joined the strikers, nor did a majority of studio staffers. They rallied behind Walt, who took the walkout very badly and fought back emotionally, labeling the strikers Communist dupes. Larson described the strike as a "bombshell" and a "heartbreaking thing." Nevertheless, he was not a union man, as he explained to Michael Barrier years later. "My dad in his business was very anti-union. I was raised anti-union. I sympathized some with what the guys wanted, but I think it was the wrong way of getting it. I was one—along with Norm Ferguson, Ollie Johnston, Frank Thomas, Ward Kimball, Wilfred Jackson—who worked our tails off to get that thing straightened out. When you go through a picket line for ten solid weeks, mister, it takes something out of you." Each morning as Larson arrived at work, Art Babbitt hollered into a bullhorn: "There goes Eric Larson. He belongs out here." Said

Slow, calm, and deliberate Larson brought to life two very quick, vivid, and nervous birds: the madly destructive South American Aracuan, seen THIS PAGE in Melody Time *(1948) and,* OPPOSITE, Sasha, *a passionate, caring Russian sparrow in* Peter and the Wolf *from* Make Mine Music *(1946).*

Larson, with residual anger nearly four decades later, "I never belonged out there, period!"[59]

Soon after the studio became unionized, Larson was elected president of a union unit, a position which he claimed he "didn't like." But he was known and respected throughout the studio for his quiet, mature judgment; when conflicts arose at union meetings, Larson invariably soothed everyone with what Ward Kimball called his "pour-oil-on-troubled-waters speech."[60] Straddling the fence in conflicts between the union and the studio brought Larson problems with Walt, who "would think I was double-crossing him." A labor-relations advisor explained to Walt why Larson took difficult positions. "I don't think he ever held it against me," said Larson. "But there were times that I felt he did."[61]

When the Animation Board was formed in the early 1940s, Larson was a charter member. "We hired, we fired," said Larson. "That's an awful thing to say, but we passed on the quality of people's work, and he [Walt] listened. We could simply say this person is not cutting it, or this person is doing an excellent job and should be advanced." The board also suggested moving personnel around according to their strengths and weaknesses as animators, assistants, and in-betweeners. "Then everybody in the group knows exactly what's contained in a certain amount of footage that the animator's supposed to get on the screen, so they have a positive interest in it."

Aside from his involvement in Disney studio politics, Larson continued to turn out exceptional animation. In the 1940s, he animated a couple of unique birds whose flightiness (pun intended) was the opposite of his slow, deliberate, dignified demeanor. The insane Aracuan Bird first appeared in *The Three Caballeros* (1945) and, though allotted little screen time, made a strong impact.

With his bright red topknot, rhythmic mutterings punctuated by sharp cries, and annoying, anarchic personality, the Aracuan resembles a South American Woody Woodpecker. Larson animated the mad bird like a mechanical doll, puttering along, turning an occasional cartwheel as it goes on its giddy way. The Aracuan is a spirit of the film medium itself and its ele-

ments: in *The Three Caballeros* he first pops out of a home movie that Donald Duck is showing and walks up the film projector's light beam.

Magically and illogically the Aracuan appears in quick peek-a-boos from one side of the screen, than the other, now from the top, now the bottom. With childish, mindless glee he disrupts the narrative—it changes direction or stops whenever he shows up—and alters other characters' actions (he steals a cigar from the parrot José Carioca in the middle of a soliloquy; forces an anthropomorphic train to radically detour). He toys with the substance of film itself and its mechanics—literally running off the film frames as they race by—thus affecting the audience's perception of what they are watching. Tex Avery, the great Warner Brothers and MGM cartoon director, reveled in such self-referential distancing devices that foreground the process of animation, rather than audience-involving stories and believable characters; but in Disney films, the use of such devices was unusual.[62]

Another memorable Larson bird character is Sasha from "Peter and the Wolf" in the postwar omnibus feature *Make Mine Music* (1946). Although resembling the Aracuan (in beak shape, coloring, and quickness), Sasha is petite and (more importantly) a caring and generous, if nervous, personality. By comparison, the Aracuan is mindless, an amoral automaton. Sasha is loyal (to Peter), forgetful (of his hat and his safety), angry (with the wolf), grief-stricken (for his careless friend Sonia the duck), calculating (in figuring how to vanquish the wolf), and joyful (when Sonia survives). Larson's animation of tiny Sasha is admirable for its depth of feeling and the clarity of its pantomime within a constricted time frame—the movements of the fidgety, Cossack-hatted bird was dictated note by note by a flute. "I had the musicians put down on the exposure sheets [charts that detail the action, dialogue, and music frame by frame for a scene] each and every note that involved Sasha," said Larson, who did most of the drawings himself.[63]

After the war, the Disney brothers struggled to return to making full-length animated features. But money was scarce and

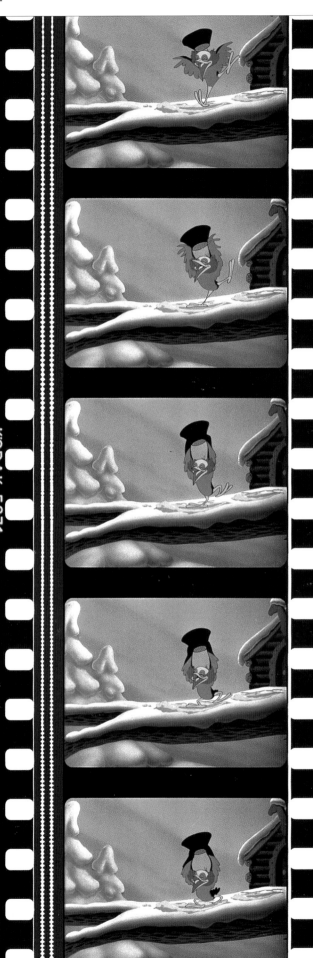

In the 1950s Larson animated his share of humans, such as Cinderella, THIS PAGE, *seen with frames of the live-action reference film, and,* OPPOSITE, *Peter Pan and Wendy flying to Never Land.*

there were a number of detours on the way to their production of *Cinderella* in 1950, including combination live action-animation features such as *Song of the South* (for which Larson was a directing animator of the "Laughing Place" sequence).

The Adventures of Ichabod and Mr. Toad, a weak feature released in 1949, truncated and combined two projects originally conceived before the war as separate full-length features: *The Legend of Sleepy Hollow* and *The Wind in the Willows*. Before *Wind* was shelved in 1942, Larson, Milt Kahl, Frank Thomas, and others had animated several sequences. When the project was revived as *Mr. Toad*, director Jack Kinney took over and gave animator Don Lusk the roughly animated sequences to sort out. In the final film, much of the original animation was used, but somehow Lusk got screen credit for scenes Larson had done. And Larson received no screen credit at all.

In the past, Larson had volunteered to supervise or animate sequences knowing he would receive no screen credit; he didn't mind helping a friend, such as Ben Sharpsteen, who asked him to work on the *Dumbo* "lullaby" sequence of baby animals cuddling with their parents. But the inexplicable, involuntary lack of credit for *Mr. Toad* angered Larson and for years he expressed his resentment: "Some of my favorite scenes," he

lamented, "like Ratty saying, 'Sorry, Toad. We misjudged you!' The best dialogue thing I ever did."[64]

As always, Larson got emotionally involved with the characters. "I guess Toad was [one of] my favorites," he told a television interviewer. "I think some of the most enjoyable actions I was ever able to get on the screen was [Toad's] defense of himself in court. I felt that I did get [a] tone that is the peak of arrogance in that figure of action, in that particular bit of business."[65]

Larson was the first to animate the heroine in *Cinderella*, whom he saw as a sixteen-year-old with braids and a pug nose. Marc Davis next came onto the production with a version of Cinderella that was, according to Larson, "more the exotic dame." Davis drew her with a long swanlike neck "as only Marc can draw," said Larson admiringly. These draftsmanship divergences were not apparent to moviegoers after a gifted cleanup artist named Ken O'Brien made, as Larson put it, "Marc's gals and my gals look like the same gal."[66]

During the fifties, Larson directed animation in *Alice in Wonderland* (1951)—notably the haughty caterpillar sequence— and in *Peter Pan* (1953), he oversaw the spectacular flight from London to Never Land of Peter Pan, Tinker Bell, and the Darling children (Wendy, John, and Michael). The sustained

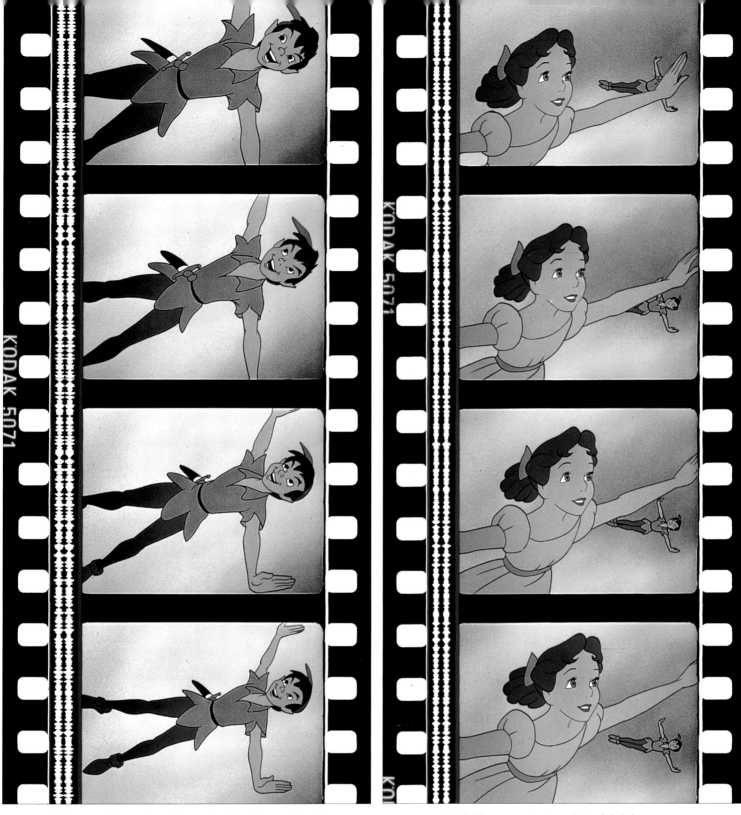

flying scene has a three-dimensional quality as the characters elegantly swoop toward and away from the camera, pass over London Bridge, and glide down the Thames toward "the second star to the right and straight on to morning."

Said Larson:

We not only used [the] multiplane [camera], we had to work the hell out of that camera-per-fields [the area actually photographed by the camera] and in-and-out exaggerations, going away from you and coming at you. Besides drawing that, we put emphasis on it by using [camera] tilts. It was a very beautifully worked-out thing mechanically. In planning it all I said, 'I wanna be

at certain fields at certain times.' We didn't have a computer. The guys had to figure it out on their fingers and on their slide rulers. So it was really a terrific job, and they did a very, very commendable job on it. It has a certain thrill to it: we can fly, we can fly, we can fly![67]

Cleanup artist Dale Oliver was astounded, he says, by the complicated "mechanics of that scene. Eric was a master at laying out mechanics."[68] In *Lady and the Tramp* (1955), Oliver also cleaned up most of Larson's drawings for a showstopping sequence starring Peg, an over-the-hill, singing canine showgirl formerly "in the Dog-and-Pony Follies."

Though a bit long in the jagged tooth, heavy of bottom, and

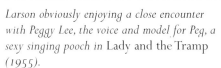

Larson obviously enjoying a close encounter with Peggy Lee, the voice and model for Peg, a sexy singing pooch in Lady *and the* Tramp *(1955).*

throughout, such as an over-the-shoulder smolder as Peg says the word "scoundrel," and a knowing eye squint on "cad." On the lyric "he gives you plenty of trouble" a lascivious tongue pops out of Peg's smiling mouth, and her hot-flash eye flutter indicates that the lady doth protest too much and wouldn't mind the return of that special "trouble."

Larson, the good Mormon, clearly enjoyed working on this naughty assignment. He "always laughed about it," recalls an associate. "He always felt [coworkers] thought he must have been in a brothel when he was doing it."[70]

imprisoned in a dog pound, Peg can still strut and belt out a torch song ("He's a Tramp") with sultry sizzle. Larson, who reminded Oliver of "a dignified banker," brought to the brief performance a sly sexiness and subtle humor. "His taste was so good," says Oliver, "so discreet."[69] A rolling piano, bass, drum, and cymbal establishes a stripper's beat, as Peg moves into a key light to lament her former boyfriend, a "no-'count pup" with "an eye for the well-turned paw." Peg's ample rear end bounces lightly as she sashays in rhythm with the music's beat.

Larson places wonderful little personality touches

Peg's fur alternates between a boa and a sable, which lends softness to her hardened Vegas swagger. Her peroxide-blond peekaboo bangs (hiding one of her pretty blue eyes) recall Veronica Lake, Joan Blondell, Jean Harlow, Marilyn Monroe, and other sexy screen blondes. Larson claimed he based Peg partly on Mae West and a lot on Peggy Lee, who composed the song and sang it in the film.

"The way she sang the song was a great inspiration," he said. "Also the way she walked. Because she had a pretty nice movement and these are things that you try to pick up from the human being and translate into the animals."[71] Right. Production photos show Ms. Lee laughing with an obviously smitten Larson, who clearly enjoyed a close-up "study" of the glamorous star. Says Burny Mattinson, who worked on *Lady*, "He said he thought she was real sexy, Peggy Lee."[72]

In late 1953, Wilfred Jackson suffered a heart attack and Walt asked Larson to take over as supervising director of *Sleeping Beauty*. "That was my downfall," Larson said years later of his participation in the troubled production.[73]

A script for the film was started in 1951, but there were numerous revisions and delays, most caused by Walt himself. Since the war, the diversification of the studio's product had left him with less time and energy to devote to animation. In the 1950s, live-action film productions, such as *The Story of Robin Hood* (1952), *The Sword and the Rose* (1953), and *Rob Roy, The Highland Rogue* (1954) engaged him; then came a weekly network television program, *Disneyland* (which premiered in fall 1954) and the daily *Mickey Mouse Club* (1955); and there was the planning of the huge Disneyland theme park, which opened in Anaheim, California in 1955.

A large layoff of studio personnel occurred when *Lady and the Tramp* was completed. Most of those remaining were assigned to the theme park or TV series. "Eric got his first sequence to work on [in *Sleeping Beauty*] and had very little help," remembers storyman Burny Mattinson. "Even his longtime assistant George Goepper was modeling things for Disneyland." Walt micromanaged every project on the boards from films to amusement parks, and his personal okay was required for all scripts, storyboards, casting, costumes, film dailies, pencil tests, designs, building construction, and so on. "So everything moved very, very slowly," says Mattinson.[74]

73

Discussing storyboards in 1958 for the troublesome Sleeping Beauty *(1959) are, left to right, supervising director Eric Larson, storymen Joe Rinaldi and Don DaGradi, and animator Marc Davis;* OPPOSITE, *the very expensive scene 31.*

"We were just going over and over the story and nothing was getting done," said Larson.[75] Finally, Walt gave the word: "Let's get this thing in animation." And the glacier began to move. Storyboards for sequence #8—princess Aurora meeting the prince in a forest—went from the story room across the hall into the director's room. "And away we went," said Larson.

"What we want out of this is a moving illustration. I don't care how long it takes," Walt told him. Larson was determined to give him what he wanted. The "illustration" Walt favored, however, was not simple. Eyvind Earle, the film's art director, based his designs on opulent medieval tapestries, illuminated manuscripts, Persian miniatures, and the paintings of Brueghel and Botticelli. Walt liked the look of Earle's distinctive concept paintings—elegant, cold, dark, angular, and extremely detailed—and insisted that the *Beauty* crew get "that" into the picture.

Trying to please Walt by integrating three-dimensional characters into Earle's stylized, color-saturated flat backgrounds frustrated the production's layout artists and animators. Earle, secure in Walt's backing, stubbornly refused to compromise, and his argumentative temperament and sharp tongue alienated many, including Frank Thomas and Ollie Johnston. Eric (oil-on-troubled-waters) Larson, however, got along with him fine.

"Personally, I was deeply moved by what Eyvind Earle did. And Walt was, or he would never have put him on there. He may have been too strong in some instances, but I can't tell you of any place in the picture where the character didn't read."[76]

Larson shot live action as reference for animators Marc Davis and Milt Kahl, who started to bring the heroine and hero (respectively) to life. Burny Mattinson never forgot scene 31 in forest sequence 8 because it was forty-three feet long, an extraordinary length of screen time. It was Mattinson's job to in-between the animation in rough form; then a clean-up artist (Clair Weeks) went through the key poses and Mattinson in-betweened it again. Walt looked at it and said the sequence was "dull as the devil! Get some life into it!"

Suddenly, Kahl was designing animals, story people were inventing new bits involving the princess and the animals, and John Lounsbery was animating the critters. Iwao Takamoto cleaned up the new material in scene #31 and Mattinson once again in-betweened it. "Marc and Milt felt so sorry for me," Mattinson says, "they took me over to Alphonse's, the old watering hole, and bought me lunch. Then they brought out a cake that said on top of it 'Happy 31!'"

Don Bluth, later the director of the animated features *An*

American Tail (1986) and Anastasia (1998) was in 1955 an eighteen-year-old assistant to John Lounsbery. "The girl [Princess Aurora] was such a holy precious thing that we were only able to carve out one [clean-up drawing] a day," he said recently. "That means during a full month of almost twenty-four working days you'd get a second on the screen. One drawing per day! They measured the width of the line, the density of the line, the taper of the line. 'Cause we thought we were making the Lord's Prayer for sure."[77]

One day the budget department phoned Larson to ask if he realized he had spent $10,000 in clean-up on this one scene alone. "I said, hell no! Nobody sent me an idea of what we're spending." The expense stemmed from Larson's perfectionism—trying to be perfect for Walt's sake. "There's no reason why it should ever cost that much," he later said. "It was just one of those things that got out of hand."[78]

A quota system was then put in place. A drawing count was initiated, Bluth recalls, "where you had to do eight girls a day, thirty-two medium sized birds a day, twenty-two squirrels a day, if you were on squirrels, so you had a specific number of drawings to do per day. That's how they got through it. And even at that Sleeping Beauty was going tremendously over budget and Walt was getting afraid of it." It wound up costing nearly $6 million, the most expensive animated feature to that time.

"Eric was one of those very precise people," says Mattinson, "so when he handed out sweatbox notes, he told you precisely, exactly how to correct the situation. The notes were very long and detailed. I think management looked at those notes and thought, This guy's making too much work for people. It was wrong that he got a lot of the blame for it."[79]

Ken Peterson, Sleeping Beauty's production supervisor, believed that "Walt never really appreciated Eric" as a director. "I felt sorry for Eric when they put him in as director on Sleeping Beauty," recalled Peterson years later. "It just slew him, really. He wasn't up to dealing with Walt on that level at all. He was almost speechless when Walt was there. He should never have been placed in that position. It was a bad bit of casting."[80]

Comic relief from the constant stress arrived when Larson took on an assistant animator named Roland Crump, an athletic amateur magician full of joie de vivre and high spirits.[81] Crump, who became an important designer at Walt Disney Imagineering, was, according to fellow assistant animator John Ewing, "almost completely unrestrained." When "winsome lasses from Ink and Paint might stroll by," Crump would shout out lewdly "Eatchabox!", careful "not to be looking at any one particular lass when he gave his call."

Crump's antics amused the straightlaced Larson, who, in spite of himself, was "dragged reluctantly, but smiling, at least a little distance from his shell." "I was thrilled to work for him," said Crump recently of Larson. "I knew he was going through a bad time. Our rooms were side by side and I only played his favorite easy-listening music. I brought him Sparklett's water, and every afternoon I'd give him a backrub. Because I really loved the man. He was a polished, perfect gentleman. A sweetheart."[82]

Toward the end of the production, an efficiency expert from Cadillac was brought in, as pressure built to get the picture out. After working on almost three-quarters of *Sleeping Beauty*, Larson was replaced as the film's supervising director by Gerry Geronimi. (In the film's credits, Larson is listed as a "Sequence Director" along with Wolfgang Reitherman and Les Clark.)

"Eric was one of the most lovable people you ever met," notes Dale Oliver. "And sincere. He wanted good work done, of course, but just such a kind, loving person. He would get angry but he would never display it. He would tell you about it: 'Boy, was I angry yesterday!' But you'd never know it."[83] His only public expression of the hurt and anger he felt at being demoted on *Sleeping Beauty* was typically mild; years later to writer Howard E. Green, he simply said: "I was a little bit disgusted toward the end."[84]

After *101 Dalmatians* (1961), for which he was a directing animator, Larson never again received a directing assignment. He is credited as a "character animator" on *The Sword in the Stone* (1963), *The Jungle Book* (1967), *The Aristocats*, (1970), and *Robin Hood* (1973) and an "animator" on *Mary Poppins* (1964), *Bedknobs and Broomsticks* (1971), and *The Many Adventures of Winnie the Pooh* (1977). He provided the staging for the titles for *The Rescuers* (1977)—evocative sequential still pastels of the ocean by Mel Shaw—and served as "animation consultant" for *The Black Cauldron* (1985) and *The Great Mouse Detective* (1986).

In the early 1970s, the studio belatedly realized that its veteran animators and craftspeople were retiring or passing away at an alarming rate. Disney needed to attract and train new young talent in order to replenish its dwindling ranks of artists, especially animators. Soon after Walt's death in 1966, there were rumors of phasing out the animation department, the better to concentrate on more lucrative enterprises, such as theme parks. But the continuing financial success of Disney's feature-length animated films, both rereleased and newly produced, convinced company executives to invest in the development of new talent. There was also the fact that animation is the core of the organization and everything springs from it.

In a 1978 interview, animation production manager Don Duckwall stated that "The key to understanding a Disney financial statement is the realization that the taproot of all the fantasy and imagery . . . is the body of creative work in the Disney film library . . . both replenished and reissued. What I hear from Ron Miller [Walt's son-in-law and at the time the executive producer of all Disney motion pictures] and Card Walker [then president of the Disney company] is 'Why can't we double the size of our animation department? Why can't we cut that three or four years of production on features

down to two years at least? We need 'em! We want 'em!'"[85]

At first, the studio tried to train their assistant animators, but after eight weeks of instruction and tests, the top animators "came down on them" hard and "didn't like the work." Not only did this result in general discouragement and hurt feelings, but the animators began to lose their best assistants when one man angrily quit and others fled to the story department. Resistance on the part of certain of the Nine Old Men toward nurturing new talent was a factor in the depletion of the ranks of first-rate animators.

Even great and proven animators found the studio gates closed to them. After leaving in 1943, Vladimir Tytla tried in vain for years to return, even writing a pleading letter the year he died (1968) to Woolie Reitherman. "We have not forgotten that you are anxious to animate here at the studio," Reitherman wrote back. But "so far we can just barely keep our present crew of animators busy . . . rest assured you have many friends here at the studio who are pulling for you." But not enough of them. Privately, Reitherman told John Culhane "there are people who don't want a restoration of a situation that existed, for reasons of their own." For example, what kind of assignments would go to this uniquely gifted animator and who would he compete against to get them?[86]

A second group of studio employees was put through training, including Don Bluth, Burny Mattinson, and two others. "This time they were a little nicer about it," recalls Mattinson. "Eric had basically showed me how to do it and not fall on my fanny, so I got the okay and could start animating on the feature *Robin Hood*. Ollie [Johnston] didn't feel like he was a teacher, nor did Frank. And Milt was never a teacher. But who really was wonderful, and everybody came to see, was Eric. So Eric got the job by default and he loved doing it."[87]

The establishment of Larson as the head of a talent search and trainee program breathed new life into him and his career. It was true that Larson "liked to teach because he loved young people," as Andreas Deja puts it. But there was a stronger motivation: despite rough patches in their relationship, Larson had a continuing loyalty to Walt. "He probably had a greater effect on me than any other [person] in my whole life except my own father," he said. "I grew to appreciate the boldness of this person."[88] Larson saw his teaching as a calling, not just a job. He intended, through the trainee program, "to revive" Disney animation at the studio and "to build" it through gifted youngsters. For the love of Walt, he was "not going to let this thing die!"[89]

Larson visited art schools and colleges throughout the country and put out the word internationally that Disney was soliciting portfolios. He wrote (and Burny Mattinson designed) a pocket-sized recruitment brochure. Thousands of hopefuls responded, but few were chosen. During the thirty-day tryout period, Larson advised the trainees one-on-one regarding their personal black-and-white test films. They were paid a small

Larson was a directing animator on 101 Dalmatians (1961), but for most of the 1970s and '80s he was the revered teaching head of Disney's training program for new, young animators.

salary and at the end of thirty days their tests were reviewed. "We're looking at the action on the screen, at the motion, not how well they draw the character. Do they have a statement to make? Do they stage it well so it gets across? Do we get a lift out of what we see?"[90]

A review board (made up of top animators, directors, and others) looked at the tests; some trainees were asked to extend their stay for another thirty days and make more tests. Those with exceptional promise were assigned to a crew on an actual production and learned to do in-between drawings; at night and on weekends they also worked on personal tests. A few were promoted to assistant animator. "After you were tutored long enough by Eric," says Glen Keane, "you were pushed out of the nest so you could fly. Your little chicken wings carried you enough and you landed with one of the other guys, Frank or Ollie or Milt."[91]

There was the tacit hope that the new people would continue to grow and progress in their careers at Disney and eventually become leaders. "The idea that we're just training somebody to animate is a bit misleading," said Larson. "It's a case of getting hold of someone we think might be a leader, aggressive in thought, imagination, and constantly on the move."[92]

"Eric was more comfortable with handing on the baton than any of the other Nine Old Men," observes animator (and former Larson trainee) John Pomeroy. "While the remainder of the giants here still were furthering their careers, Eric saw a need to pass on this language and this knowledge."[93] The trainees became the childless Larson's surrogate family. To the trainees, Eric was a roly-poly grandfather who indulged his young brood when they ran through his room having rubber-band fights. "This place was like a great big fraternity," recalls Pomeroy.[94]

His involvement with young people and teaching intensified when, on September 30, 1975, his beloved Gertrude died after a long battle with cancer. He once said his wife got along better with Walt than he did because "she wasn't afraid of him. I was!"[95] Larson was "devastated" by his wife's death, according to animator Jane Baer, a friend from the *Sleeping Beauty* days on.

At the home he and Gertrude bought in 1941 in the Flintridge section of Los Angeles, "he kept her little dressing room with her perfume bottles exactly the way she left it."[96] Three years later, he continued to mourn Gertrude in a poem he wrote called "Why to Cry?":

77

*Eric and Gertrude Jannes Larson, his beloved wife
of forty-two years.*

Last night I cried.
I cried for one I held and loved for a few fleeting years.
But whom I lost, oh, so long ago it seems.
I cried because of the fault I would find with some
    things she did,
Forgetting her great love for me.
I cried because she I can have no more. . . .

I cried in pity for myself.
The days are empty and I cried because I face them
    alone.
I cried because I love without restraint.
I cried, and my tears dampened my pillow
And I fell asleep.[97]

Not far beneath his dignified exterior, there was a part of
Larson that was mischievous and full of fun. After all, he did animate the Aracuan and Peg; and one of his favorite performers
was the "Brazilian Bombshell" Carmen Miranda; and in his desk
drawer he kept a little hula dancer on a spring that shook her
hips. His students loved bringing that part of him to the surface
and to make him laugh, to see his beautiful smile. Few were as

successful as a tall, platinum-blond trainee animator and eccentric dance performer named Betsy Baytos. "I used to try and
break him up as often as I could," she says. "He'd get so embarrassed. He was just so cute. I'd say I wanna do this kind of a walk
and I'd get up and dance. He loved that."

One time, after correcting her animation, he told Baytos,
"Okay, you can split now." She immediately fell to the floor in a
dancer's split, her legs extended in a straight line at right angles
to her body. "He couldn't believe it!" she recalls, laughing. Then
from the floor she continued with an old Ray Bolger routine
"where you try to pick yourself up by the seat of your pants. I
said 'You gotta help me! You gotta help me!' He was trying to
help me up and I purposely made it difficult."

Baytos, who is making a documentary film about the history of eccentric dance, says talking to Larson "was like talking
to one of the great comedians. He loved movies and comedy. I
think he was very much in touch with that. Eric was the first
one who helped me integrate my theatrical and dance background, and show me how to apply it to my animation."[98]

Gentle and fun-loving as he was, Larson also took animation very seriously. "Animation is darn hard work," he told this
writer in his large sunlit office one morning in 1978. During
that visit, Larson expressed how animation is a thinking person's art, at least the way he and the other Nine Old Men did it.
His journalism background enabled him to distill a lifetime of
personal experience into a few words.

Following is his succinct explanation to me of the principles of animation in general and Disney character animation in
particular. It is a revealing example of Eric Larson not as a cuddly grandpa, but as a focused and authoritative teacher:

There's only two things that limit animation. One is the
ability to imagine and the other is the ability to draw
what you imagine. The basic thing that animation has to
have is a change of shape. If I hold my finger there and I
bend it down to there, I've changed the shape from that
to this. A crude example is the animation you put into
a fellow who is fighting a strong wind. First, he's so far
off balance leaning forward, his body is almost parallel
with the horizon. And his feet are never going to get
out in front of him. A gust of wind hits him and he's
suddenly staggering backward trying like everything to
keep from falling over. You've changed the perspective
of shape. Now the charm of animation is how you time
that after you've gotten all the character into the pose
drawings. There's weight to be concerned with. We
don't take steps, we fall into them. You take what you
know is real and honest and you exaggerate it, you caricature it for all it's worth. Then you begin to get the
humor, whether it's an action, expression, whatever. On
the screen we may have less than half a second to put

over a point. That's where simplification of drawing comes in. The interpretation the animator gives an action will depend on the quality of that animator. You take Frank Thomas and he'll get a heck of a lot more into it than an ordinary animator could. It's like night and day, 'cause Frank is thinking of that character he's putting on that paper as being alive. And real. If we can't relate to that audience, we might as well give up. This is what Walt wanted.[99]

Larson explained Disney animation's illusion of life goes beyond mastery of technique. "We don't say to the trainees, 'Do this, do that,'" said Larson. "We say, 'What can you do to entertain us?' Figaro could throw tantrums. Thumper could get himself into apologetic situations with his mother. They were *kids*, characters that are alive. They're on the screen to entertain people and they'd better have personalities that are going to register with people. Now *that's* Disney!"

Twenty-five new artists were hired between 1970 and 1977, and the first real collaboration between studio old-timers and the new recruits occurred on *The Rescuers* (1977). The film proved to be a box office hit (it earned $16.3 million domestically) and more trainees were hired. "The studio when I was there," says Betsy Baytos, "was like a 1940s college campus. Everybody knew everybody. Eric was the professor. He had his definite role, his place. The Firehouse Five band would play outside the commissary at lunch time. It was a great environment, a real family kind of feeling."

But underneath the animation department's surface homogeneity, discontent bubbled. The studio was split three ways: there were "Walt's boys" (veteran animators, such as the remaining Nine Old Men; layout and story people who had actually worked with Walt), the "Cal Arts kids" (dewy-eyed trainees, most of whom were recent graduates of the animation program at the Disney-funded California Institute of the Arts), and "Bluth's boys" (older, former trainees recently advanced to positions as animators and assistant animators).

Don Bluth (age forty in 1978) had emerged as the leader of the latter group, and management recognized his potential to become a director. "I think Ron Miller felt that Bluth was going to be the second coming of Walt and really take over the whole thing," says Mattinson. "It was almost preordained, probably after *Rescuers*, that he was going to be the next guru." Betsy Baytos notes that Bluth's group "were starting to get more and more control and the animators were starting to separate into groups. I could sense that Eric was getting upset and concerned." "Eric was sidestepping," says animator Jeffrey Varab, "saying, Concentrate on the art."[100] Bluth and company were unhappy with the cost-cutting of recent features and they sent pointed memos to studio head Miller that said (in essence) "we can do better movies." "Bluth was concerned with where the

Disney studio was heading," says Dan Haskett. "He thought it wasn't Disney enough. From my viewpoint, he wanted to bring back the 1930s in a big way."

The Small One (1978), a twenty-minute featurette, brought things to a head. The film originated in Eric's wing of the studio in order, according to Burny Mattinson, to "have something for all these talented new people who were coming in to work on. Their own picture under Eric." The slight, predictable Christmas story was found in the studio library of optioned properties by Pete Young, who "was learning to do storyboards. So Eric let him do it." Young developed *The Small One* with veteran storymen Vance Gerry and Mel Shaw, and then took it to Ron Miller, who pronounced it a story with "heart." Other executives saw repeat possibilities in the property, so it received a green light for production.

Larson assumed he was directing the film and asked Mattinson to help him reboard the material ("detailing it out more"). He invited veteran animator Cliff Nordberg to work with him on some of the animation, which he planned to hand out to the trainees and newer animators. "So we came in on Friday, everything was happy," says Mattinson. "Monday, everything in our rooms was gone. Everything! Every storyboard, every drawing we had on it. The rooms were wiped out." Over the weekend, management had decided to give the project to Don Bluth.

Betsy Baytos was in the office when Larson was informed of the change. "I got so upset because he was very, very upset," she says. "He just shook his head and knew that he wasn't being appreciated. He felt the old days were gone." "He was hurt something fierce," says Mattinson. "It was a horrible thing to do. It originated with Eric. It was for Eric's use and then these guys just moved in. Eric stayed in teaching, but things were never the same."

Asked recently about *Small One*'s production, Don Bluth indicated it was his understanding that Larson was not deeply involved. "*Small One* was something I directed to get the crew busy until *Pete's Dragon*," a live action-animation feature released in December 1977. "[Larson] might have [been involved] in the storyboard area. [But he] didn't get to direction. I think he elected to [teach]," says Bluth. "Eric was a very charitable guy and he could see the writing on the wall. There were fewer than nine of them left and unless something was done there wouldn't be anyone to animate the pictures."

In any case, Larson was quietly devastated by the event. "It would have been reason enough for him to leave," observed Andreas Deja, "but he loved the studio so much he still stuck around." It was a good thing he did. In September 1979, Bluth resigned from Disney to found his own studio, taking fourteen animators and assistants with him. It was a major shakeup that caused the release date of *The Fox and the Hound* to be moved back one year. Ron Miller felt betrayed and outraged. Talent recruitment was stepped up and the loyal Larson, now the last of the Nine Old Men remaining at the studio, continued to supervise their training.

In the late 1970s, Larson took a vacation cruise on the *Royal Viking Sky* to the South Seas. Some years before, he and Gertrude had sailed on a sister ship, the *Viking Star*, from Los Angeles to Copenhagen. Now he would visit Bora Bora and Tahiti, then go to New Zealand to see old friend and former Disney assistant animator John Ewing, then on to Tasmania and Australia. He brought "work to be done and choice books to read" and it "felt good to again stand at the rail overlooking the bow and feel it lift and fall as it responded to the gentle dictates of the rolling sea."

Larson wrote about the trip in a memoir titled "Soliloquy," which demonstrated that (vacation or no) Larson was like his mentor Ham Luske: an animator who constantly observed people:

No two people walking the promenade deck, for exercise or show, walked or dressed alike, except of course those lovey [sic] couples in their "his and hers" get-ups. As in skiing or tennis, golf or jogging, swimming or sunning, promenading demanded proper attire. The women were sexy or sexless, depending on the age and how they shaped up. The men, in numbers, strutted like male peacocks in full plumage and pride. Walking styles are not set. Each to his own. There were those who walked in a slouched reverse S curve and slithered along. There were those who leaned forward, determined, as if in hot pursuit, and there were those who leaned way back as though descending a steep stairs if bracing against a stiff wind from the rear. . . . There were ladies who smilingly flaunted their bosoms and men who ogled and awed. On warm days, navels peeked out from open shorts and sometimes a sudden, teasing wind out of nowhere dipped under a loose skirt sending it skyward and the lady, face flushed and hands grabbing at it, would make a quick and desperate recovery. Older couples, with coats tightly around them, beaming in the joy of being alive, walked slowly, quite content to go back and forth on the port or starboard side, which ever might be the more pleasant, never venturing around the windswept bow.

The athletes hurried by in quick and measured stride, waving, smiling, sometimes sweating. . . . Others like the wincing, overweight lady, obviously troubled with weak ankles, shuffled along in traumatic style, seeking neither encouragement nor sympathy, looking as though they had to do it because it was the thing to do.[101]

On the trip, he was accompanied by a woman named Hazel, "a nice lady from Atlanta who ran museums," according to Deja,

"and they would travel together." Deja had corresponded from his native Germany with Larson, who encouraged him to come to Disney. They first met when Larson and Hazel stopped in Hamburg during a cruise through northern Europe.

When Larson and Hazel visited John and Jenny Ewing in Auckland, New Zealand, Ewing found the great animator "to be almost melancholy about some things" and "he displayed a sadness I found disturbing. To me," wrote Ewing recently, "he was far more than just a good animator. He was one of the Nine Old Men, and therefore very special to me. I found myself offering, very deferentially to be sure, encouragement to him, a reversal of roles unimaginable a few years earlier." Ewing got the impression that "the lady Hazel meant far more to him than anything else at that time." She was "very charming," thought Ewing, "with a plain face that could never be called plain because of her smile." Larson's face "lighted beautifully when he talked of her," and Ewing felt "Eric was a lucky man if he indeed could manage to hang on to such a creature."[102]

Back at Disney, the reasons for Larson's melancholy became all too clear. In mid-1984, the very survival of all things Disney was threatened by a tumultuous and highly publicized takeover attempt by financier Saul P. Steinberg. That battle ended with Ron Miller's resignation and the establishment of a new management team made up of men from live-action backgrounds: Michael Eisner, Jeffrey Katzenberg, and Frank Wells. "Rumors that the animation department might be eliminated were fueled by the decision to move the artists off the lot and convert the animation building into offices," writes Charles Solomon. "Those fears were allayed when Roy Edward Disney (Roy Oliver Disney's son and Walt's nephew) took charge of the department."[103]

Larson continued on through the release in July 1985 of *The Black Cauldron*, a disastrous animated feature that can be traced back to 1971.[104] Years in production, the overly ambitious feature ended up in the hands of mediocre studio talents long suppressed by the Nine Old Men, plus a slew of eager but inexperienced younger artists. Eisner, Katzenberg, and company were horrified by *Cauldron*; it failed at the box office and got poor reviews for its narrative, its design, and even its animation. Big changes needed to be made if animation were to continue at the "new" Disney studio.

The animation department was indeed moved out of the Burbank studio and set up in cavernous industrial buildings miles away in Glendale. "It seemed like a kind of warning," Andreas Deja told Christopher Finch. "We were being sent out into the wilderness and told it was time to get our act together. But at least we were given a chance."[105] Larson had to abandon the sunny office he'd occupied since 1940 for a smaller space with no windows on a bottom floor in a former warehouse. The move, Betsy Baytos felt, "was a real slap in the face. He felt this new regime, they didn't care. Their whole sensibility was alien to him." She remembered going to see Larson at his new quarters: "I walked in and his head was down and he was asleep. He was just biding his time and it was time to leave."

Larson finally retired on February 28, 1986, at age eighty-one. In a newspaper interview that fall, Larson was described as "openly homesick" for Disney since his retirement a few months before. In an accompanying photograph he appears gaunt; his diet was restricted due to a blood disease (hemochromatosis), which produces too much iron in the body.[106]

"When he left Disney, he was very despondent," says Jane Baer. "He went into a terrible depression. He didn't want to retire, but he did because he didn't like the new management, the Katzenberg–Eisner group that came in. He was so loyal to Disney, he just adored Walt Disney. So when he left he packed up everything that was in his room, his lifetime at Disney's, everything. And took it home and put it on the dining room table and covered it with a piece of plastic. And there it stayed till he died. He'd spend all of his time in his den, in a tiny little room, just sitting there."

A number of Larson's former trainees often phoned him or took him to lunches and dinners to cheer him up. Glen Keane and Howard E. Green once enticed Larson out of his house to a lunch where Keane gave him a drawing from *The Fox and the Hound* inscribed "To Eric, my rock!" Former trainees continued to visit Larson even after he entered a Pasadena hospital, where he died on October 25, 1988.

Through some mysterious alchemy, or childlike sincerity, Eric Larson was able to instill his cartoon dogs, cats, and birds with qualities that audiences recognized as their own. Larson was personally beloved for his warmth, compassion, and humor, which found their way onto the movie screen in performances that are among the finest and most unforgettable ever animated.

Memorable animation is only part of his legacy. His accomplishments as a gifted tutor are of equal significance. Larson's nurturing of new talents handed down to a new generation the technical and aesthetic aspects of Disney animation; but he also inspired them, for he was a direct line to Walt Disney's own spirit of dedication, discovery and striving for quality.

Eric Larson's work, both on and off the screen, was always a sincere communication from the heart. To use his favorite word, he lived a "positive" life, and in a poem written in 1976, he celebrated his philosophy and the eternal "newness of things":

It has been said there is nothing new in this world.
Quite to the contrary: everything is new.
As we're born into the world and until we leave, we
    find it so.
In childhood everything is new . . . strange . . .
    acceptable.
In our youth, all is new . . . we have never been this
    way before.
As a teenager, all is new and challenging.
When an adult, all is new to us.
In middle age it's new and
In old age, our life is new.
So, everything old as it is, is new.
We discover it!
We use it!
We live by it!
So everything is new and will be forever.
So who can say in honesty that "there's nothing new
    under the sun"?[107]

THIS PAGE, *a few of Ward Kimball's creatures: The Three Caballeros from the 1945 film of the same name, the Cheshire Cat from* Alice in Wonderland *(1951), and Mickey Mouse in* The Little Whirlwind *(1941);* OPPOSITE TOP, *Kimball at nine months looking at a toy train;* CENTER, *Kimball in 1941.*

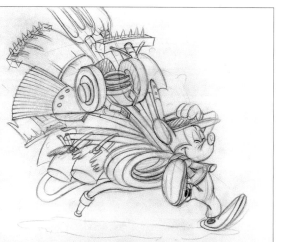
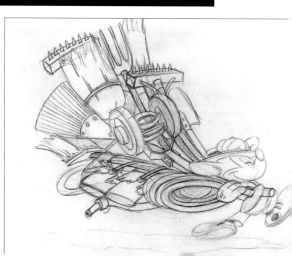

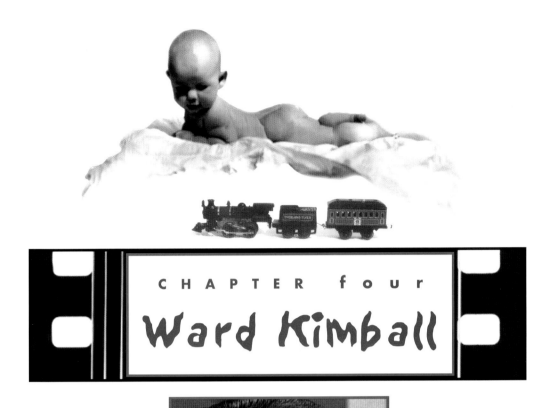

CHAPTER four
Ward Kimball

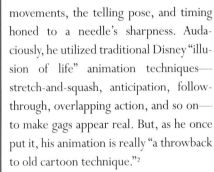

I f one were to select the quintessential Ward Kimball sequence from the scores he animated over the years in Disney films, the title song from *The Three Caballeros* (1945) would do nicely. Certainly it is high on his personal list of favorites. "That's the only animation I ever did that I'm uncritical of," Kimball told this writer in 1973. "I look at that damn song I did, and I laugh and I grin just as hard as the day I did it."[1]

Exuberant humor, zany as well as sardonic, pervades all of Kimball's work and reflects his personality. It informs how he draws his characters, their relationship to each other, their emotions as well as motions. Not for Kimball sincere emotional displays; he savages sentimentality, routs hypocrisy, and gleefully pokes a finger into tearful eyes.

For years, Kimball advocated "limited" (or, as he prefers to call it, "stylized") animation: the opposite of full, flowing, naturalistic Disney animation. Kimball communicated with selective movements, the telling pose, and timing honed to a needle's sharpness. Audaciously, he utilized traditional Disney "illusion of life" animation techniques—stretch-and-squash, anticipation, follow-through, overlapping action, and so on—to make gags appear real. But, as he once put it, his animation is really "a throwback to old cartoon technique."[2]

Ward Kimball was a most un-Disneylike animator. Of all the Nine Old Men, he would best have thrived in the 1920s in the studio that produced the magical animated universe of Felix the Cat; doubtless, he would have fit in comfortably at the wisecracking Warner Brothers cartoon studio (animating Bugs Bunny, Daffy Duck, *et al*); or at U.P.A. (United Productions of America), a studio whose stylized moving graphics of Gerald McBoing Boing and Mr. Magoo were inspired by Modernist art and design.

The Three Caballeros amply demonstrates Kimball's unconventionality. In the film Donald Duck teams up with Brazilian

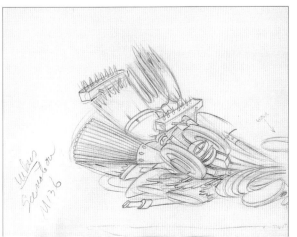

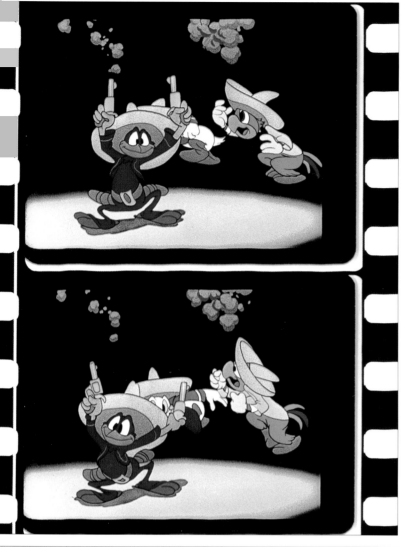

parrot Jose Carioca and Mexican rooster Panchito for a song of friendship and loyalty. The song's finale, the funniest section, has no lyrics, but is a pure Kimball improvisation. Panchito holds a high note seemingly forever as Donald and Jose try to make him cease. They douse the rooster with water and spray him with DDT; they nail him into a coffin; they try to saw a hole in the floor beneath him, but only the ground under Donald and Jose falls; they water pots of plants that grow instantly in front of Panchito and are then torched. Throughout, the rooster's note remains constant, his body fixed in a blissful singing pose, unmoving except for his quivering throat and wagging tongue—Kimball's stylized animation in action.

"If animation is giving lifeless things movement and living things a different kind of life," says animation historian John Culhane, "Ward could invent a different kind of life that you and I would never think of."[3]

Witness Kimball's animation of Lucifer, a villainous cat in *Cinderella*, whose stylized movements bring unexpected life to the character. Lucifer's search under teacups for a mouse is a marvel of comic timing worthy of Chaplin. The cat's lethal shell game is repeatedly interrupted by Cinderella, which makes Lucifer so agitated he becomes downright twitchy. Finally, he locates the correct mouse-filled cup and Kimball allows the cat a moment of unabashed joy. In one of the funniest "takes" ever, Lucifer's arms wave wildly side to side, while his face registers wild-eyed, tongue-lolling ecstasy. So unexpectedly wacky is the action, it invariably garners loud laughter from audiences.

Subsequently sneaking up a marble staircase, Lucifer molds his body to each step, giving him a zigzag look as he passes by. Only Kimball could get away with such cartoony animation in a feature slavishly tied to live action. But Lucifer's front and back legs move naturally as he zigzags, maintaining a cat-like quality in the highly caricatured feline.

Kimball's warmest, most sincere animation occurs in *Pinocchio* with Jiminy Cricket, a character he developed and whose animation he directed. The bug's flip irreverence and brave pluck is welcome comic relief when Pinocchio confronts dangerous characters, such as Stromboli, Monstro, the Pleasure Island coachman, and others. As Pinocchio's conscience, Jiminy is deeply concerned with his charge's welfare; he sympathizes with his plight (to the point of tears in one scene), thus giving depth to the character's personality as few of Kimball's assignments ever did.

LUCIFERS THE CATS
ROUGH MODELS

In the mid-1950s Kimball came into his own when he produced and directed an infotainment series about outer space for the Disneyland TV program. *Mars and Beyond* (1957), in particular, is a brilliantly entertaining mix of fact and fancy, presented with panache and humorous, imaginatively designed "stylized" animation.

A man of enormous energy and bursting with artistic talent, Kimball excelled in painting, music, and mechanics; even

*Man of many talents: animator of (*OPPOSITE*) the zany trio in* The Three Caballeros *(1945) and the evil cat in* Cinderella *(1950);* THIS PAGE, *collector of life-size vintage locomotives, musician in the Firehouse Five Plus Two Dixieland jazz band, and painter: "Sunday Morning," an oil from the mid-'40s, was Walt's favorite of Kimball's paintings.*

his hobbies became extraordinary successes. In 1948, he formed the Firehouse Five Plus Two, a Dixieland jazz band that he led (playing trombone) for more than two decades. Made up of Disney personnel (including Frank Thomas on piano), the band became internationally famous through twelve record albums, personal appearances in nightclubs and theaters, and network television shows.

Kimball's lifelong love of trains and locomotive lore led him, in 1938, to create the Grizzly Flats Railroad in the backyard of his home in San Gabriel, California. His personal railroad featured two full-size vintage steam locomotives operating on 900 feet of narrow-gauge rail. In addition, he has for years maintained one of the world's finest collections of miniature trains, toys and related ephemera. Walt Disney's own interest in vintage trains (recalled from his Missouri and Illinois childhood) was rekindled by Kimball's passion for *his* hobby.

Kimball's mocking attitude, wild sense of humor, and often eccentric clothing choices amused Walt (up to a point); as Steven Watts writes in *The Magic Kingdom*, Kimball's "irreverent, mischievous personality seemed to hold a special appeal for his work-driven, straitlaced boss."[4]

In *The Story of Walt Disney*, the 1956 biography by Walt's daughter Diane, Walt stated that "Ward is one man who works for me I am willing to call a genius."[5] That startling remark, says

Kimball, "brought me a lot of enemies" at the studio, and Walt sometimes turned it into a taunt. "For years when I'd run out of time on a project, I'd go to Walt and say, 'I can't make it in time,' and he'd say, 'Why, I called you a genius, didn't I?'"[6]

Ward Walrath Kimball was born on March 4, 1914, in Minneapolis, Minnesota. That was also the birthplace of his mother, Mary Nancy Walrath, from whom Ward inherited a quirky sense of humor. A graduate of the University of Minnesota, she loved to repeat a grotesquely funny story about dating a medical school student who held a nude corpse up in a window "and made it wave to her for all to see."[7]

His musical talent also came from Mary, an accomplished pianist who played the Maple Leaf Rag in a fast tempo. Her father, J. Parker Walrath, a well-to-do Minneapolis surgeon, "loved motor cars" and purchased the seventh automobile ever seen in Minneapolis.[8]

Often, the Walrath's visited friends in Parsons, a small town located about 500 miles south of Minneapolis in the southeastern corner of Kansas. To do so, they rode the fancy Rock Island Line railroad, which traveled through Kansas City. At a church service one Christmas day in Parsons, Mary met Bruce Kimball. He was the eldest of five sons born to Charles H. Kimball, leading lawyer for the Missouri, Kansas & Texas Railroad (MK&T), whose central offices were in Parsons. (Trains figured in Ward's life even before he was born.)[9] Charles, who later became a state senator, was famed for his elocution in front of juries. "He could sway anybody," says Ward, with his "Cross of Gold speech à la William Jennings Bryan."[10]

Bruce Kimball was "very, very smart" and loved filling three-by-five-foot sheets of butcher's paper with complex algebraic formulas. "That was his hobby," says Ward. He sang "tunes from grand opera and he used lots of Latin phrases, a holdover from law school." At Kansas University, Bruce was a lightweight quarterback on the football team. A small, compact man (like Ward), he often recalled the time Kansas was behind by one touchdown and close to the goal line; "in what would be a quarterback sneak today," says Ward, "the halfback and fullback picked up my father, tossed him over the goal line, and won the game by one point!"

After leaving the university, Bruce bickered with his brothers and declined to join a family venture: the Kimball Investment Company. For the rest of his life, Bruce was fated to be "on the move all the time," always "a little outside of the law a lot."[11]

Bruce and Mary Walrath fell in love, courted, and, in due course, were married.[12] When Mary became pregnant with Ward, she believed (as did her mother) that the child was "a rebirth" of her brother John, who died at age five and had been her mother's favorite child. She later insisted that Ward was a "marked baby" because of his early interest in railroads. She often repeated, he once wrote, "the story of how just before she went into labor, she had watched from her hospital window as a Soo Line freight train cautiously crawled

across a high bridge that had been officially condemned.[13]

"It worried her that she might be witness to a catastrophic train wreck! This was her reasoning for the fact that my first drawing effort of anything recognizable was a childish scribbling of a steam locomotive which I called a 'Choo-choo.' I was three years old."[14]

Ward's amusing story masks the essentially negative opinion he held of his mother. "Once he turned to me," says Ward's eldest daughter Kelly, "and said, 'The problem with my mother is she was just dumb!'" He may have reached that conclusion when, after he was employed at Disney, his mother destroyed all the life drawings in his portfolio and only saved the cartoons. "He claimed that she did it because they were nudes," says Kelly. "She liked cartoons and didn't place much value on the other. There were a lot of stories like that."[15]

Bruce and Mary had a terrible argument over what to name their firstborn. Bruce wanted to name him after himself or one of his brothers; but Mary thought Webster, Pierre, Paul and Charley "were all irreverent clowns who laughed at 'nasty' Charlie Chaplin movies," says Ward. "On a whim, she chose to call me the 'nice' sounding 'Ward' after Etta Ward," an elderly woman who lived on the same street as the Kimball family in Parsons. When Mrs. Ward died, she left her namesake $1,000, which he used in 1939 to build his $10,000 house in San Gabriel.[16]

The Kimball side of the family "were all great humorists," according to Ward; even Grandma Kimball was "a funny old girl. When I had dinner with my uncles at the table, and if I was gobbling up the food too fast, she'd ring the little bell she had there for the hired cook. I'd look at her and she'd crook her little finger and say, 'Piggy piggy piggy.'"

Uncles Webster and Paul took young Ward bullfrog hunting. Webb wielded a fly rod, Paul a shotgun. After the hunt they introduced the kid to the gustatory joys of fried frog's legs. "I thought it was great!" said Ward. For the most part, though, his four uncles were spoiled frat boys who played tricks on their young nephew.

One Halloween night, at the three-story Victorian Kimball mansion on Morgan Avenue in Parsons, they brought their nephew into a dusty, little-used parlor. "I walked in there," recalls Ward, "and here was this hooded ghost sitting on a throne and he had this blinking light under a sheet that made a big red spot. This was King Hal." Actually, it was alcoholic Uncle Paul "dressed like the Ku Klux" who asked the frightened youngster if he had been a good boy. "Somehow they thought this was funny," Ward said years later.

Another prank: Ward was afraid of a big fish mounted over a mantel in the dining room. "I couldn't believe that they caught a fish that big. Every once in a while, if I was acting like a bad boy, they'd grab me and hold me up to the fish like it was going to bite me! And I would start screaming!"

When Ward was nine months old, the family celebrated

CLOCKWISE, STARTING TOP LEFT, *father Bruce
Kimball holding Ward at age five weeks; brother
Webster, sister Elinor, mother Mary, and Ward in 1917
in Parsons, Kansas; Ward, age three, with toy train;
Ward's early drawing of a streetcar in 1921;
grandmother Helen Kimball holding six-month-old
Ward in September 1914.*

"baby's first Christmas," as his mother wrote in his baby book. His uncles's gifts to the infant were sophisticated toys, such as a limousine auto, a turtle that walked, and a windup train. "They got these toys just so *they* could play with them!" claims Ward.

A family album holds a photo taken over seventy-five years ago of Ward's uncles and his father dressed in summer whites and Panama hats—the very picture of midwestern Americana straight out of posters by J. C. Leyendecker and Norman Rockwell (or Main Street, Disneyland). Ever candid Ward recently offered verbal snapshots of each man, revealing the skewed reality beneath the perfect imagery:

> Uncle Webster would come visit my mother and father for many summers after our family moved to California because Uncle Webb had an eye for mom and was kind of miffed that his brother Bruce was the one she married. . . . [Webb] was a real Beau Brummel who always wore a white "Death in Venice" Palm Beach suit. . . . This is Uncle Paul, who ended up an alcoholic . . . and so did Uncle Webster. . . . Uncle Paul always had a little thing where he'd take gunpowder, go clear in back to the carriage house . . . pile it on our walk . . .and we would see this—POOM! I thought it was the greatest thing. . . .
>
> This is Uncle Charlie, the brain of the uncles, ended up living in southern California, spending his last years writing how-to-fix-it books for people who were building houses. . . .
>
> One of them, Pierre, decided not to follow law and became a Dodge automobile representative in Parsons . . . he went to war [photo of Lieut. Pierre M. Kimball, 1918] and he sent me a pair of little Belgian shoes. These baby shoes that were built with metal toes. . . . [17]

As for Bruce, Ward remembered his father as a man with a good sense of humor and many interests; for example, he explained carpentry to his son and how to use tools. Most importantly, he supported Ward's leanings toward drawing. When Ward was eleven, Bruce enrolled him in the W. L. Evans School of Cartooning, a correspondence course and his first formal art training. "I'm one of the few people that finished all twelve lessons," he bragged years later. When drawing, Kimball tended to grimace, and he fondly remembered his father telling him, "You got the expressions, but you're drooling too much!" [18]

Unfortunately, Bruce Kimball failed at all of his business enterprises. "Do you know how my grandfather became poor?" asks John Kimball, Ward's son. It seems that Bruce dropped out of university to develop, with an associate, a process for making oral thermometers. "But they had no marketing or advertising experience," says John Kimball. "So they couldn't get people to put them in their mouths 'cause they had mercury in them,

which is poisonous. So Honeywell, this small company, bought them out. They lost their shirts."

Bruce tried farming for a short while; then ran a public swimming pool in Oklahoma, where wife Mary made hamburgers and sold candy; another business endeavor was the Goody Pastry Shoppe, where Ward loved the donut-making machine. "They gave me the round holes," he recalls. But unfortunately, says John Kimball of his paternal grandfather, "everything he tried didn't work out."

Finally, Bruce Kimball became a traveling salesman for the National Cash Register Company, and his family—which now included a daughter, Eleanor, and another son, Webster—lived even more like gypsies than before. Ward recalled attending a total of twenty-two different schools all over the country by the time he reached college age.

Some were awful; some were "very wonderful," he says. "Nice schools in Minneapolis, two or three of them. Some for just a half a semester, then we'd move on. A school in Oklahoma that was built on a pier over a lake. There were just three buildings and I remember the engine oil mixed with sawdust on the floor. And another real old, ancient school in Oklahoma where we sat on bleachers facing the teacher." He remembered how the Oklahoma farm kids smelled "like bacon grease in class."

During summers, starting at age five, Ward accompanied his father on sales trips to various cities. "Most of the trains were rickety, all-wooden baggage cars and wooden coaches," he says. "I was scared to death cause I had always ridden on fancier cars on the Rock Island Line." Bruce, Mary, and the kids frequently traveled on the better line from Minnesota to Kansas when visiting their respective families.

Once, young Ward made a trip north to Minneapolis by himself with just a tag pinned to his shirt stating his name and destination. "The conductors would take care of you," he says.

At the end of a trip on the Rock Island Line, Ward's parents always took him to shake hands with the train's engineer. "He would take off his goggles and gloves and shake hands with me, and that was a big thrill," says Ward, whose fascination with trains was fortified by such experiences.

In 1921, seven-year-old Ward's traveling parents were in difficult financial straits; they sent him to live for a year with his widowed grandmother Walrath at the old Hastings Hotel in downtown Minneapolis.[19] "She had a little money left over," he says.[20] He retains happy memories of time spent with his loving granny, who later kept scrapbooks filled with press clippings about her grandson's academic and professional accomplishments.

"She was a white-haired, velvet-lined, J. C. Leyendecker type who gave me plenty of affection along with pencils and hotel stationery on which to draw," he later wrote. "She taught me how to spell by learning the names of the Minneapolis street car lines."

During summer, they took a trolley that traveled through people's backyards to Lake Hennipin, ate watermelon and went

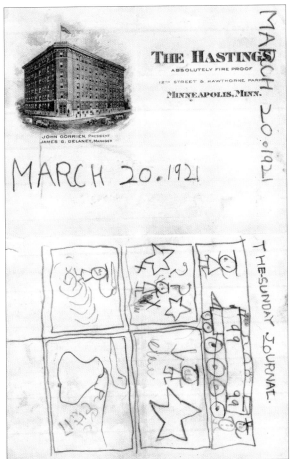

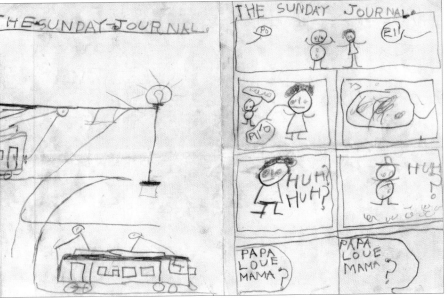

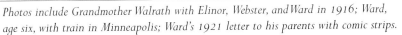

Photos include Grandmother Walrath with Elinor, Webster, and Ward in 1916; Ward, age six, with train in Minneapolis; Ward's 1921 letter to his parents with comic strips.

on a steamboat ride. "And all these people that had docks that backed into the lake were all swimming and waving at us," he recalls. "Then we'd ride home and I'd always ask for trolley transfers. I filled a big scrapbook full of trolley transfers" and dirty cigar bands. Ward and his grandmother always rode to the end of the line sitting behind the motorman, then "the conductor would get out and change the trolley pole around so we could go back."[21]

Kimball drew these memorable excursions by the hour on hotel bond, coloring the street cars bright yellow with russet-red roofs. "I also had a big collection of little dime store trolleys," he says, "and I would simulate real operation by tying strings to the legs of the furniture to serve as trolley wires."

A hand-printed letter by Ward (with help from grandma) was sent to his absent parents and siblings on his seventh birthday:

Dear mama and papa,

Thank you for the nice books you sent me. I got some acrobats for my birthday and a cake and seven pink candles and orangeade. Grandma and I had a good time. We wished you were here and Elinor and Webster. I am having a good time with Grandma. Grandma bought me a train of cars. I saw Mary Greer [a child actress in a stage production]. She is a nice little girl. Lots of love and kisses for you all.

Ward W. Kimball.[22]

It was also during his yearlong stay with his grandmother that Ward "developed an avid fascination with newspapers, especially the multicolored comic pages of the *Minneapolis Journal*. This early love affair with comic strips inspired me to 'publish' my own edition of the Sunday paper with most pages filled with my quaint versions of 'The Gumps,' 'Hawkinshaw the Detective,' and 'Gasoline Alley.' I drew them in pencil and filled in with watercolor."[23]

Constant traveling and precarious finances brought tensions to the Kimball marriage. Ward recalls that his parents had many arguments and one in particular resembled a cinematic cliché. "I remember in Kansas a rainy day, my father bought an old crappy car. My mother got mad because they were being strapped for money. It was raining, and standing at the front door she couldn't swear but she [said] 'You dirty good-for-nothing!' Used all the swear words she could think of, but proper. And as she shouted at him, he took his grip and got in the Oakland and drove away. That reminds me of all the situations in movies today: they always have to have it in the rain." In real life, however, his father always came back. "They'd make up," says Ward matter-of-factly.

Adjusting to new locations, schools, and playmates was difficult for the Kimball kids. They were "yanked around," and Ward admits, "sometimes I would silently cry."[24] He developed an outgoing, assertive personality to enable him to make friends immediately. "Ward has to have things where he's the focus of attention," says his daughter Kelly. "He's directing, he's giving orders, he's in control. Going into a new neighborhood [as a kid], it'd be hard work to get that started quickly."

Vaudeville offered the youngster a diversion and a chance to act out. Most of Kimball's animation has a show-biz, show-off quality, stemming directly from his memories of vaudeville performances he witnessed and sometimes participated in. "This is a part of my life that I always smile when I think about," he says.

When his mother worked as a salesperson at the Martha Washington candy store in Minneapolis, she would give Ward a dime to see the matinee vaudeville show at the Hennepin Theatre. "I just loved that," he says. "I always sat in the front row because the comedians, magicians, musicians, et cetera, these guys would sometimes look down for a helper in their act: 'Hey, buddy! How'd you like to do this?' And I'd get up and hold something or let them try out a trick, whatever it was. I saw all those old vaudeville shows, years of them. I must have seen Jack Benny, Fred Allen, and the crazy carpenters who would try to build something. Bill Briton's band—they would ruin or smash all their instruments. I'd just laugh like hell at all that stuff. So that I think these experiences instilled in me a show-business approach to later staging of drawings I did."

The Nifty Nineties, a 1941 Mickey Mouse short, contains an evocation of Kimball's fond recall of his vaudeville youth. In the film, Mickey and Minnie catch the bill at a cozy turn-of-the-century vaudeville house (not unlike the Hennepin Theatre),

which features a boisterous patter-and-dance team: "Fred and Ward—Two Clever Boys from Illinois." Kimball animated with gusto the exaggerated caricatures of himself and Fred Moore—paddle-footed runts who move in tandem. Their smooth routine features a little hoofing and some cornball jokes, with punch lines accented by Ward trouncing Fred with a cane. That violence, plus the cartoon team's repetitive, spotlight-hogging final bows echo a real life competitiveness, anger, and superiority Kimball felt toward the alcoholic Moore. "I would always be called in and take over Fred's drawings," he complains, "re-expose them and do all his changes and finish up for him. I felt sorry for Fred."[25]

Vaudeville's effect on Kimball's animation timing and movement cannot be underestimated. His love of performing—being "on"—spilled over into his personal life in the often clownish, attention-grabbing way he dressed; also in his professional appearances with the Firehouse Five Plus Two, and in amateur theatricals. "Whenever there'd be something in the community," says Kelly Kimball, "or a Christmas program at the school that they asked him to get involved in, he just loved the little skit. I can remember him getting into costume and working out the gag, going across the stage. He loved this."

Kimball studied all the performing arts, including ballet. Once he proved to his doubting daughter Kelly (then a preteen studying dance) that he knew all the classical ballet foot positions. "He did everything perfect," she discovered with amazement. "He had his body right, he had his arms right. I realized this is a man who watched ballet and he really is what he says you have to be as an animator. You just have to know everything!"[26]

In 1923, Ward's father decided it was too cold in Minneapolis and the midwest, so he got the family tickets on the Overland Limited to sunny California. Ward remembered seeing his first palm trees while coming down from San Francisco on the Coast Route. In the Ocean Park section of Los Angeles, they rented a house.

It was there that Ward discovered sex, or at least the sound of it. He recalls that he and his siblings were "introduced to the sounds of hanky-panky" by listening at their parents' bedroom door "as my mother and father would make out. We'd giggle a lot."

In California, the family's nomadism continued. After he briefly attended an Ocean Park grammar school, the Kimballs moved to Glendale, where Ward attended another grammar school and Wilson Junior High, where he learned how to use a typewriter ("I still use the touch system for the letters, but I can't do the numbers.").

Without his grandmother's encouragement, Kimball's interest in drawing "slipped," until the fifth grade. Each week, the teacher offered a chocolate candy bar for the best drawing. After several unsuccessful tries, Ward finally won the prize with a simple drawing his father taught him to make of an ocean liner in scalloped waves, with hovering V-shaped birds. "The candy bar was mine!" says Kimball. "From that point on there was no stopping me. Even though I can't remember more candy, the urge to draw was established."[27]

Renting a room in the Kimball house on Glendale Avenue was Uncle Charlie, now a Christian Science practitioner. "We thought he was weird," says Ward. He and his sister and brother liked to put Charlie's cat Fuzzy on the Victrola turntable, turn it on, and watch her spin. "Then we set her down on the floor. She was 'drunk.' She'd roll over and fall down and we'd laugh!" One day, after a laugh-provoking, Fuzzy-spinning episode, suddenly "from up above where Charlie was staying," says Ward, "Boomp! [his door] opened up and a beam of light came down the stairs and he said, 'God is love,' and slam!" The door shut again.

In 1929, the family, minus Uncle Charlie, moved to West Covina, a mile-square agricultural town filled with walnut and orange trees, where Ward was bussed to Covina High School. He learned to play tennis and, during a bout of influenza, read *Ivanhoe* at home to keep up with his ninth-grade class. In 1930, the Kimballs moved to Ventura, where Ward drew cartoons for the high school annual.

The next year, Bruce Kimball got a job with the Edison Company selling washing machines and moved his family up the coast to Santa Barbara. From a cartooning correspondence course, Ward learned how to shade his drawings with crosshatching, foreshorten figures and objects, and enlarge a Thomas Nast drawing of Boss Tweed. He applied his new-found techniques on the weekly mimeographed covers for the school paper.

During his sophomore year in high school, he saw an ad for the Federal Schools, another mail-order art school, later known as Art Instruction Schools. His parents "didn't have the loot for the art course," but after "a pleading letter of serious intent and enthusiasm to my grandmother, she came to the rescue with the money." Although he was a poor student in grade school, Ward became an A honor student in high school, "all the while finding the spare time to work on my Federal School art lessons." He looks back on his teen years of self-motivated learning about drawing as "no small achievement."

Since Ward's parents and uncles were "gung-ho college persons," it was expected that he would attend college, perhaps Stanford, "settle down in some small town, and teach until happy retirement." Uncle Paul, in fact, generously offered to underwrite four years of college for his nephew.

But Ward was offered a scholarship at the Santa Barbara School of the Arts. "Kimball Gets Cartoon Award," a local newspaper article announced in June 1932. "Community Arts Scholarship Goes to Outstanding High School Student."[28] "I faced a tough decision," says Kimball. When he chose art school over college, his father "immediately banished me from the house for my adolescent temerity." Forgiveness soon followed when he explained that "eight hours a day, six days a week of

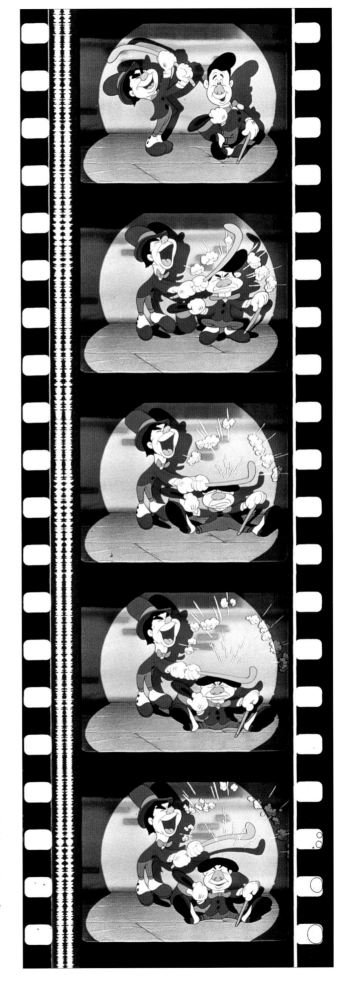

The Nifty Nineties, *a 1941 Mickey Mouse short with caricatures of Ward Kimball and Fred Moore as vaudevillians.*

LEFT, *Ward plays at football at Covina High School in 1929;* RIGHT, *a formal portrait of teenaged Ward.*

applied design, drawing, and painting was more important than pennants, pompoms and fraternities."[29]

In the fall of 1932, he entered the Santa Barbara School of the Arts, which occupied an entire city block including old adobes refurbished as classrooms. It was the height of the Depression, which took a toll on the school. Monied summer residents, such as William Randolph Hearst, slowly withdrew their financial support (eventually the school folded), and Kimball had to earn his tuition by working as a school janitor, with all the enervating duties the job entailed. But "this was okay with me," he says.

For Kimball reveled in his art education. "I was ravenous about painting portraits, slashing watercolors of California vistas, smearing oils of eucalyptus trees, designing murals for downtown bars, and sometimes receiving only a dollar-a-gallon jug of wine for pay."[30] The eighteen-year-old adopted what he calls a "bohemian" look: a reddish-black beard, bluejeans, black turtleneck, and J. C. Penney work shoes.

He attended day and evening classes, studied landscape painting with Belmore Brown (the school's dean), sculpture with Avery Simmons (a student of Rodin), and life drawing with Bret Moore. He confiscated the abandoned art materials of rich dilettantes ("especially the girl students") after they had given up on art careers. His oil palette was "a flat tin this deep,

and I kept my watercolors covered with water at night so they wouldn't dry out."[31]

Painting instructor Richmond Kelsey "gave amazing assignments." He asked his students to paint a picture in the fog; he suggested a square be divided into a pleasing design à la Mondrian; he took his classes on painting field trips in the Lompoc Valley or the Rockies in the summer. "I was impressed with Kelsey," says Kimball, whose recommendation years later led to Kelsey's being hired by Disney as a color stylist.[32]

The Depression was "pretty tough on my family," admits Kimball. "Dad was out of work most of the time and there was no welfare, so I had to pick up a little loot wherever possible." Saturdays were especially busy. Starting at five A.M. at the local Safeway—come rain, shine, or (in Santa Barbara) fog—Kimball uncrated lettuce packed in ice from Watsonville, hacked off the first few leaves and put the shorn heads in a display case. After his fingers thawed, he painted showcards ("Three pounds for a dollar") with a wide brush for display stacks.

At nine-thirty A.M., he crossed the street and headed up the block to the Fox Arlington Theatre, where every Saturday the Mickey Mouse Club congregated. Two decades before the television version, this was "a nationwide promotional thing to get the kids into the theater." The clubs had their juvenile presidents and sergeants-of-arms, and the Santa Barbara division had a special marching band made up of about ten children. Ward was paid three dollars to rehearse and lead the motley kid band, since he was already playing trombone in the Santa Barbara Symphony.

"The minute the curtain would go up," Kimball recalls, "the whole audience of kids would boo when they saw us onstage. The kids [in the band] would all be sitting there in their white duck pants and white shirts. We'd struggle through one march, all out of tune, and when we finished there would be this big, resounding boo, because the kids really wanted to get on with the cartoons."33 Kimball remembers "one day when we didn't have a lead trumpet and everybody was playing second parts on a march!"34

The cartoons shown at the Fox included not just Disney shorts, but also Felix the Cat, Popeye, Betty Boop, Krazy Kat, and Farmer Alfalfa. "After leading the kid band," says Kimball, "I would hang around and watch the damn cartoons, just for laughs, and add to the feeling that I was really earning my three dollars."35

Kimball's interests lay in fine-art painting and illustration. But his exposure to Disney's film efforts "opened my eyes to the fact that these weren't the usual crude cartoon offerings. I began to see," he later wrote, "that the Disney product was far superior and even artistic." *Father Noah's Ark*, a Silly Symphony released in April 1933, impressed him, particularly a scene in which the animals, two by two, run from a gathering storm toward the ark. "The giraffes lope like giraffes and the hippos lumber along like hippos should. Pairs of faster animals pass the slower ones. I began to see there was more to these animated cartoons than I had previously thought."

Three Little Pigs, which opened in late May 1933, "just knocked me out!" says Kimball, who saw the short "six to ten times." A phenomenal box-office hit, the short film's theme song, "Who's Afraid of the Big Bad Wolf?" became an anthem that gave a psychological boost to Depression-weary America.

"That amazed me," he says. "It was a caricature, but it was for real. You caricatured the animation."36

He was tempted to rethink his career plans when he saw in a pulp magazine a Disney ad soliciting artists. Still, he hesitated because he truly loved his learning experiences at art school. He may have been painting mailboxes for the Christian Science church for extra cash, but he was also "gobbling up" the anatomy classes, spending a week copying skulls and plaster casts of Michelangelo's David. His work in all mediums was regularly selected for school exhibitions.

The following March of 1934, instructor Channing Peague convinced Kimball to apply for work at Disney. "You have a flair for caricature," he told the twenty-year-old artist. "You shouldn't hang around this damn art school." Kimball's mother reluctantly agreed to drive him in their old Buick down the coastline to Los Angeles and the Hyperion Avenue studio "just this once." At twelve cents a gallon, they could afford barely enough gas to go down and back.37

His mother parked in front of the studio, which embarrassed Ward. Nervously, he dragged his portfolio in and announced to the receptionist, Mary Flanigan, that he was applying for a job and presented his samples. "She looked at it and it confused her," claims Kimball. "'Cause nobody had ever brought a portfolio. I said, 'Doesn't anybody want to see what I can do?'"

A "traffic boy"—a go-fer—named Gus who delivered beer to the animators every afternoon at four P.M. took the portfolio upstairs while Kimball waited. Word eventually came back that "they" would like to keep his samples for a while and make a decision later.

Kimball began to wail, "No, I gotta know today! I can't come back. I don't have enough money to buy gas to come back! Can't they let me know today?" Apparently, his portfolio was impressive; for after a lengthy phone conversation with Ms. Flanigan, "they" hired Kimball on the spot. He would start the next week, on April 2, reporting to Mr. Ben Sharpsteen.

Kimball's parents quickly arranged for Ward to stay with a Mrs. Ulman, a Civil War widow and Sunday-school teacher who lived in a house on Salem Street in Glendale. "She did all this wonderful cooking and my mother knew that," says Kimball. The widow lived alone and "liked to have somebody in there because she wanted me every night to come look under her bed. She had arthritis, [and wanted to] make sure there wasn't a man under there. That's no kidding! I filled a vacant room."

The Disney studio was still small, even with the two-story building for animators that had recently been constructed around a courtyard; there were about 190 employees, including janitors and a night watchman. In each small animation room were two animators and two assistants. "For the most part it was a crazy fun place to work and everybody was young and funny," recalls Kimball, who had a keen eye for decorative details.

"The desk furniture was something!" he says, laughing.

They decided to use the Spanish motif because the first building built on Hyperion had Spanish roof tile, so this style prevailed throughout the studio. The old sound stage looked like Capistrano Mission. The first animation desks were developed out of the function and requirements of the animators. They were painted ivory white, with the shelf edges trimmed in a sienna red. Then they sprayed a kind of dirty umber mixture inside the shelves and in the corners to give an aged or antique effect. Early Hyperion Spanish!38

The worst part of the decor, thought Kimball, were the spittoons sitting atop rubber pads next to each desk. "This was a carryover from the old days when every office had to have a spittoon, whether you used it or not. There was a big tub in the men's can [bathroom] where the spittoons were washed

This illustration caught Walt's eye in 1934 and convinced him that Ward Kimball was a potential animator.

Kimball's portfolio of drawings made the rounds, impressing everyone, including Walt. His eye was caught by an Arthur Rackham–like illustration in subdued greens and grays of a fat man and a thin man running down the darkened streets of London during the Black Plague, based on a Poe story. Walt decided the young artist should work in the Animation Department. "He liked the action," says Kimball.

To learn the ropes, Kimball was thrown into the in-betweener bullpen under the dictatorial, overtly sadistic supervision of George Drake. "He was a bricklayer having trouble feeding his family," says Kimball, "who got the job because he was married to Sharpsteen's sister." Another nail in Sharpsteen's coffin, as far as Kimball was concerned.

Kimball was paid fifteen dollars a week during this learning period, a pittance, but unusual because most tryouts were done without pay; it indicated Walt's interest in this particular talent. The in-betweener bullpen was located in a basement where in summer it was so hot the men stripped to their waists. The roomful of nervous, perspiring young men bent over row after row of animation light tables looked to Kimball like the belly of a slave ship. Making drawings between key poses was tedious, a nerve-wracking job; soon enough, many of the recruits were fired and quickly replaced by a new batch of out-of-work artists who, during the Depression, were literally a dime a dozen.

George Drake crudely corrected the in-betweeners' efforts ("That's not the way to do it!") with a bumptious demonstration ("Lemme show you how!") After tortured scribblings, much erasing and cursing, the paper ended up "like old Confederate money." Working at this new job made Kimball "very nervous."

In those pre-union days, it was also dangerous. During that hot summer of 1934, in-betweeners had to contend with a noisy, dusty excavation next door, as yet another building was added to the rapidly expanding studio. "This big Caterpillar tractor was growling away," recalls Kimball, "when all of a sudden *WHAM!* It sounded like a bomb hit the building." The tractor driver had lost control of his machine and smashed through the wall, stopping three feet from Kimball's back. "Dust, plaster, wood splinters and everything, flying all over my work," he says. "Everybody comes running down the stairs to see what happened. When the dust settles, I find my nose is bleeding all over my face. Just shows you how tense learning to in-between was!"

Balmy summer evenings after work, the exhausted young man walked up Hyperion Avenue to cross the Hyperion Bridge where the Pacific Electric line curved up Brand Boulevard toward Glendale. Kimball caught a Big Red streetcar, leaned out the window to catch the breeze, and sometimes fell asleep watching loose screws twist in and out of the wooden window frames. Sometimes, he slept through his stop at Broadway. "Jesus, I'd get mad because I'd have to stand and wait for another car to get back. Such was the life of a Disney in-betweener."

nightly and some guys were horrified one day to see me taking a bath in the spittoon tub after a hot game of volleyball."[39]

Kimball's eye also keenly sized up people, and he rarely altered his first impressions. For example, on his first day he dutifully knocked on the open door of Ben Sharpsteen, the older, uptight studio manager and director.

Sharpsteen gives me a quick glance and he goes right on working. This action tells me right away that I'm meeting one of the straw bosses. So he lets me stand there. Jesus, it seemed like a long time. I finally asked, "Mr. Sharpsteen?" Another long wait before he asks, "You Ward Kimball?" I say, "Yah." He studies me up and down slowly, then says, "I expected a much older man." I told him I was sorry. He condescendingly told me my work showed a lot of talent, and maybe I just might fit in. [40]

Kimball soon concluded that Sharpsteen was "Walt's whipping boy," an insecure man who was "very sensitive about the fact that he couldn't draw and that he had no talent himself. This made him slightly sadistic with the new, young artists who were coming in at the time."[41]

After supper if he wasn't too tired, he'd work on his hobby: model railroad building. On a workbench with a Sears Roebuck drill press he had set up in his room, Kimball started building full gauge quarter-inch model trains, "which he had always wanted to do." Next day, it was back on the Big Red to the Disney bullpen. The first films he worked on (as an in-betweener) included *The Wise Little Hen* (a Silly Symphony released in June 1934 that marked the debut of Donald Duck) and a Mickey Mouse short, *Orphan's Benefit*, released in August 1934.

"Each of us would get a small section of a scene to work on. We never knew quite how our contribution fitted into the story until we saw the completed picture in the theater," he says. Shorts were usually previewed at the Alex Theater in Glendale, followed by a sidewalk critique from Walt.

The tedious in-betweening and retracing led to shortcuts, especially in drawings of Mickey Mouse. "If he was small, we'd use a dime to draw or scribe his head and body circles. A nickel was used for the next size, then we'd go up to a quarter or a fifty-cent piece for medium size, and for close-ups, we'd use a silver dollar. That is, if we had one! There was a pliable accordion effect between these head and fanny parts, but the head and fanny circles themselves were very rigid." "Loose-change animation," it was called.

"You'd do anything to relieve the monotony," Kimball recalls. The in-betweeners risked Drake's fury by spontaneously humming a chorus of the "Song of the Volga Boatman." "Sheer desperation seemed to bring out a never-ending stream of humor." Inevitably, the humor turned risqué. "In those days we spent endless hours drawing gags and sometimes pornography," says Kimball. "The first pornography I think came about when we were working on *The Goddess of Spring* [released in November 1934]. Two likely subjects: Pluto and Persephone! These were drawing collections that everybody would contribute to."

Kimball quickly made an impression on his fellow "slaves," by the way he dressed: dark pants with a dollar-fifty white shirt and a five dollar pair of shoes purchased at the Famous Department Store in Glendale. At work, he changed into cheap little leather slippers with Indian heads burned on them and donned a green eyeshade.

He loved inciting his coworkers' jealousy. The widow Ulman kept him well fed and often a jar of fresh strawberries appeared in his lunch box. At three P.M., when the Good Humor man came through the studio, most of the men bought ice cream bars. Kimball, however, ordered a vanilla ice-cream cup and added the strawberries. "Everybody would look with envy at my mix," he recalled years later with relish. "The other guys just couldn't get over the fact that I was able to do this right here in this dumb little in-between room."[42]

Production managers continued to irk Kimball. When he ambitiously wrote *Toby Tortoise Returns* (the short was released in August 1936), he expected the usual hundred-dollar bonus, which was "a lot of money then." But Paul Hopkins of Personnel delivered a check for half that amount. When Kimball balked, Hopkins said that *he* had decided to make it less because Kimball hadn't been there very long. "I'm sure Walt was not aware of my getting scalped," says Kimball. "So at an early age I learned about injustice. Hopkins is long gone, but even to this day, the deed sets me off."[43]

One day, the paternalistic Sharpsteen asked Kimball how he liked Disney so far. "Great, great," said Kimball, adding with typical boldness, "but you ought to have a shower somewhere where a guy can clean up after he plays a dusty game of volleyball." Sharpsteen coldly replied, "There's nothing in your contract that says you have to play volleyball."[44] Kimball grudgingly continued to bathe in the spittoon tub.

Kimball's strong anti-authoritarian streak can be traced to a visiting art teacher in grammar school who suggested how and what to draw, which annoyed Kimball, who balked. At the studio, "Disney despots" earned his scorn—the bureaucratic production managers who were "always trying to show the talent who was boss." He hated their "daily cornball speeches about how we should work harder for ol' Walt, et cetera. They would do childish things like betting a carton of cigarettes that they would get the picture out ahead of schedule. So then we'd all have to work overtime, usually during the hot summer evenings of August. There were no unions then, see. Later, the straw boobs wondered why we had the big strike in 1941!"[45]

After about six months, Kimball was promoted to assistant animator under Ham Luske, whose previous assistant, Eric Larson, moved into a junior animator position. Kimball's promotion saved him from being fired by Drake, who had caught wind of Kimball's devastating impersonation of him and caricatures that emphasized Drake's *Dumbo*-like ears. "Ham wanted me there. That pissed off George Drake."[46] Recently, he noted that "If George Drake [had] fired me, I'd probably [have] gone with Warner Bros. [But] it wouldn't have been the same."[47]

Kimball assisted Luske on the classic Silly Symphony *The Tortoise and the Hare* (1935); a goodly portion of Kimball's weekly twenty-two-dollar salary he sent home to Santa Barbara. "My father financially supported his parents from the time he was twenty-one," says Kelly Kimball.

Working with the analytical Luske was "a good break for me," says Kimball, "because Ham gave me a lot of responsibility and that's the way you learn. He'd give me little secondary things to animate in his scenes, like if he did some dance animation, I would do the drapery follow-through. This is the way I learned the rudiments."

Luske told him "you cannot caricature until you can analyze, draw, and show the real object, the real character." He explained:

Say a character puts on a coat or takes it off . . . in this particular scene. Then I'd really for the first time be analyzing something I'd taken for granted before. The step-by-step process of how putting on a coat is different from taking the coat off. And by analyzing a coat: how it was stitched and . . . how a tailor put it together, by approaching this from all angles, I did a better job and this was teaching me something that I'd never learned before. Something I had to learn to become an animator.⁴⁸

On Friday nights in summer, Kimball and Larry Clemmons (1906–1988), another newcomer at the studio, would go to Ocean Park, which was teeming with people escaping the heat. Sitting on a bench eating Cracker Jack and popcorn, they analyzed every person who walked by.

What *he* must do for a living . . . how would you like to be married to *that*? And *they* came down here with all their kids! But what we were doing and having fun with was analyzing people: what made them tick, and going into the psychology of the persons. When you're an animator, all these things have to be considered along with the hardware or the mathematics of making the scene work. The use of the camera *and* the drawing. What does it add up to personality-wise? Is the character a scheming, conniving individual? Then he walks differently, and how do you also make it funny?

You have a pianist like Horowitz or a fiddle player like Heifitz: they have such command of their instruments that then they can go beyond with their interpretation. But animation, unfortunately, was always tough for everybody, and you never got to the point where you could just jug with the tips of your fingers. Every time you animated a new scene, you thought you might have licked all the problems, and every time you would run into a new set of problems.⁴⁹

Kimball "was a great observer of life," Ken Peterson once told Frank Thomas and Ollie Johnston, "but he saw something funny in everything, and sometimes it hurt!" Frank Thomas felt Kimball would have made a great political cartoonist. "He would get right to the point and *that's* what hurt. He had everybody pegged. His sense of entertainment was based on cutting things down to his size. He had to be on top of everything, better than. That was his basis of showing what was funny about something."⁵⁰

Ham Luske often left quite a bit of animation for Kimball to finish. "Where other animators wanted to do all the work themselves and leave very little to their assistants, [Ham] would give me things to animate where I said, 'Gee, Ham, I can't do that!' 'Oh, sure you can!' Just go ahead.' This happened on *[The] Tortoise and the Hare*," released in January

1935, in which Kimball animated "things like the flowers blowing over after the hare rushed by and signs flipping over."

Animators received bonuses based on the weekly footage they were able to turn out; with Kimball helping him, Luske's bonuses tripled. Gerry Geronimi, an animator from New York, told Kimball he was "a sucker," saying "*you* do all the work and he gets all the money!"

But Kimball didn't mind because he was "having the opportunity to learn the craft and not everybody was afforded that." After a sweatbox critique of pencil tests, Ham would make Kimball do the corrections that the director and Walt demanded:

And so Ham would say to me, 'Here are the notes on the scene. Walt thinks that I should jump the hare higher, which means we have to run our camera up higher. Maybe we should put it two inches higher, you decide where . . . Well, that wasn't necessarily reanimating, but I was learning how to make those changes and how to make the scenes more active, and how to slow in on top of the movement and slow up when he came down. All those mechanical things you had to do.⁵¹

By 1935, Walt was fully committed to producing his first animated feature, *Snow White and the Seven Dwarfs*, "which was sort of a shock to all of us," says Kimball, "because we knew how hard it was to do a seven-minute short." Recruitment of new talent was stepped up in all departments. "These were exciting times, because everything was opening up and expanding. New talent was coming in. I was convinced by then that animation was my bag and I didn't want to be a magazine illustrator after all.

"There was more to the cartoon film business than I ever dreamed," he says. "You had to first be an artist, a draftsman, an actor, and you had to use mathematics to make it all work. And most of all, you had to have patience."⁵²

George Drake's patience was at the breaking point with what he perceived as Kimball's antagonistic, mocking attitude and poor work habits. Apparently Kimball was still under Drake's purview, or at least Drake believed that he was; on June 19, 1935 he wrote Kimball an angry two-page letter, saying "it is impossible to reach you through the medium of conversation."

The letter implied Kimball would be fired if he didn't "set [his] house in order." Drake's main complaints were three:

First—You spend too much time away from your work . . . many of the animators have voluntarily remarked to me and others that they did not know how you ever accomplished anything because of the fact that every time they saw you, you were fooling around. You have also the reputation of being cocky and disrespectful.

Second—You spend too much time on your hobbies and on unproductive drawings and caricatures during working hours. These things have their place and I do not object to a little of it. However, you have certainly abused the privilege.

Third—You enter into discussions between Ham and others who come into your room which do not concern you or your work. . . .

Sometime ago you received an increase in salary. Let me state emphatically that I was obliged to do a lot of convincing before that increase went thru [sic]. You received that increase to spur you on and to snap you out of your present condition as much as you received it for recognition on our part of the added value of your services. . . . Bear in mind you do not owe me any respect personally—but that you do owe my office and my responsibility the respect that any executive has a right to expect from those in his department.[53]

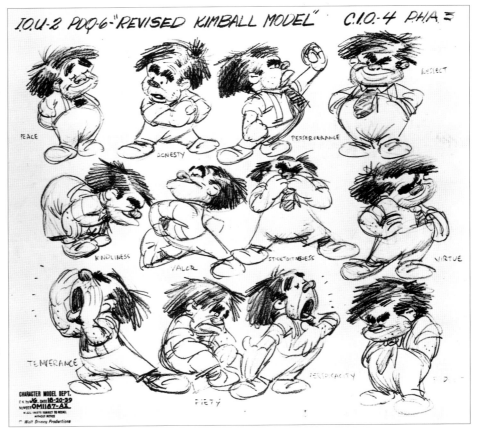

Between the lines hear the moans of a humorless straw boss severely wounded by one caricature or impersonation too many from an anti-authoritarian twenty-one-year-old. The insolent whippersnapper antagonized coworkers and thumbed his nose at authority figures. But he was not fired. Powerful Ham Luske appreciated his talents and protected him. In fact, not long after Drake's letter, Kimball was promoted to "junior animator," the next plateau in the animation hierarchy. Now he had more responsibility and worked closely with several of the film directors "doing fill-in scenes of less importance like mob scenes, smoke, dust, and maybe some angry bees who chased Donald Duck."[54]

Kimball's first effort as a solo animator was the insect dancers and jazz musicians in *Woodland Cafe*, a Silly Symphony released in March 1937. "*Woodland* was great!" said Kimball years later. "It had a great campy Roaring 'Twenties look about it." The film is rich with cartoon art-deco touches, saturated color, and lovely special effects; especially impressive is a ballroom of dozens of bugs dancing under a mirror ball made up of glowing fireflies, as dandelion puff "balloons" float and gently fall. The surprising delicacy prefigures the nature ballet in *Fantasia*'s "Nutcracker Suite." Character designs are halfway between the old circle-and-rubber-hose style and a newer, more sophisticated caricature of human (and insect) anatomy; they anticipate similar designs used sixty-one years later in *A Bug's Life*.

The film ingeniously parodies 1930s New York café society.

Kimball's self-caricature once appeared on a fake model sheet; BOTTOM, *Ward Kimball, man of many sides.*

In a huge underground nightclub (furnished with mushroom tables and a leaf dance floor) segmented centipedes and ladybugs strut and bump into each other dancing to "Tiger Rag"; old snails take it easy in a sedate, clumsy two-step; and two Lindy-hopping worms together make up one long-legged dancer. There is also an old, gout-ridden beetle with a young curvaceous June bug (they resemble William Randolph Hearst and Marion Davies); when she entices the old man into an ill-advised Charleston atop a table, the exertion sends him to the hospital, albeit with a smile on his face.

The stars of the show—a lively grasshopper orchestra—are caricatures of Cab Calloway and his musicians. As was typical in Hollywood movies of the period, African Americans are stereotyped as entertainers who perform exclusively for the pleasure of monied white dancing couples. In *Woodland Cafe*, however, this casual racism is muted because the "white" and "black" characters are every gaudy color except white and black; also, the exaggerated design of the elongated musician grasshoppers, dressed in bright green coats, spats, and white gloves, leaves naught but their enlarged lips to give the game away.

Kimball specialized in African American musicians and other performers; one year after *Woodland Cafe*, he again animated Cab Calloway in *Mother Goose Goes Hollywood* (1938), and three years later the singing-and-dancing crows in *Dumbo* (1941) became one of his most famous assignments. Kimball brought great affection and empathy to his animation of musical characters. As a musician himself and a man with high energy and an idiosyncratic personal style, he literally put into them a lot of himself. *Woodland Cafe*'s music makers explode with exuberance and fun, and Kimball's ebullient, elegant animation raises them far above crude racial caricatures.

In scene 106 in *Woodland Cafe*, a smiling, openmouthed grasshopper flails away at a bass fiddle to the tune of "Everybody's Truckin'," as his foot taps out the rhythm, and his head (and antennae) toss back and forth in ecstatic abandon. Consisting of fifty-seven drawings shot onto film at one frame per drawing, scene 106 lasts about two and a quarter seconds on the screen. Years later, Ken Peterson recalled it as the first Kimball scene that impressed him. "Ward explained how he did it with just two cycles [of animation] worked together. It was quite mechanical," thought Peterson, "but what a talent!"[55]

"I look back on it," said Kimball recently. "I moved stuff too fast, but at least it hit the beats, and Walt was always saying, well, Ward is a good musician. Let him do that."

The *Woodland Cafe* scene in question is a continuous action that does "cycle"; that is, the bug musician's hand hits the bass eight times (four large slaps on the instrument's strings followed by four smaller hits) and the character's head works back and forth like a metronome. But there are subtleties as well. The bug's leg straightens upward into his body as his foot taps, but somehow his height never increases; also the bass-slapping, white-gloved hand is enormously foreshortened as it moves on zany spaghetti-arms that contain no joints whatsoever. Kimball not only caricatures the character, but also the out-of-this-world emotional state of the musician.

In fact, Kimball caricatures the entire old cornball style of rubber-hose-and-circle animation. In his showy draftsmanship, his ease with complicated mechanics, and his graceful rhythm, Kimball is thumbing his nose at predecessors, while announcing his arrival as a gifted animator, saying in effect "Eat my dust!"

On August 15, 1936, Kimball married Betty Lawyer, a petite, pretty blonde who had been working in the Ink and Paint Department for a year; as of this writing, the couple have been married for nearly sixty-five years. "They wouldn't let me visit

  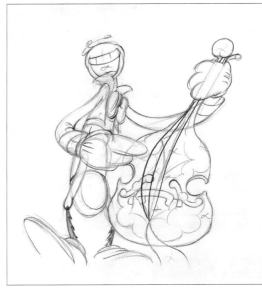

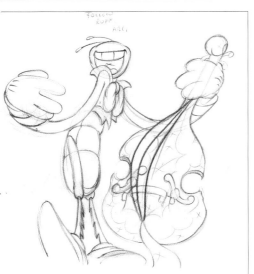 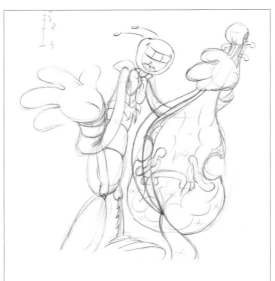 

Kimball's first important solo animation is in Woodland Café, *a 1937* Silly Symphony *featuring insect musicians.*

Ward after we were married," said Betty recently. "They liked to keep us [Ink and Paint women and the animators] separate." But from 1935 to 1937, many Disney employees married because "we worked nights and we'd get together. We'd been working and we became friends. There wasn't much mingling before that, but during *Snow White* the inking and painting people mixed in with the animators and there were a lot of marriages that occurred."

For their honeymoon, the Kimballs loaded a Ford with cameras and art supplies and headed to California's Sierra Nevada to explore abandoned settlements in old logging towns. All that remained of one place was a post-office building quaintly called "Grizzly Flats."

Ward and Betty liked the name for its whimsy and historical connection with the Seal of California (which features a grizzly bear). When they returned home, the Kimballs intended to bestow the name upon their quarter-inch (O-scale) model-railroad layout. However, as full-sized trains entered their lives, plans for the

smaller layout were abandoned. The Grizzly Flats name was applied to the Kimballs' backyard narrow-gauge line.[56]

In 1938, Kimball bought rolling stock that was about to be scrapped from the defunct Nevada Central Railroad, including a vintage 1881 steam locomotive named "Sidney Dillon." He paid $400 for the Victorian coal-burner and spent several years restoring the train, renamed "Emma Nevada" after an early Nevada opera singer. Over the years, he and Betty acquired a 1907 steam engine (named Chloe after one of their daughters), and built "an engine house, a fully detailed Victorian-era depot, a windmill, and a water tower." Other Grizzly Flats rolling stock included an 1881 passenger coach, a 1906 boxcar, and a caboose, all fully operative on 900 feet of narrow-gauge rail. "The Kimballs," writes Michael Broggie in *Walt Disney's Railroad Story*, "became the nation's first private owners and operators of full-sized steam railroad equipment in a residential backyard."[57]

By 1936, Kimball was animating on *Snow White*, which became a frustrating experience when his two sequences—a

THIS PAGE, *Betty and Ward Kimball, circa 1938; three of Ward's vintage locomotives (located on his home property);* OPPOSITE, *a sequence of rough animation by Kimball of* Pinocchio's *Jiminy Cricket.*

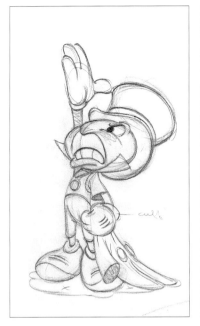

soup-eating musical number and a bed-building song, both performed by the dwarfs—were cut from the final film. "When all the sequences were put together and Walt saw the overall timing of the show, he could see that we didn't need those sequences 'cause they held up the progress of the story." Some Kimball animation remains, such as *Snow White* waking in the forest, and the opportunistic vultures following the witch, and a gag he suggested in which each dwarf's phallic nose pops out over a bed on which *Snow White* is lying.

Kimball felt "not bitter, but discouraged because I had worked so hard." He took the deletions personally, thinking there was something wrong with the way he animated. Deciding to quit the studio, he made an appointment to see Walt. Sensing why Kimball was there, Walt waxed eloquent about the next project. *Pinocchio* was going to be a wonderful picture, said Walt, and he wanted Ward to personally to take charge of this cricket character. "God, he did such a wonderful job," says Kimball of Walt's salesmanship, "that I walked out very happily and said, 'What a wonderful place this is!'"

But Kimball was never happy with Jiminy Cricket's design. "How do you make a cricket endearing and cute?" he has often

asked rhetorically. "There's no way. We got down to that nothing character, which is a blob!"[58] In mid-1939, Kimball wrote four pages of detailed comments on the anatomy of The Cricket (whom he never referred to as Jiminy):

> If the mouth is drawn too close to the nose, it makes him look too cute. Mouth works as though on a hinge. . . . Don't draw a tricky Mickey Mouse mouth, which seems always to be working on the side.
>
> The two antennas have been shifted to the back of the head to look like two wisps of hair.
>
> In drawing the Cricket, try to figure him like Mickey. Divide him into thirds, then make the body like a teardrop in normal relaxed poses.

Barely hiding his contempt for Jiminy's final design, Kimball wrote:

> By comparison, the first Cricket we drew was taller and closer to a grasshopper or bug. He had a smaller hat, smaller head, long thin arms, legs, etc. It is not much

Bacchus and his steed Jacchus, in the "Pastoral Symphony" in Fantasia, *were animated by Ward Kimball. Although full of lusty high spirits and jovial inebriation, Bacchus was not a favorite assignment for Kimball, who would have preferred animating the parody of ballet in* Fantasia's *"Dance of the Hours."* OPPOSITE LEFT, *Ward, Walt, Ub Iwerks, Fred Moore, and live-action director Alfred L. Werker on the set of* The Reluctant Dragon *(1941);* RIGHT, *humorist Robert Benchley meets Kimball and Moore in* The Reluctant Dragon, *whose storyboard is seen* BELOW.

off a pool table's edge and "holds" in midair for four frames—an unreal, Tex Avery–like delay that invariably gets a laugh.

Kimball's put-down of Jiminy as "a lousy character" and "nothing like a cricket" is self-defeating, according to Frank Thomas, "because the things that made him a cricket were not the things you wanted to show." Continues Thomas:

It had nothing to do with his personality. I would have looked at the cricket in terms of the voice and what he has to say, and attitudes he has to express. And hopefully I'd come out with what he ended up with. . . . [Kimball] elevates himself by running it down. I don't think that's fair to either the cricket or actually to Kimball.[60]

For *Fantasia,* released the same year as *Pinocchio* (1940) Kimball animated drunken Bacchus astride a tiny, equally inebriated mule (Jacchus) in the "Beethoven Pastoral" section. Weaving about, waving a never-empty wine goblet and chasing comely "centaurettes," obese Bacchus looks (as Kimball wrote on the character model sheet) "like the balloon in Macy's parade."

trouble to make him cute—but try to make him funny. . . . In other words, be sincere and realistic in the drawing always. You must make him real as much as possible because to begin with, he is neither a man or a child, but an abstract design of something that is small and cute."[59]

Still, Jiminy Cricket is arguably the warmest, most sincere, and psychologically three-dimensional personality that Kimball ever animated. Some of the spunky character's best acting occurs in the Pleasure Island pool hall when he chastises Pinocchio and tells off Lampwick, a streetwise brat. Kimball's staging, timing, and poses of the cricket are wonderfully exaggerated, but sincere; and, in one scene of pure Kimball arbitrariness, Jiminy steps

Again, he was displeased with his assignment ("My efforts on this opus were nothing to shout about"); he wished he had animated "Dance of the Hours," a satirical ballet with hippos, ostriches, and crocodiles.

Kimball appears on-camera in *The Reluctant Dragon* (released in June 1941), a quickly and cheaply made tour of the new Disney studio in Burbank, interspersed with animated segments.

Humorist Robert Benchley visits various departments (sound, camera, ink and paint, among others) including an animator's room, where Fred Moore skulks silently in the background.

Twenty-seven-year-old Kimball, however, sits at a desk animating with a cocky air and a condescending smirk on his young face, making smart-aleck remarks and flipping drawings for the hapless Benchley.

In this section of the storyboard for the live-action portion of The Reluctant Dragon, *Benchley, Kimball, and Moore are caricatured in the first row of drawings; the second row features a caricature of Norman Ferguson (who also appeared in the film) drawing Pluto.*

The feature's title refers to a book Benchley wants Walt to produce, based on Kenneth Grahame's story about a fire-breathing but pacifist monster. Kimball animated most of the twelve-minute *Dragon* short, including a number of scenes assigned to Fred Moore, whose alcoholism made him increasingly unreliable.

Kimball particularly enjoyed the outrageously fey dragon because it tweaked traditional sensibilities. The creature is so effeminate, he would make Quentin Crisp seem butch. "*The Reluctant Dragon* was a very revolutionary-type of Disney cartoon," recalled Kimball three decades later. "[For] some of the old conservatives at the studio, it was like looking at the *Yellow Submarine* to them. They felt it was too sophisticated, and they resented the fact that the dragon sounded pretty gay. You couldn't tell if he was a male or a female, but it got big laughs. The first night we ran it at the studio, it killed everybody!"[61]

One day in the studio parking lot, Walt told Kimball the plot of a new circus picture called *Dumbo*. "He went through the whole story in about five minutes," Kimball recalls. "'I want you to do the dance sequence where the crows teach *Dumbo* how to fly.' And listening to him tell the story, I could tell that the picture was going to work."

Actually, the crows sing and dance a song of derision, making fun of *Dumbo* and his friend Timothy Mouse for suggesting that an elephant might fly. Ultimately, the black crows empathize with *Dumbo* and his outsized ears, for they, too, are social outcasts because of their physical appearance; they teach him not to fly but to have confidence in himself. Besides *Dumbo*'s mother and Timothy, the crows are, in fact, the only sympathetic and generous characters in a film full of cruel tormentors (*Dumbo*'s fellow elephants) and selfish exploiters (the ringmaster, the circus clowns). Kimball's stylish animation gives the crows warmth, panache, and individuality. "The crows are stereotypical blacks," writes Michael Barrier in *Hollywood Cartoons*, "but rescued from embarrassment by the immense good humor that suffuses Kimball's animation, the voices, and the crows' song, 'When I See an Elephant Fly.'"[62]

Production on *Dumbo* was interrupted in late May through September 1941 by an acrimonious employees' strike. Kimball remained loyal to Walt, but sympathized with the strikers. "I was quite liberal," says Kimball, "yet I didn't go out on strike. But I knew something had to be done. And I agree to this day

DUMBO "JIM CROW" CLEAN-UP MODEL - 2006 -

Ward Kimball's exuberant animation of the musical crows is a highlight of Dumbo *(1941).*

that it was a good thing that it happened,"—an opinion that put him at odds with the other Nine Old Men. "There were unequal things going on there, salarywise, a lot of people being exploited without Walt's knowledge. People's screen credits, for instance, were cleared up."[63]

Kimball lost his best friend at the studio because of the strike: assistant animator Walt Kelly, who helped Kimball meet a close deadline on the crow sequence in *Dumbo*. Deciding to try some other line of work, he left for New York. A few years later, Kelly became famous for his comic strip *Pogo*.

At Disney, he and Kimball were close (Kimball named his eldest daughter Kelly). They were studio "bad boys" notorious for daily practical jokes and the outrageous gag cartoons they drew for each other; and for singing "Alabamy Bound" at the top of their voices with wastebasket accompaniment; and for playing "Darktown Strutters Ball" on tin whistles in the men's room because the reverberation there "makes you sound like a flute player in the Los Angeles Philharmonic."

With Fred Moore, they organized boisterous football games in the studio's narrow corridors. One day, the trio answered Roy Disney's call for volunteers to draw cartoons at two kiddie matinees at the Wiltern and Fairfax Theaters in Los Angeles. "Hell, yes!" shouted Kelly, a sure sign of trouble ahead. On the Saturday in question, the boys loaded up Moore's beige Buick with easels and black chalk, then loaded themselves up at a bar along the way. At both theaters, Kelly stood at a microphone cracking convoluted Irish jokes, while Kimball and Moore furiously scribbled Donald Duck and Mickey Mouse. Things went as well as could be expected until a small bottle of gin fell out of Moore's coat, which brought the festivities at the Fairfax to a swift close. "You boys have got to get off," said the theater manager. "This is not good for the youth of America!"[64]

Kelly's departure in 1941, says Kimball, "was a great loss for me because up until this time I had no friend whom I felt

Donald Duck, Jose Carioca, and Panchito sing the title song of The Three Caballeros *with Kimball's iconoclastic gusto and zany wit.*

thought as I did or did things that I liked to do. It wasn't until about two or three weeks had gone by that I really felt the loss of this guy. I didn't realize until then that we'd had so much fun and I depended so much on Kelly for a few laughs." Essentially a loner, Kimball never again had as close a buddy at the studio.

Little more than a month after *Dumbo* opened, the Japanese attacked Pearl Harbor and the USA entered World War II. Almost immediately, the Disney studio began turning out war propaganda and training films. "Walt hunted down war work to do," Kimball once told Rick Shale. "This deferred a lot of his talent. Hell, I'll be the first to admit I wasn't 1-A because I was working on war work. . . . The draft boys never came down and said, 'Hey, Kimball, why aren't you working on a training film on how we're going to land on Iwo Jima?' No, I was up there laughing and living it up."[65]

Kimball's war film assignments tended toward humor, even in one of the grimmest shorts Disney ever made: *Education for Death* (1943), which follows one German boy from birth to manhood and his indoctrination into Nazism. Frank Thomas and Milt Kahl struggled with realistic acting scenes and phonetic spellings of German dialogue for lip sync, while Kimball sailed through a satiric section: an operatic love duet between Hitler and an obese Hermann Goering dressed in Brunhilde drag as Germania. Kimball's animation makes it clear that while hoisting gross Germania onto a horse with great difficulty, Hitler gooses her. "It got tremendous laughs," he says, but "they made me cut down on her expression because they didn't really want people to think she got the finger or something. It was all suggestion." Kimball blamed the toning down of the vulgarity to the timidity of director Gerry Geronimi, which was ironic since stories of Geronimi's own vulgarity were legion at the studio. Once he attacked Kimball's buxom assistant. "Gerry grabbed Mary by the knockers," as Kimball deli-

cately puts it. "I mean that's terrible! That's not a class act!"[66]

Several animators had their battles with Geronimi on the features. "Walt had this way of playing one guy against the other," says Kimball. "He knew Gerry didn't like the animators and the animators didn't like him. [Walt] figured that's a way of getting good work out of us. Maybe this was Walt's secret." Kimball enjoyed goading Geronimi, who didn't like anyone sitting in his chair or on his desk. So, of course, when Kimball came to pick up a sequence, he'd stretch out on his back on Geronimi's desk. "Okay, Geronimi," he'd say, "give me the scenes. Tell me what's funny about it," and pretended to go to sleep. Geronimi would "go crazy," yelling "Get off my desk!"[67]

Another insecure director, Jack King, in another war short, *The Spirit of '43.* (1943), nearly ruined a Kimball scene that experimented with limited animation. Donald Duck, dressed in a zoot suit, stands on a street corner twirling a key chain. "To look real cool," explains Kimball, "I put his body on a held cel and just had him twirl his key chain, and his other hand was in his pocket. Just holds the pose and rolls his eyes." King, "who always lived in great fear of Walt Disney," panicked when he saw the stationary Duck and added some movement to the hand in the character's pocket. When the pencil test footage came in, Kimball blew his stack.

"Here's Donald Duck standing there, twirling his key chain, and his hands are playing with himself in his pocket! He's moving it around like some sex pervert!" King confessed, says Kimball: "He was afraid that Walt wouldn't like the fact that I held a cel, a body drawing, for that length of time, not realizing I did that on purpose. And so he had taken it upon himself to sit down there and put a cycle of this guy's hand moving in a rotary motion, and it was very suggestive." Kimball threatened, "[I'll] tell Walt on you," then he tore King's drawings out of the scene and threw them away.[68]

Kimball animating Pecos Bill, hyperbolic hero of the mythic Wild West, in the postwar omnibus feature Melody Time *(1948).*

Kimball's biggest battle during the war years was again with director Geronimi over the illogical entrances, exits, and jump cuts in the title song of *The Three Caballeros*. "All those were very new and progressive ideas that had never been tried. Gerry didn't want to show that sequence to Walt because it had 'bad cutting.' In other words, the Duck would run out on the right of the screen, and he'd come in through the top. All that magic stuff. Which is done all the time now. He didn't want to show it to Walt. He wanted me to change it. I said, I'm not going to. Stuff it up your ass!" Geronimi reluctantly showed the test footage to Walt, who "thought it was so great," says Kimball proudly. "He said, 'Jesus, this is it.' Gerry says, 'Well, we're going to change it. The Duck goes out there with some bad hookups.' 'Gerry, don't touch it.' [Walt] gave him hell about even thinking of changing anything."[69]

After the war, Kimball contributed to the "package" features—shorts strung together with popular music. In *Make Mine Music* (1946), he animated Willie the Whale in a satirical "opéra pathétique" called "The Whale Who Wanted to Sing at the Met." In "Peter and the Wolf," the oddly shaped Russian hunters balance Yascha, the smallest of the trio, between

Mischa's buttocks and Vladimir's paunch, and save the day by performing impossible Kimball choreography; he also brought his inimitable humor to an especially hilarious "take" when Ivan the cat sees the wolf: outstretched arms trembling, Ivan flies through the air screaming and trailing saliva.

In *Melody Time* (1948), "Pecos Bill" showcases Kimball cleverness; he animated the goofy-looking Texas superhero's roughhouse actions (digging the Rio Grande, riding and taming a cyclone, and so on) with exuberance. He worked in tandem with Milt Kahl's refined animation of Pecos Bill's girlfriend Sluefoot Sue, a superheroine whose feats match Bill's and then some. Ken Peterson thought the combination of loose-as-a-goose Kimball and uptight Kahl resulted in fine animation: "They were both raised to a height that they could never have done alone. Milt broadened out his caricature and held Kimball down a bit." Personally, the two animators (whose personalities and approaches to animation were diametrically opposed) gave each other "wide berth" throughout their careers at Disney.[70]

Kimball being Kimball, he claims he sneaked a bit of ribald humor into a Pecos Bill pencil test animated by Milt Kahl: when

Sue kisses Bill, his excited guns jump out of their holsters to shoot off continuous rounds. Kimball's phallic humor went right by Walt Disney ("You could never tell him a dirty joke," says Kimball) and the visual joke remains in the film.

The seeds for Kimball's Dixieland jazz band, Firehouse Five Plus Two, were sown in the mid-1940s. A June 15, 1944, newsletter of the Disney Studio Labor-Management Commission newsletter noted:

Ward Kimball's Huggajeedy 8 is doing a swell job of entertaining the boys in

Two tintype photos of Walt and Ward taken during a 1948 visit to the Henry Ford Museum & Greenfield Village in Dearborn, Michigan.

the hospitals. Next trip will be to the Norconia T.B. Ward, where they'll try a new act, complete with "chalk-talk," skits and jam session.

Formed casually around 1948, The Firehouse Five Plus Two, with Kimball leading on trombone, played at noontime dances on the studio sound stages; sometimes a famous visitor, like Benny Goodman, joined an impromptu jam session. Kimball's group began playing on weekends around Los Angeles and gradually, as Diane Disney Miller (Walt's eldest daughter and one of the band's fans) wrote, "to their great surprise, they became famous and began to make money.

More for kicks than anything else, they began to play Monday-night engagements at a little Los Angeles night club when the regular orchestra was given its night off . . . called the Beverly Cavern.

The Fire House Five soon moved to the Mocambo to fill in on Monday nights there. In fact, Monday night became known as their night, and before long they were so popular with prep-school groups that they were always going off over weekends to play for school dances. Their next step was to become a recording ensemble.[71]

The group recorded a dozen albums, and made numerous guest appearances on national TV shows (starring Milton Berle

and Ed Sullivan), including Walt Disney's television debut "One Hour in Wonderland" (broadcast on December 25, 1950). All this show biz activity was in addition to their regular animation duties at the studio. Eventually, the Firehouse Five wound down and quit, "tired of the late hours, the extra effort, and the frenzy."[72]

Walt Disney's attitude toward the band was always supportive. "I think what they're doing is swell," he said. "It's not only good for them, but it's good for their work at the studio." Walt openly admired Kimball and his varied talents and noted, "Kimball is always relaxed."[73]

Although he never allowed himself to become too close to his artist-employees, the interest Walt shared with Kimball in trains sparked a friendship of sorts between the two men. Its high point occurred in August 1948 when Walt invited Kimball to accompany him to the Chicago Railroad Fair.

Walt's financial problems during and after the war had changed him into a bearlike, brooding, irascible personality. Diversifying his product with live-action films took more of his time and made him less hands-on than he had been before with animation, an area in which decisions fell increasingly to the Nine Old Men.

Walt's workaholic habits and depressed outlook began to affect his health; he suffered from chronic muscle tension in his neck, which he attempted to relieve after work with a massage and "a couple of belts of booze."[74]

The trip to the Chicago Railroad Fair, accompanied by one

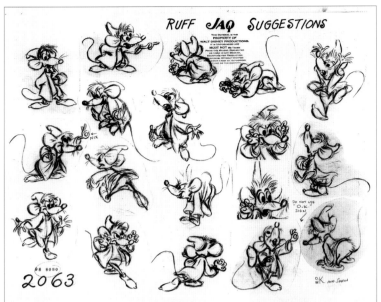

Kimball had fun animating the mice and cat in Cinderella *(1950)
because the characters were not restricted by live-action reference
film footage, which was used for* Cinderella, *her stepmother and
stepsisters, and the Prince.*

of his most lighthearted, impish employees, was literally what
the doctor ordered.

"I couldn't believe it," says Kimball about Walt's phone invi-
tation. "First of all, he never took time off. And so when I really
knew it was Walt talking I said, 'Sure! Sure!' So our wives put us
on the Super Chief, which left Pasadena, and we spent about
three days going to Chicago."

During that time, Kimball got to observe and know his
boss as few others did. He "encountered the domineering
Disney temperament when Walt insisted on ordering for him at
mealtimes and saw the familiar Disney obsession with work,"
writes Steven Watts in *The Magic Kingdom*.[75] "Sooner or later, no
matter what you were talking about, he'd get back to this god-
damn studio," Kimball told Richard Hubler in 1968. "He
wanted to talk about it. This was him! This was his *sex*! This was
everything!"[76]

Walt tried to pry information from Kimball about the studio staff's feelings about him ("Any gripes?"), a subject Kimball
unsuccessfully avoided. "This would usually happen just before
dinner in the dining car where he'd pull out this cut-glass
decanter of whiskey and pour me a shot. I hated Scotch whisky."
When Kimball did level with him, Walt always became defensive: "He took it as personal and so he explained it away."

When the pair arrived at the Railroad Fair, Kimball says,
"they found out it was Walt Disney, so they gave us special treatment, took him behind the scenes." "Walt and Ward were
amazed," writes Michael Broggie.

The museum's crew had constructed a huge, 450-foot-
long stage—big enough to hold a football field and a
half. Situated on the shore of Lake Michigan (which

Alice in Wonderland *is a veritable vaudeville of Kimball's comedic gifts. His tea party is filled with slapstick, but his Cheshire Cat is coolly insane.* OPPOSITE, RIGHT, *Walt admires Kimball's Mad Hatter sketch.*

provided a natural backdrop) . . . across the stage, differing gauges of track had been laid to accommodate presentation of famous old steam engines as well as modern streamliners. Opposite the stage was a large stadium for the audience.[77]

"And in the morning before the play was put on with Lake Michigan as a background [and a] two-hundred-foot proscenium arch," recalls Kimball, "they let Walt and [me] run the old locomotives. We'd get up on the Thatcher Perkins and the nine-ninety-nine and the Tom Thumb, and I had the time of my life pulling the throttle and making these old museum pieces go across the stage."[78]

Walt was born in Chicago, spent part of his youth there, and "was very preoccupied with his own history," Kimball says. "He spent two nights telling me his entire history from the time he was a boy, sold papers, and the whole thing." He also told how Oswald the Rabbit was stolen from him and he came back with Mickey Mouse. "He just loved telling that story. 'You see, I was right, [said Walt]. You see, I got back at them and they lost their ass!'"[79]

Besides attending the Railroad Fair, Walt insisted on dragging Kimball each night to ride on the Chicago elevated train system. "We'd get off at the station and he'd say this was where

he had delivered some mail or something like that. We'd walk over and catch another train. We'd ride the god-damn elevated half the night! He'd be looking out the window reliving his childhood," says Kimball. "And this thing for nostalgia was part of what later became Disneyland. He relived it with money. He grew up working his ass off for pennies, but he appreciated the Horatio Alger aspect even though it was tough."

Kimball also saw Walt relax and have fun, which began on route to Chicago when a conductor invited the two men to ride in the diesel locomotive's cabin. "Walt got to pull the whistle at all the little crossing signs that said W, which means whistle. I shot movies of this . . . he was like a little kid. He'd never done anything like this." Summing up their sojourn to Chicago, Kimball says, "We had the time of our lives!"[80]

Unfortunately, back at the studio, Walt's "euphoria soon wore off and he was back to his own unpredictable, grouchy self, shouldering all the studio's troubles and facing the return of his neck problem—which he hadn't mentioned once during our trip to Chicago."[81]

Cinderella's critical and financial success in 1950 ended the studio's postwar slump. By animating the mice and their bête noire, Lucifer the cat, Kimball escaped the confining live-action reference footage that Walt insisted be used to animate the human characters to save time and money. "The other

animators knew that Kimball was enjoying himself, and they resented it," notes Michael Barrier. Kimball "always had a talent for protecting himself," Frank Thomas says. "He'd smell which way the wind was blowing on each picture, and take advantage of it."[82]

Alice in Wonderland (1951) is a Kimball showcase of insincere animation. Walt, the story people, and most of the animators had trouble finding warmth and sincerity in the original literary property. But Kimball had a lark supervising sequences involving Tweedledum and Tweedledee, the Walrus and the Carpenter, the Mad Tea Party, and the Cheshire Cat, in which each character was madder than the next.

Kimball comments that the film "turned out to be a vaudeville show."

But that should not be taken as a complaint from the animator who headlined that particular Disney vaudeville bill, and who fondly remembered the shows he witnessed as a child at Minneapolis's Hennepin Theater. "He stills talks about vaudeville," said Kelly Kimball of her eighty-four-year-old father in 1998. "It's still one of his loves."[83]

Animating bizarre and insane Wonderland characters, Kimball was literally in his element. The Tweedles Dum and Dee move like water-filled balloons in patterned choreography reminiscent of an early Silly Symphony; the Mad Hatter and March Hare turn a jolly tea party into an anarchic Marx Brothers romp; and the purple, striped Cheshire Cat, speaking

in a cool Peter Lorre–like monotone with a dazzling smile pasted on his face, is perhaps the maddest of all.

The Cheshire Cat wreaks havoc most blithely, then disappears stripe by stripe, leaving only a crescent-moon grin. "You may have noticed that I'm not all here myself," he puns to a bewildered Alice. "Here I learned a big lesson," wrote Kimball in 1977. "Actions that are supposed to be violently crazy are sometimes not as mad as more subtle, underplayed treatments." Accurately (if immodestly), he called his animation of the slow-moving, quietly grinning Cheshire Cat "a masterpiece of understatement."[84]

By the mid-1950s, Kimball was bored with animating. Sincere personality animation obviously wasn't his "bag," to use an old hep-cat musician's expression he favors. He was isolated from the other Nine Old Men, who found in so-called "illusion-of-life" personality animation a continually exciting challenge to their artistic development. "Kimball was always kind of a baggy-pants comic, and he was unable to do things where the character was believable," Milt Kahl once told Michael Barrier. "He was good at making fun of things, doing something that was satirical. He didn't have the feel for getting into a character's personality and making him believable like Frank or Ollie or I did."[85]

It must have rankled Kahl that Kimball, unlike the other Nine Old Men, didn't often come to him for drawing pointers, since he worked on characters that basically he himself had

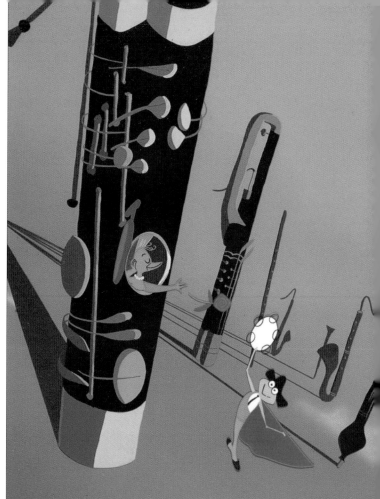

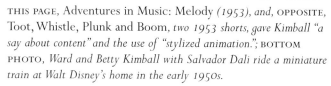

THIS PAGE, Adventures in Music: Melody *(1953), and,* OPPOSITE, Toot, Whistle, Plunk and Boom, *two 1953 shorts, gave Kimball "a say about content" and the use of "stylized animation.";* BOTTOM PHOTO, *Ward and Betty Kimball with Salvador Dali ride a miniature train at Walt Disney's home in the early 1950s.*

designed. Kimball also made fun of the painstaking, detailed character animation Kahl and the other Nine Old Men excelled in. He'd sail into Kahl's office to quip, "You know, you guys are just embroidering angels on the head of a pin."[86]

Kimball even dared to poke fun at Mickey Mouse, which made Kahl "very pissed off at him," according to Richard Williams.[87] "Mickey was the one character in our whole cast that was not believable," Kimball complained often (but well out of Walt's earshot). "What the hell are you going to do with a mouse that's three feet high, where his ears just float? They don't turn in perspective. [He] has this black-and-white division, has garden-hose legs. We could never figure out what to do with him. Who is Mickey? What does he like? Is he mean? Is he happy? Is he a Boy Scout? Does he play with himself? No one knew. And so, he finally became a symbol!"[88]

In the features it became more difficult to find opportunities for Kimball to gag things up; in *Peter Pan*, he was relegated mostly to minor characters, such as the Indian chief. Looking at Disney's future feature lineup, what (he must have wondered) would he do in the warm and cuddly *Lady and the Tramp* or the terribly serious *Sleeping Beauty*? He did test animation for the Siamese Cat song in *Lady and the Tramp*, but it was rejected as too stylized.

"He was so far out with his drawing," said Milt Kahl years later of Kimball's Siamese cats. "Nobody liked them and I had to redraw them. So it was like being his cleanup man."[89] "He tried to do something new in his cat designs," says John Kimball. "The other animators [said] his design does not fit into our picture. They were continuing with the warm, rounded look. He had more of an edge to the characters. He got really upset."[90]

Once again sensing discontent bubbling inside one of his favorite animators, Walt assigned Kimball to two special projects involving music. *Adventures in Music: Melody* (released on May 28, 1953), which was the first 3-D cartoon; and *Toot, Whistle, Plunk and Boom* (released November 10, 1953), the first CinemaScope cartoon, which won an Academy Award for Best Cartoon Short. Kimball was allowed to direct both shorts as he saw fit and his pent-up creativity exploded on the screen in two of the freshest works in Disney's oeuvre.

"I was so relieved to get away from animation," says Kimball. "I knew how to do it. I wanted to have a say about the content."[91]

In both "edu-tainment films," a Professor Owl elucidates on components of music and the orchestra, respectively. The sassy scripts are unsentimental to the point of cynicism, and Kimball indulged himself in brightly colored, flat graphics for backgrounds (most by Eyvind Earle, who later styled *Sleeping Beauty*); he also used limited (stylized) and full animation as needed. "There was an attempt to get a decorative feeling in the

movement by limiting certain parts of the animation," says Kimball. "This was almost sacrilegious at the time," he recalls. "Walt was in Europe. We had glued things down like old-time valentines and used various techniques. On a lark, we said, 'Hey, let's try to modernize the style a little.'"

The two films look like what UPA might have done if they had had Disney's budgets. The pared-down, flat design is rich in color and detailing, and works well with the animation. Kimball was sensitive about comparisons of his work to that of the studio that gave the world Mr. Magoo ("I got accused of imitating UPA," he says.). But he admired UPA's films, found them inspirational and a confirmation of his views about how animation should look and move. "My father was very much influenced by

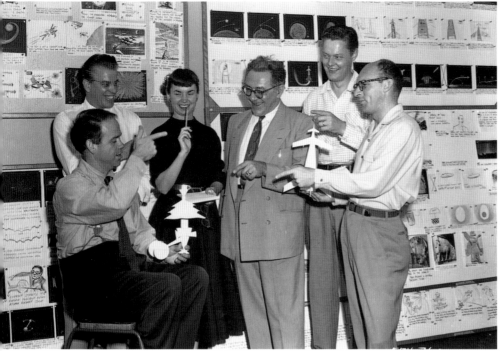

Working on the Man in Space TV *program in 1954: (seated) Ward, (left to right) Charles Shows, Ruby Barbera, scientist Willy Ley, Julius Svendsen, and Bill Bosche. Film strip shows a man from* Mars and Beyond *(1957).*

what was happening at UPA," says John Kimball. "A feeling of modern painting qualities in their character design."

Some studio veterans were appalled by Kimball's experimentation, others were puzzled or jealous. John Hench (now a veteran Walt Disney Imagineering executive) was a background stylist who was Salvador Dali's assistant during his brief tenure at Disney in 1946; the aborted Dali project told Hench something about the limitations of experimentation at the studio and he cautioned Kimball: "You don't think you're going to get away with this, do you?"[92] "You can't imagine the contrast it had to what we were doing when it came out," says Kimball, who was undaunted and unabashed. "And everybody thought Ward was going to get the ax for doing it."

But Walt "bought it," as they used to say. As usual, he didn't express his approval directly, but asked others to take a look at what Kimball had wrought. Of his work on the two films, Kimball said gleefully, "We broke all the rules."[93]

In 1954, Walt asked Kimball to produce and direct the *Man in Space* series, three one-hour programs for the Disneyland TV program on space travel: *Man in Space* (which aired on March 9, 1955), *Man and the Moon* (December 28, 1955), and *Mars and Beyond* (December 4, 1957). Given unprecedented freedom to explore the subject, Kimball took full advantage of the opportunity. "Those were the days," he says, "when [Walt] didn't have any contact with the picture. He was too busy getting ready with Disneyland and we had free rein. This was the most fun we ever had 'cause no one bothered us."[94]

In the 1950s, limited animation was the technique of choice for a TV cartoon series. Because large amounts of animation had to be produced quickly, economics dictated the use of fewer drawings to tell stories. The form is exemplified by the talky, minimally animated Hanna-Barbera series starring Huckleberry Hound, the Jetsons, the Flintsones, and many others. But Kimball used it creatively.

"My contention was there were certain types of comedy staging that were best done with limited animation," says Kimball. "A *lack* of

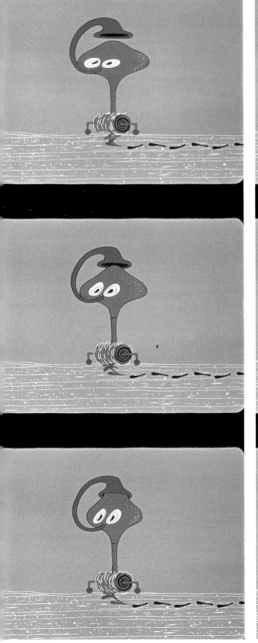

An acrylic painting by Ward Kimball: "Ladies' Hat Contest," circa 1960; BELOW, *"Asinine Alley," one of a series of comic pages Kimball drew for over thirty years for "Horseless Carriage" magazine.*

movement would put over the gag." As with *Melody* and *Toot*, the TV series had both full and limited (stylized) animation.[95]

Kimball wasn't allowed to use experienced story artists, who were all busy on *Sleeping Beauty* and the Disneyland theme-park attractions. So, he wandered down to the in-betweening department "to see what gags they were drawing on the side." Among his discoveries were John Dunn, "a crazy kid who had a lot of great ideas," and Con Pederson, now a special-effects "guru" who also worked on *2001: A Space Odyssey*.[96] "The ideas they threw out were just so great," recalls Kimball. "And we'd be laughing all morning. People walked by and wondered, What the hell are you guys working on? There were people there that hated us because we were having fun!"[97]

The space shows entertainingly blend fact and fun—Kimball's fresh, zany humor alternates with factual research by three expatriate German rocket scientists—Wernher von Braun, Willy Ley, and Heinz Haber. *Mars and Beyond*, the last of the series, contains a memorable fully animated and realistically rendered speculation on possible life forms on the red planet; this contrasts with a funny parody of a typical science-fiction movie in which a secretary is attacked by a robot who carries her (on a flying saucer) to the lecherous king of Mars (a fat, green, fish-tailed creature who sports Kimball's thick, black eyebrows).

Kimball called the space series "the creative high point of my career."[98] The shows, says his son John, "were like a shot in the arm for my father. He was into what was happening on the threshold of space. He was really into it. He'd go to work early in the morning, stay till late at night. He was working with people he really respected, like Willy Ley and von Braun, who he felt were far above him in intelligence."[99] More importantly, the space programs pleased Walt; when the first of the series was tested in a theater to get an audience's reaction, "Walt was laughing through it," and he turned to Kimball to ask, "How in the hell do you guys think up all that stuff?"[100]

In the late 1950s, Kimball was at the top of his game. The degree of personal creative freedom he was allowed at the studio was extraordinary; that his distinctive graphic style and point of view—so contrary to traditional Disney animation principles and entertainment philosophy—could flower within the belly of the beast was nothing short of amazing.

In addition to his work at the studio, Kimball energetically continued pursuing his hobbies: painting portraits of his family and others in a style that is part surrealism, part Thomas Hart Benton; music gigs with the Firehouse Five; contributing a monthly gag cartoon to the *Horseless Carriage Gazette* (which he did for more than thirty years starting in 1955); continual improvements to Grizzly Flats, the railroad and depot in his backyard, as well as additions to his extensive rare toy-train collection.

In addition to life-size vintage locomotives, Kimball (here wearing a conductor's uniform) also owns one of the world's finest collections of miniature trains. OPPOSITE, *Kimball rides the Chloe at Grizzly Flats Railroad on his home property.*

groves barefoot. There were wooden fences, the only thing that divided one area from another. A wholesome rural farm kind of feeling."

With his big Victorian train and depot plopped in the middle of this rustic setting, Ward Kimball lived in his own personal time machine and could easily time-trip back to his Midwestern childhood; but now he was in control of that world. It was permanent and stable, not ever-changing because of a peripatetic, loser father. Walt Disney did the same thing, but on a grander scale, with Disneyland.

Many Kimball family activities "when it came to big events, revolved around what he was doing," says John, referring to his father's hobbies and job. There were, for example, exciting impromptu jam sessions with musicians. John remembered as a child crawling in and among the players, listening to the music that played into the night, being a part of this whole thing. Some of the musicians stayed overnight and left the next day.

There were production "wrap parties" with performers, scientists, artists, and craftspeople at the Kimball house after Ward finished a TV program. The family sometimes accompanied him on "horseless carriage tours" to different parts of the country in the Model T Ford he owned. Visitors came from around the world to see Grizzly Flats, and Ward and Betty had annual spring "steam-ups": parties for railroad enthusiasts and friends, which Walt Disney sometimes attended. Once Dave Garroway with a TV crew interviewed the entire Kimball family live on national television from Grizzly Flats.

"His mind just never stopped with stuff while he was working at the studio," says Kelly of her father. "We couldn't do anything except just worship him. He was so interesting! Embarrassing at times. Oh yeah! Little kids going out with an extroverted father who acts up in public. We still tell him we can't take him anywhere. He's awful in public, especially if he gets bored. You have to watch out."

"He wore a multicolored plaid sport coat," writes Eric Larson about the eccentric attire Kimball wore one evening to the theater. "The pockets bulging with big manila envelopes and notebooks, a nauseating heavy plaid shirt, a rainbow tie, droopy red sox, brown shoes, and dark slacks with a yellow stripe running vertically belt to cuff." And oversize, round-lens, dark-framed glasses. "His wife, trim and blond, was elegantly dressed in black. My doctor friend, a psychologist,

What was it like growing up with Ward Kimball as a father? "Not normal," admits Kelly Kimball. "That was one of the wonderful things—the fact that he was involved with all kinds of different things. And it would seem to erupt in the household." But "it was hard for us to know how different we were."

"We didn't think it was unusual for someone to have a train in their backyard," says John Kimball. "People think of Ward as a wild, creative guy, but he was also a good family person." It was a family that valued creativity and involvement in the arts. There were drawing sessions in which everyone sat around the dining room table making sketches. "He was always encouraging the art work," says Kelly. "He never discouraged it, ever. [He'd say] 'This is keen stuff. Do more! Do more!'" When presidential conventions were first broadcast on television, each of the Kimballs drew an impression of the show and the candidates, then "put them up and looked at them."

It was a home where to be nonconformist was okay. Ward and Betty "passed a lot of that on to us," says Kelly, who designed costumes for DreamWorks' animated feature *The Prince of Egypt* (1998). Someone gave youngest daughter Chloe a paint-by-numbers set as a birthday present; she ignored the mapped-out horse's head in a floral horseshoe and painted an original desert scene over it.

Betty and Ward were liberal parents, but when Ward got angry, "he made lots of noise," says Kelly. "We called him 'The Bear' 'cause he would roar." The dinner table became a place where you let out your feelings about what was going on "'cause he did it." The Kimball kids—Kelly, John, and Chloe—were often "rowdy" and "took over." "He said we gave him indigestion," jokes Kelly.

In the 1940s and early '50s, the area southeast of Pasadena comprised acres of orange groves. "I grew up almost like a farm boy," recalls John Kimball. "Used to run through the orange

attending the Center Theater with me, motioned toward Kimball and said: 'There's a guy with the biggest inferiority complex I've ever seen.'"[101]

Kimball has described himself as "a little gruff" at work because of "a basic insecurity in my character."[102] His penchant for wearing loud, ill-matched wardrobes is perhaps an overcompensation for any public insecurity. It was protective armor or a camouflage, like those bitter-tasting insects whose bright coloring warns hungry birds, "Don't tread on me." With his blue-black five-o'clock shadow, unruly hair, and thick eyebrows, Kimball was easily caricatured on paper and on film. His looks and blunt, uninhibited personality were appropriated for the little caveman who symbolizes extreme

emotions in the wartime short *Reason and Emotion* (1943).

Kimball loved to play sly, sadistic practical jokes on coworkers; for example, he carefully pushed cans of film to the edge of a desk, so that when a poor schnook happened by, they fell noisily. During the war, Kimball's assistant Fred Kopietz was always trying to find scarce material to sell for big money. Kimball faked a phone call to Betty, making sure Kopietz overheard, advising her to get extra coat hangers at the cleaners because they would be scarce and worth something. Kopietz immediately called his wife and told her to do the same.[103] "Everybody of his generation all had this mean streak," said John Kimball. "They all played gags on one another and to them this stuff was funny. A lot of it seemed to me to be mean-spirited."

Don Bluth, who started with John at Disney, recalled Ward as "a mean old thing. You're not going to stop that one unless you have a wooden stake. He was pretty tough."[104]

One of Kimball's more elaborate and dangerous practical jokes involved Milt Kahl and played on their wariness of each other. At a Disney studio party, Kimball and the Firehouse Five were entertaining the employees and their families. All of a sudden, Kahl rose from the table he was sharing with his wife and kids, and yelled, "I can't stand this shitty damn music!!" He pulled out a gun and shot Kimball (using blank bullets). Kimball, the complete ham, did his best James Cagney impression: he grabbed his chest (and broke a capsule of ketchup on his shirt) and keeled over, spraying "blood" everywhere. Kahl had finally cracked and killed Kimball! Panic ensued. People screamed and ran. Recalls Kahl's daughter: "They just got way beyond what was socially acceptable in a practical joke."[105]

At another studio social function, a young man approached Betty Kimball to say, "I just wanted to tell you I can't understand how you could stand to live with *that man!*"[106] There is to that man, however, a soft and gentle side that he keeps fiercely private. "We, as family, have been privileged to get glimpses of a more vulnerable side," says Kelly. "I can remember that I disappointed him when I was a teenager and caused him to cry. He felt really bad. I was so struck that I witnessed him crying. 'Cause we'd never seen him get that kind of sadness. We'd seen him depressed. We'd know when things didn't go well at the studio. He'd come home and be mopey and blue. He'd be upset with himself."

"Sometimes he was very tender and sensitive about my needs," says son John. "One time he told my mother, 'You know, I'm not spending enough time with John.'" Instead of taking his son to school that day, Ward (a licensed pilot since 1946) took him to the airport, rented an airplane, and let John help him fly it.[107]

Organized religion did not play a role in the Kimball family's life. Betty, whose distant relatives were Mormons, is "so anti-religion, she won't even go to big religious epic movies."[108] Ward was raised a Christian Scientist, but "he wouldn't have anything to do with the church," says Kelly Kimball. "He did retain an interest in the Bible as a series of stories, as history. And he knows it so well."

Ward believes in and trusts his inner self. For years, he has maintained a personal journal and continues to write in it daily. He also believes in "biorhythms," "this thing I don't talk about much, but I know it's there." An intuitive process, it involves allowing one's body to go through a negative period rather than resisting it. Before starting a project, Kimball would wait until he "felt real good" because "we have times when we can't face problems. I never fought it. If I didn't like going to work or I was supposed to do a lettering job on a railroad car and I didn't feel like it, I'd sit it out." He'd watch TV, listen to a symphony, or take a nap in Griffith Park and listen to the merry-go-round.

"Then all of a sudden the answer comes. I race to get it all down. Do it with a fresh feeling. Creative. All of a sudden—BOOM! I had it! All these creative juices."[109] Kimball claims that he "always worked better when I felt in harmony with what was going on," he said.[110]

"He is strongly affected by the human condition," says Kelly Kimball. "Stuff bothers him, gets to him. Inhumane things that occur on a local level or a worldwide scale." His disgust with the Vietnam war and politicians who prolonged it led to his own animated film titled *Escalation* (1968).

"I decided to do a cartoon on my own. First time I'd ever done that. I did it all with my own money, a three-minute picture." *Escalation*, which cost $3,000, is a joke about power, truth, and sexuality: President Lyndon B. Johnson's lies cause his nose to grow (Pinocchio-like) into an erect penis and explode. The ribald short became an underground hit on college campuses. When it was shown at the Disney studio, "the conservatives," according to Kimball, "laughed their ass off because I was making fun of a Democrat. The liberals, at the other end of the spectrum, roared because it was a satire on our whole involvement in Vietnam. The people who didn't like it were the middle-of-the-road, armchair, Roosevelt New Deal Democrats who just thought it was despicable. The liberals, all the kids—pizza-eating, acid-popping, marijuana-smoking kids—laughed their ass off because this is how they felt."[111]

Regarding drugs, Kimball (a nonsmoker with a low tolerance for alcohol) claimed in 1978 to interviewer Thorkil Rasmussen that he had "tried them all, and found that LSD opened my thinking and new challenges that I had never experienced before. Which I was grateful for."[112] He was "the world's first hippie thirty years ago!" commented Disney archivist David R. Smith in 1973.[113]

"My father grew up around a lot of musicians," says John Kimball, explaining that in their company he occasionally smoked pot. "In the sixties, he experimented along with what everybody else was doing. He'd take things like peyote and LSD, not necessarily with the best results. I don't think I would categorize him as a druggie," cautions John, who once shared peyote with his dad. "He was very liberal and tolerant of what people did as long as they didn't harm themselves or get out of control. That was the whole thing about his life: he liked to take chances," explains John. "And experiment."

At the studio, Walt's estimation of Kimball's work continued to be extraordinarily positive. At one meeting during the making of the space shows, Walt gave him symbolic approval when he handed a spiral notebook and pencil to Kimball and told him, "Write your own ticket." At a party celebrating the Moon program's completion, a somewhat tipsy Walt put his arm around Kimball and called him "son." "A lot of people noticed that," says Kimball. "I don't know what it meant."[114]

Longtime Walt-watchers, however, wondered how long it

would be before he reasserted his dominance and power. It happened during the making of the studio's first live-action musical *Babes in Toyland* (1961), which starred Annette Funicello (from the Mickey Mouse Club TV show), Tommy Sands, and Ray Bolger. Three scripts, based on Victor Herbert's operetta of the same name (1903), had been attempted and now Walt asked Kimball to take "a crack at it." Kimball thought the original script was "terrible, absolutely nothing," but he loved the songs and reshuffled them to moments he thought appropriate in "an ironclad little plot where you know who the villain is and why."

At first, claims Kimball, Walt wanted him to direct the picture. Then, he decided to give it to Jack Donahue, a television director. "Walt had a way of typecasting," says the frustrated Kimball. "You did one thing and then you did it for the rest of your life! He just didn't see me. I could have done it easier and even done a better job, I always thought."[115] Kimball had, in fact, gone to New York to scout suitable Broadway talent for the film. "Then Walt said you have to use Annette and Tommy Sands in it. 'Annette can't sing as good as the talent I found,'" says Kimball, who complained to his son, "I can't get Walt to agree with me." In addition, says John Kimball, "he had gotten into a fight with Walt over politics and other things."

Marc Davis recalled hearing a rumor that after Walt viewed Kimball's version of the script he "ripped Ward to ribbons" and perhaps fired him. "He went on bended knee and Walt took him back."[116]

The direction of *Babes in Toyland* was taken away from him; he was relegated to directing the animated-toy sequence—the march of the wooden soldiers—for which he received no screen credit. (He is listed with two others for the script.) Ultimately, the film was a box-office flop. "There is no heart to the film," writes critic Leonard Maltin. "Every movement, every gag, every gimmick has a preplanned, mechanical look about it that in its very calculatedness leaves the viewer cold."[117]

Kimball was subsequently assigned to animate (but not direct) Ludwig Von Drake, Donald Duck's eccentric uncle, in the Disneyland TV series. John Kimball saw it as Walt "putting [Ward] in his place after [his success with] the science stuff." "In the period 1960 to the time of Walt's death," recalls Ward, "I was sort of sidetracked working on those horrible Von Drake television shows. I had to go back to animation and that's when I became bored with the place."[118] "He hated working on Ludwig Von Drake," confirms his son.

Kimball put his anger into the animation. "He decided to go as far as he could. See what he could get away with." On the first show he made Ludwig perform an outrageous Elvis Presley impression. "It's one of the great bits," quips John. "He just went berserk on it and carried the character as far as he could." Kimball now raced through his animation chores, did seventy-five feet in two or three days, then sat around watching televi-

sion or chatted up his comely female assistants and studio secretaries.

John Kimball, now a television animation director, was at the time working at Disney as an assistant animator, sometimes for his father on Ludwig, mostly for other animators. Ward preferred that his son be an architect and gave him halting encouragement when he joined the animation profession. "My brother made the decision to go into animation," says Kelly, "which we thought was risky because of the competition, father-son thing. But he was determined." In the early 1960s at Disney, it was difficult to advance from an assistant to a full animator; the Nine Old Men had those positions sewn up. "I'd get depressed because I really wanted to be an animator," says John. "I'd go up to see Ward and he'd be sitting there with his feet up. 'Hi, what's going on?' I'd complain about this or that. He'd lean back and say, 'Well, that's character building.' That just made me furious."[119]

"To relieve the day-to-day pressures of making films during the 1960s," wrote Ward, "in my spare time I began to experiment with 'Kinetic Constructions.'" These were paintings and sculpture combined with machinery and electronics that not only moved but emitted audible sounds as well. Thirty of his works eventually traveled to galleries and art museums. He also began teaching Action Analysis classes in the evening at the film graphics department of Art Center College of Design in Pasadena. Among the tips Kimball dispensed:

Elimination makes your drawing better.

A cartoon character who is funny to look at before he is animated is going to be made funnier by the movement.

The young filmmaker should draw what he or she pleases, not what any adult tells him or her to do.

He often looked at a drawing backward in the mirror, a technique Dürer also encouraged for focusing on the geometry of a picture rather than on the subject.

From a different viewpoint I might catch the final thing it needs. . . . The problems of animating bring out the faults of your design, and you can correct them.

In 1966, the year that Walt died, Kimball published *Art Afterpieces*, a humorous book that parodies great paintings (Whistler's Mother watches television, for example, and Michelangelo's God the Father reaches out to Adam to light his cigarette.). It took Walt's death to spring Kimball from animation back into direction again.

"Walt's passing was a terrible blow to the studio and its creative structure," he wrote. "The studio had always been a one-man operation, and without the man around to inspire and lead

Kimball with the Oscar he won for the irreverent 1969 short It's Tough to Be a Bird.

about. Our sponsor at the time was Gulf."[120]

Less than two years after Walt's death, Kimball candidly told an interviewer that at the studio "some things are better and some things are worse." He noted that "the pressure of trying to please an egocentric man like Walt became an unbearable load for a lot of people there," no doubt a reference to himself. A project was neither good nor bad until Walt pronounced it so; now, decisions were made by a group rather than one man. "It will take a little adjusting for them to realize that you can't just sit and worry about making the right decision because you don't have the man upstairs guiding you," said Kimball. "With Walt gone, there is a hesitancy and a confusion."[121]

In 1972, Kimball produced and directed "The Mouse Factory," a half-hour TV series for adults. Live action and animation combined in a quick-cut, rapid-fire gag format with guest star hosts, similar to the popular *Laugh-In* variety show. Kimball filled his show with silly, irreverent jokes and clips from new and old Disney films, edited to poke fun at the Disney image. Horrified, management canceled the show after two seasons. A new Kimball short, *Play Now Work Later*, a satire about man's leisure time, had a biting script about a cartoon dog in a real world. The film was shelved in mid-production because it was "un-Disney."

These two blows to the ego forced Kimball into a self-imposed extended "vacation," which led to his official retirement on August 31, 1973. One month before, this writer met and interviewed the master animator-director at his home.

Still smarting from his recent experiences, Kimball complained that the studio was "recalling things out of this image of Walt Disney and exaggerating to the point where these little things become important and you can't do anything controversial at all! Nothing! If you don't have satire, you've lost eighty percent of the basis of humor. All our old shorts, Goofy—making fun of drivers, hunters shooting down everything in the forest—that's an indictment of mankind. But it was acceptable. Walt never questioned it. That was pure satire. I'm a plague now," he said of his status at the studio. "You just can't be free and open about things. That's the way I've always operated there and I've gotten in trouble. But Walt always appreciated the fact I was trying

the way, many of us had to shoulder more responsibility than ever before." Kimball wasn't complaining; he loved being in charge of a new series of Sunday-evening TV shows. Especially one dealing with birds, their contributions to mankind, and fight for survival.

It's Tough to Be a Bird (1969), a twenty-two-minute free-wheeling, gag-filled, stylized production, is Kimball to the max. As such, it was received coolly by the new studio managers who, after Walt died, spent a considerable amount of time second-guessing what Walt might have thought or done. Kimball's bold-as-brass, take-no-prisoners approach gave them pause. "Instead of sugarcoating a picture like we generally do in our True-Life Adventures," he chuckles, "why we kinda made fun of things, and when a bird sings a song and says he's stepped on, he's kicked, and everything else, there was an unspoken resentment because you're attacking an institution—man and his goodness—and that's 'Disney,' and you can't even in a subtle, subconscious way make fun of that."

Kimball felt vindicated when the film won an Academy Award. Kimball's appearance at the Oscar ceremonies was memorable for his tart acceptance speech. "They didn't like my speech at the awards when I made my condolences to the unfortunate seagulls of Santa Barbara because that was the one thing we couldn't touch on—the oil spills and what birds suffer from them every year. Most of them you never hear something. I just can't honestly continue to work within that framework or that climate, with these people who have set themselves up as judges as to what is totally 'Disney' and what isn't. Everybody says, Aren't I thinking about doing something, and I said no. I've done it for thirty-nine years. I'm gonna try other things. Right now I'm playing with my trains."[122]

Nearly twenty-five years later, the same writer returned to visit Kimball in his home. About the only thing that had changed was the donation (in 1992) of some Grizzly Flats rolling stock to the Orange Empire Railway Museum in Riverside County.[123]

Kimball, now in his mid-eighties, hadn't changed a bit. Over the past quarter century, he had retained his energy, enthusiasm, and boyish sense of fun and mischief. He entertained (overwhelmed) the visitor with a five-hour, nonstop monologue, hopping (cricketlike) from one subject to another while showing (in no particular order) scrapbooks, family photo albums, and art works. He also gave a leisurely tour of Grizzly Flats (alternately imitating and threatening to shoot a neighbor's barking dog), as well as his toy-train collectibles and (poking fun at his mania for collecting) a gag collection in small bottles of "things that you don't know you're collecting," such as table crumbs, sprung bobby pins, fingernail clippings, fine print in contracts, and cuff stuff ("What gets caught in your pants").

What *has* changed is that today's management at Disney seems comfortable with one of its grand masters of animation and his irreverent humor. Kimball's 1991 parody of a Mickey Mouse model sheet was even printed on T-shirts and sold at the Disney Studio Store. Over the years, Disney has helped Kimball (and the surviving Nine Old Men) gain a measure of public recognition by arranging personal appearances (he was "conductor" on

a cross-country "Birthday Special" train tour for Mickey Mouse's fiftieth birthday in 1978), and interviews on national television and videos.

What has also changed is that Kimball has lived long enough to see his brand of satiric humor (similar to Warner Brothers cartoons) become dominant on animated TV series (*The Simpsons, Beavis and Butthead, Ren and Stimpy, King of the Hill, MTV's Liquid Television, Dr. Katz*, commercials, et cetera). It has also turned up in recent Disney features: *Aladdin*'s shape-shifting blue Genie and nonlogical quick cuts, for example, and the streamlined design and facetious approach to narrative in *Hercules* are Kimball-esque.

Ward Kimball's contribution to Disney animation was unique; it represents an exciting alternative approach to character animation and narrative—open, fresh, and experimental. It reflects the man himself, who had within him the spirit of an independent filmmaker; indeed, he is the only one of the Nine Old Men to have made his own animated film. It is something of a miracle that his unique and contrary vision not only survived but thrived within the Disney studio. It is also a tribute to Walt Disney for recognizing Kimball's special gifts and allowing them to flourish so freely for so long.

Kimball still enjoys meeting young animation filmmakers, and he always encourages them to follow their own path as artists and to be open to life. "My final two cents' worth of advice," he once wrote, "is to develop an all-consuming curiosity for things both exotic and ordinary. Read, observe, analyze, and become involved with a variety of interests. Study, practice, delve, probe, investigate and, above all, be flexible. Keep an open mind. The world is changing fast. Don't get caught in the corner of the ring.

"Keep moving and have fun. Take it from me, it's worth it!"[124]

THIS PAGE AND OPPOSITE, *Milt Kahl's superb Shere Khan, the villainous tiger in* The Jungle Book *(1967), and Madame Medusa from* The Rescuers *(1977); photos show Kahl in retirement in the early 1980s and at age three in Oakland, California.*

CHAPTER five
Milt Kahl

A t the Disney Studio in Burbank in the early 1970s, the first floor D-wing of the Animation building was known as "The Hall of Kings" and "The Ivory Tower." That's how awestruck assistant animators and young trainees referred to the section containing the offices of four of the Nine Old Men: Frank Thomas, Ollie Johnston, Eric Larson, and Milt Kahl. "All the best animators were in this part of the building," says director Dave Michener.[1]

Ward Kimball was upstairs in the television offices, Woolie Reitherman was elsewhere in the director's unit, Marc Davis was at Walt Disney Imagineering in Glendale, and Les Clark and John Lounsbery were in the B-wing of the Burbank studio on two different floors.[2] There was a "subtle separation" between the B- and D-wings, according to John Ewing, once an assistant animator to John Lounsbery. "We in B-wing were considered by D-wing to be nice-enough folk, but definitely lacking the heft, talentwise, of the folk in D-wing. They

were correct, of course, and that didn't help our view of their view one bit. But it meant that Frank and Ollie and Milt and Eric very seldom came over for coffee."[3] Lounsbery and Clark were considered by D-wingers to be "bread-and-butter" animators, but B-wing folk and others thought the two men were grossly underappreciated.

Don Bluth recalled D as "the big holy wing" and noticed "a pecking order" among the Nine Old Men. Each of the nine master animators excelled in his own way, but if there was a King of Kings among them in terms of draftsmanship, that particular crown would go to Milt Kahl. For Bluth and many others "Milt was the head. He was the guy who set the style and set the pace and everybody tried to reach up."[4]

Kahl himself would be the first to agree.

"I didn't have any limitations," he once told a television interviewer. "I could do anything."[5] Of his animation of the villainess in *The Rescuers*, he said, "I think my Medusa stuff will stand out

so damn far."[6] Regarding *Song of the South*, he felt "the best animation in it was mine on the rabbit." Ignoring the contributions of story artist Bill Peet, Kahl claimed, "I probably had more to do with the development of all three of those characters [Brers Rabbit, Fox, and Bear] than any one person. At the risk of sounding immodest."[7]

It was a risk Kahl often took. "The first time we met," says Julie Kahl, his third wife, laughing, "he told me he was the best. The greatest."[8]

Milt Kahl was always direct, almost childlike in assessing his own worth and stating his opinion in general. "I have a knack for alienating people by being a little bit outspoken," he once said— a gross understatement.[9] But there was truth in his self-aggrandizing honesty. For Kahl's gifts as both a draftsman and an animator were extraordinary. "I'm perfect for this medium," he once crowed.[10]

Praise for Kahl's drawing ability by his admirers tends toward hyperbole. "He's my favorite draftsman, probably of all time," marvels animator Andreas Deja, who has long studied Kahl's work. Kahl's colleague Ollie Johnston once compared Kahl's drawings to Michelangelo's. "I've never seen a finer draftsman," he says.[11] After seeing Shere Khan, the menacing tiger in *The Jungle Book*, animator-director Richard Williams sent his first fan letter to Kahl, saying, "you've transcended the medium."[12]

From the late 1930s, when Kahl's redesign of Pinocchio was approved by Walt, until his angry departure from the studio in 1976, Milt Kahl usually took the lead in designing characters for the animated features. He first did exploratory animation (about a hundred feet) of each character; key drawings from these tests were pasted onto character model sheets, which became blueprints for the animation crew. "My usual function on these pictures is to get a character started, to say, 'This is the character,'" explained Kahl. "I move around the picture a lot, helping people with drawings and that sort of thing, and actually animating later."[13]

Kahl was often frustrated because he rarely animated a character throughout an entire film. "Somebody else takes over the rest of it and I'm embarrassed by the result!" he complained. Exceptions were Shere Khan in *The Jungle Book* and Madame Medusa, the self-absorbed kidnapper in *The Rescuers*, characters Kahl animated nearly all the way through. He also animated major scenes featuring Pinocchio, Bambi, Alice, Peter Pan, and the princes in both *Cinderella* and *Sleeping Beauty*, among other films.

Because of his superb draftsmanship, an inordinate number of scenes involving human characters came to Kahl; especially vexing were the handsome princes, whose masculinity was difficult to maintain without making them as stiff as posts. "I can remember Milt complaining," says Ward Kimball, who infuriated Kahl when he said that Walt chose him to animate the princes "because you're so good at doing that dull stuff."[14]

For all his complaints, though, Kahl enjoyed the ego-

A LAST SHOT FOR STAN —
PLEASE DRAW HER
BETTER THAN THIS!
Milt
29·4·76

OPPOSITE, *Medusa in* The Rescuers *(1977); Kahl animating* Brer Rabbit *from* Song of the South *(1946);* THIS PAGE, *Kahl's sketch of Snow White's prince, and a final drawing of Medusa made for his assistant Stan Green, when Kahl abruptly departed the studio;* ABOVE RIGHT, *a gag drawing by Ward Kimball who enjoyed goading the volatile Kahl.*

massaging salve that came with being The One to Whom All Others Must Turn. Through the years, a steady stream of animators (including each of the other Nine Old Men) and their assistants came to Kahl's door seeking counsel and/or a single drawing to define a character, strengthen a pose, suggest a gesture or an expression. Some wanted merely to keep a character "on model"—that is, looking exactly as Kahl had decreed. Even Kimball, who often goaded the volatile Kahl, concedes that Kahl "had a knack. He'd look at a character, go over it and make it better."[15] Says Frank Thomas, "I was very appreciative that his drawings would make my scenes work so much better."[16]

"Unlike many irascible temperaments who have filled the halls of history," write Thomas and Ollie Johnston in *The Illusion of Life*, "Milt had a very sweet, helpful side, when he chose. He gave unstintingly of his time and talent when it was to help the picture and almost as often to help a fellow artist who had a problem. However, he expected everyone coming for help to have worked hard and tried everything—to have done his best before coming."[17]

Kahl's impatience and short-fuse temper often abruptly ended many a consultation. "I suggest you go back and work a little harder!" he loudly bellowed to one hapless artist, followed by a string of expletives. "We don't even *draw* this way here!"[18]

"He was scary," says Richard Williams, an admirer and friend of Kahl. "Because he was for real. He was the authority. That's always scary. Like talking about the violin to Isaac Stern. You'd be careful."[19] Kahl, claims Williams, "regarded most animators, you could almost say all animators, as lazy bastards. Milt didn't want to mess around."

"His drawing, animation, character design, acting, what-have-you were guideposts for all," his longtime assistant Stan

PROD.	SEQ.	SCENE	FOOTAGE	ANIMATOR	SHEET
2519	007	307	9⁰⁰	MILT KAHL	1

STAPLE HERE   STAPLE HERE

P-148A (R-3) 8X

SCENE SYNOPSIS

C.U. MEDUSA'S REFLECTION. SHE REMOVES SECOND FALSE EYE-LASH AS SHE TALKS TO O.S. PENNY.

OPPOSITE AND THIS PAGE, *Milt Kahl's exposure sheet (a timing chart used by animators) for a scene with Medusa in* The Rescuers.

Green once said. "He was responsible for the quality of a film and he would not compromise."[20]

Individual Kahl drawings are beautiful to look at. The design, composition and complex detailing are perfection. "I just happen to love every train of thought he has," enthuses Andreas Deja. "The way he defines a belly or a shoe or a finger. There isn't something that isn't beautiful in those drawings. It doesn't exist."[21] Even a homely character with an ugly person-

ality, such as Madame Medusa, has visual appeal in the carica-ture Kahl fashioned. She is, notes John Culhane, "like a drawing from Daumier's 'Sketches of Expression' series—but in move-ment!"[22] Kahl's tour-de-force animation of the middle-aged, self-absorbed frump in her boudoir removing her eyelashes is so unsparing in its depiction of a female ritual, it borders on the misogynistic. (A Kahl caricature of John Culhane, by the way, developed into Mr. Snoops, Medusa's comic henchman.)

Kahl's key animation poses are invariably strong and full of an inner vitality. "I haven't seen a bad drawing of Milt's ever," says Deja. "Every pose holds up as a still, as a design, the way it sits on the paper, the way it's composed, the way it's drawn." "Milt's drawings hold still better than anybody else's," agreed Marc Davis, Kahl's closest friend at the studio.[23]

In motion, Kahl's sequential drawings offer elegant patterns of action. In *101 Dalmatians*, as the birth of a puppy litter is announced, the dog Pongo jumps into the lap of his human owner, Roger; a simple action, but in Kahl's hands it becomes a polished and refined (even beautiful) movement that belies its simplicity. It is a showcase of Kahl's sophisticated application of the principles of character animation, such as anticipation (a preparatory movement in the opposite direction preceding a main action), squash-and-stretch (revealing the elasticity of flesh and even bone), arcs (a graceful path of action), overlapping

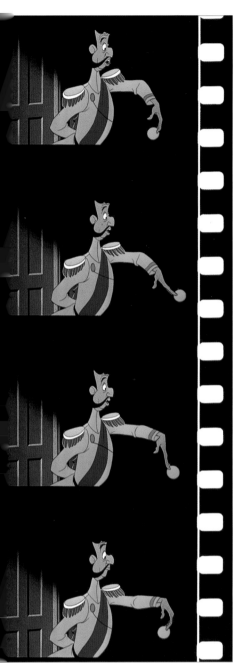
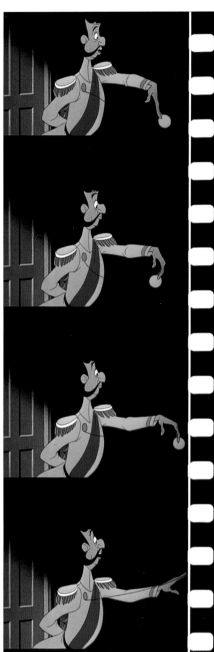

action (not everything on a figure moves at the same time), follow-through action on secondary movements (in Pongo's ears and tail, and so on). "He always has the most graceful moves in animation," says Deja, "designed in a glorious way."

Also in *101 Dalmatians*, Pongo unexpectedly licks Roger's hand. The pipe the surprised Roger is smoking flips upward and he grabs it in a marvelously choreographed pinwheel twiddle of both hands. The original drawings reveal the care (and joy) the animator took in rendering the shape and position of each finger, knuckle, and cuticle. Hands are notoriously difficult to draw, and doubly toilsome in motion. Kahl, however, obviously enjoyed drawing hands and showing off how well he could do it. For *The Sword in the Stone*, he created model sheets devoted *only* to the hands of the ancient sorcerer Merlin—wonderfully gnarled digits rendered in exhaustive gestural explorations. In *Cinderella*, he used hands to "put across acting through subtle body language," according to Iwao Takamoto, one of Kahl's former assistants. During a talky scene between the Duke and the King, Kahl had the Duke take off his monocle, put it onto his hands and roll it between his fingers, in order, says Takamoto, to "give him something to do during this reflective dialogue. He often drew his way out of problems."[24]

Kahl's drawings and their movements are completely thought out, yet seem spontaneous and

OPPOSITE, *Kahl caricatures himself and John Culhane for a lecture at New York's School of Visual Arts in 1973; sequential drawings of a scene from* 101 Dalmatians, *and film frames of the Duke from* Cinderella.

inevitable, like all great art. They mesmerize and hold your attention, "draw you into the film" (as Richard Williams puts it) to become "compulsive viewing."[25] Unlike the naive immediacy of Fred Moore's drawings, Kahl's sketches are not innocent and were not easily made. They are "very, very involved," explains Deja, and all about "having high opinions about things. Uncompromising. It's very honest. It's trying to be perfect."[26] Unlike Frank Thomas's animation, which (though thoroughly analyzed and thought out) retains an incredible warmth, or Ollie Johnston's, which exudes pure emotion, Kahl's work is ultimately cooler and more detached.

Yes, he could be warm and cuddly when need be; see Thumper in *Bambi* reciting a tedious bromide for his mother ("If you can't say something nice . . ."), or *Bambi* jumping awkwardly over a log. But so much is going on in Kahl's work *graphically* that ultimately *that* is what takes precedence—particularly late in his career when he developed an interest in Picasso and his designs became more angular and complex. "Milt's stuff is cooler, like a Japanese print, like Utamaro," observes Williams. "It's so refined and boiled down. You could say it's more intellectual. You could say that, but I don't think it is. It's cold fire."

Ollie Johnston once said that Kahl was "inclined more toward action than acting. He could draw so well, he'd choose a way of making the character do something that required the kind' of draftsmanship nobody else in the place could do." Kahl, claims Johnston, secretly liked the prince roles for that reason. "'Cause it showed him off. They were the things nobody could do as well."[27] Using designs dictated by Kahl, most of the other Nine Old Men struggled with their drawings; among the exceptions were Marc Davis, whose fine draftsmanship Kahl himself admired; Ward Kimball, an excellent draftsman who traveled his own graphic path; and John Lounsbery, who could follow Kahl's most complex designs.

Kahl stammered, cursed, and tipped over many a wastebasket when the muse proved elusive; but his struggle was not so much with pencil and paper. It was with his own impossibly high standards and his ferocious attempts to reach the Shangri-la of perfection that he held in his mind.

Milton Erwin Kahl was born on March 22, 1909, in San Francisco, the son of Erwin Kahl, a German immigrant from Hamburg who came to the United States at age twenty; Milt's mother Gracie's parents were from Birmingham, England.[28] "I would say 'that explains you, Milt,'" Richard Williams told Kahl years later. "It's the German precision and the English humor."[29] Milt's mother, whom he adored, had an imaginative sense of fun; once, she put Milt's head through the middle of a slatted dining table and decorated it with vegetables.

Erwin's occupation is listed on Milt's birth certificate as "bartender," but he later drove limousines for the William J. Gallagher Company and became a superintendent there. His maximum salary was about thirty-five dollars a week and the

family, which included two daughters (Dorothy and Marion) as well as Milt, was "terribly poor."[30] Milt may have developed rickets as a child from malnourishment, although his mother became furious when a doctor suggested it. Nevertheless, although he grew to be over six feet tall and stood straight, from childhood on Kahl had a pronounced hump on his back.[31]

Milt hated his father because Erwin abandoned the family. Then his parents divorced. Years later, Erwin Kahl would visit his son and his wife and kids in Los Angeles. "My mother was a catalyst that made sure he was always around," says Milt's daughter Sybil Byrnes. "But I don't think my father really ever forgave him. Because it put them into really hard times." Grandpa Erwin—heavyset, gray-haired, bespectacled—looked "like a Santa Claus, very kindly." Hoping to ingratiate himself, he brought gifts to Milt's children; often he sat in his car outside Kahl's home smoking one cigar after another, and talking with Peter Kahl, Milt's young son, promising to send the kid five dollars.[32]

Ironically, Milt inherited his drawing talent from Erwin, who drew car leasing/rental newspaper ads for his employers. "My father had a little drawing talent," said Kahl dismissively. But "he was not an educated man in the least bit. And didn't have any artistic training at all."

Milt Kahl claimed his earliest drawings were on toilet paper ("I tore up the paper a lot"); he enjoyed sketching motorcycles, and his grandparents saved a drawing of a Mexican in a sombrero made when he was seven. He also recalled a detailed drawing of a lace curtain blowing in the wind, perhaps his first attempt to transfer an animated action to paper.

Grace remarried a man named McKinnon and they had two daughters (Audrey and Gladys); the family moved to Oakland, but again there was little money and Milt didn't get along with his stepfather, whom he described as "vulgar" and "a little bantam rooster." Milt attended Horace Mann School in San Francisco; then, in the East Bay area, he went to Fremont High School, but didn't graduate. He quit school to help out with the family's finances, first by delivering prescriptions on his bicycle, then by working at an engraving company. "I left home as soon as I could," he said.

Kahl's limited formal education always bothered him. His daughter Sybil says that "he was kind of compulsive about being right. Maybe that's how he compensated for his lack of education." Throughout his life he challenged himself, not only in animation; he timed himself doing crossword puzzles, learned to play chess by mail (six games at a time), was an avid reader, and became a first-rate fly fisherman who tied his own intricate lures. "My dad epitomized the self-made man," says Sybil.[33]

Surprisingly, Kahl didn't really like to draw, or so he claimed. His childhood delight apparently changed when he began drawing to make a living. "As soon as I became a professional," he told Robin Allan, "which was [when I was] very

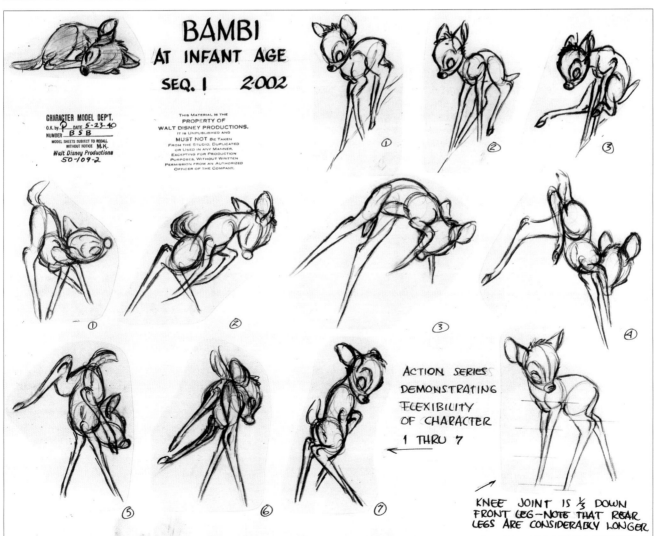

Milt Kahl's rough animation sketches exploring movement and designs for Bambi *(1942).*

young, too. I found it got to be work."[34] After retiring, he told a television interviewer, "I'm not one of those people who draws compulsively. I don't draw unless I have to. I actually don't really enjoy it. I got my kicks at the studio from putting a performance on the screen."[35]

In 1925, when he was sixteen, Kahl got a job in the art department of the *Oakland Post Enquirer* (now the *Oakland Tribune*) doing pasteups, layouts, photo retouching, and spot cartoons for twenty-five dollars a week. Covering local boxing matches in Oakland barns, he developed an interest in prizefighting; then he wrote about

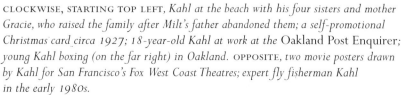

CLOCKWISE, STARTING TOP LEFT, *Kahl at the beach with his four sisters and mother Gracie, who raised the family after Milt's father abandoned them; a self-promotional Christmas card circa 1927; 18-year-old Kahl at work at the* Oakland Post Enquirer; *young Kahl boxing (on the far right) in Oakland.* OPPOSITE, *two movie posters drawn by Kahl for San Francisco's Fox West Coast Theatres; expert fly fisherman Kahl in the early 1980s.*

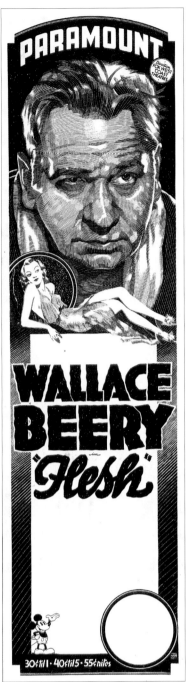

and drew the results for the paper's sports section. While at the *Enquirer*, he worked with a sweet-tempered, eighteen-year-old University of California at Berkeley graduate named Hamilton Luske, who contributed a two-by-four-inch column/cartoon on local merchants. A decade later, Luske affected the direction of Kahl's life.

After three years at the *Enquirer*, Kahl was offered a job at the *San Francisco Bulletin* at forty dollars per week, which was raised within a few months to forty-five. His ability to get drawing jobs (and raises) at an early age indicates how impressive his talent was even then. The next year, 1929, the stock market crashed and the *Bulletin* was sold to Hearst. Kahl was among the many who lost their jobs. "So then, I was very fortunate," he recalled. A friend named Rufus Blair "almost immediately" got Kahl a job working with him at Fox West Coast Theaters drawing "car cards": movie advertisements for the front of street cars. Again, Kahl's talent and seriousness of purpose impressed

his bosses: "They moved me into doing the theater ads in the newspapers."

The ads were based on stills from current films, such as *The Island of Lost Souls* (1933), starring Bela Lugosi and Charles Laughton. Kahl and Blair modeled their technique after Franklin Booth, a landscape artist known as "a pen-and-ink painter." "We sort of adapted that style for these theater ads," said Kahl, "because we got better reproduction on the drama page, where they don't get very good printing."[36] Around this time, Kahl's hot temper got him fired: he exchanged angry words with a theater manager who refused to honor tickets Kahl had left at a box office for a friend.

Kahl freelanced and shared a penthouse studio with artist Fred Ludekens, who "helped me a great deal with my work." Ludekens was art director for the Lloyd and Thomas ad agency for which Kahl drew numerous advertisements; for example, Sunmaid Raisin Growers. Ludekens later became a top American magazine illustrator, along with the likes of Albert Dorn, Al Parker, Jon Whitcomb, and Ben Stahl. Once, Richard Williams casually mentioned to Kahl that his work reminded him of "this guy who did a lot of animals and western illustrations called Fred Ludekens. Milt jumped in the air and said, 'Jesus Christ! He was my friend and teacher! We had a studio together." Williams describes "an analytical thing" and "precision" in Ludekens's drawings that undoubtedly influenced Kahl.[37]

Kahl attended art classes in and around San Francisco, faithfully participating in a figure drawing session two nights a week at the San Mateo home of commercial artist Louis Rogers. There was no instructor, but you paid your money and drew a live model for three hours. The group included Stanford art students, among them Frank Thomas and Ollie Johnston. The pair didn't formally meet Kahl at those drawing sessions, but years later they remembered his displays of temper.

"Five guys came down from San Francisco who all seemed to know each other," Thomas recalls. "One of them was engaged to a girl and she had broken it off and he couldn't get his ring back from her. Each week they would all have some gag about 'How you doing with that ring, huh?' Make all sorts of silly suggestions." Kahl, the spurned Romeo, would growl angrily at the jokesters: "God-damn you guys!" Thomas thought, "Gee, he's a touchy guy." Years later, Thomas and Kahl discovered they had both attended the San Mateo drawing sessions: "You knew Louis Rogers?" "Yeah, I knew Louis Rogers." "Ever go down to his place?" "Hell, yes, I was there every week for the model." Thomas gingerly broached an old subject: "Did you by any chance . . . ?" And Kahl answered, laughing, "Damn it! I never did get that ring back!"[38]

Toward the end of 1933, illustration jobs began to dry up for twenty-four-year-old Kahl. "I was quite a successful commercial artist in San Francisco, but the damned Depression began to hit that field," he said forty years later. "The field started using photographs and doing things the low-budget way, and meanwhile your rent and phone bill and all that stuff keeps going."[39] Ham Luske, his former newspaper pal, was now a respected animator with a steady job at the Disney studio in Hollywood; when he suggested Kahl join him, Kahl seriously considered it. He had always enjoyed cartoons—in newspapers it was the Katzenjammer Kids, and in films Felix the Cat was a favorite. In 1933, along with millions of other Americans, he saw Disney's *Three Little Pigs*, which he said "just really captivated me."

Since the wolf was literally at Kahl's door, he appreciated the film's social symbolism ("People today have a hard time realizing the impact that a cartoon like that had."). He was particularly impressed by the painterly Technicolor of *Three Little Pigs*. "When you get color that is projected and has a transparency to it, it has a lot more vibrance to it than color in a painting on a canvas or paper."

Another reason Kahl sought steady employment was that he had fallen in love with Laura Nordquist from Kellogg, Idaho. One year older than Milt, Laura lived with her sister in San Francisco and held a degree in journalism from the University of Idaho; that academic accomplishment sometimes rankled the undereducated Kahl. "I think that may have been a little bit of a thorn in my dad's side," says their daughter Sybil. But the young couple were both fun-loving and shared much in common, including political beliefs: "They were adamant Republicans who hated Roosevelt," according to Sybil. "They could have

died the night Hoover lost!"[40] Kahl started work at Disney on June 25, 1934; soon after the couple married.

Kahl began in the in-betweener bullpen at twenty dollars a week, but quickly advanced to assistant animator under Bill Roberts, "one of the fast-action boys."[41] Roberts was the opposite of the thoughtful, analytical, subtle animator Kahl would become. But "you learned something from everyone," said Kahl. "Even if they didn't have something to teach you, it was stimulating."[42] He enjoyed the palpable competition and macho give-and-take between the artists. He recalled first meeting Vladimir (Bill) Tytla, also newly hired, but five years older than Kahl, who had a reputation as one of the finest animators in New York. Kahl was part of the crew on Tytla's first Disney picture: *Mickey's Fire Brigade* (1935). "I'm in the in-betweener pool," said Kahl. "Oh yeah?" replied the intense Tytla. "What scenes have you screwed up lately?"[43]

Kahl was ambitious from the start. "I bought a stopwatch after I'd been at the studio a week," he said. "And I'd time people walking."[44] At evening art classes at the studio, he was stimulated by Donald Graham, whom Kahl thought "a very fine art instructor." That did not stop him from disagreeing with Graham "on almost everything, as far as drawing was concerned. But he made me think. When you say someone's wrong, and he's given it some thought, you've got to defend your point of view. And it makes you think."[45]

"In 1934 when I first met Milt at the studio," says art director Ken Anderson, "his language was peppered with cuss words and you'd never have guessed that he had a very high IQ." Kahl was unaware of his blasphemous tongue until he met a man of the cloth whom he admired at a party, in whose presence he became tongue-tied. "This collar of mine sure puts a stop to your saying anything, doesn't it?" said the reverend slyly. "From that moment on Milt changed," said Anderson, "and he cultivated good linguistic habits." At least in front of clergy.[46]

Anderson also fondly remembered Kahl as the bad boy of the in-betweener pool whose displays of musical farting were among "his early supreme achievements." Kahl could perform the opening bars of the "Star-Spangled Banner" through quick bursts of perfectly pitched crepitation. His performances took place in the lavatory adjacent to the in-betweener's room. "It was his habit to back up to the thin, ventilated plywood door, which reverberated with his efforts," recalled Anderson.

Once Walt had some important guests and they were standing in the in-between room right next to the lavatory door discussing the meaning of *in-betweener*. We, the in-betweeners, had always enjoyed [Milt's] performances. But this time we were terrified. Hopefully, Milt would somehow know that guests were there and hold off. But no—Milt had already backed up to the door and it exploded right beside Walt and his guests. Before they could recover, the unsuspecting Milt, flushed with success, opened the door and asked, "How was that?" Walt and his guests departed promptly without comment.[47]

Kahl learned the rudiments of the craft of animation quickly in order to climb to the position of animator. He remembered when director Ben Sharpsteen cautiously tossed him his first small bits of animation in *Mickey's Circus* (1936). "Talk about control!" said Kahl years later. Sharpsteen insisted that he make pose drawings for each scene to "show him what I was going to do with it." Kahl brought the drawings in and Sharpsteen looked at them, then sat staring out a window for what seemed a very long time. "Oh, Jesus!" thought Kahl anxiously. Finally, Sharpsteen said, "All right, that looks pretty good," but Kahl "nearly had a heart attack in the meantime."

"My first memory of Milt," recalled Marc Davis, "was in early 1936, when he was animating in the annex, a training building across the street from the Hyperion Avenue studio.

> Milt and several other young animators were working in what they called bullpens. These were rooms farthest from the street. This seemed to us to give quite a sense of security, since the front of the building housed the new arrivals and trainees such as myself. Being close to the street was like being in a revolving door. People came in, tried out, and left—never to be seen again.[48]

Kahl shared a "bullpen" with "junior animators" Ken Anderson, Frank Thomas, Ollie Johnston, and James Algar, among whom a rivalry sprang up from the start. "We were encouraged to compete for scenes to animate, working at night," Anderson once recalled. "Milt would usually win the plums, and even today some of his scenes are still being studied by aficionados of the art." Kahl contributed to several shorts, including *Mickey's Service Station* (1935), *Elmer Elephant* (1936), *Lonesome Ghosts* (1937), *Farmyard Symphony* and *Ferdinand the Bull* (both released in 1938). In the latter film Kahl's voice is heard on a line of dialogue from the gentle, pacifist bull Ferdinand— obviously an in-joke, considering Kahl's warriorlike personality.

When *Snow White* went into full production, Kahl moved across the street to the main studio, where he animated the animals, alongside Eric Larson, Louis Schmidt, and James Algar. "We had one big room, where all of us animal boys were," he said. Kahl worked out the timing of a turtle falling down stairs with pianist-songwriter Frank Churchill. "He was the best musician we ever had in the place," according to Kahl. "He worked out a musical pattern for it. He helped me decide. You know, I said, the guy ought to pick up speed [going] down [the] stairs. And [so] we've got a thing at the foot of the stairs where he slides across and hits the wall, so we can make it as long as we

Kahl and first wife, Laura, whom he married in 1934, the same year he started at Disney.

have to, to get the proper length into the timing." "His animation of the little turtle has always stood out in my mind," said Marc Davis. Kahl also animated some of *Snow White*'s prince, according to Davis: "This was the beginning of many such assignments because of his great skill in drawing the human figure in animation."

Pinocchio brought Kahl to Walt's attention, starting him on a major career path at the studio. Production of the studio's second feature was stalled for months while Walt pondered how to make Pinocchio a more appealing character and the episodic story cohesive. The story artists and Fred Moore (who supervised test animation) followed the original book's depiction of Pinocchio: as a brash, selfish, amoral wooden marionette. Stiff and jerky in movements, odd in appearance, with no warmth. Some lead character, thought Walt glumly.

"They were obsessed," said Kahl, "with the idea of this boy being a wooden puppet. My God, they even had this midget who did the voice for 'Call for Philip Morris' [a radio cigarette ad]. It was terrible!" Kahl was, of course, outspoken about what should be done. He asked Ham Luske, why didn't they forget that he was a puppet and design Pinocchio as a cute little boy? "You can always draw the wooden joints and make him a wooden puppet afterward."

Luske suggested Kahl redesign the character and animate a test on his own. Kahl did: a scene of Pinocchio with donkey ears under the sea walking up to a large oyster, knocking on its shell and asking the whereabouts of the whale Monstro. The frightened shell snapped shut, causing a swell in the water that

affected Pinocchio.[49] "I made kind of a cute little boy out of him, and Walt loved it." "Walt flipped," concurs Ollie Johnston. "Real fine drawings. [Walt] liked them much better than what Fred had done. That was the beginning of the domination of Milt Kahl in character creation."[50]

"This was actually my big chance," remembered Kahl. "It was my move into being one of the top animators."[51] Indeed, Kahl's ascendancy marks the beginning of Fred Moore's eclipse at the studio. Walt assigned Kahl, Johnston, and Thomas to be the main animators of the new Pinocchio. No longer would animators beat a path to Moore's office to admire or copy his appealing drawings, or ask his advice. Kahl was the new design

guru; a draftsman *and* animator more formidable than Moore ever could (or ever wanted to) be.

As Walt discovered the extent of the talents of his young, art-school educated animators, the more he used them to push the perimeters of character animation. Fred Moore might have survived had he the will to train and develop his limited draftsmanship, and if he had not eroded his talent by abusing alcohol. Significantly, there was no role for him to play when the ultra-realistic *Bambi* came around; as for *Pinocchio*, Moore animated the comparatively small role of Lampwick (said to be a self-caricature): a cocky and wasteful juvenile delinquent who self-destructs by literally making an ass of himself. "My God, that

OPPOSITE, *Kahl in 1940;*
his redesign of Pinocchio
made the wooden puppet more
boyish, which impressed Walt;
THIS PAGE, *Pinocchio turns*
into a donkey in a dramatic
scene animated by Kahl;
the animator in a 1983
television documentary.

Milt Kahl can draw. Jesus!" said Fred Moore when he first saw Kahl's Pinocchio redesign; little did he realize the impact those gorgeous lines would have on his career.[52]

The trouble with Kahl's redesign of Pinocchio is that he is so charmingly boyish throughout the film that when rewarded for his bravery at the end by becoming a "real boy," he has nowhere to go in his transformation. In fact, his real-boy proportions are less appealing than his boyish design as a puppet; he is too close to live action and therefore less right for animation. It would have been better if an even compromise had been struck between Moore's wooden and Kahl's soft designs.

Be that as it may, Kahl's reputation with Walt and the rest of the studio was made by *Pinocchio.* For the next nearly forty years, Kahl *was* Disney graphic style, a fact he proudly touted:

> I felt a little bit like the chess champion of the world at one time who was a Franco-Russian by the name of Alexander Alekhine. Someone—an onlooker—mentioned to him, "Mr. Alekhine, that isn't a book move you made there." He said, 'I *am* the book.'"[53]

Kahl also came into his own as an animator in *Pinocchio,* which is brilliantly demonstrated in scenes of the puppet's metamorphosis into a donkey. The boy's disbelief, terror, and eventual panic are convincingly portrayed as, against his will, he changes piece by piece into an animal—a textbook example of screen horror.

Another Kahl scene that the ambitious student or serious professional animator should study involves Jiminy Cricket. It is morning and Jiminy is late for his first day on the job as Pinocchio's conscience. The little insect runs and hops breathlessly from distance to foreground and off into the distance

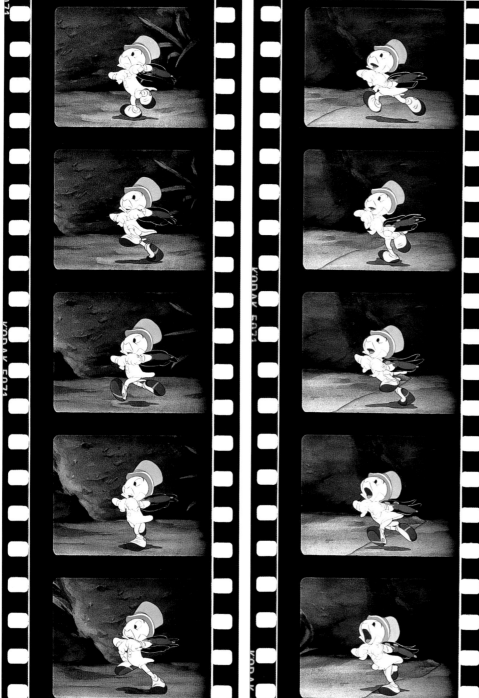

Late for work, Jiminy Cricket dresses on the run, a Kahl masterpiece of animation timing, staging, and acting.

again, all the while getting dressed and taking himself to task: "Fine conscience I turned out to be . . ." et cetera. To the general public, the scene is amusing and entertaining; to animators, however, this scene is one of the greatest ever animated, a miniature masterpiece of staging, timing, organization, clarity, acting, and personality.

Kahl elegantly caricatures an everyday process: putting on clothes to go to work; he emphasizes some actions (stuffing shirt in pants), disguises or simply gives an impression of others (tying an ascot). It is wonderful to see his solution for the problem of perspective; how he emphasizes words by stressing certain actions; how he maintains the pace of Jiminy's run, now hopping on one foot, then two, never losing his speed; how eas-

ily he makes the whole damn, complex thing flow. Undoubtedly, Kahl worked extremely hard on it; the planning alone required superconcentration, which he had in abundance. "He could concentrate like nobody else," confirms his wife, Julie. "He played chess by mail and when the move arrived, I'd say, 'Well, he's gone into his den [in his mind] for hours.' He'd play the *New York Times* acrostic puzzler in ink. Took three, four hours. He must have been the same way at the studio."[54]

He was. Frank Thomas admired the Jiminy scene because it is so "well thought out," and commented ruefully that it was made "during a stage when Milt was just right for himself and for the studio." By the 1970s Thomas had serious misgivings about Kahl personally and his drawing's usefulness to the films at that time.

In the early 1940s, however, working on *Bambi*, Thomas

and Kahl "got along hand in glove." Kahl's work in the film, in Thomas's opinion, "was the best thing he ever did at the studio," especially his animation of the child-rabbit, Thumper. The first scene of Thumper reciting one of his father's boring speeches is another masterful Kahl performance worthy of close scrutiny.

Kahl once spoke in a lecture about this scene as an example of how graphics, sound, and acting can put over a subtle idea:

The situation: Bambi is learning to walk. He takes some steps and falls down. And Thumper says, "He doesn't walk very good, does he?" And his mother admonishes him. ["What did your father tell you?"] So in this scene he says, "If you can't say something nice, don't say nothing at all."

We try to squeeze every last drop out of each scene. The kid who supplied the voice was only four or five years old, and he had a little trouble remembering the lines . . . and it showed. So we got the same hesitation into the animation. We even added time between "nice" and "don't." So he says "nice," takes a breath, and nothing comes out. He suddenly can't remember this thing. He's fooling around with his foot and looking at his mother out of one eye. He tries real hard to remember and almost has to squeeze this second part of the line out. Then he's proud that he remembered it and he turns to his mother, and she gives him this admonishing look, and he's sort of sheepish. . . .

The main thing is that in this case you have fairly subtle ideas, but the change of mood he goes through are strong enough to make the scene successful. They sell themselves to an audience.[55]

In *Bambi*, Kahl's streamlined, highly animatable graphic solutions were a world apart from the deer in *Snow White* (sometimes described as grain sacks on legs). "We had to make certain concessions away from the [real] animal in order to make it animate," said Kahl. He continued:

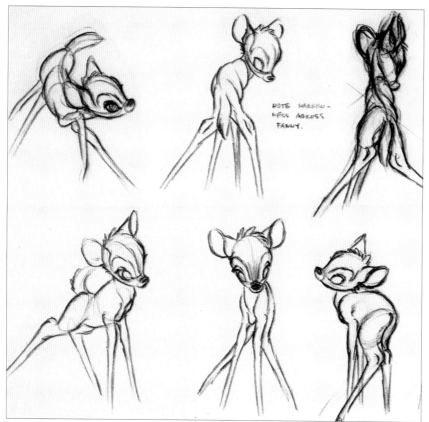

Kahl's streamlined designs for Bambi and Thumper; OPPOSITE, *Milt, a man of many moods.*

this is a compressed shape. You have a whole new set of proportions. This fawn is just about as close as we could get to the real thing.[56]

Throughout his career, Kahl frowned on the extensive use of live-action film as reference material for animation. He did study live action on a Moviola (a clattering upright projection machine with a tiny screen) and made notes, but he never used a rotoscope, a device that allows film frames to be projected onto an animator's drawing board and traced; nor did he use frame-by-frame blowups on photostats. "Milt could analyze so thoroughly from live-action film, he didn't need rotoscopes," says director Dave Michener.[57] Kahl often railed against those who did. "These lazy bastards around here get to counting on it, relying on it blindly, and they don't give thought to their scene," he said. "That's a helluva way to work. I think live action stifles whatever little creativity these guys have, which isn't much!"

Bambi's head had to be designed in such a way that we had a full expression . . . but [in a real deer] the head is not in proportion that way. The eyes and mouth, two important elements for expression, are widely separated. You have to have a mouth [such that] you can do something with its teeth and in turn with an eye. You've got to have a squash-and-stretch and give it a change . . . you actually have to have a different shape than an actual deer's head. Where there should be a long, thin shape,

He recommended, instead, habitual consultation of photographer Eadweard Muybridge's famous nineteenth-century studies of humans and animals in sequential motion. "Study these actions thoroughly and then apply your analysis to your work," he advised.

> It's almost like studying film itself except you have a lot of time to research it and you don't have to run back and forth over it to get the action. You've got it all on one page and they have check[ered graph] lines behind the characters so you can see where the lows and highs [of the body positions] are in the pictured action, and just where the weight is and where the switch of weight occurs. It's damned interesting.[58]

During the war years, Kahl's versatility was put to use in both serious and humorous projects. He and Frank Thomas struggled with the animation of phonetically spelled German dialogue issuing from the mouths of realistic human characters in *Education for Death*, a 1943 propaganda short. "I remember a scene when this mother is praying over her child," Kahl said. "I guess she didn't want him swept up in this Nazi movement. I found quite a bit of satisfaction in getting a good performance out of that one little thing."[59]

The Winged Scourge (January 1943) is a World War II informational short in which the Seven Dwarfs demonstrate methods of controlling malaria-infected mosquitoes. In Ollie Johnston's opinion, Kahl's animation of the Dwarfs "had much more subtlety in the drawing than what Fred [Moore] and Bill [Tytla] did [in the feature film]."[60]

Saludos Amigos, the 1943 feature that was Disney's initial Good Neighbor Policy plunge, showcased the lighter side of Kahl. When tourist Donald Duck visits Lake Titicaca in the Andes, he tries to communicate with a llama by playing a native flute. The stolid, dignified beast of burden reacts with pain to Donald's initial off-key pipings. When the Duck slips into a 1940s jitterbug rhythm, the llama's body can't help but follow—bouncing, breaking into a loose-kneed Charleston, leaping through the air—as his face registers puzzlement and annoyance with his uncontrollable bottom half. Kahl clearly expresses the silent llama's thoughts throughout this comic gem of pantomime and choreography. At the end, the reluctant dancer lands in a heap like a furry haystack; and there is no doubt his attitude toward Donald the Ugly American is one of pure disgust.

Kahl welcomed the opportunity that *Tiger Trouble*, a 1945 short, offered to prove he could handle the broadest type of comedy. Ken Anderson once noted that Kahl was "the butt of remarks" implying that he "wasn't capable of animating the outlandish cartoon characters. Then one day he got a far-out cartoon tiger to animate and the results were so fantastic, they quieted the remarks forever. He could animate anything better than anyone else and he'd proved it."[61]

Kahl was little challenged by his postwar assignments. He loathed Johnny Appleseed (in *Make Mine Music*): "There's nothing harder to do in animation than nothing. Appleseed was such a mild character. He never got mad. He was never elated about anything. Everything was kind of in the middle. He was a weak character. Insipid."[62] Pecos Bill's girlfriend (in *Melody Time*) bored him, although (according to Thomas and Johnston) Kahl's animation of her "sassy walk with the swinging hips has been copied widely throughout the animation industry."[63] It's not that Kahl slacked off when his assignments disinterested him. Quite the opposite; he tried all the harder to make the character or action interesting. "I'm not a lazy bastard," he stated often and emphatically.[64]

OPPOSITE, *the comedic llama from* Saludos Amigos *(1943), a jitterbug in spite of himself;* THIS PAGE, *a square-dance caller in* The Martins and The Coys *from* Make Mine Music *(1946) moves in ways beyond the range of live action.*

In *The Martins and the Coys* (another section of *Make Mine Music*), for example, he put a strong personal stamp on a vigorous square dance performed by a clutch of country folk. Even the square-dance caller, a nonentity who appears in a three-second scene, is worthy of our attention. Richard Williams, in fact, analyzes the caller's animation in detail in his master-class lectures; he notes how Kahl usually gives "an extra drawing" to a gesture to make it more powerful, dynamic, or lively. One such drawing allows the caller's arm joints to bend and break in a way that is beyond the range of live action.

With the return of true animated features at Disney in the 1950s, Kahl found the work more interesting: "Oh, God! Everyone was delighted to get back to work on something that was important."[65] During the next two decades, he was responsible for the final design of most of the characters; but he complained of being saddled with animating damnable non-comic human characters who were difficult to move believably, such as Cinderella, her Prince, the King and the Duke, Alice, Peter Pan and Wendy, Princess Aurora (in *Sleeping Beauty*), *her* Prince, the King, and so on.

There were those who thought King Kahl (or "The Mighty Milt," as some called him) protested too much. "Milt took any scene that no one else could draw," says Frank Thomas. "He had to

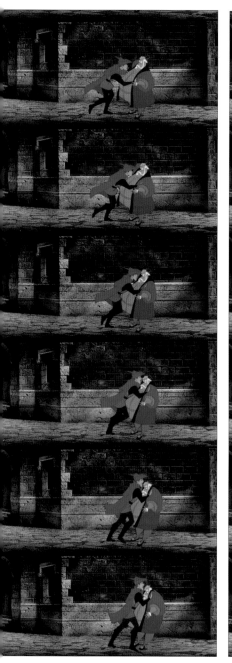

be pretty sure that not only could no one else draw it, but everyone else in the studio *knew* that no one else could draw it!"[66]

Still, his standards were incredibly high; he drove himself with an intensity, "a fever that was unbelievable," according to Dave Michener. First, he thought about his scenes for a long time, before making dozens of thumbnail sketches of ideas for staging and poses. ("God, those beautiful thumbnails," recalls Michener.) From behind his closed door, his assistants heard angry mutterings and paper yanked violently off the light table's pegbars, crumpled and thrown into a wastebasket, which was kicked for good measure. They heard a series of pencils emphatically shoved into a hand-cranked sharpener, then more muttering as the creative search continued. "When he blew up and trampled his drawings in the wastebasket, it was real frustration," says Frank Thomas, "self-criticism, feeling of being inadequate, pure concentrated torture."[67]

"To Milt, the project he was on was the most important thing," wrote Stan Green to Richard Williams. "Animation was his medium, his creative expression, and he gave it his all. His concentration and intensity [were] amazing. His drawing and animation were guideposts for all. So often I would go into his room and Milt would be so involved in what he was doing that I would just leave. And he was never aware of my presence. His face would be about six inches from his board, his glasses hanging from one ear—intensity abounds and drawing away!"[68]

"When I'm exploring what I'm going to do with a sequence," explained Kahl, "I'll thumbnail it out. I'll figure out all my business and any staging. By the time I start animating I know exactly what I'm going to do. I'm not going to surprise myself. I'm going to stick to that plan pretty much."[69]

Once, on *The Jungle Book*, he crumpled paper for hours

OPPOSITE, *the Prince in* Sleeping Beauty *(1959) playfully lifts his hefty father, the King, an action animated with grace and believability;* THIS PAGE, *Kahl grudgingly "stuck with" animating the difficult prince and his horse.*

trying to make a difficult layout work. He persisted, instead of staging the scene an easier way. "You never pick the simplest way to do a scene," he told Michener, "you pick the best way. If the best way is the hardest way, then that's the way to do it."[70] He expected others to follow suit.

On *101 Dalmatians*, Kahl went to great pains to perfect a tiny scene in which Pongo, after finding out he is the father of fifteen puppies, walks in a wobbly, "drunken" way. To a group of animators and assistants on the film, Kahl offered a lengthy demonstration: how he

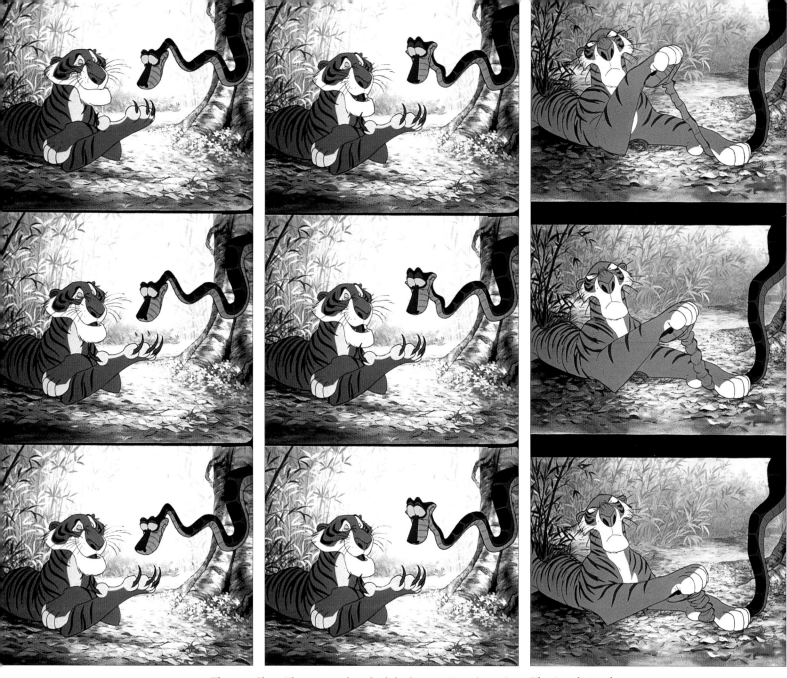

The tiger Shere Khan toys with and subtly threatens Kaa the snake in The Jungle Book.

analyzed a normal four-footed walk, how he changed the placement of the feet, timing, and patterns for the drunken walk. Later, when he heard that one animator had said, "I don't want to work that hard," Kahl hit the roof. "You work a *damn sight harder* if you don't know what you're doing!" he bellowed. "I think a lot of people are a lot lazier than I am," he told a different audience years later. "I really do believe this."[71]

The complex animation of the villainous Shere Khan in *The Jungle Book* was certainly hard to do, starting with the tiger's anatomy, all liquid movement and shifting weight. Kahl made the character a triumph of personality animation, a perfect and memorable performance of cool menace. Elegant, condescending, preening Shere Khan, whose contained exterior masks a savage heart; dangerous, creepy Shere Khan, whose sadism is revealed as he questions the python Kaa, sticking a sharp nail from his claw into the snake's nostril and slowly outlining it.

The tiger's personality and looks were primarily based on actor George Sanders, who recorded the character's voice. At lunch with the animators, the imperious actor did not hide his boredom and disinterest. Offered a drawing of the tiger signed by Walt Disney, Sanders sneered, "How utterly absurd!"[72] Kahl's sharp observational skills caught Sanders's cold disdain. Shere Khan is also partly a self-caricature of Kahl in appearance and manner, as well as a superb caricature of a tiger.

Richard Williams once asked the master how he made the cartoon tiger's weight so convincing. "The stripes helped, gave it shape," replied Kahl. "But on every drawing I know where the weight is. I know where the weight is coming from, and where the weight is just traveling, and where the weight is transferring to."[73] Shere Khan is another sheer Kahl tour de force in terms of subtle acting, sophisticated draftsmanship, and nuanced application of animation's basic principles. Kahl was allowed to concentrate on this one character and to animate all his major scenes, which he reveled in.

But there were always interruptions. Through the years, a steady stream of people came to Kahl's door for help with their drawings; some were top animators, many were assistant

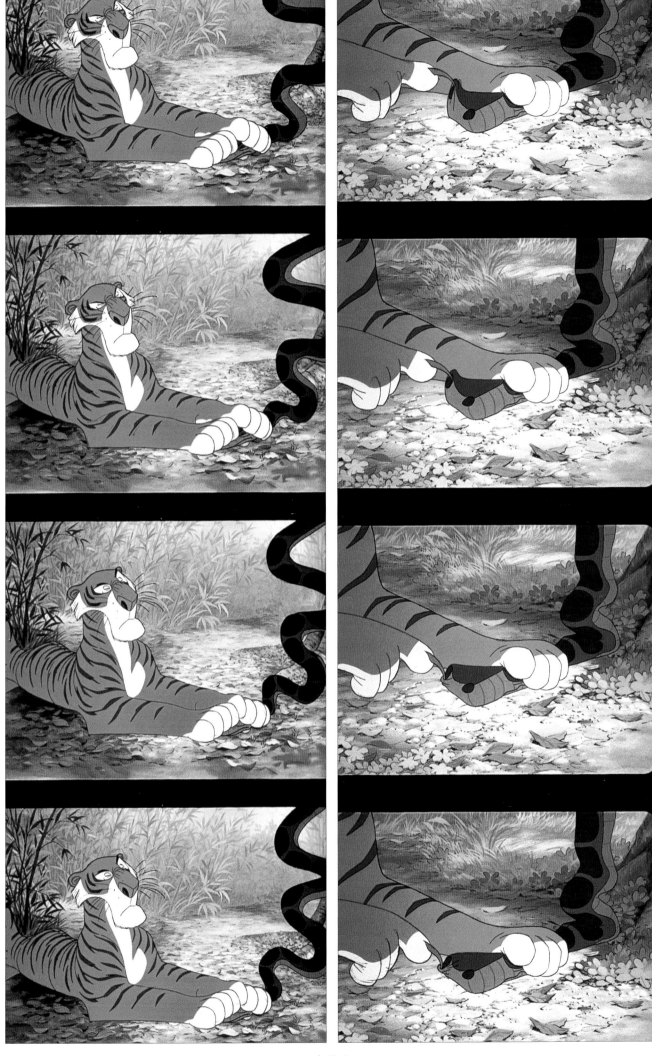

149

JUNGLE BOOK

2179
Shere Khan

A character model sheet for Shere Khan made up of a variety of expressions and poses from Kahl's animation.

animators or layout artists sent by a director. At the studio, a mystique grew around Kahl: "If you want your scene to look good," said John Lounsbery, "go get one drawing from Milt."[74] "He could do one drawing for a scene and it would set you up for days to come," says assistant animator Dale Oliver.[75] Inside his office, "there was Milt, who did the magic," says Don Bluth, "spun straw into gold and then put it under the door."[76]

Everyone was in awe of what Milt did; seeking his guidance became a ritual, like entering the cave of the oracle. He even had his own guards: first, a corridor secretary passed you on to one of his assistants, who always knocked timidly on his closed door (whether it was to deliver coffee or to introduce a supplicant seeking aid). For many years his top assistant was Stan Green who, in this particular Disney pecking order, was "a very high chicken indeed."[77] Green, who had an assistant of his own, was in charge of Kahl's other assistants, in-betweeners, and breakdown sketchers. Though a good animator himself, Green "realized how great Milt was" and was content to work under him. He had, says Richard Williams, "developed kiss-assery to a fine art."[78]

"*Yah, c'min!*" Kahl would holler impatiently from his desk. His room was spare, basically a Picasso print on the wall, a trash can, and desk. "It wasn't like a warm and cuddly place," recalled Glen Keane.

"Whatizit?!" he'd demand.

"Milt was always out of patience," says Bluth. "'*Just go draw the damn thing!*' [he'd say.] As if everybody could do it." On *Robin Hood*, Bluth asked for a drawing and Kahl swore and yelled continuously as he drew it. "All the time he's trying to talk to you, which he didn't do well."

People secretly made fun of Kahl's inarticulate sputterings. But "they were stupid" to do so, says Williams, for "he was trying to formulate, prepare the answer. So you were a damn fool if you didn't hang on."[79] John Ewing recalls that Kahl's "tongue-tiedness made him angry and he would kick his wastebasket for relief."[80] "Milt was very, very tough to talk with," says Dale Oliver. "He was a moody gentleman. Sometimes you'd walk in and he'd be just marvelous, helpful. Other times you'd be met with expletives and four-letter words. You knew you better get out."[81]

According to Jane Baer, Kahl "was Jekyll and Hyde, or could be. He was always polite and nice with the ladies. With the guys he could literally pick them up and throw them out into the hall. Then doors would slam and the whole D-wing would be silent. You could hear a pin drop."[82]

John Ewing experienced the two sides of Kahl. On *The Sword in the Stone*, Ewing did "minimal touch-ups" in a scene that had been animated by another "mere mortal." The scene contained one of Kahl's characters, so director Reitherman suggested Ewing pass the drawings by the master. When he did, a "mini-tornado" took place in Kahl's room. "It is best to say he was disappointed in what I had done," says Ewing. When he tried again, the scene passed muster, "due entirely to the things Milt pointed out to me." Later, he and Kahl rode the same elevator to lunch. "Listen, John," said Kahl, "I really got a lift out of how you fixed up that scene. And I'm sorry if I seemed a bit rough." Ewing, an ex-Navy man, laughed and said he'd had stripes torn off during admiral's inspections. Kahl smiled and "for me, on that occasion," says Ewing, "there was never a more beautiful smile."[83]

"He seemed to appreciate anyone who was willing to extend themselves in terms of hard work," says Iwao Takamoto, a Kahl assistant for fourteen years, starting with Pecos Bill's girlfriend broncho-busting a giant catfish. "Consequently, he never raised his voice at me. He was very kind. He was not a man who taught. He wasn't a natural pedagogue. You learned from him by studying what he did."[84]

"Many thought of Milt as crass and emotional, especially when he was critical of their work," Stan Green once said. "No one was treated with kid gloves. He was very verbal. If he liked something, he used the same energy for praise and was just as verbal. He was completely honest and vented his feelings. It was the product that he set the pace for and demanded that everyone keep. Some may think it unreasonable, but that attitude is what made the Disney films what they were."[85]

Some animators, who saw underneath Kahl's irascible exterior that he *needed* to redo people's work in his own style, took advantage of him, until he caught on. "People's assistants would come in," he complained to Richard Williams in 1987. "I'd end up being a cleanup man for this bastard! Because he's sending his assistant in all the time to have me make good drawings for him. And I had to put my foot down on that stuff. People will run all over you if you let 'em do it, you know."[86]

Kahl was particularly brutal in his critiques of the work of two of his peers among the Nine Old Men, Les Clark and John Lounsbery, both of them in B-wing. In fact, he went out of his way to run down the gentle, insecure Lounsbery in public. "Lounsbery was a very good animator for slapstick stuff," Kahl said *on camera* during a filmed interview for a television show. "But if you gave him a scene that had any subtlety to it, he'd fall on his face . . . I could do stuff that Lounsbery would do, you know. I could do better than that, better than he did."[87] "He has

limitations," he told author Christopher Finch regarding Lounsbery. "He's real good on some stuff and then some stuff he can't do. I, on the other hand, can do anything!"[88]

But Lounsbery was a very strong draftsman who could "imitate anybody's style of drawing,"[89] according to Frank Thomas. Therefore, he was often chosen to follow up Kahl's characters "because he's good enough to follow Milt."[90] Kahl's public savaging of Lounsbery was a way of protecting his turf and reputation as the greatest.

Kahl was as hard on himself as on others. Stan Green once wrote about a day when Kahl returned from a meeting with Walt and others on early tests of *Sleeping Beauty*. He stood at the window of his office "and just stared. It was easy to see he was quite bothered. After a long silence he finally said, 'Walt thinks the prince's head is too flat.'

> To most of us it would seem a simple adjustment, an easy thing to alleviate *[sic]*. Not to Milt. As far as he was concerned he had faltered. But that would pass. What had concerned me more than anything was the group that came into Milt's room when he left for lunch. Some animators who heard of Walt's criticism and just wanted on the bandwagon. "Yeah, his head is flat"; "Not too good, huh?"; "Walt is sure right"; "I wouldn't do it that way"; and so on. I was in my room listening to all of this and I remember thinking "What a bunch of vultures."[91]

Marc Davis was Kahl's best friend at the studio—"Brothers couldn't be closer," comments Davis's wife Alice—and the only animator whose draftsmanship he respected and praised.[92] "Marc is such a damn fine artist, you know," said Kahl. "An excellent draftsman. He makes me look sick, as far as that's concerned." Davis and Kahl sent each other a steady stream of gag drawings back and forth through the years, many off-color; Kahl's penis as a fishing pole figures in several.

Until he moved to WED Enterprises, Davis's office was next door and he had total access to Kahl all the time. Others often consulted Davis regarding the master's mood: A silent shake of the head signaled it was not a good time; a quick "Yep!" was practically an "open sesame."

One of Disney's most versatile artists, Davis specialized in animating the human female form. As such, he relieved some of Kahl's burden with *Cinderella*, Alice, Wendy, and Princess Aurora. Among the women characters that Davis handled by himself are Tinker Bell, Maleficent, and Cruella De Vil. The two animators worked together several times, wrote Davis, on "characters that had physical contact with each other. He did Peter Pan to my Tinker Bell. He did the wonderful fairy godmother to my Cinderella, the Prince to my Maleficent in *Sleeping Beauty*, and Roger to my Cruella De Vil in *A Hundred and One Dalmatians [sic]*. I don't remember ever having a real

WHO SEZ WHO'S MILT KAHL

problem with Milt in this kind of difficult collaboration. It was always interesting to see his approach to animation."[93]

For all their camaraderie, Kahl could not suppress his competitive nature, even with his best buddy. "I remember when he did [Madame Medusa in *The Rescuers*]," said Davis. "He said, 'I'm gonna top your Cruella De Vil.'" In Andreas Deja's first fan letter to Kahl, he praised his work on several characters and mistakenly included Cruella. Kahl replied politely: "Thank you for all your compliments, but I didn't animate Cruella De Vil. She was animated by my friend Marc Davis and, unlike Medusa, was based on live action."[94] Even an unknown fan had to understand that Kahl was king.

Kahl's relationship with Walt Disney was one of mutual respect. "The man was a genius and we all recognized it," said Kahl. And Walt certainly appreciated the invaluable contributions Kahl made to the films. "Where's the genius?" Walt would often ask Stan Green as he stuck his head inside Kahl's door.[95]

Kahl could argue with Walt and let loose his explosive temper. "Well, he was the boss, but we could disagree," said Kahl. "And did. What was he gonna say? Fire me?"[96] Kahl knew his worth and Walt knew he had a human Shere Khan by the tail; a unique and temperamental talent who needed to be handled with kid gloves.

Kahl played chess at lunchtime and if he was losing he often violently tipped the board over. Walt would phone to see how the game had gone. Sometimes Iwao Takamoto took the call. "Did he win?" asked Walt. If the answer was positive, he'd say, "Okay, tell him to call me when he gets in." But if Kahl had lost, Walt would say, "Well, I'll get back to him in a couple of days." "He wasn't about to sit there with a grumpy Milt," says Takamoto.[97]

"Walt would call me on the phone every once in a while," said Kahl, "and it wouldn't be to compliment me. It would

HOLD IT, JOE! I WON'T DRINK A TOAST TO A (expletive deleted) LIVE-ACTION PICTURE!

TOP, *A Ward Kimball caricature of Kahl and his healthy ego;* ABOVE, *Kahl shares a drink with best buddy Marc Davis (right).*

always be to raise hell about what's happening!" Once he phoned to complain about "that damned Peter Pan." In some scenes the character looked too old and muscular. "Something's wrong down there," he barked from the Olympian heights of the third floor. "What the hell's the matter?" Kahl gave what he later called "a rather classic reply." It was certainly classic Kahl: "You really want to know what's wrong? You don't have any damn talent in the place! *That's* what's wrong!"

Years before at a preview of *Snow White* for studio staff members, one audience questionnaire came back with the blunt statement: "Stick to shorts!" The anonymous insult rankled Walt deeply and for years he tried to discover its author. A decade later, after a preview of the surreal "Bumble Boogie" sequence in *Melody Time*, Kahl yelled in Walt's face, "How any sane man could put his money in a piece of shit like that, I just can't understand!" To which Walt angrily replied, "You're the son-of-a-bitch who said, 'Stick to shorts!'"[98]

"I don't think anyone had to worry about talking back to Walt if he had a point," said Kahl. "Walt was anything but difficult to work with. When you were having a conflict with Walt you were having a conflict with someone who probably had more on the ball than you had, and whose judgment was probably better. It was a hell of a lot easier than trying to get a point over to someone who couldn't understand what you were talking about."[99]

Kahl even made jokes about Walt's ideas in his presence and lived to tell about it. At a story meeting for *The Jungle Book*, Walt suggested how the wild child Mowgli might be lured away from the jungle by falling in love. Kahl thought that a "lousy idea," and sarcastically suggested they retitle the film *The Call of the Tame*. "Jesus, he didn't see anything funny about it at all," laughed Kahl. "He just looked over at me like I stunk, went on, and completely ignored it."[100]

In the mid-1950s Walt's interest in films decreased in direct proportion to growing enthusiasm for his new "toy": the Disneyland theme park. To invent and design rides and attractions for the park, he hired creative personnel from the animation department, and sometimes they didn't return. For example, Marc Davis, after animating on *101 Dalmatians*, worked exclusively as a theme park designer. Kahl became alarmed when Walt recruited Ken Anderson to design for Disneyland. "I told him we needed Ken because he was the strongest art director we had, and I thought our product was the main product, and he was spreading us too thin. It was a pretty sticky situation," said Kahl, but Walt finally allowed Anderson to work on *101 Dalmatians*.

Later, he wanted to "borrow" Anderson for the "It's a Small World" exhibit at the 1964 New York World's Fair. Kahl phoned Walt to boldly say, "he couldn't have him." More than a little annoyed, Walt said, "I only want him for two weeks, goddamnit!" "You borrowed Marc Davis for two weeks," Kahl countered, "and we'll never see him again!" Not used to having an employee tell him how to run his business, Walt exploded. "He bawled the hell out of me," said Kahl. "Told me I was getting too big for my britches and I was an overbearing bastard and all that stuff." Then Walt hung up and phoned Anderson to tell him to forget about the World's Fair.[101] Kahl's talent was a veritable shield of kryptonite that rendered him invulnerable even to Walt's wrath.

Kahl became angry if he felt that people in general, or Walt in particular, weren't paying him *enough* respect. He would use any incident—the Camera Department shot his pencil test wrong—to burst into a tirade. "Can't they do anything right?" he'd yell, slamming about and rattling papers, as Stan Green tried to calm him. Then he would charge down the hall headed for Walt's office, leaving his assistants fidgeting at the door. He'd demand to see Walt and would, of course, gain immediate entry. Walt would proceed to play him like a Stradivarius, allowing him to vent his anger and even goading him on. Kahl would take the bait (like one of the trout he fly-fished) and become so angry he would threaten to quit. Walt would then laugh and masterfully reverse the tension, calming Kahl with lavish praise: he was a wonderful artist, a genius; no one in the company could do what he did so well, and so on. Kahl left with his ego thoroughly massaged and, to top it off, Walt sent him to the studio nurse for a vitamin B_{12} shot. When Kahl floated back to his office, his assistants were delighted to find he was downright jolly.[102]

Kahl, his wife, Laura, and children, Sybil and Peter, lived in a lovely house atop the Los Feliz hills with a view of the ocean. A maid and a gardener, a dog and a parakeet completed the family. After work, Milt and Laura wound down with cocktails in the den, while he solved a crossword puzzle and listened to classical music on 78 RPM records. The couple were fun-loving partygoers, who enjoyed socializing with friends. "My dad liked nothing better than to have a good time," says daughter Sybil Byrnes. "Laughed a lot, he was very verbose, very outspoken, kind of conceited about where he was in life."[103]

As a father, though, Kahl's two children found him distant; he and they became closer after they reached adulthood. "I don't think he loved kids, being a father," explains Peter Kahl. "He would like to do things with you that he liked to do."[104] That meant fly-fishing, and Peter's "fondest memories" are of fishing with his dad at Lake Sherwood forty miles north of Los Angeles, or at Hot Creek (Milt's favorite place) ten miles south of Mammoth off highway 395. "If I went fishing with him, he would love it," says Peter. "If I was to ask him to play football with me, he would probably say, 'Why?'"

"He had quite a temper," recalls Sybil. "As we grew up he grew to love us. He wasn't one of these great dads with kids. No. If the two of us started fighting he had this philosophy that we both got spanked no matter what."[105]

Fault lines developed in the Kahl's marriage in the mid-1950s. Laura "didn't think life was fulfilling,"[106] she was "not very contented,"[107] and developed a drinking problem. "She didn't drink that much," says Peter, "except she couldn't handle what she drank at all." "Everybody drank a lot," recalls Sybil,

A family photo from the mid-1940s of Laura and Milt Kahl and their children, Peter and Sybil.

"especially people like my dad who were clever and artistic and man-about-town type of thing. He never had a drinking problem 'cause he was always just up all the time. She wasn't, I guess. Maybe the fact that she was a woman over fifty. Maybe these things just hit her wrong."

The couple argued over money ("He was very happy and didn't need much money"[108]) and a brief extramarital affair he had had. (In a 1954 Disney studio questionnaire, under "hobbies" Kahl listed "sexual intercourse.")[109] "They would start fighting," says Peter Kahl. "My sister was away at UCLA at the time and I was confused. Maybe I should run away from home. I never did. I just put up with it and that led to some pretty depressing years."[110] Kahl said he went fishing "to get away from my wife."[111]

Laura quit drinking and for a while "their marriage was fine." Then, after both children moved out, Milt insisted the house and furniture be sold. They moved to a smaller place on Griffith Park Boulevard, which Milt furnished sparely in Danish Modern. "Laura liked showy things," so she was "very unhappy" in the new house. In fact, the move caused "the biggest rift" yet in their marriage. Alice Davis recalled her friend Laura giving

her an antique secretary ("The first piece of furniture Milt and I bought when we were married"), which she couldn't bear to sell to strangers.[112]

In mid-December 1966, Kahl wept upon hearing the news of Walt's death, and he wept at his funeral. "Our best man died," said he, speaking of Walt as the irreplaceable head of the team. Six months later, Kahl received a shock closer to home.

While on a fishing trip in the High Sierras, his wife Laura died at age sixty-one of a self-inflicted gunshot wound to the head. Kahl insisted her death was accidental. He had bought her the gun because she feared being alone during his trips away, but she had never learned to use the weapon.

When Kahl read the coroner's report listing her death as a suicide, he was devastated. He yelled and cried hysterically, according to his son. Later, Kahl quietly apologized to Peter for his outburst and said it was time he got on with his life.[113]

And so he did. Kahl purchased a sporty Jaguar and rented an apartment in the La Brea Towers in downtown Los Angeles. The first items he bought for his so-called "bachelor's pad" were teak furniture and a four-inch-thick, fire-engine-red shag carpet. His bachelor life didn't last long: eight months

Fly fisherman Kahl poses with a mechanical model used in Disney's 20,000 Leagues Under the Sea (1954); Phyllis Bounds, who became Kahl's second wife, painting cels for Dumbo in 1941.

after Laura's death, he married again on Valentine's Day 1968.

Marc and Alice Davis introduced the nearly sixty-year-old Kahl to forty-nine-year-old Phyllis Bounds, the wealthy niece of Walt Disney's wife, Lillian.[114] Fun-loving "Phyl" (as she was known to friends) was a hard-drinking, hard-smoking former TV-commercial coordinator and talent scout at Disney. She had also spent time heading an ink-and-paint TV-commercial unit in the late 1950s that had experimented with Xerography instead of hand inking. Kahl was her fourth husband; previously she had been married to a Disney studio gas station attendant, a Disney storyman, and the fashion photographer George Hurrell.[115]

"What a sybaritic life they led!" says Kahl's daughter. Phyllis owned two buildings on a corner of Melrose Place, one of which she rented to the fashionable Le Restaurant; the other was an elegant brick and wrought-iron one-story studio decorated in pumpkin and black with living quarters in the back; the front housed the Bounds Gallery, which sold posters and graphics by Picasso and other modern masters. Phyllis was artistic, loved luxury, was tough and opinionated—"very much her own self"—and grandly generous.[116] Peter Kahl remembered when he and his wife visited Phyl in a mansion she later owned in Pacific Heights in San Francisco. "We walked out of there with about twenty Picasso exhibition posters," he said. "She'd just give you anything, just open champagne up, bring out caviar. She was great. A real sweetheart."[117]

Kahl was dazzled. During their ten years of marriage, Phyllis would add a great deal of flair to his life. The newlyweds moved to a penthouse in Century City, which Phyllis decorated with a $200,000 set of furniture from a French chateau, with Louis XIV armoires so big they had to be hoisted by a crane through a window. "It was the most beautifully furnished, elaborate house in the world," says Kahl's daughter.[118] The other half of the penthouse floor was shared with actor David Janssen and his girlfriend, who hung stereo equipment on the wall adjacent to the Kahl's bedroom and played rock and roll. Loud! The two neighbors were "forever yelling, screaming at each other."[119]

The Kahls traveled frequently to Europe; Phyllis to meet artists and buy art for the gallery, Milt to fly-fish (one of his fishing buddies was Charles Ritz of the Ritz Hotels). Through Phyllis, Kahl discovered a new world of art: Picasso, Chagall, and Henry Moore. "After marrying Phyllis Bounds," says Alice Davis, "he grew like you can't believe." Never particularly concerned about his appearance, Kahl now "became the most marvelous dresser you ever saw, everything just so" after Phyllis introduced him to fine haberdashers.

"The only problem," observes Mrs. Davis, "was that all that she was teaching him, he became better at than she. And that didn't work well. She started tap dancing and he started tap dancing better than she. And then she started playing the piano and then he started playing the piano better than she." "That's

ABOVE, *Phyllis and Milt Kahl on a fishing trip in England circa 1970;*
OPPOSITE, *exploratory sketches by Kahl of Madame Medusa, his final assignment at the Disney studio.*

just the way he was with my mother, too," says Sybil Kahl Byrnes. "Phyl was a lot tougher than my mother was. Therefore, there was a lot of bickering between them."[120]

Richard Williams remembered Phyl as "the Kahl girl," who "talked like a producer and tucked the alcohol away." He remembered an evening at a restaurant when Phyllis was "tanking up." Kahl sat watching her, his fingers repeating a double tap on a table top, "the exact thing the tiger did" in *The Jungle Book*. Williams thinks Kahl modeled some of *The Rescuers'* Medusa's "aging sex-pot" looks and flamboyance on his second wife.[121] Jane Baer knows it to be true, although "Milt never admitted it. I gave him a bad time about it. Phyllis wore boots. Medusa wore boots. In that scene where she's pulling off the eyelashes, I said, 'That's Phyllis!' 'What makes ya think that?' 'Well, where would you know how a woman takes off false eyelashes?' 'Well, I know about these things.' It was always a kidding thing," says Ms. Baer, "but you just knew."[122]

Peter Kahl believes that they were "too much alike. Too much conflict there."[123] Phyllis and Milt amicably divorced in 1978 because, he claimed, she "got tired of being a wife."[124]

By that time, Kahl had been "divorced" from the Disney studio for two years (his official retirement date was April 30, 1976) and the parting was anything but amicable. Since Walt's death a decade before, things had not been the same at the studio for Kahl, or so he thought. He certainly did not feel the bedrock of support from the top that he had with Walt. "Ron Miller and I didn't get along to start with and so I just decided, the hell with these guys. And I made a lot of demands. I wanted a separate card on the titles saying that I did Medusa . . . and Ron wouldn't go for any of it. He didn't give me a goddamn thing!"

Also, regarding his toilsome drawing style, he felt that "no one was following him anymore," says Frank Thomas. Kahl once showed Don Bluth a book on Picasso and exclaimed, "Have you ever seen such genius? Look at this stuff. Look at it!" "I could see

he was influenced by it," says Bluth, who cited a scene in *The Rescuers* as an example. It is where Snoops, Medusa's foil, attempts to explain away his incompetence in forcing the orphan girl Penny to find a submerged diamond: "But the water was rising and the tide coming in and all she did was fuss about her teddy bear getting wet." Bluth notes that Kahl's animation of the character is expressionistic—the shape of Snoop's arms crossing in front of his face like a tidal wave, and so on. Bluth witnessed Frank Thomas confronting Kahl: "What kind of a scene is that? Look at that! It's all sort of designy stuff happening and not so much the acting or the character." Thomas was "the antithesis" of that approach, says Bluth. Kahl was offended by the criticism. "That might have been part of what caused them to drift apart," Bluth theorizes.[125]

While Thomas admired Kahl's drawings, he also felt that "they were [of] less and less use to the studio." Ollie Johnston agreed, of course; toward the end of Kahl's tenure at the studio, says Johnston, "he was trying to get us to follow his design on certain characters that just wouldn't work for us anymore. It was a design that lacked appeal."[126] Some drawings were so formidable

WHAT DOES THAT DUMB (expletive deleted) WOOLIE KNOW ABOUT ANIMATION!

TOP, *Kahl grimaces while drawing Sir Kay from* The Sword in the Stone; ABOVE, *a photo with a dialogue balloon prepared as a gag by studio associates for one of Kahl's birthdays.*

and so much Kahl's personal signature style that director Reitherman dared not assign them to junior animators because Kahl would "hit the ceiling." "So, gee, we were cutting his scenes out," says Thomas. "It started back— well, Walt was still alive. *Jungle Book.* [On] *Robin Hood* he was impossible. He was a little better on *Rescuers* 'cause he was doing one character all by himself."

"The more you find out about animation," says Andreas Deja, "the more you realize that it's not all about drawing. It's more about feeling." Deja believes Kahl's animation affects the brain more than the heart because the drawing ultimately takes precedence. "Toward later years, when he refined his drawings more and more," says Deja, "I see patterns in the acting. I see walks on characters that he applied to other characters before. There's the Medusa walk, or Sir Hector and Kay [from *The Sword in the Stone*]. They all walk a certain way. I don't think Frank [Thomas] would ever do something like that."[127]

"I do not want to convey the impression that I thought Milt was the finest animator the studio ever had, because I don't believe he was," Ollie Johnston once wrote to Andreas Deja.

With his superb draftsmanship he moved the characters beautifully and always convincingly, but there have been those few who could make their characters give acting performances that touched the audience in a way that Milt's work never did. I bring this up not to put Milt down in any way but only to put his work in the proper perspective. Milt had a wonderful gift with his remarkable drawing—others had great talent in other areas of the medium—and they complemented each other.[128]

"Milt was always hung up so on the drawing," laments Frank Thomas, "and good thing he was, too. But there were so many things, particularly in the last few years, we had to throw out because he wouldn't change it. He wouldn't accept that they needed to be changed. He'd say grudgingly that since we were all dumb shits who couldn't do anything in the first place, it didn't matter whether we threw it out or not!"

The Rescuers *heroine Penny, a spunky little girl, and her nemesis Medusa, as drawn by Kahl.*

Brad Bird, director of the Warner Brothers animated feature *The Iron Giant* (1999), was a trainee animator at Disney in the late 1970s and considers Kahl his mentor. He challenges the notion that Kahl's drawings were rejected at the studio because they were too "graphically oriented." "What are they rejecting and for what movies?" he asked recently. "That's the kind of statement you really have to investigate. Is Medusa too graphic?" he asks incredulously. To Bird and other admirers, Kahl brought the highest-quality animation and a strong personal style to what are essentially bland, styleless films; the other animators, Kahl's supporters contend, should have worked harder and/or held higher standards not only in drawing but in picture making. "Milt always felt people were not trying to match [his standard]," says Bird. "He felt they were not applying themselves. He didn't feel

he was good [just] because he was naturally talented, [but] because he didn't quit."[129]

Medusa is a shot of absinthe in an ice-cream sundae. The screen tingles with excitement when Kahl's scenes appear. The great Geraldine Page's over-the-top voice characterization encouraged the great animator to find a visual equivalent. "She's a magnificent actress," said Kahl. "She forces you to 'plus' things!" He even borrowed from Page's performance in *Sweet Bird of Youth* (1962) when she keeps her boyfriend (Paul Newman) away by putting her foot in his gut; in one scene, Medusa keeps the child Penny away from her the same way.

Kahl searched for entertainment possibilities in the character's voice, costume, and props. In a phone conversation with Snoops, for example, Medusa believes that he has found the diamond, and Kahl said he "injected this little girlish thing like, 'You found a present for *me*!'" The fifty-something harridan becomes briefly a coy (if grotesque) coquette. "What do you do with a dame talking on the telephone?" asked Kahl rhetorically. His solution was to make the phone represent poor Snoops: When Medusa pokes her finger into the receiver, she really is poking Snoops's chest (or his eye); using both hands to hold the phone, she is also grabbing Snoops's lapels or choking him.

FOR CRISSAKE, LARRY, YOUR DIALOGUE IS A BIG CROCK OF (expletive deleted)!

This gag photo jokes about Kahl's bluntness and salty tongue, but is based on his real behavior.

Slamming the phone into its cradle is a resounding smack across his face. "There's a lot you can do if you start looking at the possibilities," said Kahl of props.[130]

Unfortunately, Medusa is more of a star turn than an integrated part of an ensemble acting troupe. It would have been more effective (and affecting) had there been a true sharing of the limelight with the other animators. And the film in general would have benefited had there been more cooperation between Kahl and the remaining Nine Old Men.

The isolation of the Medusa character and the fractured quality of the film itself reflect a war that went on behind the scenes. Kahl made his last great animation fling virtually by himself alone in his room. Communication was impossible, says Frank Thomas. "He would have thrown a chair at anybody who tried to come in." He brooked no suggestions regarding the character, and his criticisms of the rest of the film's animation were "so crude you always had to talk with someone else to clear your head up."[131]

Kahl claimed he got tired of "bucking egos" and having his efforts "both resented and resisted. And I just got fed up with it. I just divorced myself from the whole place and did the damnedest best performance I could do with these two characters [Medusa and Snoops] and forgot the rest of it."[132]

Over time, Kahl's explosive, often abusive outbursts had made many reluctant to follow or support him. "I found I was getting people so nervous they couldn't work," acknowledged Kahl. "I hated to hear that crybaby crap!"[133] "I was losing respect for him because of the way he was treating Larry Clemmons and others," says Thomas. Storyman Clemmons had lost a son in an auto accident and recently returned to the studio. At a story meeting, Kahl upbraided him without mercy before the group: "You never had a decent idea! You're ruining this picture with your lousy dialogue!" and so on. Afterward Kahl came to Thomas's room and laughed. "Why I sure dished it out to old Larry," he said. Thomas replied that he was surprised by the attack, considering Clemmons's loss. "Oh," replied Kahl suddenly recalling. "That's right. He did, didn't he. Yah, well." Thomas claims, "It was harder for me to be jolly with him. There were so many things I didn't think were right." For example, Kahl's continually harsh treatment of Les Clark and John Lounsbery. When Thomas tried weakly to correct him, Kahl countered with a sledgehammer: "Aw, ya dumb shit! You never know anything in the first place." "After five or six years of that," says Thomas, "I was gradually losing respect for him all along the line."[134]

Animator Eric Cleworth was aware of "the forces gathering

against Milt," even if Kahl was not. "They hated Milt," he told Richard Williams. When Cleworth quit the studio in 1970, Kahl said, "Jesus, I can't understand your leaving. The only way I'll ever leave is, they'll drag me out kicking and screaming!" Cleworth thought to himself, "I'll give you five years."[135]

Kahl had built up a litany of complaints since Walt's death about the way things were run at the studio, his coworkers, and the films. He suspected a conspiracy between Thomas, Johnston, and Reitherman that guaranteed that Frank and Ollie would get the "best" roles and he'd be stuck with the difficult-to-draw ones. He lamented not having animated Captain Hook, or the Queen of Hearts, or even Ichabod Crane, all roles that went to Thomas.

Kahl literally ran hot and cold regarding Woolie Reitherman, alternately praising and damning his leadership and directorial efforts. "Oh, God, this guy, he's just growing into the part," he would coo to Richard Williams. "He's really doing it. He's growing and he's just wonderful." Nine months later, he'd call the director a "Goddamn junkman!" for retracing old animation from *Snow White* and using it in new scenes for *Robin Hood*. "Can you believe the bad taste? I mean, what garbage. Garbagemen! Garbageman!" he'd sputter. A few months later, his opinion changed back again, and so forth.

Little more than two weeks before officially retiring, Kahl showed rough footage of his scenes in *The Rescuers* to animation students at the California Institute of the Arts and publicly vented his grievances. *The Rescuers*, he said, was "mediocre" and, like *Robin Hood* and *The Aristocats*, was full of "bad taste and terrible judgment." He hated that the giant alligators in *Rescuers* were played for laughs and were not "a convincing menace." He deplored the reuse of voices from other films, such as Phil Harris and Eva Gabor. "There's a tendency nowadays to find something that works and use it forever," he said. "That's a rotten way of looking at the business. We've always had our quota of crap in every picture," he concluded. "This is something you have to be philosophical about. The last half a dozen or so, the quota's been too great."

Perhaps the final straw for Kahl occurred when Ollie Johnston gave Glen Keane, then a novice animator, a *Rescuers* scene slated for Kahl. "The only way you could get promoted in the animation department," explains Keane, "was to do a personal test and show it to the Review Board." With Johnston and Eric Larson advising him, Keane worked for months on a scene of the little girl, Penny, running

An example of Kahl's delicate wire sculptures, a hobby he took up after retiring from Disney in 1976.

away. When it was shown to the Board, Kahl hit the roof. He took it as a personal affront that a scene scheduled for him to animate had been given to a neophyte for a test. He hated what he saw and eventually did the animation himself. Keane, whose scene never got into the film, bravely approached Kahl in his office to ask why he was so negative toward it.

"Well, Milt, my name's Glen Keane, and I, ah, just showed an animation test of Penny to the Review Board—" "Oh, yeah, yeah, yeah!" said Kahl. "I heard that you had some thoughts about it and, um, I wonder if you could let me know what you were thinking?" "Ahhhhmmmm. No. No. I don't think so." "Okay," said Keane gingerly. "Maybe another time?" "No. No! Never. Never!" Keane shut the door and left.

"I couldn't imagine the rivalries going on," he says, "and I had walked right in the middle of a minefield." Later, Kahl was always cordial to Keane when they would see each other around the studio. In the war of the titan animators, Keane felt "it was almost as if I didn't exist."

"I'm really rather bitter," said Kahl six months after he retired, "about some of the people who I thought considered that we were working together, and I find out we really weren't. Here I am, a person at the height of my powers, and I feel there's not a place for me any more. I don't want to be involved. I can't fight this thing."[136]

Stan Green recalled Milt's final working day at the studio: "He came to my room, shut the door, and said, 'I'm getting the hell out of here, and I want you to finish the balance of the Medusa animation.' He handed me a personal drawing, a pile of exposure sheets, his stopwatch, and his own little refrigerator—then zipped out."

Kahl headed back whence he came: the San Francisco Bay area, settling in Greenbrae, a little town north of Sausalito. Besides constantly fly-fishing in the area and once a year in

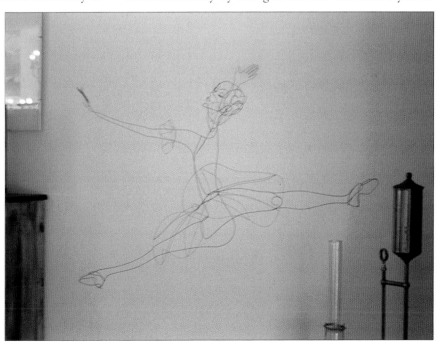

Milt and Julie Kahl in northern California, circa 1983.

"He felt the Disney films weren't worth his animation," says Brad Bird. "But the whole time he was retired, I felt he was in search of an art form that gave him as much pleasure as animation. And I don't think he ever found it."

His next door neighbor, an Italian dentist, was a drinking buddy. Once they drained a bottle of Remy Martin while taking turns shooting Kahl's German luger air pistol at targets on an antique desk; BB shots peppered the walls of Kahl's living room, a reminder of how bored and lonely he was.

That all changed when Kahl's daughter introduced him to a Marin General Hospital librarian twenty-some years his junior, who was an accomplished pianist and student of ballet. "We were together two years," says Julie Kahl, "before we married on March 21, 1980," the day before his seventy-first birthday. "I was fascinated with him. Something about him. His voice was enough to . . ."[138] The couple shared interests in music and dance, and it was a happy marriage. "Julie just had my dad completely boondoggled," says her friend Sybil Byrnes. "All these things he liked to do and she wanted to do."[139] "Julie's a very open person," remarks Richard Williams. "Milt was crazy in love with her and she with him."[140] "This was probably his best marriage," commented Ken Anderson, "because he was no longer the boss. But he was in love with the boss."[141]

Europe, Kahl began making eighteen-inch-high wire sculptures of ballet dancers based on Degas paintings. "They give me something to do besides making love to women and fishing. It makes a good third hobby," he quipped to a local newspaper. "All I know is I'm having a ball."[137] But eventually he lost interest in the sculptures which, though three-dimensional, could only be viewed properly from one or two positions; more significantly, they didn't move.

Occasionally, Kahl returned to the Disney studio as a consultant. "He went a few times, but knew it wouldn't work," says Julie. "'They didn't even know who I was,' he said. He could be so honest, it was childlike."

Kahl had prostate cancer, but it was under control. However, an embolism in a stomach artery required an operation, which

Alice struggles with a giggly flamingo in complex animation by Kahl for Alice in Wonderland.

left him with less energy. One day after lunch, he mused, "I wonder if this is the last good meal I'm going to have on this planet." On a Wednesday very soon after, he entered a Marin hospital with a respiratory infection that developed into pneumonia. It was soon discovered he also had baseline lung cancer. He quickly died the following Sunday; it was Easter, April 19, 1987, and he was seventy-eight.

Milt Kahl left an indelible imprint on the art of animation in general and Disney animation and graphic style in particular; for almost forty years he *was* Disney style. His work possesses an amazing beauty of form and movement. He took on some of the most difficult animation assignments ever and made them work; he made them look easy, though his personal struggle to do so was enormous.

"I almost think that Milt's influence is a bad one," says

AN EXAMPLE OF THE OBSERVATIONS THAT MIGHT BE MADE BY FLIPPING AND STUDYING JUST THESE TWO DRAWINGS. BY SHIFTING YOUR EYES FROM ONE DRAWING TO THE OTHER YOU CAN SEE THESE THINGS HAPPENING. WATCH THE NEGATIVE SHAPES CHANGE ALSO.

NOTE CLEAR SILHOUETTE THROUGHOUT

FLESH CONTINUES DOWN (OVERLAP) AS UPPER BODY SPRINGS OFF, SHOWING WEIGHT AND PULL OF GRAVITY.

TOP OF HEAD USED AS SPEAR TIP TO ACCENT DIRECTION OF THRUST. NOTE SIMPLICITY OF LINE OF ACTION.

WHISKERS DRAGGING

EARS DRAGGING

STRIPES USED TO INDICATE PERSPECTIVE, VOLUME, SQUASH AND STRETCH, AND BODY CONTOUR

WHISKERS NOW DRAG IN OPPOSITE DIRECTION.

JAW DROPS — TO SHOW WEIGHT AND FORCE OF UPWARD THRUST

THE PATH OF THE RUMP, IN THIS CASE THE PRIMARY ACTION, IS FOLLOWED BY THE TAIL, A SECONDARY ACTION

FRONT LEGS PUSHING OFF (STRETCH)

HIND LEGS COIL IN ANTICIPATION FOR PUSH OFF (SQUASH)

ELBOW BENT IN ANTICIPATION FOR PUSH OFF

OVERLAPPING ACTION (FRONT VS HIND QUARTERS) INCORPORATES SQUASH AND STRETCH IN SAME DRAWING.

CONTACT AND DIRECTION OF FEET INDICATE PERSPECTIVE

LEGS STRETCHED FOR CONTACT

STRAIGHTS IN LEGS SHOW TENSION OF STRETCH.

NOTE SHAPE OF RUMP IN ⑥: ◯ (STRETCH) TO ⑦: ◯ SQUASH.

Richard Williams of the master's effect on animators who attempt to emulate him. "Because if you're copying the surface aspects of Milt's work and you're not a skilled draftsman like he was, you're going to screw it up." Many of today's skilled draftsman-animators can move human figure designed with Kahl-like complexity, as seen in *Pocahontas* (1995), *Anastasia* (1997), *The Road to El Dorado* (2000), among others; but much of their work is bland and lacks that something extra—a vitality, or perhaps a sense of play—that Kahl was able to inject in his work.

Pick a scene, any scene, and marvel not only at Kahl's drawing skill, but also at his inventiveness and unerring instinct for entertainment. Alice's fight to gain control over a daffy flamingo in *Alice in Wonderland* is complex from any point of view: drawing, mechanics and staging, acting, timing, and so on. So is the old lawyer in *The Aristocats* who loses and catches his balance as he nonchalantly goes about his business. The lightest side of Kahl is revealed in the bouncy fun of Tigger in *The Many Adventures of Winnie the Pooh* (1977).

But Kahl *always* found a humorous dimension in his animated characters; even murderous Shere Khan and mad Medusa have their funny quirks and moments. In *Sleeping Beauty* he even managed to lighten up the straightlaced prince, who affectionately lifts and swings around his portly father, the king, in a mock waltz turn. Kahl, always the proudest of men, was rightly immodest about the "dance" of the royals. "I did that damned thing and it's believable," he said. "The king has weight, but the prince is strong enough to lift him off the ground, and it looks convincing—as convincing as any of the stuff that was taken from live action. I can do that and I think that other animators should be able to do it. I don't think the surface has been scratched, really, with our kind of picture," he said. "I think you should be able to animate princes or princesses, or any kind of difficult character, and make them believable. I don't mean realism, I mean you should be able to do things with them that a human being wouldn't be able to do. But make them convincing, make people be able to believe in them."

Kahl's contentious personality exacerbated rivalries at the studio, which unfortunately undermined his influence there and cut short his tenure. "That was

A diagram by Walt Stanchfield analyzing two Kahl animation drawings of Tigger in Winnie the Pooh and the Blustery Day *(1968); a film frame of the old lawyer in* The Aristocats *(1970).*

sad," comments Brad Bird, "'cause I think you could have gotten another great ten years out of him."

During retirement, Kahl eventually came to see the achievements of the Nine Old Men as a whole and was proud of them. Even at the height of his antagonisms at the studio, he always praised the work of Davis, Thomas, and Johnston, making it clear that he never included them in his rogues' gallery of "lazy bastards." But he never made peace with the latter two animators, although he wrote them that he thought their book, *Disney Animation: The Illusion of Life*, was "great."

Near the end of his life, Kahl continued to protest when people said his animation was better because of his superior draftsmanship. "I think that's sort of cheapening it," he told Richard Williams three months before he died. "It's selling it short because it's not the draftsmanship. It's the conception."[142] Quite rightly he insisted that he was a *thoughtful* animator, who worked out problems in his head (like his beloved crossword puzzles) long before his pencil ever touched the paper.

His thoughts were often occupied with the difference between animation and live-action film performances; in the latter, he said, "an actress or an actor can make a complete expression and mood change with a little motion of the eye." Animators, however, must devise more obvious ways to communicate emotions. "What you have to do," said Kahl, "is to display it to the audience. I always try to make it goddamn clear that people see what you're trying to do."

> What I like to see in animation, I like to see that change. I like to see that contact . . . [where] you'll have something that's fairly straight and then, as the weight comes into it, you'll get the bulging of the muscles, what you'd call the squash-and-stretch kind of thing. But I like to see that change taking place . . . I always get a kick out of that in drawings. I always admired Degas, where he has a nude with soft flesh leaning against something hard, like a bathtub or something that's rigid. And where the flesh gives with this.

It makes a more interesting drawing because you're displaying something. You're saying this is hard and that's soft; that's rigid and this is not. You're making statements when you do that. . . . You're making an editorial opinion. I think that's what makes a good drawing. And I think that's what makes good animation. . . .

> Another thing I do is, if a character is reading a book, say, and something over here makes a noise, something startles him. . . . I'd try to get a very complacent and maybe amused expression, so you'd have something to change to. So you'd make the change strongly . . . you see the change of expression and it reads to you. . . . You've got to have it in a place where the audience can see it. I think that's an awfully strong point . . . it not only applies to animation, I think it applies to top drawing and painting. . . . To look for the contrast. You need something to change from. . . .[143]

In a talk to students in 1976, the year he retired, Kahl was unusually articulate in summing up his thoughts about the art of animation: "It's a very difficult medium," he reflected. "Animation requires a pretty good draftsman because you've got to turn things, to be able to draw well enough to turn things at every angle. You have to understand movement, which in itself is quite a study. You have to be an actor. You have to put on a performance, to be a showman, to be able to evaluate how good the entertainment is. You have to know the best way of doing it, and have an appreciation of where it belongs in the picture. You have to be a pretty good story man. To be a really good animator, then, you have to be a jack-of-all-trades.

"I don't mean to say that I'm all these things, but I try hard. I got accused over the years of being a fine draftsman. Actually, I don't really draw that well. It's just that I don't stop trying as quickly. I keep at it. I happen to have high standards and I try to meet them.

"I have to struggle like hell to make a drawing look good."

Frank Thomas catches trout in the High Sierras on his sixteenth birthday in 1928. Some of the characters Thomas brought to life at Disney include Captain Hook *in* Peter Pan, *two squirrels in* The Sword in the Stone, *and the Queen of Hearts in* Alice in Wonderland.

OPPOSITE, *Thomas drawing a canine model for* 101 Dalmatians *in 1961.*

CHAPTER six

Frank Thomas

imilarities abound between great actors and great animators. Both keenly observe the behavior and movements of humans as well as animals; both are masters of timing and gestural nuance; both prepare for a performance through rigorous study, research, and analysis. The animator's thumbnail sketches and filmed pencil tests are equivalent to an actor's rehearsals.

Like actors, animators become immersed in their roles and their character's story. "The actor creates his own universe, then peoples it—a giant puppet master," writes Laurence Olivier. Exaggeration in performance (a believable caricature of life) and clarity of staging (the presentation of an idea to an audience) are used by animators and thespians alike. "The trick is to make the audience feel that they are observing reality, and this isn't easy, because," notes Olivier, "you have to exaggerate subtly, ever so slightly highlight. Lead the audience by the nose to the thought."[1]

Frank Thomas is a great "actor with a pencil," as animators are sometimes described. In fact, some liken him to Laurence Olivier because of the variety of roles he has played and the depths of emotion he has wrung from them. During his forty-three years at the Disney studio, the versatile Thomas convincingly portrayed villains (such as Captain Hook in *Peter Pan* and the stepmother in *Cinderella*), innocents (Bambi and Pinocchio), and even an inanimate object (the doorknob in *Alice in Wonderland*). He also animated Mickey Mouse, the three good fairies in *Sleeping Beauty*, the mad Queen in *Alice in Wonderland*, and the dancing penguins in *Mary Poppins*.

Thomas is particularly known and admired for his ability to animate emotionally sensitive material; the saddest scenes, the most romantic, most deeply felt sequences, the sincerest heart-tuggers usually found their way onto his drawing board.

To mention a few Thomas gems: the lovesick female squirrel whose heart is broken in *The Sword in the Stone*; the first date and spaghetti dinner in *Lady and the Tramp*; Thumper teaching Bambi to ice-skate; Pinocchio trapped in a birdcage by the evil puppeteer Stromboli; Baloo the bear attempting to tell the boy Mowgli that they can no longer be buddies—each of those screen moments evokes in moviegoers joy or sorrow, and sometimes both in the same sequence.

Thomas's assignments demanded a believability unusual in animation, and skills of the highest order in acting, dramatic staging, subtlety of gesture, expression, and timing. And something more: an x factor, a special alchemy that occurred at the drawing board between Thomas and the characters he animated.

167

"There was a feeling that as you started to work on a scene," he once explained, "you had a contact with the magic that was behind the drawing. Not the drawing itself as much, but this whole feeling of 'this is a room, this is a forest glade, this is a rock, this is a castle.' And you had to be able to see your character working in three dimensions, going in there and living in there. And *you* want to live in there."[2]

The act of drawing never came easily to Thomas, who always felt his draftsmanship was inadequate. He struggled mightily with the graphite lines that were necessary to express his ideas. And so he dug deeper, analyzed more fully in order to, as he put it, go "behind the drawing" and to mine the gold in a scene or character. "Frank's stuff is absolutely incredible because of the way it feels," says Andreas Deja. "He wins that struggle with his drawings. He has something in his mind that he's after. Just getting there is a little hard for him."

Thomas lacked Milt Kahl's graphic facility, and their ways of animating were decidedly different. Thomas's drawings do not settle, like Kahl's, into readily identifiable key poses that express the essence of a scene. "You try to find that particular drawing or several key drawings with Frank and you can't," explains Deja. "It's all solved through motion. Frank has a way of moving through it in very subtle ways. Its the series of drawings that sell the thought."[3]

Thomas once articulated the differences between his and Kahl's approach to acting in animation:

The type of thing I've had the most luck [with is] working on it, wrestling with it, scratching on [the drawings], flipping [them] until the character's doing what I conceive of it doing. Milt will work just as hard on getting drawings that look as though the character's doing it. If he's got a drawing that says this, then he puts in in-betweens and makes it move nicely. But it's not the same type of acting. My emphasis is on character and acting. He'll say, 'Sure, I can do character and acting, too.' But primarily he handles graphics and if the graphics are right then the scene is right. Which, for him, is right. . . . As I say, Milt does most of his work through drawings, but even so he has a great feeling for acting, he has a great feeling for character, and you have to have.[4]

Although one of the most intelligent of animators, Thomas's work never smacks of dry intellectualism; rather, his ideas about what a character should think and feel are always in the service of high drama and sincere emotionalism. The depth of his analysis was painstakingly thorough. No one analyzed a scene, a sequence, an action, or a gesture quite the way Frank Thomas did. His intensity and tenacity often overwhelmed assistants and associates, and sometimes himself.

"And if the phone rang," he recalls, "it was like a real dream, you know? It's hard to come out of this concept. I'd pick up the phone and think, 'Where am I? What's going on here today? Oh, who's this?' Because you would enclose yourself in this, ah, it was a high-class escapism to be able to go into this magic land with this character, whoever he was, and spend a couple, three hours, creating something there between him and you."

After experiencing something akin to a long pregnancy and birth pains, Thomas felt a fatherly pride and affection toward his creations. "Sculpture, painting, drawing, etchings, none of it can give you that same feeling of life that you get out of seeing this doggone little character projected up on the screen," he said. "You feel like a parent who's just sent his kid away to school, you know. You don't really own this guy up on the screen anymore. You did for a while and you're very close to him for a while. But now, all of a sudden, here he is, apparently making decisions on his own, doing quite well without you, thank you. It's kind of a sad moment, but it's also very fulfilling and rewarding."

Some actors claim that comedy is harder to play than drama. But with animation that is not the case. For if a drawing looks funny to begin with (according to Ward Kimball, clown prince of animators), you are halfway there in making an audience laugh; add funny movements to an amusing gag and laughs are almost guaranteed. But to make audiences believe in animated drawings so much that they cry or are deeply moved is vastly more difficult. One must, first, suspend disbelief that the characters are mere graphic lines; they must be perceived as real creatures of flesh and blood, capable of feelings. In Disney features, audiences are asked to believe that a cartoon is really alive: its safety is at risk, its very "life" in danger. Second, the cartoon must convincingly express love, grief, passion, anger, hate, and jealousy.

This special communication between moving drawings and moviegoers is a strange and wonderful magic, and Frank Thomas was a pioneer of the form. His sequence in *Snow White*—the Dwarfs grieving and crying at the dead Princess's bier—was a major breakthrough. It could have been ludicrous: seven toons weeping over another "dead" toon. Instead, thanks to Thomas's superb analysis, taste, and judgment in timing and motion, audiences shared in the Dwarfs' mourning; the tears shed on the screen and in the audience in 1937 were the waters of baptism for a powerful new kind of animation.

Six feet tall and lanky, Thomas, with his crooked smile and ready sense of humor, has a friendly, just-folks manner. But as one of his former assistants puts it, "You didn't mess around with Frank."[5] Underneath the unassuming, easygoing exterior is a driven perfectionist whose relentless work habits often exhausted him and coworkers. *Disney Animation: The Illusion of Life*, the definitive book on personality animation that Thomas wrote with his close friend Ollie Johnston, describes those working under Thomas's supervision as being "subjected to the most rigorous training imaginable. As one young animator said, 'It is impossible to please that guy. He's never satisfied.'"[6]

This Snow White *sequence, animated by Frank Thomas, was a breakthrough in depicting believable emotions.*

"Frank was a taskmaster, but wonderful," concurs Dale Oliver, who assisted Thomas for twenty years. "Very exacting, very demanding. He knew precisely what he wanted." Thomas micromanaged his assistants; often, when they were at lunch, he left notes written in red Scripto attached to drawings. ("This is the shape of a mouth in dialogue. This is the shape of an eye. The eye has an orb. In the orb is a pupil. When it moves, it moves like this. Now let's see if we can draw eyes more like this.") "He worked over his drawings and you better have it right," says Oliver, who admired Thomas as an "absolute master."[7] Another assistant comments that when he left Thomas to work for someone else "it was like taking off lead boots!"[8]

John Pomeroy recalls animating one scene in *Winnie the Pooh and Tigger, Too* under Thomas's supervision nearly twenty times. "I got very frustrated but never angry because I knew I was working for a genius," says Pomeroy. "There would always be something wrong. As Tigger trudges away in the snow he was going up too high or going down too low in the squash [position], or the tail is too active, or the stripes [aren't] working right, or the overlap on the ears. Everything had to be perfectly choreographed, especially on a pathos scene. 'Cause you never want to be aware that it's drawn. You want this illusion complete and if there's any little thing wrong you spoil it. So Frank was teaching me how to keep my guard up. Always to sustain that willing suspension of disbelief."[9]

"He's very jovial, but also extremely driven and competi-

tive with himself," says his son, filmmaker Theodore Thomas. "If he's going to do something, he wants to be good at it." His intention is, "I'm going to be better at this than anybody else."[10]

Most of Thomas's associates mention his pedagogical approach, which perhaps came naturally, considering that his father and two brothers were in the teaching profession. "I learned tons of things from that man," says Don Bluth. "He showed you how to organize your scene and exposure sheets, how to focus your scene so you were giving the audience the right message. But he didn't mess with you. If you didn't take him seriously and do what he asked you to do, he let you know that [you were] wasting his time. He'd simply say, 'I told you what to do. What's your problem?' Then he would joke with you in a way. He'd say, 'Aw, this is easy. Everybody can do it, right?' So it's got a cut in it a little bit."

Thomas's opinions are invariably sharp and plainly expressed. It was startling to hear bracing, candid declarations from the mild-mannered, easygoing "professor"; they often took away the breath of the unwary. "You'd never see him overtly getting angry with you or disappointed," says Bluth. "It came out in the form of sarcasm or a cutting little remark. I'd say, 'Wait a minute. I think that was an arrow.' He'd always do it with a smile on his face so it was always deceiving." Bluth recalls that Thomas's secret nickname was "The Velvet Needle" because "you didn't really know that you were being stuck till after you were stuck.[11] I think Frank prided himself on being prickly," says Bluth.

Indeed, Thomas always enjoyed director Richard Williams's description of him: "Frank Thomas is as cuddly and innocent as a roll of barbed wire." Williams developed quite a thick skin after years of seeking Thomas's opinion of his films and animation. "Frank was typically Frank," he says. "Very strong criticisms of my work and my approach and everything. And at the same time enormously helpful. Just very friendly *and honest*. Very generous." Williams felt he "could come back and attack him, too." Once, for example, he told Thomas, "'I don't believe all this James Stewart aw-shucks stuff because you're fiercely competitive!'" Thomas reacted with a folksy chuckle.

"In Frank's work," observes Williams, "he can snuggle right up to you. He's got this incredible charm, and he has it personally, too.

"But," says Williams admiringly, "he's also a killer!"

Franklin Thomas was born on September 5, 1912, in a house on Tenth Street one block off Wilshire Boulevard in Santa Monica, California. The *Titanic* had sunk nearly six months before and "they were still talking about it when I arrived," he recalls wryly.

His father, Frank W. Thomas, was an Indiana farm boy, the youngest of fourteen children whose English ancestors had come to North America in the 1600s. *His* father was a Southern Baptist minister "and a long line of ministers preceded him," but Franklin's father "went more toward Congregational."[12]

Frank W. largely raised himself; he taught in a one-room schoolhouse at age sixteen, learned Latin and Greek, earned a masters degree in education at the University of Illinois.[13] He met his future wife, Ina Gregg, singing in a church choir in Tuscola, Illinois. She was Scotch and Irish, "very compassionate, very spirited." Her father raised sulky race horses at a racetrack on their property called Greggland; one of their horses once beat out the famed Dan Patch. Her grandfather founded the Christian Endeavor Organization, moved west in a covered wagon, then returned to the midwest and "cut down all the trees in old Illinois so they could have farm land."

Frank W. and Ina married and two boys were born before Franklin: Lawrence (who was three years older) and Craig (one year older). Frank W. came to California to be interviewed for the position of principal of Santa Monica High School; when he was hired, he sent for his family in Illinois.

Franklin remembered Santa Monica not at all, for he was one year old when the family moved to Sacramento, where his dad became the principal of another high school. Four years later Frank W. Thomas accepted the position of president of Fresno State College.

Fresno was a small agricultural town in 1917, the so-called "garden spot of the San Joaquin Valley," home of the annual Raisin Day Parade and the motto "We're raisin' raisins in Fresno!" The Thomases were a family "very interested in educational things," the arts, and "mostly intellectual games." But

"still associated with people who were close to the soil," Thomas says, adding, "and I always felt that makes a difference in your appreciation and your feeling about humor and about animals and people. You get down to basic personalities and you see it in the animals and everything around."[14]

Mr. and Mrs. Thomas were "very supportive" of their children, but "very direction-oriented. They didn't care what direction I took," says Thomas, "as long as it was honorable." However, they did not want their youngest son to become a grocer or a shoe clerk "no matter how honorable" these professions were; instead, they ambitiously hoped young Franklin might someday become a doctor or a lawyer. "His was a family of people excelling," notes Theodore Thomas. "I'm quite certain [Ina] instilled real standards of excellence in her three boys."[15]

Eventually, both of Franklin's brothers followed their father and became teachers at the college level. Laurence Thomas, in fact, received his Ph.D. from Yale in 1938 at the same ceremony that conferred an honorary degree on Walt Disney (as the "creator of a new language of art"). Walt later told Thomas he had met his brother back east. "Wow, he's sure got a lot of degrees. Must be pretty smart. What are you? Black sheep of the family?" he teased. An old sibling rivalry made Thomas want to respond "No, I'm smarter than he is. But," he says, "the words wouldn't come out."[16]

The Thomas family was "middle class in terms of morals and behavior" and "barely" comfortable financially. A family of five, living on an educator's salary—even a college president's—only went so far. During World War I, graham crackers with milk was considered an expensive luxury, Thomas remembers. "For a while we churned our own [butter]. Lot of those things survived from the farm age. Made jellies, canned things like that. My mother didn't really like it, but she felt it had to be done for the family."

In fact, Ina Gregg Thomas did not enjoy the life of a college president's wife; she disliked the mandatory social obligations: evenings spent sponsoring student dances activities, and stuffy faculty teas that she was obliged to host twice a year. "It was very rigid socially in Fresno," says her son Frank.

> If you had a tea for lady friends, you had to have at least eight of them there to qualify. Then the [newspaper] social editor would come out to your house and find out if you had the little nut cups [for] only the acceptable things, hazelnuts maybe. But no pistachio, any strange thing. Nothing from a foreign country. Had to have those little dishes, some no bigger than this! Had to have all the courses for a luncheon. Flowers arranged a certain way. [Women] just killed themselves to put these on.

Ina dreamt of being a singer or a librarian, "where you're creating something of yourself." But her ambitions were frustrated because of her duties as a wife and mother of three. "I never heard them argue," says Thomas of his parents. "I just sensed things were tense every so often." Years later he learned from his brother Larry "things my mother was unhappy about. Her wish that her life were more full."

Ina was critical of her husband "as she should have been," says Thomas. "Because they got him off the farm, but they couldn't get the farm out of him." She balked when he suggested washing up in the morning in a horse trough outside the house "because he liked the out of doors." As it was, he drove his wife crazy making sounds when he washed his face ("B-b-b-buh-buhbuh-bbbb!") because it reminded her of the farm hands who worked at her family's racetrack.

Frank Sr. was successful in his career as president; he had the common touch and an ability to talk to anybody; he enjoyed relaxed one-on-one conversations with colleagues and students, especially those in need of guidance. Ina preferred the stimulation that was available at a university as opposed to a state college environment. There were only six state colleges in California at the time, each independent of the other; thanks to Ina's influence, Fresno State had more guest speakers, concerts and plays than the others.

"He wasn't a rough guy," says Thomas of his father, who appreciated the arts and literature as much as Ina. "But he did like the outdoors and the streams and the view and the smell and the fishing. I thought he was great!" Every summer Frank, Sr. took the whole family camping in the mountains as part of Fresno State's Sierra Summer School. Along with other faculty members, they went fishing and hiking, backpacking on mules, cooking and sleeping under the stars; it was all a bit too strenuous for Ina, who backed off after a couple of trips.

But young Frank enjoyed playing with the kids of the faculty at the summer retreat, who were "a very creative group." He was usually a solitary child. The Thomases lived on the outskirts of Fresno where "there weren't any other kids to play with." Until high school, he "didn't have any playmates or friends. I read, I drew, I had games of my own, took a few piano lessons. There wasn't much else to do except build a fence." He always quipped that his mother "is the necessity of invention," for each week Ina suggested her boys build bird houses, household tools, and the like.

Franklin hung around with his brothers, but Larry always picked on him and did "diabolical things," such as making him walk on painful sand burrs. He helped Larry raise rabbits, which Franklin thought "real cute." But "that didn't last long. Larry took the rabbits to market when they were old enough to eat. I had to stay home and clean out the pens." Craig was considered "the artist in the family." He drew well, particularly birds (he raised fantail pigeons), and also played music by ear, sang, and won school contests. He also had all the traumas and troubles of the middle child: a need to be noticed and to prove himself.

TOP, *infant Franklin with mother Ina and brothers in Santa Monica, 1912;* ABOVE, *Frank W. Thomas, Sr., president of Fresno State College, poses in 1919 with sons (left to right) Frank, Jr., Craig, and Lawrence.*

Franklin's drive and competitiveness surfaced early. When he was four, he stomped around the house in a major temper tantrum because he wanted to go to school like his big brothers. "His parents actually ended up putting him into school a year and a half earlier," says Thomas's son Theodore, "because he was a holy terror about being kept out."[17]

Franklin started drawing, he said, "because Craig was drawing. It always seemed to be natural to draw. I never thought much about it. Particularly when there was nothing else to do, no one to play with. I read a lot and discussed books and ideas and like that. In the meantime, I was usually drawing." He was nine when he asked his father if there was "any job where you just sit around drawing funny pictures all day." "Yeah," replied Frank Sr., "that'd be a cartoonist," a word Franklin had never heard before.

To Frank W., his youngest son's curiosity about cartooning was amusing, a passing fad. But in Fresno High School Franklin developed his interest in drawing; he drew cartoons for the school paper and annuals and received support from several teachers. He and Craig attended Fresno State College for two years because, he says, laughing, "we knew the president." He enrolled in courses in music, theater, and drawing; his art teacher was a "very good painter," a woman from Nova Scotia who had trained at Columbia "back when very few girls went to university."

The summer after his freshman year, Frank took courses at the University of Southern California in Los Angeles to "get my science requirements out of the way." (His dad taught there in summer and his son was allowed in at half the tuition.) "I took a course in botany and they worked my little old tail off. I had to know the name of every tree in Exposition Park, over a hundred!"

He also saw an amateur movie made by USC students based on a Hollywood film about Harold Teen and college life. "That appealed to me," said Thomas. Upon returning to Fresno State, he became sophomore vice president, responsible for furnishing entertainment at class meetings. "So I suggested that we make a movie." The resultant thirty-one-minute, 35mm film titled *The Soph Movie*, was, says Thomas, "a great episode in my life." Several students pitched in, but Thomas was the producer, cowriter, director, editor, and lead actor. He "learned an awful lot about picture making. Trying to get your gag over, difficulties, one thing or another." He also learned about people: "How unreliable they are, how many excuses they can give you. All the things I've used the rest of my life. I learned." The experience interested him in "making movies and communicating with people."

Everyone in town wanted to see *The Soph Movie*, "and see it over and over again." It was shown up and down the coast at local theaters, rotary clubs, and schools at twenty-five cents a screening "which was big money then." It brought in $1,000 above the cost for his sophomore class. Drawing cartoons for the school paper couldn't compare to the thrill of a theater filled with people laughing at his film. "To suddenly hear this crowd of a thousand voices: '*HA-HA-HA-HAHAHAHAHA!*' Belly laughs coming!" Thomas recalls with glee.

It became obvious to Frank, Sr. that his youngest son was headed toward a career in the arts. But first he wanted all his kids "to have the best education he could afford," and that meant Stanford University. Larry and Craig were already there, so he made a deal with Franklin: if the boy would attend Stanford for his final two years of college, after graduation Dad would pay the tuition for two years at any art school he chose. "If you want to go to Paris and live in a garret or something, I guess that's what artists do," said his father. "That's all he knew

about it," says Thomas. "I thought it sounded pretty good."

In 1931, Frank Thomas entered Stanford as a junior transfer. Located 150 miles from Fresno, the sprawling campus in the California countryside was nicknamed The Farm "because it had farm buildings on it from the Stanford family." It was a stimulating yet relaxed campus with strong sports and academic programs. "Everything about it seemed to be pretty easy," says Thomas.

He drew cartoons for the school humor magazine, *The Chaparral*, where he met two young men who would later work with him at Disney: copy editor James Algar from Modesto (working toward a master's degree in journalism) and art editor Thorington (Thor) Putnam from Berkeley. The art program at Stanford barely existed; only four students enrolled in Landscape Painting, which was "the first and only art course they had."[18] Before the start of the first class, Thomas introduced himself to Oliver (Ollie) Johnston, who became his lifelong friend.

Born in 1912 in nearby Palo Alto, Johnston grew up on the Stanford campus, where his father headed the Romance Languages department. "We just sort of drifted together," recalls Thomas. "Found that we had the same sense of humor and the same interest in things, particularly with the landscape class." The boys would load up Johnston's roadster with art materials, put the top down, drive to a scenic spot, and paint using the seatbacks as easels.

"Later [Stanford] had a class in perspective," recalls Johnston, "but there were no models" for a life drawing class. "Mrs. Stanford walked in on a class in 1900 and there was a nude model. She said, 'There'll never be another model of any kind at this university.'" Therefore, art instructor Ed Farmer made arrangements for his students to attend an unsupervised life drawing class in San Mateo. Thomas, Johnston, and Putnam drove up twice a week to sketch from the live model. "Lots of times on our way back," recalls Johnston, "we'd stop at this speakeasy up on a hill off the road. Frank would play the piano and they'd give us this horrible beer for nothing. We'd maybe leave a drawing with them." "We felt like we were right in with those top painters of the day," says Thomas. "Go out and make a painting, come back and trade it for dinner. We were artists!"[19]

Thomas's first impression of Johnston was that he was "more outgoing," but not any more "brash" than Thomas himself. "He was not particularly compassionate or interested in other people's feelings any more than I was, maybe any more than anyone is at, what were we, eighteen, nineteen?"[20] Their personalities and interests complemented each other: Johnston was energetic and involved in sporting events, while unathletic Thomas "always just sort of stood there and frowned," he says, "trying to sort things out." Thor Putnam recently recalled that Thomas's outstanding trait was "a good sense of humor even then," while Johnston "was more serious."[21]

Thomas tended to "jump into things headlong" and

Johnston was "always much more thoughtful" and, says Thomas, "saved me from a lot of difficult situations." While Thomas would happily develop and embroider the kernel of an inspiration forever, Johnston has always been able to help his friend let go and move on. Johnston also, according to Theodore Thomas, has "been a lot stronger in common sense things," such as money matters, buying property, and so on.

"I think that Frank was probably more mature than I was when we first met," commented Johnston in 1993. "I would probably have more unusual ideas that would lead us in a new direction, while he would analyze things more. I liked his ideas because he stated [them] well and they were well analyzed, while mine were more spontaneous, more emotional reactions to what we were doing. It just seemed like we had some kind of vibes creatively that seemed to communicate. We'd look at each other's work and criticize and give helpful suggestions. But I never got mad at him about a criticism and I don't think he did me either."[22] "The incredible thing about their friendship," observes Theodore Thomas, "is that there is not one who was the leader or one who was the follower." They are true equals.

They discovered unusual similarities in their backgrounds: both of their mothers were born in Tuscola, Illinois (although fifteen years apart, and without knowing each other); both of their fathers grew up on farms and became scholars and college teachers; both boys enjoyed reading the great romantic historical novels, such as *Ivanhoe, Robin Hood,* and *Scottish Chiefs.* The "twinning" aspect of their lives continued and intensified through (at this writing) nearly seven decades of friendship, including more than forty years working together at the Disney studio.

When Thomas graduated with a Bachelor of Arts from Stanford, his father made good on his promise. The twenty-one-year-old decided to attend the Art Center in Pasadena, because he wanted to study with designer Kem Weber: "I developed an interest in commercial design-toasters, hairdryers, egg beaters." He arrived in June 1933 only to find that Weber wasn't teaching that summer. Thor Putnam, his Stanford *Chaparral* buddy, had been in town for a year studying with illustrator Pruett Carter at the Chouinard Art Institute at 7th and Grand in downtown Los Angeles. "Thor said . . . commercial design doesn't sound like as much fun as we're having in illustration," recalls Thomas. By the end of that summer, Thomas "was hooked on Chouinard" and enrolled in Carter's class, which included several students who later worked at Disney, such as Hardie Gramatky, Phil Dyke, and Lee and Mary Blair.

Thomas felt fortunate to be supported by his father in his pursuit of an art career at the height of the Depression. Putnam recalls "people coming to your door carrying babies, begging for money to eat. It was as bad as that."[23] Thomas moved in with Putnam at a boarding house at 1012 North Edgemont, just off Santa Monica Boulevard in back of the old UCLA buildings. The landlady, a Mrs. Charles, barely spoke to her husband, a retired

mortician who had lost their life savings to a con man. Their son, an aspiring undertaker, practiced what he called "grass funerals" in the backyard beneath Thomas and Putnam's window.

The two art students shared a "little bitty old room with two twin beds, a walk between them, little table down there, [and] a mirror we put up back here so we could look at our paintings from a distance. You'd do like in an optometrist's office: have a hand mirror and you'd look in a mirror behind you thirty feet away." The toilet was down the hall.

For Thomas it was "a loose, happy time," but at Chouinard he "didn't feel like [he] was progressing." In fact, instructor Carter suggested that he study life drawing and composition in order to "know more about what [he was] talking about." Thomas did so, including taking a course with Donald Graham, who in little more than a year would become the head instructor of an art-training program at the Disney studio.

Hardie Gramatky urged Thomas to rejoin Carter's class: "Just show up. Don't say anything." Thomas did, and again drew illustrative compositions for various stories each week. But he got hung up researching details for the pictures or laboriously rendering color values to the detriment of the illustration's emotional content. "The things I was trying to do with the illustrations," he explains, "always shot too far. People on a train or a bus, I had to find a picture of the inside of what a bus looked like." "The interesting thing," says Ollie Johnston, "is that when we got to the [Disney] studio, all the emotions that he didn't get into the illustration material seemed to come out in his work there."

Johnston visited Thomas and Putnam in the winter of 1933; a football team manager, he came down to Los Angeles for the Stanford–USC game. So impressed was he when Thomas showed "all these keen drawings he was making in art school," Johnston went back and convinced his parents that he should do the same. In January 1934, the middle of his Junior year, Johnston transferred to Chouinard. He, too, rented a small room—a former

Old friends: Ollie Johnston and Frank Thomas in the 1980s.

closet with a makeshift window—in the same eccentric boarding house that housed Thomas and Putnam. Each morning, the three happily drove in Putnam's car downtown to the art school.

In July, Jim Algar, another Stanford *Chaparral* alum, arrived unannounced in Los Angeles. He was in town for a tryout at the Disney studio, an opportunity that came in a roundabout way. It seems Gilbert Guest, also a Stanford graduate, responded to a magazine advertisement and applied for a job at Disney with samples of his artwork from *The Chaparral*. Ben Sharpsteen saw Algar's cartoons on the same pages and inquired, "Who's this fellow?" In July, a letter from Sharpsteen arrived in Modesto where Algar had summer employment on his hometown newspaper. "We were all starving for a job and I was lucky I had one."[24] The letter requested he come to Los Angeles for a two-week tryout for an unspecified job in animation at Disney. "I'd seen *Steamboat Willie* and Mickey Mouse," said Algar, "but I'd never dreamed of doing it."

When he arrived in Los Angeles, he looked up Thomas, Johnston, and Putnam, and again Mrs. Charles found a tiny spare room for the latest upstate refugee. Algar struggled for two weeks trying to make in-between drawings for Fred Moore's *Three Little Pigs* poses, which were "awfully hard to copy, never having done them." At the end of the test period, Algar was in and became employee #207, but his friend Gil Guest was out.

In August, Putnam, Thomas, Johnston and other students appeared in an "art class scene" in the Universal feature film *I Give My Love* starring Paul Lucas ("They cut most of us out," says Johnston.) Come September and it was back to real art classes at Chouinard; but Putnam decided to follow Algar's lead by trying out at Disney. "I knew it was a good starter place for that period," he says. In other words, it was a place to draw and paint all day like Chouinard but for pay, during a period in which there were few opportunities to do so. Putnam was hired on September 17, 1934.[25]

Frank Thomas was also interested in trying out at Disney. He remembers that he and Putnam flipped a coin to see who

would go first. "We thought, well, they're only taking one person a week. We don't want to both go out the same week." What motivated Thomas to consider animation at the time? Years later he claimed the Silly Symphony *The Flying Mouse* (released in spring 1934) sparked his interest. He found the film "different than any of the other cartoons" because "this one had more pathos and more feeling for the characters and more acting. And it really grabbed me," he says. "It wasn't just a series of gags. I thought, 'Gee, this *Flying Mouse*, if they're going to go that direction, there might be something there that would interest me.' The idea of bringing a character to life really began to fascinate me."[26]

With two of his Stanford buddies employed, Thomas's competitive side may also have come to the fore. But in a 1981 two-page studio information sheet Thomas wrote that he came to Disney "on advice of Pruett Carter, who did not think much of Frank's future as an illustrator."[27] "I thought it would be easier to do these little characters who run around and bop each other on the head," said Thomas recently. But he was cool toward animation, for he still harbored hopes that he might go into commercial design. "I wasn't lying awake at night," he says of the Disney tryout period. "I really wasn't into it. I thought of it as a fill-in. I still had a year of my dad's promise. I thought I'd go over to Art Center. See if I liked Kem Weber."[28]

Thomas took his portfolio to the Hyperion Avenue studio and gave it to Clarence "Ducky" Nash, whom he later discovered was Donald Duck's voice. Collecting and delivering aspirant's portfolios was an extra job Walt gave Nash "just to keep him around so he wouldn't go wandering off to work for someone else." Thomas's tryout started the end of that week: "They worked a half day on Saturdays." He was quickly hired (he became employee #224) and began on September 24, 1934.

For six months Thomas toiled in the large in-betweener room, where behind a plate-glass window George Drake glared at the backs of the workers. It was a scene out of Kafka. The in-

The Flying Mouse (1934) contains scenes of sincere emotion and pathos that appealed to Frank Thomas. "If [Disney] is going in that direction," he thought before applying for work at the studio, "there might be something there that would interest me."

betweeners couldn't see over into the next row, so high were the stacks of paper on their desks. "So we all learned the noises they made," says Thomas of the steady buzz in this peculiar beehive. "One guy'd be nervous, tapping a cup. 'Hey, knock it off!' Another guy'd be doing Mexican accents," and so on. Wadded up paper and spitballs flew about the room when Drake wasn't looking. Several men with newspaper experience goofed off whenever they could; it was just another job to them. But this was Thomas's first real job and he had a self-described "Boy Scout attitude" about "participating in the whole thing" and doing what he was hired to do.

The first drawings Thomas in-betweened "didn't impress" him, although, he adds, they "were harder to do than I thought they would be." He recalls a scene of a mill pond with a reflection of the moon that was so small the pencil lines looked like black ants. But "the things that should have been tedious, and would be later on, were fascinating," he says.

He was earning seventeen dollars a week ("I could live very comfortably on that as a bachelor."); and he enjoyed having a "regular job, eight to five," although unlike school "you couldn't go down to the beach if you weren't drawing any good and if you didn't like the model." But his school days weren't all behind him, for Thomas was among a half dozen animation beginners selected for art training after hours at the studio. The instructor was Donald Graham, formerly of Chouinard, who was hired the same day as Thomas.

"Almost immediately this easy life of sitting there and drawing little pictures and laughing disappeared," he says. "Walt put us into art class, he put us into studying action analysis, looking at old films, studying characters, studying filmmaking. These are things that appealed to me." Like *The Soph Movie* of happy memory, the medium of animation became an opportunity for Thomas to use all of his talents. Ambitiously he decided

to one day "create a sequence, scenes, drawings that the audience could identify with and be wrapped up in."[29]

After six months, Thomas was promoted, which saved him from being fired. Unpredictable George Drake, the Inbetweener Department head, was irritated by Thomas's crooked smile and how he talked out of the side of his mouth. Thomas moved into Fred Moore's unit and became the star animator's assistant.

Thomas was delighted to work with the animator whose scenes he had admired in *The Flying Mouse*. "Fred was tops," says Thomas. At first he cleaned up Moore's rough drawings, but soon was asked to make changes in the animation itself. "Fred would just rough them out, 'Do this and this and that, three frames here, make a little longer and hold on this.' Okay. I'd set the drawings up and do 'em, then show them to him. He'd make a few little changes in it, but not much. Then I'd go back to the regular cleanups. The other fellows in the unit would finish the in-betweens." Gradually Thomas was given larger chunks of animation to complete.

He marveled at Moore's ease in making beautiful drawings and how quickly he captured the emotional content of a scene. Moore taught by example, but also made suggestions that guided Thomas for years; such as, "Don't clutter up your scene with a lot of extra bits of action. Do one thing at a time." And "Don't move too much while you're doing it. Hit a pose and get the expression you want, and then move on."

Moore was only one year older than Thomas; although he had four years more experience in animation, he was literally a peer of the young men he supervised—a fun-loving, easygoing fellow. But Thomas noticed a dark side as well. "He reminds me more of Chopin than any artist or artistic person I [have] read about," he says. "The flair and almost, I would say, undisciplined feeling—the pure emotions that would come out, and then his dissatisfaction, the torment." Moore was, says Thomas, "the first real artist that I'd run into" in terms of temperament.[30] On days when the muse avoided Moore, he would mope and wander about the studio unable to work. "He had to be well-balanced, like a diver, before he could draw," observes Thomas. When he reached that elusive mental alignment, Moore perched happily on his chair humming a tune; he'd quickly pull down one sheet of paper after another, as animation smooth as satin flowed from his pencil.

Thomas learned, too, from the highly analytical Ham Luske "because Fred admired Ham very much. They'd both come up together" at the studio. Luske "was always the under-control thinker, plotting things out," says Thomas, in a description that could also fit himself. He recalls how Luske used to say, "If you're going to spend two days on a scene, you ought to spend the first day with your arms folded staring at a blank piece of paper. Because until you can visualize the thing and know *exactly* what you're going to do with it, you can't draw it."[31]

Thomas also found Les Clark and Wilfred Jackson, two of Disney's earliest employees, to be extremely generous with advice and offers of help. After nearly a year with Moore, Thomas had acquired quite a bit of experience.

Ben Sharpsteen often gave "Freddy's guys" tests "to see if they were ready to start animating."[32] Thomas's test of a slapstick bit with Goofy was considered to be "pretty good" by Sharpsteen. But a test Thomas did in Graham's class really impressed him: a girl waiting at a train station hears her dog bark from inside her suitcase. "You have to show without any sound that something attracted her attention," Thomas recalls. "She thinks, 'Oh, I remember that.' Squats down, opens the suitcase and lets the animal out." In addition to the subtle action, Thomas paid attention to how the girl's skirt hung and didn't cling to her leg, how the pleats worked with the action, and other details. Animator Fred Spencer saw the test and told Sharpsteen "This kid Thomas is doin' real good stuff!"

Based on that test, Thomas became one of a half dozen junior animators at the studio. Ollie Johnston (hired in January 1935) now became an assistant to Moore in March 1936. Thomas's first solo animation appears in three scenes in *Mickey's Circus* (1936): trained seals swarming over Donald Duck at feeding time; "quite a change from the little girl opening her suitcase," quips Thomas. He had the pleasure of flipping the seal drawings for movie star Douglas Fairbanks and his wife Lady Ashley, two of the many celebrity guests who often paraded through Walt's dream factory curious about "what makes 'em move."

The seal animation proved successful and in the fall of 1936 Thomas was next assigned a large 150-foot section (including fourteen scenes) of *Mickey's Elephant* (1936), in which a ball Pluto plays with is sucked through a fence by an elephant. "That was fun to do," says Thomas. "Course I could run to Fred anytime and say 'Hey, draw me an elephant here. What am I doing

Mickey's Elephant (1936), starring Pluto the pup, contains one of Thomas's earliest solo animation performances.

wrong?' He'd laugh and draw me an elephant, a Mickey, a Pluto. All these drawings. He could do 'em so fast. He liked to work over someone's else's drawings. Milt [Kahl] liked that too. It bolstered their ego[s] 'cause they were the top authority on this. You're pretty good, sonny. But I'm better."

Mickey's Elephant solidified Thomas's reputation as an up-and-comer. He jokingly contends he made his mark with a scene in which Pluto wrests his tail from the elephant and tucks it underneath his belly. Intent on exaggerating the bit to make it read well, Thomas naively "tucked the whole end of the body under him with a black line for the tail coming straight out of it. I never thought of the implications." The crew howled with laughter when the pencil test of Pluto's "erection" was screened and Thomas immediately became well known throughout the studio. The scene was "corrected," but Thomas was sure Walt heard about it, although he had yet to meet the boss.

That happened soon after Thomas's work appeared in *Little Hiawatha* (1937). For a scene of the child Hiawatha and a bear cub in a nose-to-nose confrontation, Thomas again asked Moore for help. "Fred made beautiful drawings. I just copied them as best I could." But on his own Thomas "put in all the action of the feelings—startled or scared, or surprised, or what the feeling was and what they do about it." Ever the tough critic, even of his own work, Thomas thought "part of it was pretty good."

Apparently Walt agreed. For word came from David Hand, supervising director of *Snow White and the Seven Dwarfs*, that Thomas was to begin work on the feature. His rapid ascent

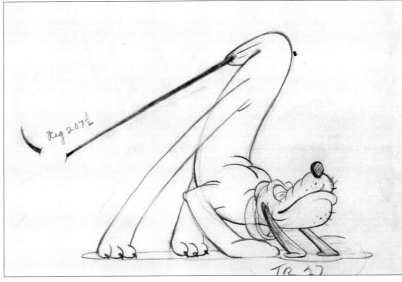

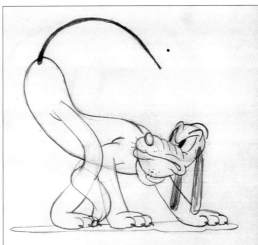

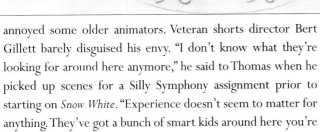

annoyed some older animators. Veteran shorts director Bert Gillett barely disguised his envy. "I don't know what they're looking for around here anymore," he said to Thomas when he picked up scenes for a Silly Symphony assignment prior to starting on *Snow White*. "Experience doesn't seem to matter for anything. They've got a bunch of smart kids around here you're not supposed to touch," he said, staring at twenty-four-year-old Thomas. "Just give 'em scenes and not tell them how to do it or help them or anything. So here you are. Take 'em!" Gillett said, tossing him the scenes.

"Walt let it be known," says Thomas, "he wanted the guys who had been into cartoons in school. Had college training." Ham

Luske, for example, was the first to come to Disney's with a college education, and Walt "knew that he was head and shoulders above the other guys as far as working out problems of animation." Walt was "looking for people who had a creative spark in them."

Animator Bill Roberts called the art school-trained junior animators (who by that time included Milt Kahl, Ward Kimball, Eric Larson, James Algar, Wolfgang Reitherman, and Ollie Johnston, as well as Thomas) "a bunch of Cinderellas."

For *Snow White*, Thomas was one of eight animators who concentrated on the Seven Dwarfs in three sections of the picture. "You were always looking for some way of making the character come to life, enriching him, making him a little different," comments Thomas.33 For a sequence in which the Dwarfs are ordered by Snow White to wash before dinner, Thomas noticed that story sketches of Dopey suggested a hitch step so he could keep up with the others. Ever the industrious Boy Scout, Thomas inserted a hitch step into his pencil test and Walt was delighted: "Hey, we oughta use that hitch step throughout the picture." Done, Walt! All scenes of Dopey walking were recalled and many were reanimated using the hitch step. Within a day, several animators dropped by to tell Thomas what they thought of him and the extra work he had inadvertently given them.

Thomas took his responsibilities seriously and cared a great deal about the picture. "There was a section of *Snow White*," he recalls, "where they'd given some very important footage on the Dwarfs to a lesser man and it just killed me!" He came back nights voluntarily to redo the animation.

Two sequences in the film's final section showcase Thomas's special gift for "realistic, sincere, believable action": the Dwarfs in the cottage in the evening grieving over Snow White's inert body, and (next day) putting flowers around her coffin, kneeling down, and so forth. The latter scene, Thomas heard later, was exactly "the way Walt wanted to see it. And he was told no one could animate it—it was too realistic! So with a sly smile, [Walt] said, 'How about Thomas?'"

The sequence in the cottage required taste and judgment in drawing poses that expressed emotions in a convincing manner. "I made a lot of drawings," Thomas told this writer in 1973 of his working process. "Are [the Dwarfs] better looking straight ahead? Are they better grouped together two or three looking around? And, of course, you always have help. Someone in story sketch, someone like Albert Hurter, or Don Da Gradi will make drawings. Don was great at getting the essence of the character. If it was sad, he'd make twelve drawings of a sad guy. You'll only use one in your scene, but you're ninety percent there.

"Now if you can think of some kind of movement, not too much because this is sad and you want minimum movement; but in 'sincere' animation you find out if you do not move the character he goes flat and it kills it, and you can't make your point. In doing a sincere thing, in order to believe this guy is real, he's up there feeling this part, you have to keep him moving."

Thomas found that he could "hold" a character—that is, freeze his position—for two or three feet of film with merely a tear rolling down a cheek or the camera trucking in slightly. "But you can't go over three feet. Keep him moving, which

The challenge facing Thomas with scenes of the dwarfs grieving over Snow White's body was to make the animation into "realistic, sincere, believable action."

means that in each scene you have to have at least two drawings where he's either settling into it, or the other overlaps till the end of the scene, so somebody's moving just a tiny bit."

A scene of Dopey collapsing in tears into Doc's shoulder was cut in half when a preview audience laughed; Dopey's face held an uncharacteristically pained expression which the audience misinterpreted. The final version begins as his face is nearly buried in Doc's shoulder and continues through his shoulder-heaving sobs. The most heartbreakingly successful depiction of grief is Thomas's animation of Grumpy. The so-called "woman-hater," who secretly loves Snow White, is obviously devastated by her death. A loner throughout the film, he mourns by himself. His eyes register disbelief as he turns away to bury his head in his hands. ("The only Dwarf with a major body move," says Thomas.) The brief scene is deeply moving. [34]

Technically, the slow movements of the characters required close in-between drawings, "so you have to pick an in-betweener that you can either whip or lead or inspire," says Thomas. There could be no distracting wiggle or flicker in the movement. Thomas finally sat down with a conscientious artist named Bob McCrea and convinced him he was the chosen one.

"Essentially," concludes Thomas regarding ultra-sensitive or sad scenes, "it's what drawings you can get that will sell it, 'cause you're going to have minimum action to begin with. When somebody's very sad that way they don't act." [35]

Thomas was one of three Disney Studio wunderkinder to be asked to animate the star of *Pinocchio*. The others included Milt Kahl, who redesigned the character to Walt's liking, and Ollie Johnston, who became an animator on *Brave Little Tailor* (1938). Thomas found the assignment less interesting than it might have been because of Pinocchio's watered-down personality. "Jiminy Cricket took all of Pinocchio's personality and

left Pinocchio to say 'Why?', 'Will she?', and 'Who did?'" What *was* challenging to Thomas and the others was the wooden boy's naïveté; he was a blank page experientially, emotionally, and morally. "You had to always watch out that he moved and acted in a very innocent, unskilled way. Every movement had to be as if he was born today and had no history."[36]

Thomas did remarkable animation early in the film of the lifeless Pinocchio manipulated on strings by toymaker Geppetto; he also animated highly emotional scenes of the sentient Pinocchio frightened and desperate when kidnapped by the puppeteer Stromboli. Thomas also gave us a joyous Pinocchio singing and dancing in Stromboli's puppet theater. Belting out "I've Got No Strings," the wooden boy exudes the undisciplined eagerness of a gauche amateur performer.

"I felt pretty strongly that it ought to be very amateurish," says Thomas, who discussed his concept with Kahl. "He's never rehearsed this," explained Thomas. The performing puppet "doesn't know what he's going to do. He's making it up as he goes along. I'm going to have him be late on his sync on some of the words."

Pinocchio gives the performance of his life on stage in Stromboli's puppet theatre, exuding the show-off joy of the amateur entertainer. His spontaneity required detailed planning by animator Thomas. The final impression is that the puppet is "making it up as he goes along." OPPOSITE TOP LEFT, *a caricature of hirsute Thomas as Pinocchio's alter ego.*

"Are you crazy? exploded Kahl. "God! That's the lousiest idea I've ever heard anywhere!"

Kahl's opinion notwithstanding, Thomas proceeded with the idea. "When Pinocchio says, 'I've got no strings to hold me down,' the gesture comes after he says 'down.' That was just what I wanted to do and no one objected, although I can still hear Milt scream, 'Oh for Christ's sake!'"

Original drawings of Pinocchio's song and dance reveal the sweat and strain of Thomas's intensive creative search. Scratchy, scribbled shapes in red pencil overlaid with black, erased and redrawn again and again, "frenetically searching for the form and feeling inside," as Glen Keane described it. "His were very thin,

little, nervous, spidery lines like touching, trying to feel inside the forms, around the eyes, the nose and the mouth. Almost like he's putting his little fingers in there trying to feel it."[37]

In movement the lines miraculously coalesce, as does Thomas's search for truth. Now his scribbles awaken to life. They brim with joy and charm as the puppet boy sings his heart out and dances with pleasure. Showing off by kicking his jointed legs backward and forward, Pinocchio basks in the warmth of the spotlight and welcomes the cheers and applause. Bravo, Pinocchio! Bravo, Frank Thomas!

Ollie Johnston, unlike Milt Kahl, was a reliably friendly sounding board for Thomas's ideas. Throughout their careers

In The Pointer *(1939), Thomas animated Mickey encountering a huge bear; attempting to save himself, he touts his celebrity: "Why, I'm Mickey Mouse. You've heard of me, I hope."*

both men discussed work-related problems and personal concerns on a daily basis; in time, their friendship became a sturdy seawall against the storms and tempests that arose at the studio.

When Jim Algar moved out of the ex-mortician's crowded boarding house to something better up the block, Thomas and Johnston went with him. And when Thomas and Johnston's salaries increased sufficiently ("I got three raises on *Pinocchio*," says Johnston), the pair moved to Fountain Manor, a two-bedroom apartment

complex at the corner of Fountain and Normandie.[38]

During this period, Thomas animated two of Mickey Mouse's finest performances. In a sequence in *Brave Little Tailor*, Mickey's enthusiastic description of how he killed seven flies "with one blow" is misunderstood by the King and the Princess (the lovely Minnie Mouse); both assume he is an accomplished giant-killer. In *The Pointer* (1939), Mickey plays himself as a hunter who hopes his celebrity will stave off an attack from a threatening bear: "Why, I'm Mickey Mouse. You've heard of me, I hope." Thomas shot film of Walt recording Mickey's voice and used his gestures as inspiration for the animation: "I always thought there was an added sincerity to Mickey's part because of it."[39]

At the end of December 1939, Thomas and Kahl became

the first artists to occupy the new animation building in Burbank, where they began test animation for *Bambi*. "We knew that Walt was determined to make something very unusual with this story and he was counting on us to bring it to life," wrote Thomas years later.[40] The feature about life and death among deer and other forest critters was in development for about three years. Now all the research, inspirational sketches, atmospheric concepts, and story constructions hung "on the ability of two men to breathe life—even more than life—into drawings," wrote Thomas. "Animated characters must be created to communicate story ideas in the most entertaining way. Just being alive was not enough."[41]

A lot was riding on *Bambi*. The war in Europe had cut off most of the studio's lucrative foreign market; in 1940, the expensive new studio, plus the box-office failures of the equally costly *Pinocchio* and *Fantasia* would force Walt and Roy Disney into a fiscal corner.

Bambi was challenging in terms of story and animation. "We had several artists who believed that the true design of the animals should not be lost," Thomas wrote in a letter to Göring Broling, a fan in Sweden, "but it was impossible to animate them in a way that would capture the audience. Many changes had to be made before we had a design that allowed the personality to shine through, and the personality is the most important ingredient in getting audience acceptance of any character in an animated film."[42]

In Felix Salten's book *Bambi* the deer were roe deer, a small type found in Europe and Asia; but in Disney's version, they became robust Virginia deer. "The whole idea of *Bambi* called for grandeur and magnificence, especially in the visuals," wrote Thomas.

How could the Great Prince of the Forest be a little animal the size of a coyote? He had to be overpowering in his size and breadth of his antlers. The oldest and the wisest—certainly not the smallest. Salten made the same type of error in judgment when he chose Faline's sickly brother Gobo to be the one shot by the hunter in the story's most dramatic moment. He had said earlier that Bambi's mother had been killed in the hunter's drive, but not even a full sentence was devoted to that incident. Of course you must remember that this was macho Vienna right after World War I. It was a man's world and women—even mothers—were not very important. The fact that a sickly male would be more important than a loving mother tells you how the Austrians felt about females! In both cases—the roebucks and the death of the mother—Walt shifted the emphasis to make a great film, certainly one that was better than the book that had inspired it.[43]

Thomas and Kahl worked together solving design and animation problems and "got along hand-in-glove," says Thomas. "We respected each other. I was very appreciative that his drawings would make my scenes work so much better. He was appreciative of the fact that I was appreciative of that. He also liked the things I did with the characters, movements I had on them. Things that were a better idea than he had had."[44]

Kahl animated a sequence in which Thumper tells baby Bambi to hop over a log and the deer gets his legs mixed up and ends up on top of the little rabbit; Thomas took on Bambi's learning to talk: saying the words "bird" and "butterfly" (as a butterfly lights on his tail) and a chase up a hill ending with meeting a skunk whom he calls a "flower." At a meeting on March 1, 1940, they showed Walt 200 feet (about two minutes) of their experiments. Thomas always recalled the emotional discussion afterward as Walt uncharacteristically complimented them to their faces.

"After seeing the footage," says Thomas, "he turned to the two animators with tears in his eyes and said, 'Thanks, fellows, that's great stuff, no kidding. Those personalities are pure gold.'" He particularly admired "the gentle flow of the action" and "'that easy pace where you're not hurrying—where you take time. You have value there." Of all Walt's words, Thomas said he and Kahl most treasured these: "It's your picture. You guys have

a feeling for this picture. You belong to this picture."[45]

Bambi went into full production and by April, Eric Larson and Ollie Johnston, just off *Fantasia*, completed the team of supervising animators. Thomas, fully committed to the film, threw himself into it emotionally and physically. He even made extra work for himself when he salvaged the now-famous ice-skating sequence. Walt had decided it wasn't working until Thomas came to a meeting armed with a "pose test" reel he'd spent three days and nights working on alone.

In the sequence, the cocky rabbit Thumper attempts to teach his pal, wobbly-legged, insecure Bambi, how to skate on ice. Thomas exploited all the entertainment possibilities: the contrasting personalities, one boastful and energetic, the other timorous and cautious; the deer's shifting weight on his uncoordinated limbs; the touch of deer hooves on a glassy surface as opposed to a rabbit's wider furry paw; the fun of two kids playing; the danger of injury; the excitement of speeding across ice and landing headlong into a snowbank. Thomas was "very sympathetic" at the time, for he himself was learning to ice-skate and "had all of the beginner's problems." Marie Johnston, Ollie's wife, recalls analytical, nonathletic Thomas skating around a rink while methodically reading an instruction book.[46] "I was like Bambi," admits Thomas. "I couldn't stay on my feet. There was always someone like Thumper who'd come racing by me, having no problem with it, going backward, frontward, doing little flips. I was dumbfounded by it all. I was stuck out there."[47] In the end, the delightful sequence was not only rescued by Thomas's efforts but expanded, and it became one of the film's most memorable.

In their book on the making of *Bambi*, Thomas and Johnston describe Walt as "trapped" by mounting debt, which forced him to make drastic cuts in the film. "Frank had tears in his eyes," they wrote of one meeting, "and Walt leaned over to him with unexpected gentleness. 'Frank, I know it hurts you, but damn it, it's got to go, that's all there is to it.'"[48]

In spite of cutting more than 2,000 feet of film, most of which was already animated, *Bambi*'s release was delayed until August 1942 by two cataclysmic events in 1941: a labor strike at Disney in May (which lasted through September) and America's entry into the war in December. Discussing the former crisis, Thomas wrote that "[a]t that time, we lived from one feature film to the next, with no Disneyland or TV shows or elaborate merchandising to bring in extra revenue. Walt wanted desperately to keep this special crew of talented artists together, but it was simply no longer possible." Thomas's weekly salary as one of the studio's top animators was at that time about $200-plus, while the compensation for layout artists and assistants was much lower, and ink-and-paint women were at the bottom earning a pitiful $18 a week. None of the top animators struck, with the exception of Art Babbitt and Vladimir Tytla. An equally important factor in the strike was the issue of job security.

The deer in Bambi, *developed by Frank Thomas and Milt Kahl, brought a rare compliment from Walt: "Thanks, fellows. Those personalities are pure gold."* BELOW, *Thomas feeds a model for Bambi in 1942.*

When layoffs began in the staff of 1200-plus, they did not spare senior employees and so, said Thomas, "[m]orale was sinking at the very time we needed the strongest resolve and dedication."[49]

In the middle of the acrimonious strike, Walt was invited by the United States Office of the Co-ordinator of Inter-American Affairs (CIAA) to make a goodwill tour of South America as part of the U.S. government's "Good Neighbor" policy. Thomas was the only animator in the group of eighteen handpicked artists, writers, and musicians who spent weeks with Walt visiting Brazil, Argentina, Peru, Bolivia, and other countries. "Supposedly we were to research each country for its folklore, its music, costumes, legends, everything that might be used in a picture about that country," says Thomas. "Mainly we were wined and dined all over the place, where it was real hard to do any work."[50]

When the group returned to the studio in the fall of 1941, the strike was settled. America entered the war at the end of the

year and Walt tried to keep the twenty-nine-year-old Thomas out of the draft. "He kept saying, 'Now don't go enlisting,'" recalls Thomas. "'I can keep you. I can keep you.'" Deferments were granted to personnel working on training or propaganda films, of which Disney turned out more than any other

1 8 5

Frank Thomas, sketching in Argentina, was the only animator among the artists, writers, and musicians Walt brought to South America in 1941.

Hollywood studio. "So I was animating real awful stuff," such as *The Winged Scourge* (1943) (about malaria) and *Education for Death* (1943); (about how Nazis raise their children).

Still, Thomas was vulnerable to the draft, and after failing to get a commission in any branch of the service, he enlisted in the Air Force in December 1942. "I wanted to break codes," not animate on training films "'cause the last year of doing that kind of animation didn't appeal to me at all." So, naturally, the Air Force assigned him to three years directing animated training films in Culver City; with former Disney designer John Hubley, he created a popular character called Trigger Joe for a series of gunnery films. Hubley and several of Thomas's Air Force colleagues were leftist in their political leanings; they kidded Thomas "unmercifully" about his being on the other side of the spectrum, once pinning an advertisement for "modern conservative" furniture on his office door.

Just before the war, at a party thrown by his brother Larry on the Stanford campus, Thomas met a young woman named

Jeanette Armentrout. Tall and elegant, with beautiful, intelligent blue eyes, Ms. Armentrout was visiting from Greeley, Colorado, taking summer classes at Stanford. She and Frank later went on a picnic, but, said Jeanette recently, "before I could get very interested, school was out for the summer and I returned to Colorado." She held a teaching certificate and began teaching at Colorado State. Strong and independent, Jeanette was always grateful, she says, for the "experience in earning my own living."

In 1945, after the war, she took a job teaching in a high school in Redwood City, California, near Palo Alto. "She started writing to me at that point," says Thomas, who was smitten after their initial meeting and had "written letters to her all along." Now that Ms. Armentrout was suddenly "in the back yard" (that is, in California) their letters became more specific. "It took me three and a half years, and a war, and teaching, to realize that he was pretty special," says Jeanette.[51]

She invited him to visit her in Redwood City; he sent her a musical piece he had written titled "Concerto by Me." When he played it for friends, they said it sounded like a proposal. "I said it's okay with me if she takes it like that," says Thomas. "Oooooh!" said his friends. "Good things happened pretty fast after that," he recalls. On a three-day pass, master sergeant Thomas stretched the fifty-mile limit allowed soldiers to 200 miles to see Jeanette. "So we proposed to each other and decided what we were going to do."[52] Thomas was discharged from the service on January 23, 1946 and the couple was married in Colorado on February 16.

Some former Air Force buddies suggested that Thomas work with them at other animation studios in Hollywood, but Thomas decided "the type of picture I wanted to make was only going to be done at Disney."[53] But when Thomas went by the Disney studio to see about getting his job back, the guards at the gate (who all knew him) refused to let him in. He needed a pass because the security setup was "all different now." In the middle of the discussion, Walt happened by. "Oh, hell! C'mon!" he said

taking Thomas's arm and personally escorting him in. He started work that day: April 1, 1946.

Thomas told Walt he wanted to direct for a while, since he had been doing that in the service. "I didn't like it as well as animating by quite a bit," he said, but after the war there were few capable directors of features left at the studio. He and James Algar tried to salvage *The Wind in the Willows*, for which Thomas had animated two sequences before the war. But Walt decided to cut it in half and pair it with *The Legend of Sleepy Hollow*; the two properties together became *The Adventures of Ichabod and Mr. Toad*, released in 1949.

In *Ichabod*, Thomas animated the first half of a sequence in which the superstitious pedagogue rides an old nag home on a dark and scary night. Keeping an eye out for the Headless Horseman, Ichabod's fear makes him see and hear ghostly specters in every tree branch, firefly twinkle, and frog's croak. Thomas was aided, he says, by "great drawings and great ideas" from storymen Joe Rinaldi and Ed Penner ("how Ichabod

   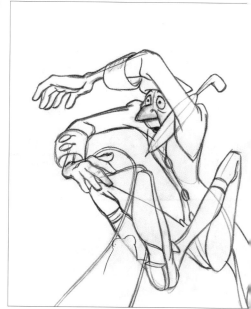

A postwar assignment: Ichabod Crane, whose fear of the Headless Horseman progresses from nuanced nervousness to full-blooded panic.

would pull his hat down over his ears and look funny," etc.); by live-action footage of eccentric dancer Gil Lamb; by Thomas's own attempts at horseback riding ("I was very sympathetic to anyone having problems on a horse."); and by a soundtrack of musician Ollie Wallace whistling as the scared Ichabod ("Boy, I hung onto that track!"). Thomas felt that between the inspirational sketches and the Wallace soundtrack he "couldn't really miss" because "the other guys had already pyramided the thing so well."[54]

Thomas added to the creative mix by giving Ichabod mood swings ranging from twitchy wariness, to jittery nervousness, to

cold-sweat, heart-pounding, bloodcurdling, Adam's apple–gulping panic. The nuanced, highly controlled comic performance builds perfectly to the wild chase that follows, animated by John Sibley (Ichabod and horse reacting as one entity) and Woolie Reitherman (the sword-slashing Headless Horseman).

Thomas was "astounded" when Walt switched him over to villainous characters starting with the Stepmother in *Cinderella*. As noted previously, the actions of the film's human characters were tightly modeled on live-action footage; in the Stepmother's case, grande dame actress Eleanor Audley lent her aloof visage and cold manner (as well as her deep, smooth voice) to the

The wicked stepmother in Cinderella *was Thomas's first villain, an assignment he found "a terrifying chore."*

character. Thomas disliked being tied down to live models and found the assignment "a terrifying chore." While the Stepmother was "very difficult to do and not much fun," Thomas also felt she was "the thing that made the picture work." Her villainy had to be convincing for audiences to feel sympathy for the heroine.[55]

For *Alice in Wonderland*, Thomas animated the overbearing, bellicose Queen of Hearts. But this villainous female was a broad, cartoony caricature and Thomas found few subtleties in her redundant hollering and slapstick belligerence. Walt was of little help in finding the character's personality. "I tried making

Thomas continued in the early 1950s to bring life to villains, some quite mad, such as the Queen of Hearts in Alice in Wonderland, *and paranoid, such as Captain Hook in* Peter Pan.

her a certain way and he said, 'Well, you've lost the menace.' So I made her meaner and tougher and then he said, 'You've lost the comedy.'"[56] Thomas had a better time with the talking Doorknob, one of the first creatures Alice meets in Wonderland; though a minor character, the Doorknob has a more three-dimensional personality than the Queen's. In his brief sequence, he is officious (faithfully guarding the door on which he hangs) and haughty ("What can I do for you?"), yet possessed of a fondness for silly puns ("You gave me quite a turn. Get it? Doorknob? Turn? *Hahahahaha!*")

In those days, Walt controlled the casting of his animators in their roles; based on a hunch or an inspiration, he shifted his best men around like pawns on a chess board. He first had Thomas "tabbed for realistic, sincere, believable action" with cuddly, cute types, such as Pinocchio and Bambi; after the war, he asked him to animate villains, thinking, "Maybe I'll get a new type of villain that won't be a big bad wolf."[57] Thomas's next assignment was Captain Hook in *Peter Pan*, a juicy part that the animator "had a particularly bad time getting started" on.

The problem lay in conflicting concepts from director Gerry Geromini and storyman Ed Penner. "Penner had always seen Hook as a very foppish, not strong, dandy type of guy, who loved all the finery. Kind of a con man. Geronimi saw him as an Ernest Torrence, a mean, heavy sort of character who used his hook menacingly. Well, Walt could see something in both approaches, and I think he delighted in thinking, 'I wonder what the hell Thomas is going to do when he gets this.'"

Thomas felt he was starting out "with absolutely nothing" and considers his first pencil test of Hook to be "one of the low points of my life." Milt Kahl was so upset, he asked Thomas not to show the four scenes to Walt and the crew. "It's nothing," he said. "Just nothing!" Thomas agreed. "It *was* nothing. This is the first scenes of him where he's walking, pacing the deck, and saying 'That Peter Pan, if I get my hook in him!' or whatever. He was neither menacing nor foppish. Sort of halfway live action and he didn't have any 'entertainment!'"

Walt watched the test and the crew watched Walt. Thomas sweated and died silently inside. He knew that if Walt expressed

the slightest doubt "fifty people would jump up thinking, 'Here's my chance to impress Walt!' They'd say, 'I think his head's too big. I think his feet are too small. I think he's too this. I think he's too that!' hoping Walt would say, 'Yeah. I think you're right.'" This time, however, Walt came to Thomas's aid. "He said, "Well, that last scene has something I like. I think you're beginning to get him. I think we better wait and let Frank go on a little further. I think you're beginning to get hold of something here," he repeated, offering a glimmer of hope to the wretched animator.[58]

Thomas later said that actor Hans Conried, the voice of Hook, helped greatly in pulling the character together. "Because he could be supercilious and he would still have this underlying strength," says Thomas. "Even when he asked for his gold-plated hook, you know, when he was going to dress up to trick Tinker Bell into revealing Peter Pan's hiding place. Even there you felt that there was strength underneath this guy. He was mean and so Peter Pan really had a problem with him."[59]

Thomas and Walt got along well, as both enjoyed tinkering and developing things endlessly. (Indeed, Walt's beloved theme parks are perpetual works in progress.) Thomas believed, however, that while Walt excelled at developing stories, he was jealous of his animators because "animation was the one job he couldn't do. And he always resented this a little bit." Walt kidded the animators, ruefully threatening to replace them with the Audio-Animatronics robots used in the parks.[60]

The close friendship and "twinning" coincidences in both Thomas's and Ollie Johnston's lives continued through the war years and beyond. In January 1943, Johnston married vivacious Marie Worthey, who worked in the Ink and Paint department. They moved into the Fountain Avenue apartment and Thomas (who was serving in the Air Corps animation Los Angeles unit) moved across the hall to a smaller place. During the war the two buddies continued discussing animation problems on training films as well as Disney's theatrical releases. Marie remembered when she was dating Ollie, he and Frank would drive her home from work on occasion. She sat between them in the front seat as they talked shop. "It wasn't very long," she says, "before I found out, you don't say a word. You don't talk, Marie, until we get to Fountain Avenue."[61]

Frank and Jeanette married and moved into his one-room apartment. When Jeanette became pregnant, Jeanette and Marie went house hunting and found a duplex in Glendale, which the two couples bought and shared for two years. "Before that even," said Jeanette, "Ollie and Marie and Frank had bought property and so we were both planning [to build] houses at the same time." The war delayed the couples' dream houses in Flintridge, a picturesque community in the mountains near Pasadena. "Then when we were ready to build," said Jeanette, "we couldn't, because it cost two much [twelve dollars per square foot], so we waited for prices to come down."

It snowed in Flintridge the day the Johnstons moved into their new house on New Year's eve 1948; some months later the Thomases moved into their home, located next door, just down a hill from the Johnstons. "That August we both had babies within a week of each other. Our first sons," says Jeanette. "They were falling off the trees on Flintridge Avenue in August," quips Marie. The Johnston family includes two sons, Rick and Kenneth; the Thomas family includes daughter Ann, and sons Gregg, Theodore, and Doug. In 1965 the two families bought and shared property in the town of Julian, California, near San Diego.

Before the freeways, it took about an hour by car to get from Flintridge to the studio in Burbank. Thomas and Johnston used their daily shared drive to build up steam to face the day's work; at dusk, the ride home became a decompression chamber during which problems and triumphs were vented and hashed over. They discussed

> the picture and what was wrong with it and what it needed and the scenes we had coming up. And even if we were on different pictures we would still know the problems that each was facing. And we'd talk about them on the way home. And you'd talk it over and talk it over, and back and forth. When you finally got to work the next morning you had a pretty clear idea what you wanted to do.[62]

They "were like split sections of the same soul," observes John Pomeroy, who worked with Thomas and Johnston in the 1970s. "And they relied heavily on each other in every way, spiritually and emotionally as well. 'Cause they went through some difficult times where they probably held each other up. They would influence each other's judgment and give each other pats on the back and reinforce, nurture each other. Every production that bond would get strengthened until they were just inseparable."[63]

After Walt cast his lead animators on a character "it was up to you to find the good stuff that was coming up," says Thomas regarding his methods for getting choice scenes. If a sequence he especially wanted was due in six weeks, and another "that didn't look too good" was available in three weeks, he would "figure out a way to stretch" whatever he was working on at the time. He might also "go up and talk to the story people and say, 'Gee, I'd sure like to work on your sequence.'

"You maneuvered to try to get the things you wanted," explains Thomas, "and you also maneuvered to try to get the footage animated the way you felt it ought to be." When his concept of a role differed from the director's, Thomas fought for his point of view. He believed that since the animator is "the actor," he "had to feel right about it. It had to come from his creative juices. There's a place where you have to do what the director says, but also other places where you can alter the interpretation."[64]

Thomas and Johnston became adept at maneuvering, particularly after Walt's death. For example, they respected director Reitherman's decisions as final, but "if they really wanted to sell something [to him]," according to Glen Keane, "they would scramble and do whatever they could to try and convince him [to go with their idea]." Once, during the making of *The Rescuers*, while Reitherman was on vacation, they storyboarded a crucial section and "actually posed out the animation for the whole sequence, so that they could convince him that this is the way that they should go with it. It worked great and that's how it is in the film. Woolie came back and loved it!"[65] Thomas once said his job was to keep Reitherman pointed in the right direction, "like a farmer with the plough."[66]

"It always varied as to who won the arguments," even when Walt was alive, says Thomas. "If you were in the middle of a real tough argument and you felt strongly about it, once again you would maneuver and you would not cut your scenes into the [story] reel until just the hour before Walt was going to look at it. So no one else could see it, no one else knew it was there. And they're all seeing it for the first time." The element of surprise at these meeting usually worked. Walt often sided with Thomas's and/or

TOP, *Frank, his wife, Jeanette, and daughter, Ann, 1949;* BOTTOM, *a Thomas family Christmas card, late 1950s.*

Johnston's cogently worked out version "even if a scene was not very good. He had faith we could come back, that we would be able to get it on later scenes and then we could come back and correct [the earlier versions]. Without that support," says Thomas, "I would have been shot down. I would have been kicked out of the studio."

Because Thomas played the game so well, some co-workers saw him as "a Cardinal Richelieu personality," referring to the seventeenth-century French statesman known for his iron will, cunning, and ambition. "He would work behind the wings," says John Pomeroy. "If someone was displeasing him he could work to get them demoted or fired or dismissed from the production or moved to another animator. He never would come right out and confront." After Walt's death, however, during the making of *The Aristocats,* Thomas did confront another animator and apparently pulled rank. Eric Cleworth, a character animator from *Peter Pan* on, animated two comic dogs and a villainous butler in a slapstick chase in the first half of *Aristocats*; the sequence was successful and a follow-up was requested from the front office. "So," says Thomas, "we wrote a sequence in for the dogs to come back and I said, 'Hmmmmm. Incidentally, that's the kind of stuff I like to do.' So I kept trying to make a deal with Eric, but he wanted to do them because he enjoyed doing them the first time around. 'Halvers? You take half and I take half? Huh?' Well, his spirit finally broke and I got all of it and then he left the studio. I don't know if that had anything to do with it or not," says Thomas disingenuously.[67]

Thomas's competitiveness was mostly triggered by his perfectionism; he could not tolerate sloppy or inadequate work, and he had an overwhelming desire to make the films as good as possible. He expected a similar dedication from everyone he worked with. But his son Theodore believes a deeper motivation for the degree to which he excelled was "because he's afraid of being hurt. To him the world is a scary place." But instead of becoming belligerent or defensive, his fear became a creative stimulus for his imagination. "I think part of his incredible mastery of personifying everything," says Theodore Thomas, "comes from a fundamental way of dealing with the world. It's the way children control their nightmares." Put a face on a scary dream "and suddenly it becomes manifest and you can deal with it."[68]

Thomas's competitiveness did not diminish with old age. John Culhane remembers that during the filming of the documentary Frank and Ollie in 1993, Frank "kicked [Ollie] under the table because he didn't want Ollie telling me [a story] he wanted to use. Frank is competitive," says Culhane, "like crazy!"[69]

Milt Kahl was no match for the nimble, determined duo of Thomas and Johnston, who formed a veritable flying wedge of purpose. While they "maneuvered" and fought for juicy characters and sequences, Kahl sat in his Ivory Tower office and took on whatever he was given. He may have bellowed loudly about animating difficult-to-draw princes and princesses, but his massive ego blindly welcomed the challenge of drawing what others could not. "Milt could have put his foot down, but he didn't realize what was happening," said Marc Davis.[70] When he finally did—and in the 1970s there were open confrontations about the usefulness of Kahl's drawings and his animation—an acrimonious rift developed between Kahl and the Thomas–Johnston duo that never healed. "I don't think it was because I was better at doing that sort of thing [drawing human characters]," said Kahl. "I think it was because I was outmaneuvered." Kahl became "rather bitter" about "some of the people who I thought considered that we were working together and I find we really weren't."[71]

"They came from an interesting time," muses Pomeroy about the Nine Old Men in general. "It was like being out in the open savanna with a lion pack. It was survival of the fittest. And because [Walt's] finances would get lean, only the best would be kept on. So these guys had an incredible rivalry."

Sometimes Frank Thomas even took Walt on. As with Bambi, he would try to change Walt's mind (a most difficult thing to do) if he saw a juicy, entertaining sequence going to waste. In Lady and the Tramp, Thomas was assigned a section where the two dogs, Lady and Tramp, go on a first date. Behind an Italian restaurant, the owner and cook entertain the pooches with a song while they dine on spaghetti al fresco, under stars

and hanging laundry. By accident, Thomas happened on an old story reel and found that most of this action had been thrown out. "Walt thought it was kind of distasteful or something or other," recalls Thomas, "but the business that replaced it I thought just didn't give you anything." Thomas called story head Ed Penner and said he'd like to give the old material a try.

"A couple of dogs eating spaghetti doesn't sound real attractive," he had to admit, "and yet I saw the real Chaplin and Harold Lloyd symbol of things." No doubt Thomas was thinking of The Gold Rush, in which Chaplin ate his shoe like a fastidious gourmet. Lady and the Tramp offered a situation of similarly delicate absurdity: two dogs inadvertently slurping the same strand of spaghetti and kissing. When their muzzles touch, Thomas had Lady arc her head away into a blushing pose, while Tramp smiles in surprised delight. With his nose he gently pushes the last meatball over to her and Lady gives him a look of love. To make this difficult business come off required consummate taste, extraordinary acting ability, and entertainment knowhow. As with Bambi's ice skating, Thomas saved a difficult (and nearly discarded) sequence. He made it work so well, the sequence became an icon not only of the movie, but of romance itself.

Thomas and Johnston both disagreed with Walt regarding the character development of the three elderly good fairies in Sleeping Beauty. Distracted at the time (the mid-1950s) by his plans for Disneyland, Walt reluctantly came to meetings on the film. When he did, he hurriedly disbursed suggestions, such as "all the fairies could be the same." Donald Duck's clonelike nephews (Huey, Dewey, and Louie) came unhappily to Thomas and Johnston's minds. Both animators hated the idea and felt that Walt would too "if he saw it in the final picture. So we figured," says Thomas, "we better stick our necks out and try to get some different personalities here that will play with each other."[72] Each fairy had to be virtuous, but "how many ways are there of being good?"

He and Johnston studied old ladies. "I spent hours in the grocery store, usually at the dogfood counter," said Thomas. Once at a wedding reception he found himself "studying all the older women there" and "picked up some excellent pointers on necks, ears, hairdos, and style of dressing." On vacation in Colorado one summer, he took home movies surreptitiously of "a perfect type" who "moved just beautifully." His research revealed that "when old ladies move, they bounce like mechanical toys. They paddle, paddle, paddle on their way. They stand straight and their arm movements are jerky. Their hands fly out from the body. The reason for all this is they're afraid to get off-balance, afraid they will fall over."[73]

Eventually the fairies took shape. "It wasn't too hard to get Flora," says Thomas, "because she was masterful and forgetful, and had an aggressive streak in her. Merryweather was the one who didn't like being told what to do, but she did it. It was hard to make

Two dogs chewing on spaghetti sounds unromantic, but in Thomas's sensitive hands, the sequence became an icon of romance.

Ollie Johnston and Frank Thomas view test animation for the three good fairies in Sleeping Beauty *on a Moviola, circa 1958. Thomas's intensity working on this film landed him in the hospital.*

her just right." Fauna, based on the Colorado old lady sighting, was serene. "Nothing seemed to disturb her. Sweet and affectionate."[74]

Thomas's intense work habits took a physical toll during *Sleeping Beauty*. "Frank was working so hard on those characters and [supervising] other animators working under him," observes Dale Oliver, an assistant animator on the film. "The stress on Frank was overwhelming. He developed a huge red blotch on his face, three inches across. [He was] going to the doctor once a week. Stress just killing him."[75]

There were also tensions with Eyvind Earle, *Sleeping Beauty*'s production designer. "Never before had Walt given one person the freedom and authority to take over the designing of an entire animated feature," wrote Earle in his autobiography. "The old-time animators, who were revered as gods at the Disney Studios, were in the habit of telling the directors of each sequence what colors they wanted their characters to be, and working directly with the ink and paint department." Earle

refused to share his authority or to compromise his stylized vision for the film. "One day two of the top animators couldn't stand it any longer," he writes. They complained directly to Walt and were frustrated when he backed Earle.[76]

Years later Thomas told Dan Haskett "he ended up in the hospital a couple of times for his intensity. Just after *Snow White* and just after *Sleeping Beauty*. He said he worked all through *Beauty* with a blemish on his face that looked like a bruise."[77]

Haskett, a trainee animator under Thomas on *The Fox and the Hound*, recalls Thomas as "an extremely methodical person." Once, reviewing a scene with Haskett took so long, the young trainee fell asleep! "God help me," says Haskett, laughing. "He'd be sitting there: 'Well, let's try this one. Well, naw, that doesn't work. Let's try it this way. Well? Naw!' I'd be sitting at his desk. He was going over and over it. He just wanted it to be just so. He would work and work and work over a thing. He was very intense."[78]

"You can't just sit down and do it," Thomas once explained about immersing himself in the animation:

> You start in there slowly and gradually you get up a head of steam and then things start to jell and work together. And it is very difficult to be interrupted in the middle of that. It intensifies your feelings and emotions and if you're happy about something that has happened, you find yourself giggling–real giddy while you're working away. Suddenly, if you're annoyed with something, you get so mad. You're filled with hate! Lots of times I'd get furious about something that's pretty inconsequential, but [it was] because I got such a buildup of nervous tension.[79]

Stress also brought on a hiatal hernia, a protrusion of part of the stomach through the diaphragm. The alarming periodic condition, which affects breathing and swallowing, became more pronounced during Thomas's late fifties.[80]

As the pianist in the Firehouse Five Plus Two, Ward Kimball's Dixieland jazz band, Thomas burned his candle at both ends; sometimes the group played engagements around Hollywood until 2 A.M. on weekends and Monday nights. Far from adding to his exhaustion, though, he claimed the music gigs refreshed him. "I did my best work on Tuesdays," he says. "I was all relaxed and no problems." His perch on the piano stool also served as a people-watching observatory. "If you sit like this for four hours, big smile to the audience, you can be thinking anything you want and studying," he says. "You get a group of eighty people, you find that they break down into very distinct groups, psychologically and in the timing. If somebody's different, they just stand out.

> Some guy will come in and he's happy, but he's elbowed his way in and he's all over the place. Or some girl is too giggly and too spirited, just too *too*. Each one is different in the way they move and their timing. So you watch these and you know that you've got a character for a picture.[81]

OPPOSITE, *Frank Thomas (far right) relaxed by playing piano in the Firehouse Five Plus Two, a Dixieland jazz band formed by Ward Kimball (on trombone) in the 1940s;* THIS PAGE, *Thomas used his piano perch for people-watching opportunities;* BELOW, *entertaining at a 1947 studio function was the Huggajeedy 8, forerunner of the Firehouse Five Plus Two. Thomas is behind Walt Disney (seated right) and Kimball stands at right.*

Jeanette Thomas recognized how "terrifically stimulating and restoring" the band was for her husband.[82] "He loves an audience," she says. "He's a ham, that's why he's a good animator." She saw his professional piano playing as "an ego booster" that provided a release from "the frustration that he had to keep bottled up during the week." He did not bring home the stresses of the studio; at dinner each evening with his family, his constant sense of humor came to the fore putting a funny spin on the day's events. In general, according to his wife, Thomas is "one of the least mercurial artists that I've ever known."[83]

The Sword in the Stone contains one of Thomas's favorite sequences. Merlin, the legendary magician, changes himself and

A sequence in The Sword in the Stone *of a lovesick girl squirrel and a reluctant human boy transformed by magic into a squirrel features one of Thomas's finest acting performances.*

the boy Wart (the future King Arthur) into squirrels in order to "learn the great truths of nature." Originally, the squirrels' main action was trying to avoid a hungry wolf; that changed when Thomas auditioned a voice actress able to improvise nonsense words ("squirrel talk") that made emotional sense. "It changed my concept of the picture," says Thomas. The sequence developed into a romantic pursuit by a young female squirrel who didn't realize she was in love with a disguised human (Wart).

Aggressively amorous, the girl squirrel's treetop chase of her reluctant swain is full of charm and delightful invention: quick kisses, aborted embraces, and her tail used as a ensnaring prehensile prop.

Thomas wanted the girl squirrel to have "an innocent animal quality." One night, playing with the Firehouse Five at a club in Burbank, he saw the right type among the dancing couples. "She just sort of radiated appeal," Thomas recalls. "She was

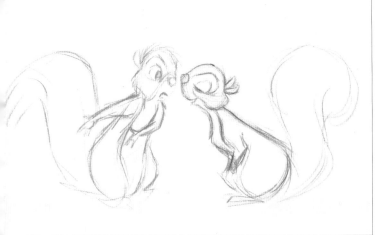

..., but not pretty-pretty. But it was mainly her timing, her movements, how quickly she moved. She was quite a gal!"[84] And she became quite a squirrel.

Walt liked Thomas's early footage so well, he suggested old Merlin get involved with a "granny squirrel." Waving her ample tail at the disguised wizard, the hefty granny playfully pulls his whiskers, hugs and tickles him; horrified by this interspecies attempt at *amour*, Merlin announces with great dignity: "I'm not a squirrel. I'm an old man." To prove it, he transforms himself and Wart back into human form. The explosive change insults and angers the elderly squirrel, but the young one is, at first, confused and uncomprehending. Then she is devastated, and so is the audience. Thomas created a perfectly structured, emotional rollercoaster and made his cast perform brilliantly. In the bargain, he broke our hearts.

The lighthearted penguin song and dance with Dick Van Dyke in *Mary Poppins* should have been a piece of cake compared to Thomas's more complex assignments. But Walt told the live-action director not to worry about the animation; that whatever he and Van Dyke came up with, his animators (Thomas and Johnston) would top them. As a result, camera setups were often too tight to accommodate the cartoon penguins that were to be animated later. On the live-action set, Thomas's warning that "this storyboard isn't going to work" was ignored. When footage came in of Van Dyke dancing, says Thomas, "here's his feet lying all around and stepping on [where] my penguins [were going to be animated]." So Thomas and Johnston were forced to make the penguins jump over Van Dyke's long legs or duck as he spun around, making the number more spontaneous and fun. "All of that worked," admits Thomas. "Walt was right. It forced us to be more imaginative and to work harder."[85]

Walt's input also saved *The Jungle Book*. When Thomas and Johnston started on the film, they were concerned, says Thomas, "because there didn't seem to be any heart or warmth to the story. It was just this kid [Mowgli] going through the jungle meeting a lot of strange characters. There was no mother's love, no romance, nothing you could really develop that would give the audience something they could identify with." And where was suspense going to come from? Should they bring the tiger in at the beginning of the picture or later?

Walt, distracted by micromanaging his continually enlarging entertainment empire, was in failing health; he would, in fact, die before the film was finished. At an early meeting, however, he told his top animators "Don't bother me with that icky-sticky story stuff. You guys just get the personality. That's what I want from you." In other words, ignore Rudyard Kipling's text and concentrate on finding entertainment in the characters.

The dancing penguin waiters in Mary Poppins *(1964), animated by Thomas and Ollie Johnston, stole the show from Dick Van Dyke.*

Frank Thomas, at age 61, working on Robin Hood *(1973).*

When Walt asked bandleader Phil Harris to record a test track for a bear (a bit or "cameo" part), the animators wondered where this old saloon singer would fit into things. But Harris's warm, happy-go-lucky vocal quality and heartfelt improvisations inspired the animators. "Yeah, we knew we were in business. We had a character," said Thomas. After the recording session, Walt did a little dance step, snapping his fingers to show how this jazzy, irresponsible bear named Baloo should act. "This marked the turning point of the picture," according to Thomas, "because from now on we had a story about Baloo and Mowgli and friendship." Thomas and Johnston worked on permeating the film with the relationship between the boy and the bear. "You never knew where it came from, but you had a feeling of a strong friendship here which we wanted and needed so badly for the picture."[86]

In a way, the two animators transmuted their own feelings regarding friendship, loyalty and trust to Mowgli and Baloo. Near the end of the film, they animated back-to-back sequences that were critical to the project's emotional life. Johnston led off with Baloo and the panther Bagheera arguing about why Mowgli must return to the man-village; Baloo is loath to disappoint the boy, who trusts him and believes they will be buddies in the wild forever. In Thomas's subsequent sequence, Baloo breaks the bad news to Mowgli, who feels betrayed. "Without these [sequences] coming off properly," says Johnston, "all this character work we had done wouldn't pay off. The section that I had certainly tested me and I think it tested our friendship, because I had to rely so much on Frank for help, and I think he relied on me for his sequence." "It also tested our abilities as animators," adds Thomas.[87]

When Walt died of cancer in December 1966, Thomas sadly remembered that "nobody could work for a couple of weeks at all." He felt, however, that they had lost Walt and his spirit years before. "Because he had been pulling away from animation as he got into other areas of the product," such as television, live-action films, and the theme parks. "We would still say, 'Walt, can't you come in and look at this? We need help on it.' And he'd come in and look at it and say, 'You're not in any trouble,' and walk out. That was sort of a cruel way of making us stand on our own. Like a mother bear shoving her cubs up a tree, or out in the river: 'Come on, kids, it's time for you to swim by yourself.'"[88]

Thomas worked on five more features between 1966 and

his retirement (with Johnston) in January 1978: *The Aristocats* (1970), *Robin Hood* (1973), *The Rescuers* (1977), *The Many Adventures of Winnie the Pooh* (1977), and *The Fox and the Hound* (1981).

"When we started *Aristocats*," says Thomas, "we were very aware of the fact that we didn't have Walt anymore to guide us, to give us a direction, to bounce ideas off of." There is, indeed, a walking-on-eggs feel to the above features; the older animators were groping their way through projects without Walt's guidance and encouragement, and working with younger, unproven talents. Nevertheless, the films became box-office hits and saved animation from being scuttled at Disney. But making them was neither a happy nor satisfactory situation. "We were never sure we were bringing it off," says Thomas, "and [sometimes] we didn't bring it off. We had parts of *Robin Hood* and *Aristocats* where we had high hopes and were pretty sure it wasn't working and didn't know what to do."[89]

Thomas once expressed his concern about *Robin Hood* in a 1973 letter to animator Larry Ruppel. "We obviously decided to keep it on the 'fun' side, but I have worried that the audiences would feel it was too flimsy—that we were not being quite serious enough with our characters.

> For instance, does anyone really fear Prince John? Is Robin ever worried about his ability to achieve something or even how it should be done? Did winning Maid Marian make any difference in Robin's behavior? In real life it would have. The audiences will not know the difference if you are serious or comic in these decisions, but they will know that they liked the characters, believed in them and enjoyed them, or that they didn't.

And if they didn't they'll tell their friends and the picture will not be a success![90]

Thomas wrote Ruppel one month after *The Fox and the Hound* opened in 1981: "I worked on it for about a year before I retired [in 1978], animating the two pups meeting and playing and laying out many other scenes for younger animators to take over."

They've been using my drawings as the basis of their publicity, so I guess I had some kind of influence on the picture. I feel that it is very straight in its storytelling and never completes any of its ideas. Nothing really comes of the birds, or the owl, or the widow, or anybody; they are too busy telling their story to develop any of the rich ideas that should have been [in] it. There. I've said my piece. . . .[91]

"The films of the fifties, sixties, and seventies," writes Christopher Finch, "were different in that they were predicated, almost exclusively, upon the character animator's ability to breathe life into heroes like Peter Pan and Mowgli, heroines like Cinderella and Bianca, comic characters like Gus and Jaq (the mice in *Cinderella*), and villains like Cruella De Vil and Shere Khan. The other weapons in the animation armory [bold camera movements, effects animation, other technical devices to enhance dramatic situations and advance the story] were assigned to backup roles."[92]

Thomas and Johnston didn't fully retire. The desire to pass on over forty years of animation knowledge led to a tome that required nearly five years of research and writing. Finally published in 1981, *Disney Animation: The Illusion of Life* is one of the finest books ever written on the development of Disney animation techniques. Certainly it is the most authoritative and articulate book of its kind, from two of the medium's greatest practitioners of personality animation. It quickly become an internationally recognized "Bible" for animation students, professionals, and Disney fans alike.

In writing the book—and subsequent books, such as *Too Funny for Words* (1987), *Walt Disney's Bambi: The Story and the Film* (1990), *The Disney Villain* (1993)—Thomas and Johnston became teachers like both of their fathers, but on a grand scale. They also became celebrities. Book reviews led to newspaper and magazine articles, and book signings led to appearances on major network radio and television talk shows.

Their grandfatherly looks, gracious manners, self-effacing humor, and genuine charm presented an appealing image of Disney animation, one that the Disney studio exploited. For over fifteen years, the studio sent the pair and their wives on grand tours (from Japan to Australia and points in between) to promote everything from feature film re-releases to video cassettes to original animation art sales. Thomas and Johnston became a fused entity—Frank and Ollie—icons of Disney animation. Through their avuncular presence, the public's affection for all things Disney was given a channel of expression.

Their deification culminated in the acclaimed documentary *Frank and Ollie* (produced in 1995 by Theodore Thomas and his wife Kuniko Okubo), which a *New York Times* film review called "an enthralling portrait of the legendary animators Frank Thomas and Ollie Johnston."[93] They were now legends in their own lifetimes. In 1999, they lent their voices and images (as caricatures) to Warner's animated feature *The Iron Giant*, directed by former Disney trainee Brad Bird.

Frank and Ollie's magic was real, as this writer witnessed during one extraordinary occasion in June 1982. It occurred in Yugoslavia, where Thomas and Johnston were being honored by the Zagreb International Animation Festival.

On a cloudless, blue-sky morning, the then seventy-year-old animators and their wives were driven one and a half hours away to the small town of Cakovec. Two limousines containing the guests, photographers and festival officials arrived to find the old town curiously empty. The local movie theater was outfitted with a Disney sign and the cover of Frank and Ollie's first book; birds chirped in the nearby forest but there were no people. It was a scene from the finale of *On the Beach*.

The guests and entourage were led in leisurely fashion under an ancient brick-and-mortar viaduct into a bright, sunlit courtyard. Surprise! There the entire town had assembled and a band of children, dressed in native folk costumes, began to play carved wooden balalaikas. The bright music silenced the birds. Two rows of children stood at attention as a couple of tiny youngsters stepped forward to present large floral bouquets to Mr. Frank and Mr. Ollie. *On the Beach* had suddenly turned into *Naughty Marietta*.

All who witnessed this charming and affectionate presentation were moved to tears, as were the two honored guests who choked out their thank-yous. The movie and still photographers went into overdrive as Frank and Ollie were slowly escorted into a carpeted, chapel-like building where the mayor made a welcoming speech. Afterward in the courtyard, children waving handkerchiefs danced and sang as the string band played again.

The formal ceremony was followed by a tour of the small Cakovec Animated Film School, where Frank and Ollie signed autographs and drew cartoons for the students. A lavish lunch featuring pilsner and pork soup was served in an outdoor restaurant in the woods, while Yugoslavian film critics and historians interviewed the two men; then it was nap time for all for an hour at a nearby motel, before Frank and Ollie made an appearance at the local movie theater, now filled with five hundred excited kids.

There, films from the Film School were screened; when

Frank and Ollie appeared on stage, the theater erupted in applause and cheers. Presented with a book on the region, they gave emotional thanks for an extraordinary day, and were then swept outside to waiting cars while Disney shorts held the audience. "Come back," shouted several tearful students who watched as the two animation gods literally drove into the sunset.

The infirmities of old age gradually slowed and eventually stopped the travels of Disney's two goodwill ambassadors. Thomas's 1998 Christmas card contained a succinct photocopied note that reported on his and Jeanette's recent physical trials, including his stroke. It is vintage Frank Thomas: breezy, humorous, and optimistic; yet unsparingly candid, astringently honest, and with not a jot of self-pity:

> Lessee now—Stroke in '96—
> Jeanette in hospital '97 and no Christmas.
> 1998, after nearly two years of trying to get my right leg to be a team player, both legs failed me at the same time and I took a header in the garden in September. There went the old left leg. So much for '98.
>
> Nine huge screws and a steel plate will hold the left leg together but the right one seems hopelessly entangled with the rosemary and thyme. So here's a big WHEE-ee-ee to '98. May your joys in 1999 be endless and remember that 2000 is not far away.

Few actors ever get the chance to play the variety of parts Frank Thomas did and fewer still are able to reach the deeper human emotions that he tapped. And he did it with drawings.

Thomas once claimed a day didn't go by that he didn't figure he "was in the wrong profession, that I should get out of animation." But he didn't quit because he recognized the unique opportunity his tenure at the Disney studio provided.

"I'd get so mad at something that was going on," he recalls. "Part of the time it was my own inability to draw what I wanted. But I'd get so mad at the setup and the people I was working under and the people that shouldn't even be at the studio, and the dumb bunnies, and all these people who were causing trouble. And I'd want to go storming up to Walt and say, 'You're wasting all your money because you've got all these stupid people!'"

Then he'd cool down or run to a colleague, mostly Ollie Johnston, but often (in the early days) to Milt Kahl to say, "Whatever happens, no matter how upset I get, don't let me quit! This place is too unique, too wonderful, too different.

"I wouldn't be happy if I missed out on this experience."[94]

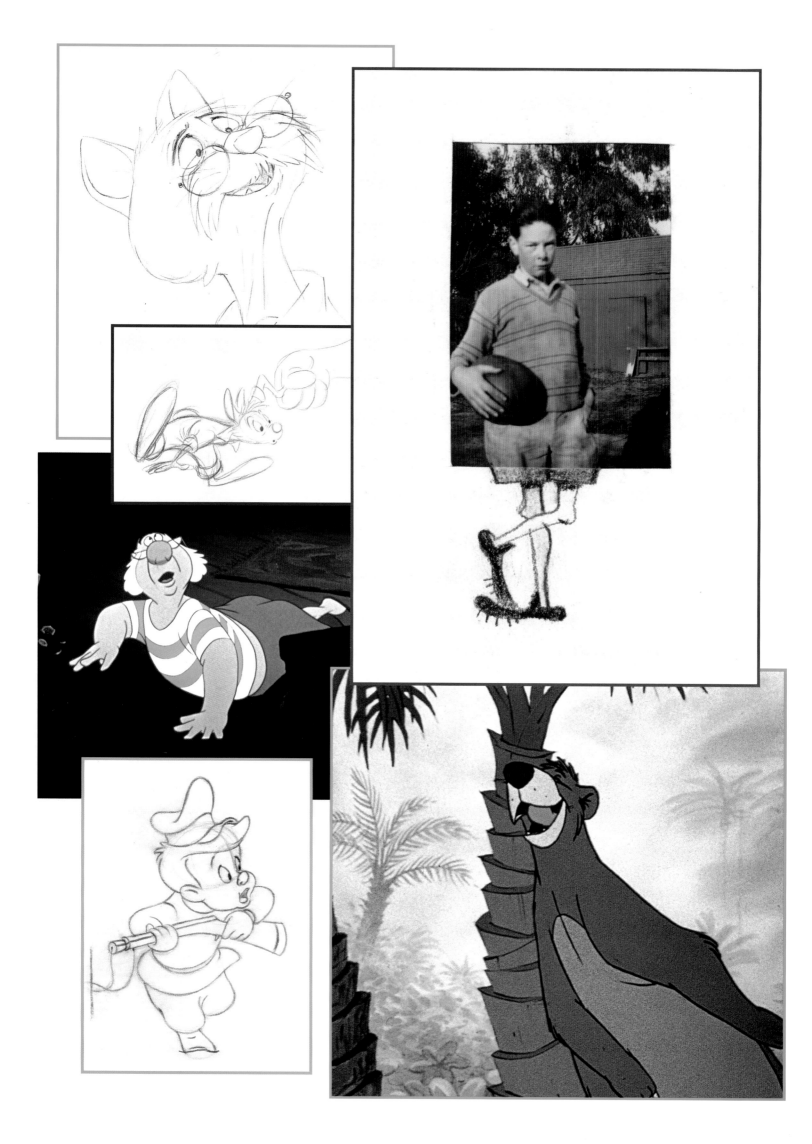

CHAPTER seven

Ollie Johnston

"I t's surprising what an effect touching can have in an animated cartoon," Ollie Johnston once said. "You expect it in a live-action picture or in your daily life, but to have two pencil drawings touching each other, you wouldn't think would have much of an impact. But it does."[1]

The Ollie Johnston touch: a super-sensitive visual tactility that deeply affects audiences. You find it in numerous Disney shorts and features. In *101 Dalmatians*, for example, Pongo comforts his mate Perdita, who cowers from evil Cruella De Vil under a kitchen stove. Although the confining space (and tight close-ups) allow little movement, Johnston elicits a range of feelings from the two dogs: apprehension and fear, sympathy and love. By the sequence's end, the delicate emotion is sealed with the Johnston touch: a "kiss" in which Pongo gently licks Perdita's tearful cheek.

OPPOSITE, *young footballer Ollie Johnston (with legs later drawn by Ward Kimball); characters who have received the "Johnston touch" include Rufus the cat in* The Rescuers, *Brer Rabbit in* Song of the South, *Mr. Smee in* Peter Pan, *Peter in* Peter and the Wolf, *and Baloo the bear in* The Jungle Book.
ABOVE, *Johnston in the 1950s.*

Throughout most of *The Jungle Book*, Johnston externalizes the close-buddy feelings between wild child Mowgli and Baloo the bear with an array of touches—everything from scratches, tickles, and punches, to literal bear hugs. The easy physicality of their relationship intensifies the strain of their disagreement and separation late in the film.

In *Robin Hood*, writes John Culhane, "there were so many vibrations passing back and forth between Prince John, the vain and mangy lion, and his gaptoothed snake sycophant, Sir Hiss, that it amounted to an animated Sensaround."[2]

Slapstick comedy emphasizes the master–slave relationship of domineering Captain Hook and his obsequious first mate–servant Smee in *Peter Pan*. When horrified Smee thinks he has decapitated Hook while shaving him, he grabs the allegedly disembodied noggin and pulls it, which enrages the captain; in another sequence, Hook's head cold becomes worse when Smee inadvertently hits the boss's skull with a hammer. Later, Hook uses his sharp namesake prosthesis to scoop Smee off his feet while pointedly issuing orders, as the stooge dangles helplessly.

Even when characters don't physically touch, Johnston keenly expresses their inner emotional life. In *Peter and the Wolf*, young Peter leaves home to hunt for the wolf by himself;

in pantomime, Johnston conveys the boy's excited apprehension as he ventures forth in the snow. Andreas Deja greatly admires that particular scene; he studied the animation closely when the original drawings were reshot for the toon mob finale of *Who Framed Roger Rabbit*. "I said to my assistant, I can't do that!" recalls Deja. "I just can't do something like that. The simplicity, the honesty, the emotion. The essence of a little kid with his toy gun going into the wood. All of that was there." It made Deja rethink his own philosophy about the animation medium, about "what's possible and what's important."

Johnston's words of wisdom to Deja years earlier finally made sense: "Ollie saying that you're not supposed to animate drawings. You're supposed to animate feelings! That's just so profound to me," says Deja. "Makes you a totally different artist once you focus on something like that."[3]

Johnston's animation drawings are graphic manifestations of his own hypersensitivity. In contrast to Frank Thomas's visible struggle with *his* drawings, Johnston's sketches appear to have been "coaxed into being," as Glen Keane puts it.[4] Light-blue lines made with the flat edge of a graphite pencil float, wispy and mysterious, on separate sheets of paper. Forms, faces, gestures, and attitudes are barely suggested. When the drawings are flipped one after the other, however, the phantasms on textured bond become messengers of emotion. And when the lines intersect—when they "touch"—sparks of recognition shiver through the onlooker.

The lines touch comically when poor Brer Rabbit cannot escape Brer Bear's viselike handshake, or when Orville, the seagull aviator in *The Rescuers*, smashes his rear end onto terra firma in a spectacularly incompetent landing. (Ouch!) Most often, though, Johnston's lines touch the heart in ways that bring forth empathetic tears from moviegoers.

An extraordinarily heartrending sequence in *The Rescuers* is by Johnston: the elderly cat Rufus commiserates with Penny, an orphan girl rejected by potential foster parents. Rubbing against the child (as cats are wont to do), grandfatherly Rufus hears Penny's sad tale, then offers her sympathy and encouragement. Cheered, she picks up her fuzzy friend and carries him clumsily (as kids are wont to do) to supper.

"I seem[ed] to have a kind of reservoir of feelings about how people felt in certain situations," Ollie Johnston once explained. "And while somebody else might be more interested in the drawing of the character in that situation, I was particularly interested in how that character actually felt." Johnston noted that he liked to watch people, how they moved and acted; but primarily he "was interested in their emotions. And," he added, "I always had been."

Oliver Martin Johnston, Jr., was born on October 31, 1912 in Palo Alto, California. His father, Oliver Martin, Sr., was the head of the Romance Languages department at

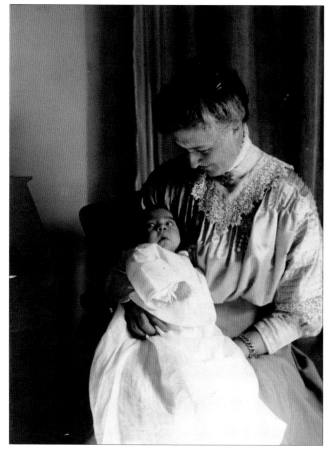

Stanford University. A self-made man, Oliver, Sr., was born in 1866 on a cotton farm in Bastrop, Louisiana; his family (which included half a dozen children) was so poor they traded cotton for food. As a youngster, to help pay off the family's debts, Oliver, Sr. worked from dawn till dusk splitting rails for fifty cents a day.

He attended school sporadically and his mother used the Bible to teach him to read. "It was the only book they had," comments Ollie on the devoutness of his Baptist grandparents.[5] Realizing how much their son wanted an education, the Johnstons allowed Oliver, Sr., to leave home at age eighteen. They gave him a mule, which he sold for twenty-five dollars, an amount that was matched by a sympathetic local merchant. After some misstarts, he ended up at Mississippi State College with his money gone. The college president took pity on him and talked two hardware merchants into sponsoring the bright lad. "Well, he stayed a year and he made the highest grades they had ever had," says Ollie proudly of his father. Back home during the summer, Oliver, Sr., earned money by teaching school, and eventually he received a Ph.D. from Johns Hopkins University.

He met his future wife, a music teacher named Arclissa Florence Boggs, in Urbana, Illinois. (As noted, she was born in 1869 in Tuscola, Illinois, where Frank Thomas's mother was born fifteen years later.) They married in 1897, the same year he was hired by Stanford. The university's president, David Starr Jordan, apparently a busy man, interviewed

OPPOSITE, *Oliver M. Johnston on mother Arclissa's lap, 1912;* THIS PAGE, *Ollie and father on the Stanford campus, circa 1914; baby Ollie surrounded by family members (older sisters, mother, aunt, and father); Ollie and sister Winifred, circa 1920.*

Johnston for the teaching position on a Washington, D.C., streetcar.

A daughter, Winifred, was born in 1901, followed a decade later by Florence; two years after that Oliver M., Jr., their only son and last child, was born. Winifred, who babysat Ollie, did not pamper the boy. "I thought she was a holy terror," he recently claimed. He spent little time with Florence outside of family vacations, for she was a sickly child with a weak heart, a condition to which she succumbed in 1936. (Robust Winifred lived until her mid-eighties.)

The family home on the Stanford campus was a "big square house that was built about 1895." Mrs. Johnston held baby Winifred in her lap on the house's second floor when the 1906 San Francisco earthquake struck. The huge seismic event was felt in Stanford: "The house swayed and everything shook," Ollie recalls his mother saying. "The chapel fell down at Stanford, buildings fell."

Aside from the occasional earth tremor, life was good for the Johnstons. They lived on an elm-lined street directly across from a vast field full of haystacks.

Beyond the field (eventually paved over for classrooms) were university dormitories, including Encino Hall, where Ollie later lived as a freshman. A streetcar ran near the house, which proved handy, as neither Mr. or Mrs. Johnston learned to drive a car. Infant Ollie rode in a handlebar basket on his father's bicycle, which sported front-wheel brakes.

Ollie's lifelong love of trains began at age three when his parents took him to the Panama Pacific Fair in San Francisco in 1915. "They had a steam locomotive there and I could get right next to it and hear the thing panting," he recalls with delight. Nearly eighty passenger and freight trains pulled by steam locomotives chugged through town each day and Professor Johnston often took his young son to watch them, to hear them, and to smell them as they passed by. The boy kept his first drawing: a train with "Oliver" written on the coal car.

Although college professors "didn't get paid very well," says Ollie, and the family "was always in debt," they ate well. They even hired an elderly Norwegian cook named Carrie Otterson, who became part of the family and helped Mrs. Johnston in the kitchen; for Arclissa, like her daughter, suffered from a weak heart. Mademoiselle Daumalle, a part-time French baby-sitter hired for a time to take care of baby Ollie, was "real mean," he remembers. He hated her *and* her amateurish painting of the falls at Yosemite, which hung with a few other mediocre paintings in the house for years.

In 1915, Professor Johnston was studying in Italy and France when war broke out. Arclissa and the children in Stanford spent worrisome days and nights until the U.S. Embassy in London arranged passage for him back to the United States on the liner *Mauretania*. The dangerous Atlantic voyage took two weeks because of the constant threat of German submarines.

At the end of every quarter, Professor and Mrs. Johnston invited the Romance Languages faculty to their home for afternoon tea. From age five until he was twelve years old, Ollie's job was to open the front door for the visitors, who invariably through the years patted his head and murmured "My, how you've grown."

Ollie was an energetic boy who loved playing in the wide field across from his home. His best friend was a faculty member's son named Calvin Coover, known by his name spelled backward: Nivlac Revooc. (Ollie Johnston, of course, was "Eillo Notsnhoj.") Nivlac's Coke-bottle-thick glasses prevented him from playing tackle football, but the boy could aim and pass a ball beautifully. So, at two-man touch football sandlot games "we always won," recalls Johnston. "No one could beat us, no matter how tall they were." Johnston played tackle football with another friend, Albert Guerard, who grew up to become a novelist and a teacher at Stanford and Harvard.

Visiting his grandmother in Urbana, Illinois, nine-year-old Ollie and the kid next door climbed a tree to smoke their first "cigarettes": coffee grounds wrapped in toilet paper, which made a large fire and a lot of smoke. Eighteen years later, Ollie's smoking partner (Ted Parmalee) ended up in Disney's special-effects department.

Ollie was also interested in electronics. He and Nivlac ingeniously rigged a wire along telephone poles so that each boy had a private phone in his respective house, in a tree house they built, and in a secret cave they dug in Ollie's backyard. "We could talk to each other and he could listen to my radio," says Ollie, whose doting parents thought he would grow up to be an engineer. They encouraged all of his pursuits, even when he woke them up in the middle of the night to announce breathlessly that he had reached Denver on his radio contraption or got as far as Salt Lake City! "That's fine, son. That's fine," they'd murmur before going back to sleep.[6]

Mostly, Johnston loved sports and outdoor activities: hiking in the wide country behind Stanford, and fishing and swimming in the lakes in the hills. At Lake Tahoe, he played Robin Hood and led a bunch of local boys as his Merry Men. On occasion, the family took a train to Mt. Herman, a Baptist retreat near Santa Cruz, where Ollie and his dad would hike a mile to Felton "where many trains came in." Together, they sat and watched the big locomotives pull into and out of the station, steaming and panting like iron mammoths.

The Johnston family was deeply religious. Oliver, Sr. later cofounded the Berkeley Baptist Divinity School, and was known by admirers as "the strongest religious force on the coast." Oliver, Jr., however, lost his fervor for organized religion in the fifth grade when a Sunday-school teacher responded angrily to his questions. "That turned me off," he says. "The longer I attended church the more questions arose in my mind." By high school, he no longer attended church with his family; however, he did go to evening church socials "where you could meet girls." Johnston considers himself religious "but in a different way. Especially since I've been reading Carl Sagan and Stephen Hawking and others." He and his wife, Marie, raised their two sons to make up their own minds regarding Biblical teachings. "The more you learn about the universe and how huge and awesome it is, it can't help but open your thinking," says Johnston. "Is there a god for every planet?" he wonders, asking one of those unanswerables that must have driven his Sunday-school teacher crazy.

The most unusual aspect of Johnston's idyllic childhood and early adolescence was the number of illnesses he suffered and survived. Frank Thomas once claimed that Johnston is "stuck together with spit and string but will outlast everyone." His poor health, inherited from both parents, was noticeable at age ten. A train trip with his father to Colorado was (at first) memorable for a stop in Billings, Montana, to attend a screening of Chaplin's *The Gold Rush*; Johnston described viewing the classic film comedy as "a big moment in my life." But the trip yields a more disturbing memory: Johnston noticed that his hand shook periodically, especially while eating. At the time, the boy didn't connect his slight tremor with the full-blown palsy that continually shook his father. "Even his jaw trembled," Johnston recalls. What he later termed a "familial tremor" has "haunted" him all his life and worsened with age. "I had great difficulty drawing Penny's close-ups at the end of *The Rescuers*," he admits. "*The Fox and the Hound* characters were broader, so I got by there." But palsy was a major factor in Johnston's decision to retire from Disney in 1978.

In 1926, Johnston contracted a veritable plague of childhood diseases, which delayed his entering high school for a year. A severe sinus problem required a doctor to remove mucus from his nose with a syringe every other day and led to continual colds and whooping cough. He also came down with both measles and chicken pox. It wasn't until his third year in high school that he felt able to return to the sports activity he loved. He could throw a football fifty-seven yards, kick it sixty-five yards, run "fairly fast," and swim "real well." He joined the football team but unfortunately "was always getting hurt." A knee injury led to a blood infection and he found he was allergic to tetanus shots. "I can remember shaking all night long while my mother and the doctor were standing there. It's a wonder I didn't die." During football season in his senior year he had an emergency operation for a burst appendix.

He performed well in a decathlon, which seemed to be a better, safer outlet for his renewed energies. "In the first big meet, I won three first places in high jump, low hurdles, and shot put," he says. "I got up to six feet and a quarter inch in the high jump. That was about the best. And I held the record in eight-pound shot—for one week," he says, laughing. But while jumping a low hurdle he fell and fractured his hip, which landed him in the hospital during the League finals.

Johnston always enjoyed drawing, especially pictures of girls, but there was no encouragement to do so in his high-school art class, which consisted of "cutting stuff out of colored papers." His doting mother intervened with the art teacher, who agreed to give Ollie credit for the girl drawings he made outside of class. While his parents were, as Frank Thomas put it, "very captive to his whims," they were reluctant to encourage their son too much in the direction of the arts.[7] How would he earn enough to live? they worried. "The only guy earning money as an artist was Norman Rockwell," Johnston recalls. "Everybody else was starving!"

It wasn't until he entered Stanford as a journalism major in October 1931 that he began to draw in earnest. He became

Ollie Johnston at Stanford, 1931.

a cartoon contributor to *The Chaparral* and enrolled in the school's first and only art course: landscape painting, which met three times a week. Johnston, who had never been to a museum or art gallery, found his first exposure to fine art electrifying. Ed Farmer, the painting instructor, opened a world to the young man when he lectured on Rubens, Michelangelo, Da Vinci, Van Gogh, Botticelli, Monet, and Renoir. Even better were the glorious prints of works by master artists that Farmer passed around in class. "I just fell in love with those," Johnston recalls. "I took them home and showed them to my folks. Said, Look at all this! This is the most wonderful stuff I've ever seen!" And, of course, "they thought so, too."

Farmer challenged his pupils to think. When Johnston and others returned from drawing classes in San Mateo, they pinned up their drawings of the nude model for Farmer to critique. "Why'd you draw that pose in that view?" he often asked. "Well, I couldn't get another seat," came the lame reply. "That's not a good excuse," countered Farmer. "You should have looked at the model and seen how he or she

Frank Thomas and Johnston goof around on the Stanford campus, circa 1932.

interested you more from here or over there or somewhere. And if you sat where you did, you should have done more with it."

Waiting for the first painting class to begin, Johnston was sitting on the curb under an arch when a young man named Frank Thomas came over to introduce himself and a friend from Fresno (Roland Pickford). Within a few days Thomas and Johnston were sketching and painting together. It was the beginning of an extraordinary friendship, which (as of this writing at the beginning of the twenty-first century) has lasted seventy years. During that time, the two men have encouraged, supported, and nurtured each other creatively and personally. Thomas, for example, was the reason Johnston got a job at Disney. "If I hadn't met Frank," muses Johnston, "my guess is I would have finished Stanford and gone to work for United Press as a reporter or gotten a crummy job as an artist somewhere."

In June 1933, when Thomas graduated from Stanford and went to Los Angeles to study commercial art, Johnston was a sophomore. He wrote sports reports for the *Stanford Daily* (known as "The Dippy") and was Stanford's United Press campus correspondent; for the *San Francisco Chronicle*'s sports page, he made wash drawings of sports figures. As a junior manager of the Stanford football team, he came to Los Angeles with the team when they won the Rose Bowl on New

Years Day 1934. He visited Thomas, who showed him artwork he was creating at the Chouinard Art Institute.

"'Wow! That's what I should be doing,'" Thomas recalls Johnston saying.[8] "What am I doing at Stanford?" Upon returning upstate, he announced to his parents, "I can't do any more of this. I want to go to art school!" As always, his parents acquiesced to their only son's wishes. ("My parents believed in me.") His father borrowed $500 for one semester's tuition plus living expenses. Johnston quit Stanford in the middle of his junior year and moved to Los Angeles.

He rented a small room in the same boarding house as Thomas, who roomed with Thor Putnam, another Stanford alum. Johnston's no-frill's weekly allowance of ten dollars to fifteen dollars, while "barely enough to live on," was adequate. "You could eat dinner for thirty cents, thirty-five," he recalls. "If you wanted a steak you might have to pay forty. And you had your lunch, maybe twenty cents: a hot roast-beef sandwich with a salad." But food was of secondary importance to Johnston who "loved" art school, especially his classes with Donald Graham and Pruett Carter. "He was great," says Johnston of the latter. "He was critical, but I happened to have something about my work, even though it was amateurish, that he liked. The emotional quality, I think."

Johnston's friendship with Frank Thomas ripened during this time. They decided to leave their cramped quarters and move to a better boarding house near by. "I thought as we were deciding to make the move," recalled Johnston many years later, "and after we had, I kept thinking about, well, it's gonna be fun kinda living with Frank here and be going to art school together. It occurred to me, gee, you know, I kinda hope that this guy and I would stay friends. That it would be a long friendship, even if we got married and lived in separate parts of town or anything. We'd still stay friends. I was enjoying the relationship, which was based mainly on our similar interests and backgrounds. The fact that we both liked to draw and both were headed toward the same type of career."[9]

As previously discussed, in September 1934 Thomas began working at Disney's Hyperion Avenue cartoon factory. In October, Johnston quit art school to take a job arranged by a "lawyer cousin" at Paramount Studios on a Cecil B. DeMille picture. Making thirty-five dollars a week, Johnston designed and drew multiple views of "lutes and owl racks, which I know nothing about," he says. After a month, he gladly returned to art school.

At Stanford, Johnston "loved to see the Disney pictures"; he and his buddies would "just kill ourselves laughing at them." Especially impressive was *Playful Pluto*, in which a hapless dog is stuck on a piece of flypaper. "It was hilarious to me," says Johnston of the pup's attempts to remove the sticky stuff. "Later on I realized the reason I enjoyed it so much was the fact that this character was thinking about what he was

"March 23, 1936, a most important day," wrote Johnston years later. "I become Fred Moore's assistant." One of Disney's most gifted animators, Moore makes a drawing for Johnston.

doing." But thoughts of becoming an animator were far from Johnston's mind; he still harbored a dream of becoming an illustrator. In January 1935 his father paid another $500 to Chouinard.

One morning, as Johnston lay in bed waiting for Thomas to finish shaving with the single razor they owned between them, Thomas said casually: "Oh, by the way, they want you to make a tryout at Disney's." Instructor Donald Graham had suggested Johnston because "they were looking for art-school talent. 'Cause Walt knew he was going to do *Snow White*."

"Oh my god!" thought Johnston. "My poor dad. What am I gonna do?" If he got a job at Disney, he decided, he would attend art school at night, use some of his salary to buy art supplies, and reimburse his father.

Johnston took the tryout for "that stupid guy" George Drake. His test was, he recalled, "a real tough one: do the three little pigs all on one sheet, one with a fife, one with a drum, another with a flag in a half an hour. By the end of the week I had an acceptable in-between. I sweated over that!" he says. On January 21, 1935, he was hired at seventeen dollars a week. "Ironic, I'd say," mused Johnston recently. "Stanford, a school with no art department, sends four guys to Disney!"

Johnston's first job in-betweening was on *Mickey's Garden* (released July 1935), which led to small jobs cleaning up animators' rough drawings. Initially, he was "snapped up by the Effects Department [which sought] men of a careful, conscientious nature."[10] Johnston felt he "hadn't done any really important clean-ups" until Gerry Geronimi's drawings for *Mickey's Rival* (released June 1936), a key sequence involving Mickey Mouse, a bull, and an automobile. Ambitious Johnston decided to "work like hell" and "make that guy's stuff look really good."

The film's director (Wilfred Jackson) pronounced

Johnston's effort "the best god-damned cleanups I ever saw!" and both Geronimi and Fred Moore vied for Johnston's services. But Moore, who needed a replacement in his unit after Frank Thomas had moved on, prevailed. Johnston was pleased because (like others) he disliked the bumptious Geronimi. Besides, Thomas had raved about how much he had learned working with Moore. "March 23, 1936, a most important day," Johnston recalled years later. "I become Fred Moore's assistant." "Not good enough for ya, eh?" sneered Geronimi as he passed Johnston in the hall.

Assisting Fred Moore, Johnston always remembered, was "the greatest learning experience I ever had." Moore was not an articulate man ("When he was trying to teach me something," recalls Johnston, "he'd say, 'You know, like we always talk.'"); he taught primarily by example. "He could make little drawings to show you. And he was a natural animator. The most natural animator that ever came to the studio." Untrained, Moore "didn't know anatomy really well, but he knew where everything ought to be." His simple drawings exuded charm and his innate feeling for stretched and squashed shapes gave his animation a juicy life and vitality.

One of the most important lessons Johnston learned from Moore was how "the acting comes from the change of shapes" in a character's face and body, and "the thought process comes from a change of expression." In a 1978 lecture to neophyte animators, Johnston discussed that aspect of animation using Moore's redesign of Mickey Mouse in *Brave Little Tailor* (1938).

Here he's crossing the bridge saying, 'I'll be back, I hope.' This is a real nice, simple shape here and you can read it very easily. See the difference between here and there where he bulges his cheeks out a little. This wasn't done

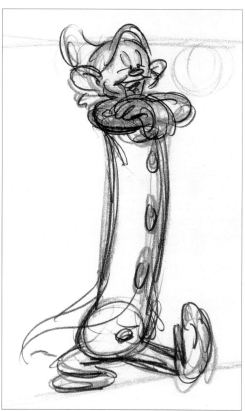

Moore's drawings of the dwarfs brim with vitality and visual appeal.

Under Moore, Johnston also "learned how important the [character's] expressions are. You can't show it unless you stage it right and give the audience time to see it. [The] same with acting and attitudes."

To counter Moore's mood swings and occasional creative blocks (during which he couldn't draw even a simple scene), Johnston and Thomas would gather around the animator to chant, "C'mon, Fred. C'mon, Fred. You know you're the greatest!" Moore invariably took the bait: "Yeah, go on. Tell me more!" The praise gradually built to such ridiculous heights ("Yeah, Michelangelo couldn't even be your assistant!") that Moore had to laugh. "Look, fellas," he'd say, "this is only a little scene. I don't need that much buildup."

Moore was assigned as a supervising animator of the Dwarfs in *Snow White* (along with Vladimir Tytla), and Johnston supervised the cleanup drawings made by Moore and all of the animators under him. Johnston also participated in all of the "sweatbox" (projection room) meetings with the top directors and Walt who "criticized the hell out of Fred's stuff. 'Cause he was using Fred as his standard."

Johnston was allowed to animate small scenes, such as the Dwarfs scurrying under a bed or Grumpy turning around. Tytla, Grumpy's main animator, was "a big influence" on Johnston. "His ability to get the inner emotions was fantastic." Tytla, born in Yonkers, New York, in 1904, was considered the finest animator in New York City when he came west to work

too much on Mickey, but if you didn't hold this too long, it looked fine. You got a nice squash here. . . . Also, notice the change in the body shape. The body should always reflect the attitude you're trying to do. It shouldn't just be in the expression. It must be in the body, too. Another important thing is that every drawing in your scene should have the right attitude. . . . Every drawing in your scene has to be acting. For example, Laurence Olivier wouldn't just have acting on poses—he moves between them. His thought processes are working between poses, and his acting is continued through every frame of film. That's the way you have to do it. So many guys will just use the extreme poses to show their acting and that isn't correct."[11]

Vladimir Tytla brought strong inner emotions to animation acting for the first time; here he draws the magnificent devil on Bald Mountain for Fantasia.

at Disney in 1934 (after much coaxing by his pal Art Babbitt, who preceded him). During a brief nine years at the studio, he brought emotional power to animation for the first time. The varied roles he played—including Grumpy, Stromboli the puppeteer in *Pinocchio*, the Devil on Bald Mountain in *Fantasia*, and Dumbo in *Dumbo*—are remarkable for their strong emotional impact on audiences, and as supreme examples of the personality animator's art.[12]

Of Ukrainian-Polish descent, Tytla was an intense man filled with barely contained feelings. One day in 1939, just after his son was born, he said to Johnston enthusiastically, "Ollie, you gotta get married and have a kid. There's nothing like it!" Tall and muscular, with thick, black hair combed straight back and a mustache, Tytla grabbed Johnston by his upper arms with both hands as he waxed eloquent about birth and the cosmos. "He says, 'You're part of the moon, the sun, the stars, everything!'" recalls Johnston. "I'm getting all black and blue. He doesn't know he's doing it. He just gets carried away."

Tytla's drawings had the right stuff emotionally, but they lacked the graphic appeal of Moore's. So Walt asked thirty-two-year-old Tytla to check in with twenty-five-year-old Moore and

"get him to make a drawing" for reference. Sometimes he told Moore to go by Tytla's office and "make a drawing" for the older, art-school-educated, and more experienced animator. It was a touchy situation embarrassing to both men. "Fred told me, 'I can't do that!' says Johnston. "So they never did. Tytla was always jealous of Fred getting all the cute stuff. Yet, Fred did a lot of Grumpy stuff that had guts to it. *Dumbo* was where Tytla got to show he could do the cute stuff."

Johnston's busy schedule also included attendance at art classes at night on the studio lot (he had quit Chouinard). But during the last four months of production on *Snow White*, all classes ceased as he and most of the artists worked from 7 A.M. until 10 P.M. each day to finish the picture.

At the time, the method for cleaning up rough animation drawings was to trace directly over the originals, strengthening main lines and erasing superfluous others. Ollie so admired Moore's scribbly sketches that he "found it hard to draw over Fred's drawings, they were so great." He saved many from the wastebasket, and even saved Moore's stubby green pencil. "You can see how worn it is here where his two fingers held it," he says in the documentary film *Frank and*

Fred Moore tries out an expression for Jose Carioca in The Three Caballeros; *the brilliant animator had a self-destructive streak and tragically died at age 41.*

Ollie, "and up here where it rubbed against the palm of his hand. More beautiful stuff came out of this pencil—it just flowed like liquid. Beautiful drawings of the dwarfs, where he'd draw the cheeks on them. Where it was a slightly wider line at the bottom of the cheek or around the nose or somewhere around the eyes, the eyelid darker."

Moore told Walt that Johnston would make a better animator than an assistant. "He pushed me on out of the nest after we finished *Snow White*," says Johnston.[13] He became a junior animator on *Brave Little Tailor*, animating crowd scenes and bits in which Mickey struggled with a giant. (Frank Thomas animated more sustained and difficult scenes, such as Mickey bragging to the king.) "They liked what I did on that picture," says Johnston, "so they put me and Frank on the character of Pinocchio." Moore supervised Johnston's scene of the boy-puppet coming to life, but Walt, displeased with the character's look and personality, shelved the production for six months. During that time, Johnston gained experience animating on *The Practical Pig* (1939), *Mickey's Surprise Party* (1939), and *The Pointer* (1939).

When *Pinocchio* started again, the title character, redesigned by junior animator Milt Kahl, was less wooden and more boyishly innocent; the new quality was enhanced by Johnston's sincere and charming animation. He literally brought Pinocchio to life after the Blue Fairy's magic touch: the inert puppet's emergence into consciousness is like an awakening from deep sleep. He also animated Pinocchio twice telling a lie: in the first, the boy twists the fabric of his pants with his fingers childishly; as he tells the second falsehood, his nose grows into a grotesquely large tree branch complete with bird's nest and eggs. Johnston animated comic scenes (Pinocchio attempts to whistle into his hat and nothing comes out), as well as sad scenes (Pinocchio trapped in a birdcage commiserating with Jiminy Cricket).

For his efforts, Walt paid Johnston a rare face-to-face compliment. "One day I'm talking with Ham [Luske]'s secretary in the hall outside Walt's office," Johnston remembers, "and Walt comes out. Oh dear god! Why did I pick this day to be loafing? Here I am trying to make a name for myself." But

Johnston literally brought Pinocchio to life in his earliest scenes.

Walt merely said in passing, "I sure like those Pinocchios you're doing." Surprised, Johnston replied self-effacingly, "Well, I'm just trying to draw like Frank and Milt do." As he kept walking, Walt fired back: "I don't give a damn where you get it. Just keep doing it!" By five o'clock the studio was abuzz. "The secretaries told everybody," says Johnston proudly. "I was elated." Walt backed up his praise by raising Johnston's salary three times during the making of *Pinocchio*.

With their increased prosperity, Johnston and Thomas were able to move into a spacious apartment at the Fountain Manor in Hollywood. They often invited other Disney friends (such as Ward and Betty Kimball, Mel Shaw, Marc Davis, David Hand, Eric and Gertrude Larson, and Milt Kahl) to perform "some crazy plays" they wrote and directed in their living room. The plays were recorded, including sound effects, such as a garbage can the "actors" put their heads into for an echo-y "underground passage." One play involved a Chinese detective named One-Guy-Too-Few (played by Ward Kimball); in another, *B-17*, a parody of a 1930s war film, Betty Kimball played the role of "Murgatroy" whose only lines

were: "I didn't do it. It was not me who. It was you who. He who. Not me who." Mrs. Kimball, who was nine months pregnant, threw herself into the part with such giddy enthusiasm she went into labor on the way home; after an emergency stop at a hospital, she gave birth to daughter Kelly.

For *Fantasia*, director Luske asked Johnston to supervise the animation of cupids and "centaurettes" in a section of the Beethoven Pastoral sequence. The winged baby gods of love were based on the plump, dimpled infant nudities made popular in eighteenth-century paintings and engravings by Francois Boucher (1703–1770); for example, "Three Putti among Clouds" in the Louvre.

The centaurettes are a Disney invention not found in classical mythology; that is, a female version of the centaur. Their design was based on countless drawings Fred Moore tossed off of sexy adolescent girls. His sensual little women— usually nude or in a state of dishabille—retain a prepubescent innocence, which did not prevent the animators from using the sketches as pinups. Constructed from simple oval and pear shapes, the "Freddie Moore girl" was highly animatable. Versions

OPPOSITE, *Johnston animated plump cupids and sultry centaurettes in* Fantasia's *Pastoral Symphony;* OPPOSITE, BOTTOM RIGHT, *a Fred Moore sketch of a centaurette.* ABOVE, *Marie and Ollie Johnston with his first steam engine at their newly completed home in Flintridge, California, 1949; Marie and Ollie and their sons on the train, circa 1952.*

of her appear in several Disney films of the 1940s, including the hillbilly bride in *The Martins and the Coys* and the bobby-soxers in *All the Cats Join In* from *Make Mine Music* (1946), the girl ice skater in *Once Upon a Wintertime* and Sluefoot Sue in *Pecos Bill* from *Melody Time* (1948). Bosomy Jessica Rabbit in 1988's *Who Framed Roger Rabbit* is a recent, more pneumatical version. Ollie Johnston's animation of the sultry centaurettes and solicitous cupids who fuss and flit on tiny gossamer wings about them is smooth and graceful; without words (and to the second movement of Beethoven's Sixth Symphony) both creatures express their thoughts and attitudes clearly, while gliding into and out of poses as languorous and coy as Boucher's.

Arrows from the bow of Johnston's personal cupid struck around this time (1940) when he saw Marie Worthey in the coffeeshop of the Burbank studio. Blond and petite, she was a new employee in the Ink and Paint Department; her mother was a widow who worked as a secretary at the Wilshire Country Club. "She had purple slacks on," he remembers, "looked nice and friendly, laughing, talking to a girlfriend." He inquired about her from an animation building wing secretary, who the next day told Marie that a guy named Ollie wanted a date. Marie asked her friends if they knew this Ollie-something and one pointed to a man with wild hair atop a brick wall imitating a monkey. Marie was appalled until she discovered that the wild man was Oliver Wallace, "a good musician, but kind of crazy!"

Johnston recalled their "first big date" attending *Fantasia*'s premiere in November; during the two-hour screening Marie took off her shoes and lost one of them. The couple drove to dates in Johnston's gas-guzzling Buick Century convertible, which he later replaced with a 1933 Model-A Ford. On January 23, 1943 the couple were married at the Stanford chapel; a torrential rainstorm prevented best man Frank Thomas and the bride's mother from attending. "The tracks were washed out," recalls Marie. "They spent the night on the train and woke up the next morning in the San Fernando Valley somewhere. They had never left the Los Angeles area."[14]

In 1945, the Johnstons looked for property to build a home on; with Eric Larson's help, they found four acres near his house in the wooded Flintridge area. Frank Thomas bought half, hoping to marry Jeanette Armentrout when he got out of the armed services. "Marie and I love the Flintridge property," said Johnston recently. Their house was built around a huge oak whose thick, wide branches provided ample shade for picnics. "It was exciting, planning our first home. Marie had great ideas." He has often praised his wife ("a very strong, determined lady") and her creativity not only in landscaping and gardening, but in "singing, piano-playing, great dancing, golfing, sewing, and cooking." Two sons eventually completed the Johnston family: Rick, born in 1949, and Ken, born in 1951.[15]

Johnston became one of four who supervised animation on *Bambi* (starting in April 1940) because of the "life and captivating personality touches" he could bring to the film's animal cast.[16] He sought opportunities for emotional changes in the characters in order "to show they were thinking." For example, the young doe Faline teases young Bambi so relentlessly in one scene that he turns from a mild-mannered fellow into an angry aggressor.

One of Johnston's best-known sequences involves a baby rabbit, Thumper, who advises Bambi to avoid the green parts of clover. As punishment for his naughty advice, Thumper's

Johnston was one of four supervising animators on Bambi; *here, Thumper advises Bambi that clover's green parts "sure is awful stuff to eat!"*

mother forces him to recite his father's dull platitude: "Eating greens is a special treat; it makes long ears and great big feet." Thumper speaks the speech with zero enthusiasm, and Johnston gives the bunny stock gestures to accompany the lines (touching an ear and sticking out a foot on the appropriate word); he performs like a kid stuck in a boring school recital. But Thumper's rebellious spark and smart-aleck attitude returns when he whispers to Bambi: "But it sure is awful stuff to eat! I made that last part up myself." "Animating is, in a way, imitating," Johnston once said. "As if you're doing an impersonation. It's more than that, but that element has to be there."[17]

During the strike at the studio, which started in late May 1941, Johnston remained loyal to Walt, as did all of the future Nine Old Men. "I couldn't see it," said Johnston of the situation. "He'd been good to me and all of us." When America entered the war later that year, Johnston tried enlisting in the armed services along with Frank Thomas, but an old duodenal ulcer prevented his joining. Instead, Johnston "served" by animating Disney's wartime training and propaganda films, such as the feature *Victory Through Air Power* (1943). Johnston found the work "tedious. There was no personality [animation] involved."

One exception was *Reason and Emotion* (1943), which, wrote Richard Shale, "probed the Nazi psyche by satirizing the theme of regimentation."[18] Inside an American female's head, two tiny women fight for control of her body and soul. The characters are sexist stereotypes, typical of the period, of women's roles and desires. Reason, prim and uptight, is dressed in a high-collared black suit and sips tea with toast; she unsuccessfully tries to subdue her "other side": Emotion, a chunky hoyden in a décolleté blouse and miniskirt loudly lusting after gooey, high-calorie desserts. "The little girl," says Johnston of boisterous Emotion, "was so flamboyant and so impulsive, and wanted to do everything that popped into her mind. She couldn't control herself." The design of the character and her actions were broadly caricatured, and Johnston enjoyed this "simpler" graphic style for female characters; it was less "restrictive" than the more realistically drawn *Snow White* and (later) the women in *Alice in Wonderland* and *Peter Pan*.

For the 1945 wartime film *The Three Caballeros*, Johnston animated numerous scenes with Donald Duck interacting with live action. "I had a scene with the Duck reacting to Aurora Miranda['s kiss], where his heart and necktie start beating to this South American rhythm. I staggered the [animation of the] tie so that it went out and then back a little, then out and back in a little again, so that it could work to this

beat." Johnston's in-betweener misunderstood and erased all of the extreme poses, "so that the necktie just floated out to meet her." Unfortunately, the error was only discovered at an important screening that Walt had arranged for Latin American executives. They were also surprised to see some Johnston scenes of the singing Mexican rooster Panchito accidentally cut in upside down. "I was sitting in the back [of the theatre] and that stuff goes by on the screen and Walt turns around with this black look on his face. It's funny now to look back on it, but, oh geez!"[19]

Johnston learned never to talk back to Walt "if he gave you a criticism." Commenting on some of Johnston's drawings of Hitler, he said, "You can probably improve those caricatures." To which Johnston replied, "Well, geez, I only started on it yesterday." Walt turned, raised an expressive eyebrow, and shot back, "You're not on *Bambi* now, you know!"[20]

Johnston has happier memories of his post-war assignments, including *Peter and the Wolf* (in *Make Mine Music*), the tugboat Little Toot and Johnny Appleseed in *Melody Time* (1948), and various characters in *The Adventures of Ichabod and Mr. Toad* (1949). In the latter, a flamboyant district attorney who sends Toad to jail was, said Johnston, "the first character I really had all by myself of any importance. I loved doing him even though there weren't too many scenes; but he was a real egotistical guy who had nothing but contempt for everybody that got on the witness stand. He'd laugh at them, make fun of them, and I got this great way of having him walk and then whirl on the character."[21]

Although Johnston shared animation of Brer Rabbit (in *Song of the South*) with other directing animators, he enjoyed the character. In one scene, dimwitted Brer Bear shakes the rabbit's hand in gratitude, unaware that he has (again) been made a fool of. The Rabbit tries to be polite while attempting to escape the massive oaf's viselike grip (for Brer Fox is fast

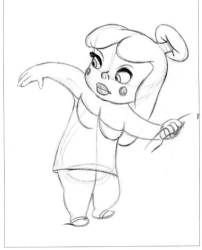

During the war years, Johnston found animating on training and propaganda films "tedious"; an exception was the boisterous little woman in Reason and Emotion *(1943).*

"The simplicity, the honesty, the emotion. The essence of a little kid with his toy gun going into the wood. All of that was there," says Andreas Deja in praising Johnston's animation of Peter in Peter and the Wolf. OPPOSITE, Brer Rabbit is all shook up by Brer Bear's grip.

approaching down the road). Johnston's problem as an animator was to convey the rabbit's flickering attitudes and thoughts (rising anxiety, pure fear, phony politeness) while trying to free himself. The bear's heavy hand, pumping up and down, keeps the lightweight rabbit off-balance; were it not for Johnston's facility, the scene's emotional gist would be lost. As Brer Rabbit's body flails like a yo-yo, Johnston contained the character's face within a comparatively small area, the better to read his wily mind through facial expressions.

The scene was "tough" but "fun to do," he says. "You like things that are complicated."[22]

After the war, Johnston and Thomas continued driving to and from work together; before freeways, their twice-daily commute took close to an hour each way—plenty of time to hash over the day's happenings and work-related problems. "We helped each other see a different viewpoint or enlarge the perspective on what it was you were trying to do," says Thomas. For a problem Johnston was having on *Song of the*

Engineer Johnston at the throttle of the Marie E. in Julian, California, circa 1994. Photograph courtesy of Michael Broggie.

South, for instance, Thomas "would suggest bits of action which I thought would fit the character." For a line spoken by Brer Fox to Brer Rabbit—"We're going to have *you* for dinner!"—Thomas suggested the fox walk his fingers up the rabbit's nose and over the top of his head.

  · Johnston, in turn, was making suggestions on Thomas's scenes regarding "what was very subtle and very deep to the character." Johnston "helped define the inner feelings of the character for me in a way that no other animator did," said Thomas. "Even Walt didn't 'get really inside' of a character," says Thomas, "what a character was made up of and how they would work."[23]

  In 1946, Johnston indulged his lifelong love of trains by building, during his off hours, a one-inch-scale steam-driven train and track in his backyard. "I've always loved trains and been fascinated by them," he once said. "I love the sound of a steam engine; it's the closest thing to a human sound that you can have in a machine." Ward Kimball shared his interest, and so did Walt Disney, who later built his own backyard one-and-

a-half-inch-scale engine. "Out of that we had quite a close relationship," says Johnston. "Almost too close at times. Some of the guys said, 'Don't dance too close to the queen.' I couldn't help it. He'd keep coming in to see me with a little brake wheel and things. He was so enthused about it that he had to have somebody to talk to, you know, to get away from his work. He used to invite me out to his place and he used to come to our place."[24]

  Besides his locomotive, modeled after a circa-1920 Baltimore & Ohio Railroad prototype, "he also has a modern diesel-electric engine, and a type of gear-driven steam locomotive known as a Shay."[25] But, like Kimball, Johnston always wanted a real locomotive and in 1962 he started trying to acquire one. It took him over six years to find a suitable model (a seven-ton 1901 H. K. Porter), refurbish it, and set the track on the Johnston's vacation property in Julian, located in the hills near northern San Diego County. "Oh, what a thrill!" said Johnston recalling the first firing up of the restored Porter.[26]

John Lasseter, the director of *Toy Story* and *Toy Story 2*, once spent a weekend visiting the Johnstons in Julian when he fired up the train, which Lasseter describes as being "like a giant lifesize train set." "It was so fun," he says. "I brought my sons and there was a potluck dinner and lot of friends," including Frank and Jeanette Thomas. He remembers Johnston's sheer joy. "Ollie was in his element," says Lasseter. "He was not an animator anymore—he was an engineer! This steam train was his baby and he loved it. You just saw it in his face. He had the hat, his overalls were dirty and oily. And he was just loving it! He would drive this thing." He allowed Lasseter into the engineer's cabin, but first gave him his cap. "'Cause you can't drive a train without an engineer's cap, and I know why!" says Lasseter, laughing. "It's because if you really give it the gas all this soot and ash comes out of the smokestack onto your head."[27]

At the beginning of the Disney Studio's comeback years in the early 1950s, Johnston was a versatile team player. He did a reliably fine job on broad secondary characters—for example, the lackey and stepsisters in *Cinderella*. He also successfully shared animation on leads, such as dainty Alice in *Alice in Wonderland*; although (unlike Milt Kahl and Marc Davis) he struggled with the "restrictive type of drawing" required for the character. "Everybody knows what a real girl looks like," Johnston says. "If you get the eyes off a little bit or the nose, it really spoils the looks of it."

Johnston's Alice shares an amusing sequence with a talkative doorknob, animated by Frank Thomas. Exasperated by the doorknob's silly puns and supercilious personality, Alice pushes her hand across her face. "It wrinkles up her nose," comments Johnston. "Now on a more cartoony character you can go so much broader. You had to handle her in a much straighter way."

Once, after running a pencil test of the doorknob sequence, Walt turned to Johnston to ask, "Did you do all these Alices?" When Johnston sheepishly admitted that, "yeah," he had, Walt enthusiastically said he'd have to assign him next to animate Wendy in *Peter Pan*. "*That'll* kill him!" said Thomas with a laugh.

Perhaps Walt took Thomas's comment to heart, for Johnston was spared the prim and "teddibly" British Wendy (who, like Alice, was modeled and voiced by actress Katherine Beaumont). Milt Kahl got stuck with her, as well as

the realistic-looking *Peter Pan*. Johnston, however, was assigned the part of Smee, first mate to pirate Captain Hook.

Johnston's Smee is a comic tour de force. The basic shape of the character's face is a variation on *Snow White*'s Dwarf design, but placed on a flabby, tall body. He has a unique, fear-ridden sycophantic personality festooned with neurotic, effeminate hand gestures, and facial ticks. Johnston used lots of eyeblinks on the character. "I use it as an anticipation lots of times," he once told a group of animation students.

> If you're going to start into a word, say with an "M" mouth, you get a little squash and the whole face seems to relate. You close the mouth and drop the eyes and then bring the eyes open on the accent of the word. Also, the blink . . . can represent a puzzled feeling. If somebody said something you didn't understand, you'd blink fast. You're wondering. There are a lot of different reasons to use a blink. A lot of them haven't even been discovered yet, I'm sure. They're all symbols that you work with."[28]

Working for the unpredictable Captain Hook had obviously made Smee a nervous wreck. "See, the thing about Smee was he wasn't smart at all," says Johnston, "and he was used as a foil for Captain Hook."[29] And at night, Mr. Smee drank to release the day's tensions. "I don't drink much," confides Johnston, "but I watch my friends drink. I get some ideas watching how late in the evening they sit there and smirk or hiccup a little bit." In a sequence in which Hook tricks Tinker Bell into revealing *Peter Pan*'s hiding place, the acting between

A Peter Pan *model sheet of Mr. Smee, who was animated by Ollie Johnston.*

Thomas's devious Hook and Johnston's drunken Smee is a wonderful ping-pong performance, worthy of Laurence Olivier and Ralph Richardson.

"Smee is one of Ollie's masterpieces," comments Andreas Deja. "I don't know how he did it—that nervous quality. So beautifully realized and so natural. And different."[30] According to Deja, "He repeatedly steals the show, even when he plays opposite Frank Thomas's terrific creation, Captain Hook." Further, Johnston "applied the animation principles he had learned under Freddie Moore's tutorship to Smee, but he went well beyond those."[31]

Sadly, Fred Moore worked on minor Smee scenes under the supervision of Johnston, his former assistant. "He didn't resent it," Johnston said recently. "He was too far gone." Indeed, alcoholism had finally destroyed Moore, the animator who was once the studio's brightest star. "Fred was trying to animate Smee, but he couldn't get to first base on it, he was so soused all the time," Johnston once recalled.[32]

Moore's chronic absenteeism and poor work had led Walt to actually fire him in August 1946. He freelanced as an animator on Walter Lantz's cartoons for a year and a half; then Walt and the studio's Animation Board felt sorry for him and took him back. "We were all real sentimental about Freddy," says Johnston, one of the Board's original members. "I know that Walt was real sad when he had to let Fred go. I think he hoped to shock him so that he would, maybe, snap out of it and come back a different guy." But Moore's life had spun out of control. On the afternoon of November 22, 1952, he and his second wife, Virginia, were involved in an auto accident on Mount Gleason Drive in Los Angeles. When he died of a "cerebral concussion" the next day in St. Joseph's Hospital across from the Disney Studio, Robert Fred Moore was forty-one.[33]

Frank Thomas, who had been "alienated" from Moore "since 1942, when he was always drunk," did not attend his mentor's funeral service at Forest Lawn Cemetery.[34] Neither did Walt Disney. Sentimental Ollie Johnston did, however, because he felt "I owed him so much. Fred made my life and Frank's life different. The flexibility he got into characters. No one did squash-and-stretch—used it properly—like he did."[35]

Colleagues had advised Moore numerous times to get professional help. "There's this thing over me," Moore once told Thomas, who asked in frustration if Moore could try to "let it go by?" Thomas was disgusted by how Moore wasted his talent. The mystery of what bedeviled poor Fred Moore was contemplated for years by his two former apprentices. Johnston thought "that he got to the top too quick. It just came so easy for him that he didn't feel any more challenge. He got bored." It was also thought that his promotion by Walt to supervisor of other animators on *Snow White* was a responsibility that Moore

An inebriated Mr. Smee is one of Johnston's finest comic performances.

Watching Johnston draw are, left to right, Milt Kahl, Marc Davis, Frank Thomas, Walt Disney, and director Wilfred Jackson.

"couldn't accept. He just kept leaving earlier and drinking more and horsing around more and next thing you know he got divorced," comments Johnston. "He had to be disciplined. If he'd been left animating he might have lasted longer."

But perhaps not much longer. There is the fact that Moore's simple approach to animation and drawing was quickly surpassed by the sophisticated work of his former assistants. A private personnel report circa 1938 indicates that the bloom was already off Moore's rosy reputation soon after *Snow White*. Director Wilfred Jackson notes that "I would place him very high on the list of animators. [But] I would put Frank Thomas above him on that."[36]

In the 1950s, Ollie Johnston animated characters in shorts, such as the spunky four-wheel star of *Susie the Little Blue Coupe* (1951) and a befuddled Benjamin Franklin in *Ben and Me* (1953); he also gave grace and warmth to two of Mickey Mouse's opening and closing moments on the daily *Mickey Mouse Club* (1955) TV series. (Baby boomers may fondly recall Mickey in cowboy garb twirling a lasso, or dressed in a tux playing a piano, both animated by Johnston.)

For the feature *Lady and the Tramp* (1955), he made major contributions to the lead characters Lady and her dog neighbors Jock and Trusty; especially memorable is the latter, a bloodhound who scratches his bony body so vigorously the loose skin envelopes his head like a monk's cowl. In *Sleeping Beauty* (1959), Johnston shared with Frank Thomas the development of the Three Good Fairies and animation of their primary scenes. "The thing that wasn't as strong as it should have been," says Johnston of the fairies, "was their relationship to the girl [Briar Rose, also known as Princess Aurora]. You never had the type of relationship that we had with the Dwarfs and Snow White where she had a different feeling about each Dwarf. Briar Rose looked at the three [fairies] as pretty much the same type of personality. Well, we considered them different, but I don't think the girl was planned that way."[37]

Johnston went to the dogs again in *101 Dalmatians*, a showcase of his increasingly delicate emotional touch with characters and situations. He eagerly took on a difficult sequence in which a pregnant dog (Perdita) cowers under a stove and commiserates with her mate (Pongo) about villainous

Examples of the emotional "Johnston touch": Nanny gives a pat and a hug to Pongo in 101 Dalmatians. "*What an effect touching can have in an animated cartoon," says Johnston.*

Cruella De Vil. "I thought, gee, this [layout] is really restrictive," recalls Johnston. "I'd rather have [Perdita] out in the center of the room. But the more I worked at it, the more I realized that that was the best place to have her because she is secluded, with her back to the wall. You couldn't move her head or anything, but in the end what moves I did put on them paid off. Particularly the little one at the end where he gives her that little kiss."[38]

During the making of *Dalmatians* in the fall of 1960, Johnston collapsed at the studio. After resting for a few days over Thanksgiving, he returned to work only to collapse again. A week's stay in Good Samaritan Hospital, then rest at home for the Christmas holidays did not help. Johnston had no strength and his doctor couldn't figure out why. He stayed away from the studio, too weak to hold a glass and "very discouraged," for three months. Frank Thomas brought his friend's weekly check every Thursday, until they stopped. "Walt is going to continue paying you out of a special fund," explained Thomas. Johnston was grateful for Walt's kindness, but moaned, "This can't go on! I want to work."

Finally, his boyhood pal Albert Guerard connected him with a U.S.C. endocrinologist who found that Johnston's thy-roid gland was not working. The reason: Johnston had contracted mumps a few years earlier from his own children. Three weeks after diagnosis and treatment, he was back at the studio. "Not at full strength, but I could work," he says. "My assistant, Walt Stanchfield, nursed me back to full strength." He was cheered to see the scene he had been working on prior to the illness was still on his drawing board.

The Sword in the Stone (1963) found Johnston sharing with others (including Milt Kahl) animation of Merlin and his charge, the boy-king Wart; for the owl Archimedes, Johnston and actor Junius Matthews created a memorable moment when the bird sustains a twenty-second laugh (one long hoot) at Merlin's attempts to prove man can fly. In *Mary Poppins* (1964), more birds for Johnston: this time a quartet of penguins (shared with Frank Thomas) who, with great charm, dance and sing with Dick Van Dyke, all for the love of Julie Andrews.

Ollie Johnston started slowly in features, working first as an assistant animator on *Snow White*; but nearly forty years later, in his final decade at Disney, he crowned his career with a series of masterly, emotionally sensitive performances. Perhaps his best-known and best-loved character is Baloo the

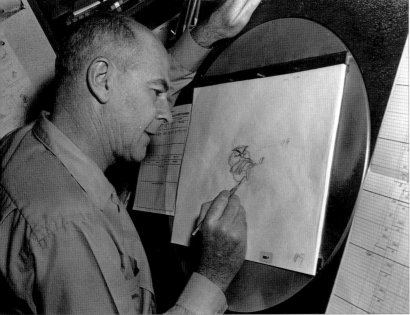

The levelheaded owl Archimedes lost his stern demeanor in The Sword in the Stone *when he sustained a twenty-second laugh, animated by Johnston;* BOTTOM, RIGHT, *Johnston and Thomas make like penguins at a* Mary Poppins *story session.*

bear in *The Jungle Book*, which he shared again with Frank Thomas. Johnston's experimental animation (using Phil Harris's voice) inspired Walt to ask that Baloo's role be expanded. ("This bear is marvelous. We gotta keep him in the picture.")

When Johnston began exploring how Baloo would enjoy (as all bears do) scratching himself, Walt suggested that he

"oughta look at that nature stuff from *Bear Country*," a 1953 Disney True-Life Adventure highlighting a montage of real bears scratching. "That's pretty great stuff," said Walt. "I don't think you can ever top it." Johnston quietly took up the challenge. Walt looked at the resultant animation and "didn't say it was good or bad. He just said, 'Now, we ought to get some music behind it to get some real frenzy in this.'" (That, of course, meant Walt approved of Johnston's efforts.) Cappy Lewis's blazing trumpet rendition of the song "Bare Necessities" accents Baloo's increasingly frenetic, ecstatic scratching of various parts of his anatomy on rocks and uprooted trees. Johnston's sequence is one of the film's funniest, most memorable moments.

It is the relationship between Baloo and the boy Mowgli, however, that is the emotional bull's-eye of the picture. "I kept thinking how can I make this bear and this kid feel closer together," says Johnston. "I think," commented Thomas, "we got the strongest friendly relationship between two characters we ever got in any picture." "We got it into every scene," Johnston explains. "How much these two characters liked each other. How much they belonged together. And everything Mowgli did, he did because he saw Baloo do it. He tried to mimic him, and the bear wanted this little guy for his cub."

As in the best Disney features, both characters undergo a psychological change during the course of the picture; they develop as characters before our eyes—

181

their emotional range expands as they overcome diffi-culties. There came a point in the story when the friendship between bear and boy was sorely tested. Baloo ceases to be a carefree buddy and becomes a responsible father figure, and Mowgli changes from an adoring chum to a rebellious kid on the verge of concupiscent adolescence.

Johnston and Thomas had back-to-back sequences to play out this crucial narrative change. "Without these coming off properly, all this character work we had done wouldn't pay off," says Johnston, whose sequence involved a panther (Bagheera) encouraging irresponsible Baloo to bring Mowgli to live in the "man village." In other words, to remove him from the wild in order for him to grow up with his own species. "Baloo had never done anything like this before," explains Johnston, "where you had to figure out a problem in your mind. Most of my sequence went on with just talking, no real movement. They're just standing there, Bagheera and Baloo, talking."

Johnston sensitively showed how the bear felt, and his changing attitude by using physical actions, such as rubbing his head and his arm, and absently

scratching his back. Now his beloved scratching was used to indicate dis-comfort and indecision (another example of "the Johnston touch"). Thomas picked up the next section where Baloo confronts Mowgli, who reacts with anger and disbe-lief. "The betrayal comes here, and this sequence had to be done right," says Johnston. "You have to make it sincere, so that the audi-ence will believe everything they do, all their feelings."

In the end, Mowgli is finally enticed into the village by a pretty little girl gathering water. When Walt first suggested that as the

"This bear [Baloo] is marvelous. We gotta keep him in the picture," said Walt of Johnston's exploratory animation. OPPOSITE, *life imitates art: Johnston demonstrates Baloo's moves for the song "Bare Necessities."*

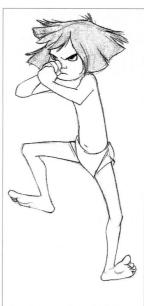

In The Jungle Book, *the trusting relationship between Baloo and Mowgli, the wild child, was crucial. "You have to make it sincere," says Johnston, "so that the audience will believe everything they do, all their feelings."*

solution, Johnston hated the idea. "Here's this tacked-on ending. How, what can you do with it?" he wondered. "I wrestled with it and the more I wrestled with it, the better I liked it. So finally, I managed to help this little girl innocently seduce Mowgli into going back." Johnston recalled that one of his last meetings with Walt before he died was to show him the little girl sequence. Just before the pencil test was screened, however, Milt Kahl distracted Walt by vigorously arguing with him about whether tigers can climb trees. (Walt believed they could.) "Milt's getting Walt all upset and I'm trying to shut Milt up," says Johnston, "but when he'd get on something he didn't hear anybody else." Finally, Walt said, "Damn it! I came in here to look at Ollie's girl anyway. So whatya got, Ollie?" Nervously, Johnston showed his animation. Walt approved it, commenting "She's sexy, Ollie."

The vain and cowardly lion Prince John and his snake lackey Sir Hiss were animated with subtlety and wit by

Johnston in *Robin Hood* (1973). The strong voices and mannerisms of actors Peter Ustinov and Terry Thomas inspired Johnston's delineation of the duo's egomaniacal personalities and gingerly one-upsmanship. "I watch those guys when I have lunch with them," says Johnston of the actors. "I can't take my eyes off them because I keep thinking I'll see something. I'd do it with Ustinov and he'd be eating and he looks at me out of the top of his eyes." Johnston claims his intense observations enter his subconscious. "You sort of saturate yourself with them, so I really stare at them. I'm hypnotized and I'm sure that there's a lot that comes out that belongs to those guys that I don't even realize because I've thought about it so much."

While Prince John is not an obvious caricature of Peter Ustinov, says Johnston, "there's something of the Ustinov quality about him." For example, the small, almost invisible movements the actor made while recording the soundtrack. "He doesn't move around a real lot," says Johnston, "and my

In Robin Hood *in 1973, Ollie Johnston's light pencil sketches conveyed animated personalities of the greatest subtlety and nuance; such as insecure Prince John and sycophantic Sir Hiss.*

conception of this guy [Prince John] is the important things on him are the little things. He isn't the kind of guy who does a lot of big movements. He really is too lazy and he only gestures. I like to see his mouth move and I like to see the expression in his eyes. Walt always said when you look at somebody, you look at their eyes."

Johnston once had a sign on his desk that read "What is the character thinking and why does he feel that way?" "He's very intuitive," said Frank Thomas of Johnston's method of animating. "He has to feel it from the inside."[39] Johnston also wants the audience to see his characters thinking: "The thoughts are behind the eyes and behind the mouth. I have rather restrained movement on him. And the snake [Sir Hiss] moves more, but I don't like to see him all over the screen. You can get violent when there's a reason to. I like where [Prince John] says 'Seize him!' and 'Stop the coach!', where he does little gestures. He wouldn't exercise more than he had to. He's a coward when it

comes to fighting. He'll tell somebody else to kill or seize but he wouldn't do it himself."[40] Johnston's two fully delineated characterizations are the brightest and funniest spots in an otherwise disappointing film.

Frank Thomas noted in a 1976 letter to a friend that *The Rescuers* (then in its final stages of production) "doesn't have the styling I would have liked, nor the type of color and painting, and the songs aren't as good as we had hoped, but somehow there is a very strong and good feeling that comes out of

Ollie Johnston put a lot of himself into his roles, especially the cat Rufus in The Rescuers; OPPOSITE, *a Johnston exposure sheet for a scene in which Rufus reacts to the orphan Penny saying she was not adopted because another girl was chosen who "was prettier than me."*

the whole situation and the characters that makes it unusual and quite appealing. It has more 'heart' than our last three [films], without losing any of the entertainment and laughs."[41]

A major portion of the film's "heart" and laughs were supplied by Ollie Johnston, who shared animation of the heroic mice Bernard and Bianca, and the orphan girl Penny. A solo role was the albatross Orville, a hick aviator-entrepreneur who runs a "fly-by-night" one-bird airline. The ironically named fowl is endearing in the unfounded confidence he has in his piloting abilities. Johnston's study of real bird actions paid off hilariously: in this case, a caricature of ungainly albatrosses attempting to take off and their sloppy, skidding landings. "It struck me so funny the way an albatross would land and knock over about three other albatrosses like he was a bowling ball. They would get up and shake and settle back down like it was a perfectly normal thing. That's what gave me the idea that this was all very routine. It finally came to life for me when we put all the [sound effects of] panting and footsteps in."[42]

The emotional high point of *The Rescuers* is Johnston's handling of the relationship between Penny and an elderly cat, Rufus (a lookalike for the animator himself, grandfatherly mustache and all). In a flashback, Rufus relates his last conversation with the missing child, which took place in a large room at the orphanage. Little Penny sits alone on one of many empty beds, her small, huddled figure facing away from us— a strong visual statement of vulnerability and loneliness. Rufus approaches slowly down an aisle and asks quietly,

"What's wrong, Penny honey?" "Nothing," says the child. As Rufus hops onto the bed, the cat's hind leg slips a bit, Johnston's subtle indication of the aging cat's fragility.

Rufus rubs against the little girl's back and leans against her arm (very catlike actions), all the while coaxing her to talk about what's bothering her. Rufus is even more magical than *Pinocchio*'s Figaro: for not only is he physically anthropomorphic, but he has the power of human speech. When Penny reveals she was passed over for adoption ("they chose a little redheaded girl—she was prettier than me"), the camera is tight on Rufus. His devastated expression—on the verge of tears with a trembling jaw—would have been too broad on Penny. But it is just right for the old cat, and through him the audience has an expressive conduit for its own emotions. Then Rufus (still in close-up) breaks the mood ("Ah, she couldn't be. . . .") and begins to encourage the little girl, to bolster her confidence. He makes silly jokes and gives her hope, as any loving granddad would.

In addition to the extraordinarily sensitive and warm acting, Johnston was responsible for the final shot selection and editing of the images. As always, he made tiny thumbnail storyboards in planning his sequence. "I changed the cutting to suit my plan," he once explained, "and get the dialogue on the right character. Sometimes on the one listening, which often exposed the thoughts of both characters." He also sat in on recording sessions "so they'd say stuff in a way I felt would promote the character."

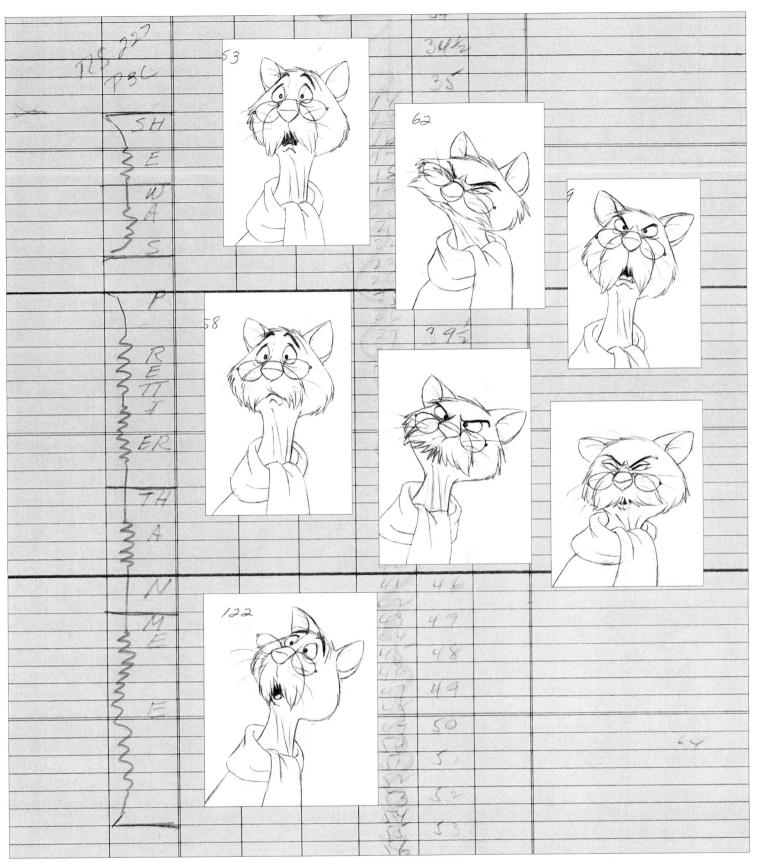

Then the master animator would "sit and sweat" at his drawing board. "Analyze what I was going to do. It's so hard to be sure you've picked something entertaining," he says. "If you haven't, what have you got? Especially in a Disney picture. With Walt, that was his strongest thing: entertainment, personality, humor. So you struggle with these drawings, work so hard to get the right expression. And the right acting on the body, the right timing."

The Rufus–Penny sequence is strong because the relationship between the characters is real. It is quintessential Ollie Johnston: deeply touching, with a straight-to-the-heart impact on audiences. It is on a par with his Mowgli/Baloo pairing in *The Jungle Book* and equal to Vladimir Tytla's *Dumbo* visiting his imprisoned mother. The sequence is the emotional zenith of *The Rescuers* and, arguably, of Johnston's career.

Johnston explored personality in key pose drawings, and also made numerous thumbnail sketches laying out action and positions for important dialogue.

Interestingly, for all the high emotionalism he brings to his animation, and the warmth and sentimentality he has personally, Johnston also has a practical, no-nonsense side. While Frank Thomas admits to a tendency to "jump into things headlong without thinking about them properly," his friend Ollie has always "been much more thoughtful. He also led in economic things, too," according to Thomas. "He would say, 'Hey, don't you think we ought to get an apartment where we can have this and that, someone come in and cook for us?' It was Johnston who suggested they both buy the Flintridge and Julian properties and split them.

Ted Thomas, Frank's son, has noted that "Ollie has been a lot stronger in common sense things [than Frank], everyday dealing-with-the-world kind of issues. Like, 'We ought to buy this property or that's a good price'; or 'That's not such a good deal.'" Creatively, too, over the many years of their friendship, Johnston has been extremely good at coming up with an inspiration, according to Ted Thomas; while "Frank has been incredibly good at elaborating on that inspiration." But it is Johnston who always recognizes "when something's ready to be let go. Ollie has been good at saying, 'Okay, let's move on.'"

While working on *The Fox and the Hound*, Johnston decided "I think it's time for me to leave" the Disney studio. His decision was based not only on health problems (the increasing tremors in his drawing hand), but also because he felt that he had "done all this before."

Another factor in the decision of both Johnston and Thomas to retire was the sudden death in 1975 of Bill Walsh. Walsh was a spectacularly successful producer of Disney TV shows and movies who, during the 1950s and '60s, was considered Walt's creative twin. In their search for an artistic ballast for the animated features after Walt's death, Thomas and Johnston trusted neither the taste or judgment of Reitherman and Kahl, nor that of the front office suits. Instead, they turned often to Walsh (who was a year younger than they) for critiques and support of their instinctual creative decisions. When Walsh died, Thomas told Dale Oliver "this is the second worst day in the history of the studio." The first was, of course, when Walt died; but Walsh's passing was almost equally traumatic because, according to Thomas, "Bill was the only artist we had in management."[43]

In the 1980s, animator/authors Frank and Ollie struck a running pose similar to one at Stanford nearly fifty years before (SEE PAGE 212). BELOW, performing for the 1995 documentary Frank and Ollie, coproduced by Theodore Thomas and Kuniko Okubo.

Both Johnston and Thomas decided to retire together on January 31, 1978 (Ollie's hire date); however, as noted in the previous chapter, their so-called "retirement" of the last twenty-some years has involved authoring several books, lecturing, and consulting on film projects around the world.

"From the beginning," says John Lasseter, director of the computer animated *Toy Story* and *Toy Story 2*, Frank and Ollie were "always very interested in the new technology and what it could do. They saw the potential of computer animation when I first started working with it. They were very excited. When I first went up to Lucasfilm, before Pixar was started, I invited them to come up for a day. They did. I had one of the first paint systems and I let them start drawing. It was so fun to see them draw. Ollie's hand, he had less control over it. He became so frustrated. He made this one comment which I'll never forget. He was so excited about what he was seeing, he

said, 'I wish I was young again!'"[44] In February 2000, the up-to-the-minute Johnston and Thomas began to create their own Web site (frankandollie.com), which will dispense advice about their kind of personality animation directly to the world at large.

As he nears his ninth decade, soft-spoken, gentle Ollie Johnston continues to be practical and tough in making life decisions. When the huge old oak at the corner of his house became diseased, he ordered it cut down rather than risk its falling on the house. When he and Marie found their mobility decreasing, he sold his share in the house in Julian and, with it, his beloved 1901 H. K. Porter locomotive. He also sold his superb collection of original animation art to a private collector; the funds went to build a small house on the Flintridge property for an au pair couple, who look after Ollie and Marie.

"He's a passionate man," says Ken Johnston of his father,

"and tries to the best of his ability to connect with the different stages of his life. Letting go of that oak tree and the train, he's kind of honoring in himself that you do let go of certain parts."[45]

Ollie Johnston has few regrets regarding his forty-three years of work at Disney. "I wish I'd worked harder on some of the stuff," he commented recently. "Thought it through more. I wish I had [had] the energy. Spent more time on the clean-ups." Zeroing in on *The Jungle Book*, he admitted, "I don't like the bear's mouth.

"But, all in all," he concluded regarding Baloo and Mowgli, "I like the emotional quality in their relationship."[46]

ABOVE, *Ollie with Mickey;*
OPPOSITE, *Christmas in Flintridge, 1984: John Canemaker seated on Johnston's model steam locomotive, with (left to right) Ollie Johnston, Jeanette Thomas, Frank Thomas, and Marie Johnston.*

Young John Lounsbery in Colorado, circa 1916; years later he animated Pluto in numerous shorts, Colonel Hathi, leader of an elephant herd in The Jungle Book, *and Ben Ali Gator in the* Dance of the Hours *in* Fantasia. OPPOSITE, *John Lounsbery in 1955.*

CHAPTER eight
John Lounsbery

S elf-effacing. Self-sac-
rificing. The soul of
kindness. A gentle-
man. Unselfish. Not
envious. Not pushy. Modest.

No, these are not the
attributes of a candidate for
the sainthood, although they
could do very nicely. They are
descriptions from colleagues
and friends of master animator John Lounsbery.

Few of the Nine Old Men
were as universally loved and
admired as a person as was the
quiet, unassuming Lounsbery.
Younger animators in particular found him a consistently
warm and friendly source of
knowledge and support. Even
in the thick of production,
"he'd always lay down his pencil to talk to you," as Ed Hansen
puts it.[1] Don Bluth, who was eighteen when he became an assistant animator to Lounsbery, notes that "John was not a preten-
tious man, but very much a teacher. Very kind and very sharing
with all of his information."[2]

His peers respected both his calm demeanor and his artistic gifts—the fact that he was "a helluva draftsman," who "could

imitate anybody's style."[3]
"John Lounsbery was one
of the superior talents at
Disney's," says John Ewing,
another former assistant.[4]

Lounsbery's sequences
usually contained broad action
and comedy. One of his favorite roles was Ben Ali Gator,
the reptilian swain of balletic
Hyacinth Hippo in *Fantasia*'s
"Dance of the Hours" sec-
tion. Equally memorable is the
wonderfully absurd elephant
march and military inspection
in *The Jungle Book*. When he
ventured into the human
realm, Lounbery's characters
tended to be bigger than life:
for example, Tony and Joe, a
volatile Italian restaurant
owner and cook (respectively) in *Lady and the Tramp*, and
George Darling, the pompous father in *Peter Pan*.

Lounsbery trained under Norman Ferguson, assisting
that early master of action on numerous shorts starring
Pluto the pup. From Ferguson, Lounsbery absorbed the
basic principles of character animation, with an emphasis on
big anticipatory moves preceding a main action, and plenty

2 4 1

of squash-and-stretch throughout. Ferguson also pioneered techniques of making characters appear to go through a thinking process, an important component of his style that became second nature to Lounsbery.

Eventually, the apprentice surpassed his mentor; Lounsbery's superb draftsmanship, control of line, and personal taste gave even the broadest actions detail and subtlety. His dogs, pachyderms, and lizards are truly alive and full of personality, qualities that even his sketches in repose maintain. Glen Keane found Lounsbery's quietude and reserve fascinating because they belied the "bold, powerful, passionate" drawings that came out of the man.[5]

But like Les Clark, another gentle personality, Lounsbery "underrated himself, underplayed his talent," according to one friend.[6] In turn, he was "vastly underated as an animator-director" by the other Nine Old Men, according to Ewing.[7] It is no accident that both Lounsbery and Clark worked in the B-wing of the Burbank Animation building, away from most of the Nine in the high-powered D-wing. Lounsbery was uneasy in the competitive atmosphere of the upper echelons of animation at Disney; particularly troubling were Milt Kahl's jealous public putdowns.

Lounsbery loved to animate, period. Late in his career when he was moved into direction, it distressed him. "They pushed me into this thing," he sadly told Richard Williams.[8] The day he was packing to move into the director's area, animator Dale Baer asked him how he felt. "He said all he wanted was just to be a good animator someday."[9] "He was just a quiet, shy person with a circus inside of him," notes John Pomeroy. "Man, this guy had dynamite in his veins and you'd never know it!"[10]

John Mitchell Lounsbery was born March 9, 1911 in the Norwood section of Cincinnati, Ohio, the second son of Mary Heath and Arthur P. Lounsbery; his father was a carriage builder "noted for his leather upholstery. He later installed specialized interiors for automobiles."[11] In addition to an older brother named Arthur (Art), John also had an older half-brother, Charles, from his father's first marriage.

Mary Lounsbery's father, Thomas T. Heath, was "quite a character," according to John's widow Florence (Lounsbery) Shaw. During the Civil War, he was a short-tempered colonel and brevet brigadier general who "had his own troop and a lot of silver mounted saddles."[12] In his long life, General Heath (who was also a lawyer) went through three fortunes, thanks to his disagreeable temperament. One fortune was made with a partner in Linotype machines; but after a quarrel, the partnership broke up. Heath's two other fortunes came from marrying rich women; both wives "got mad at him, too," and the last one divorced him when he was ninety. By the time John was born, the family fortune consisted of "lots of things that [the General] had picked up in Europe, silver and all kinds of arms. But no

money." Nevertheless, John was said to have been "always very proud of his grandfather," according to Mrs. Shaw.

When Lounsbery was five, his family moved to Denver, Colorado. His childhood there he once described simply as "typical, filled with winter sports, drawing, school activities, and summer trips to the Colorado mountains. His appreciation for the natural beauty of the area was reflected in his early artwork, as sketching and painting became his principle interest."[13] "Dad developed a deep and abiding infatuation with the outdoors," says Ken Lounsbery, John's son. He was "an active scouter" who trapped small game, but decided he "couldn't make a living as a mountain man." And so, "he turned to another love of his": drawing.[14]

Making a living became a real concern when John was thirteen: his father died of a heart attack, which forced his mother to work to support her three boys.[15] By that time, John was in East Denver High School, where his facile drawing quickly gained him a reputation as the "resident cartoonist." In the school's 1928 yearbook, seventeen-year-old Lounsbery's cartoons (initialed "JML") are on almost every other page. "Many cartoonists draw in their own image," notes Ken Lounsbery; and "many of dad's characters in the yearbook did have a relatively prominent nose," supposedly based on the artist's own proboscis.[16]

Following graduation, there was a brief period when Lounsbery traveled throughout the west by railroad, working occasionally as a lineman and pole-setter for Western Union. Years later he told his children stories about "stringing line" in rattlesnake country. "When a lineman was up a pole," explains his daughter Andrea, "they would leave [a second man] on the ground to shoot the snakes. Dad was known as the best shot." "But," says son Ken, "gandy-dancing was not his true forte."

Lounsbery's inner strength and sense of purpose were demonstrated early on when he enrolled in the Art Institute of Denver, from which he graduated in 1932. "The Depression notwithstanding, he was determined to make a living at the thing he loved doing most: creating through cartooning," says Ken Lounsbery.

Soon after graduation, though, an opportunity for further art studies appeared. Albert Giesecke, one of Lounsbery's high-school classmates and a fellow cartoonist, planned to attend Art Center in Los Angeles. "He talked John into doing the same thing," recalls Florence Shaw. Lounsbery's mother arranged for her son to have a working scholarship at the school; with the help of a stipend from a close family friend, Lounsbery traveled with Giesecke to Los Angeles.[17] Money was tight; the young man lived mainly "on Shredded Wheat" while attending classes for three years; but, notes a friend, "he was so dedicated to becoming an artist that it didn't matter." In his spare time, he took on freelance commercial art assignments.[18]

John and Florence Lounsbery, newlyweds in 1935.

It was at Art Center that Lounsbery met Florence Louise Hurd; ironically, both had attended East Denver High at the same time but never met. Florence, a scholarship student interested in landscape and architecture, started at Art Center one semester before Lounsbery. "When he arrived," said Mrs. Shaw recently, "we had a natural interest [in each other] because the Gieseckes were from Denver and we were from Denver. So we struck up a good friendship."[19] In fact, they quickly fell in love.

Florence worked part-time as a color-model designer for the new Harman–Ising animation studio in Hollywood, owned by Walt's old associates from the Kansas City and Oswald the Lucky Rabbit days, Hugh Harman and Rudolf Ising. One day a young animator named Melvin Schwartzman (later Mel Shaw) walked directly over to Florence Hurd and asked her to dinner. "I liked his appearance very much, so I said, 'Oh, yes. Sure.'" The next day he arrived early for a second dinner date with Florence and, he says, "to my surprise John Lounsbery was just leaving after taking Florence out for a luncheon date!" "Now this didn't irritate John, but it irritated Mel," says Florence. "My heart fell," admitted Shaw years later, "when I assumed that I had already missed the boat with this pretty little miss." After that dinner, he never called her again. "So eventually," says Florence, "I married John." Years later, however, after both their spouses had died, Florence and Mel renewed their friendship and in 1983 were married.[20]

As Lounsbery was about to graduate from Art Center, he sought full-time employment. When the school's Fine Arts teacher told him about Disney's talent search, the twenty-four-year-old applied. "It looked like a real utopia in the height of the Depression," he said. Lounsbery was hired on July 2, 1935, and he and Florence wed on December 7, 1935 at the Forest Lawn Chapel. The groom's starting salary at Disney—only twelve dollars a week—necessitated his taking a second job at night in store decoration at Sears. Donald Graham recognized his talent and got him a raise. "So I was able to stay on and get married." The couple honeymooned in Big Bear and lived in a rented house in Hollywood within walking distance to Harman-Ising, where Florence continued work until 1937.[21]

Lounsbery was soon assigned as an assistant to animator Norman ("Fergie") Ferguson (1902–1957), a former stenographer and animator from New York. After joining Disney in 1929, Ferguson rose quickly to become one of the studio's most creative and well-paid animators. "Fergie's bonuses looked like heaven," said Lounsbery.[22] Like Fred Moore, Ferguson was a natural; he made up for his lack of training as a draftsman with keen instincts for showmanship and the performing arts. Moore gave Disney animation its appealing shapes and designs, and he instinctively used shape-shifting principles (such as squash-and-stretch) to bring characters to life. Ferguson emphasized his characters' internal life; he showed a thinking process going on within their cartoon brains.

Ferguson created a milestone in personality animation with the famous flypaper sequence in *Playful Pluto* (released March 1934). Each time the hapless dog tries to remove a piece of the sticky stuff from his anatomy, he thinks about his predicament before acting. Ted Sears, head of the Story Department, writes that the scene "illustrated clearly all of Pluto's characteristics from dumb curiosity to panic."

> It is timed in such a way that the audience feels all of Pluto's sensations—each "hold expression" after a surprise action was carefully planned, and expressed some definite attitude causing the audience to laugh. Each small climax builds to a better surprise.

Ferguson based his simple, direct staging on old vaudeville routines and comedians he saw in New York theaters. His approach was uncinematic; his cartoons performed as if they were on a proscenium stage. He also adopted the vaudeville performer's tactic of looking directly at and commiserating with an audience; Pluto often stares into the camera to express his feelings of the moment.

Through his drawing style, Ferguson brought spontaneity and immediacy to animation performances. His first ideas—known as "Fergie ruffs"—were extremely sketchy symbols of action. The scribbles "kept the staging simple and gave him a guide that was easy to change," write Thomas and Johnston. "He could keep making fast changes, never feeling he had invested so much time in a scene that he could not

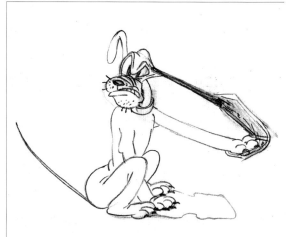

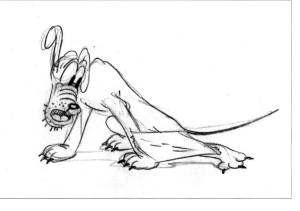

discard it and try a new idea if something was not working."[23]

"A natural action must be caricatured to constitute act-ing" in animation, wrote Disney art instructor Don Graham in a 1940 issue of *American Artist*. The article was illustrated with drawings from the Ferguson and Lounsbery section of *Pinocchio* (with the fox and cat) and the text tacitly refers to Fergie's drawing style and technique of animation.

> Economy must be exercised in the number of lines or shapes utilized. The drawings must be simple yet com-pletely expressive. Every line must be functional, both optically and structurally. Every line must be rhythmic to preserve the continuity or flow from one form into another.[24]

In 1936, Ferguson wrote an analysis of his approach toward animating Pluto. He advised roughing out the action from one extreme pose to another "as the action is visualized."

> This helps to hold the spontaneity of the situation or gag and prevents the animator from dwelling too much on an unimportant spot in the action. In going back over those drawings, extremes can be exaggerated when necessary, or a new slant may be had on different points throughout.

Ferguson was the first animator to emphasize a principle of motion later termed "overlapping action," in which not everything happens at the same time, be it the motion of parts of a body or the staging of an action. In the Silly Symphony *Frolicking Fish* (1930); one of Ferguson's first assignments at Disney, a trio of girl fish perform a fluid (no pun intended) soft-shoe in which "one part would hold [as] something else would move. So there was never a complete stop." Wilfred Jackson recalls it was a scene that "Walt made us all look at, because he said that [was] the worst thing about the kind of animation [we were] doing. Your character goes dead and it looks like a drawing."[25] Here was another way (along with stretch-and-squash and making the character "think") of strengthening the illusion that the characters were *not* draw-ings, but were real, live actors—which was essential to Walt's concept of animation.

After a screening of Pluto pencil tests, according to Thomas and Johnston, the young animators would run to Ferguson's room to study his drawings and copy the timing from his exposure sheets. Ferguson, watching the feeding frenzy with cool blue eyes, would ask laconically, "Why do you want to memorize how I did that action? I might do it dif-

OPPOSITE, the famous flypaper scene from Playful Pluto *(1934), animated by Lounsbery's mentor, Norman Ferguson.*

ferent next time." A true animation pioneer, Ferguson felt his way blindly along new paths, trying always to find ways to make characters more expressive.

John Lounsbery quietly soaked up all that Ferguson accomplished and was trying to do. They worked closely together on numerous Pluto shorts and both men loved the dog. Years later, Lounsbery complained about how Pluto was handled in his last shorts: "It always hurt me to see him get carried into human actions, expressions, even a voice. He was pure dog, that's the way Fergie always considered him."[26]

On the features after *Snow White* and *Pinocchio*, Lounsbery's superior draftsmanship and instinct for dynamic cinematic staging enabled his animation performances to go beyond Ferguson's capabilities. However, much of Ferguson's approach always remained in Lounsbery's work: a certain energy, a strong use of squash-and-stretch and anticipations, and a bold directness. And, like Fergie, he had a desire to find a different way each time to approach an assignment.

Some felt there was often too much Fergie lingering in the wings. "I sometimes have a hard time understanding his sense of squash-and-stretch," says Andreas Deja of Lounsbery's animation. "Occasionally, I think it's overused. The character goes for accents into these broad squashes and stretches more than is called for. It goes throughout his work."[27] "He was sort of a product of Fergie's thinking, wasn't he?" asks Ken Peterson rhetorically. "He didn't seem to arrive at things the same way [Frank and Ollie] did."[28]

Lounsbery assumed more responsibilities working with Ferguson on the witch sequences in *Snow White*. The leap from Pluto to "Supervising Animator" of the witch was a big one for Ferguson; but Joe Grant, who made the character's final design, states that the animator was "very cooperative—it wasn't good drawing, but he put such character into the ani-mation. Everything was extreme, you know, and it just felt right."[29] Ferguson's approach was big and hammy; it was melodramic hokum he probably witnessed in scores of the-atrical plays. It was also partly modeled on Lionel Barrymore's drag performance of an old lady in *The Devil Doll* (1935), and live-action reference footage of the character actor Moroni Olsen (also dressed in drag).[30]

The masculine models give Ferguson's witch an aggres-sive quality, rather than the frailty of a little old lady. It is as if her shape-shifting potion pushed her beyond the norm in behavior and form, beyond male or female and into another sexual category. Her overplayed dramatic gestures and poses succeed in the action scenes, and also in dialogue scenes where she comes off as truly insane and scary: mumbling and cackling to herself and her pet raven while dipping an apple in a toxic brew, and (later) cajoling Snow White to take a bite of the tainted fruit. ("It's a magic wishing apple, dearie.") The witch often speaks directly to the camera, another element of

Lounsbery's drawing skills and Ferguson's sense of timing and the dramatic meshed well together when they animated the witch in Snow White, *one of Disney's scariest villains.*

Fergie's show-biz approach; beneath her warty nose and toothless smile lurks a vaudeville baby.

One assumes Lounsbery was a great help to Ferguson. Among his duties, he worked over the rotoscoped drawings (sequential sketches made from live-action reference footage) of the witch attempting to push a boulder onto the Dwarfs and the surprise bolt of lightning that topples her off a cliff; also, a scene in which the witch feigns a heart attack, and scenes in which she rows a boat from the distance across a lake, which were challenging because of the subtle changes in size.[31] Ferguson also gave Lounsbery a scene all his own: a close-up of the witch exiting down a trap door, laughing as she contemplates Snow White "buried alive."[32]

On Pinocchio, *Lounsbery and Ferguson again worked closely together; this time, they made vivid personalities of a con artist team consisting of a dim-witted cat and a sly fox.*

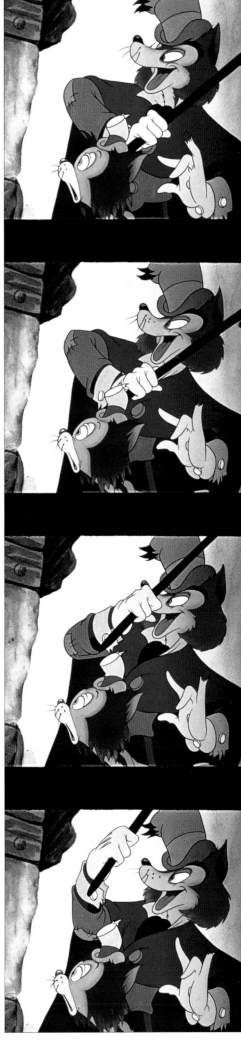

As assistant to Ferguson, Lounsbery received no screen credit on the feature; but Fergie generously made sure his assistant's work was noticed and rewarded. A memo from Walt dated May 3, 1938, awarded Lounsbery a share of the "adjusted salary compensation" in "direct proportion to your contribution toward the production and completion of [*Snow White*]." Half of the $248.78 bonus was in an enclosed check, the balance due "to be paid in ten equal weekly installments" starting the next week.[33]

In 1939, Lounsbery animated numerous scenes "under Ferguson's supervision" on shorts, such as *The Practical Pig* (released February 1939)—the wolf spanked by a complicated mechanical contraption; *Society Dog Show* (February 1939)—Pluto and his girlfriend Fifi; and *The Pointer* (July 1939)—Mickey Mouse scolding Pluto and teaching him how to hunt.

With *Pinocchio* came a change in status for both Ferguson and Lounsbery: the former became a "Sequence Director" and the latter is listed as an "animator" in the screen credits. This time they worked together on sequences involving a shabby but elegant fox named J. Worthington Foulfellow and his companion in crime, a mute and profoundly stupid cat named Gideon. Actor Walter Catlett's voice for Foulfellow, write Thomas and Johnston, "clearly suggested all the attitudes, facial expressions, and mannerisms that would be needed to capture the potential of such a character."[34] Ferguson and Lounsbery followed through superbly on the vocal "suggestions"; they built a solid relationship between fox and cat. "Fergie never displayed much emotion and kept his thoughts and ideas to himself," write Thomas and Johnston, "but this assignment was obviously one of the most enjoyable he had encountered."

Other animators might have made the Fox more dramatic, more villainous, perhaps sillier, less believable, or more sincere. Only Fergie saw the special kind of entertainment that both the Fox and the Cat could offer this picture. It was the kind of character development he understood and loved.[35]

Essentially, Foulfellow and Gideon are a vaudeville team, a pair of slapstick comedians who play off of each other physically. The fox continually uses his cane to subdue the cruder impulses of his silent partner; and, at one point, the cat uses a sledgehammer to remove the fox from his hat. Tipping funny hats and brandishing Chaplinesque canes, the pair even break into a jolly song and dance extolling the fun of being a performer. ("Hi diddle-dee-dee, an actor's life for me!") It is Ferguson's most overt vaudeville reference; no wonder he enjoyed it so much.

Lounsbery handled many scenes dealing with the pantomimic cat, Gideon; he made plain the cat's one-track mind for violence (he usually grabs for an oversized mallet before considering other options). Yet the cat is also quick enough to support the fox eagerly when he goes into one of his humbugging riffs; he plays nurse-stenographer to the fox's doctor as they try to convince Pinocchio that he's a sick puppet in need of a vacation on Pleasure Island. "A slight touch of monetary complications with bucolic semilunar contraptions of the flying trapezius!" bamboozles "Doctor" Fox regarding the kid's fatal symptoms, as Lounsbery's Gideon writes it all down (in illegible scribbles).

Four years after joining the Disney studio, Lounsbery's apprenticeship was over. For in *Fantasia*'s "Dance of the Hours" section, "Johnny Lounsbery became a star animator," as John Culhane writes in his 1983 book on the making of the concert feature.[36] "[W]hen he set the character of Ben Ali Gator in motion, it made his reputation." "It was the first time I had worked with music to that extent," Lounsbery told Culhane, "where you are completely guided by the tempo and accents of a prescored sound track . . . it was a lot of fun trying to be inventive enough to fit action to all these sounds."

"Dance of the Hours" was codirected by Norman Ferguson and T. Hee (a *Pinocchio* storyman and sequence director) as a satire on ballet and its romantic heroes and heroines; in the film, ostriches and hippos, elephants and alligators pose ridiculously, perform *entrechats* and elevations, and daintily dance on pointe. Mostly they lust after and chase

each other through neoclassical settings and choreography influenced partly by the sequences George Balanchine choreographed for Vera Zorina in *The Goldwyn Follies* (1938). Marge Belcher (the model for Snow White, later half of the dance team of Marge and Gower Champion) was also photographed performing various balletic movements.

In addition, Walt arranged for the "Dance of the Hours" creative crew to attend performances of Colonel de Basil's Original Ballet Russe, then in Los Angeles on a national tour. Irina Baronova, the company's legendary prima ballerina, dropped by the Disney studio on at least two occasions to pose for the artists and to dance in a reference film. "What a Baronova! Paris or London or New York will never see her like this," wrote Robert Baral in *The American Dancer* magazine in 1941. "Baronova picked some worn ostrich feathers from an artist's table and let herself go."

Only once did Baronova hold back. One idea man wanted the ostrich to lay an egg in a final tableau. But the entire unit rose as one man and replied coldly, "Not in our sequence." Baronova also decided that a bunch of grapes in her mouth was sufficient![37]

"It is not difficult to parody the classic dance," wrote Lincoln Kirstein in 1940. "Frequently the form itself in performance is so preposterous, affected and brittle that it becomes a parody of itself. Disney does not stoop to mere irreverence. His ballet dancers, whether hippos, alligators, elephants or ostriches, have spent their long hours at the *barre*. The *pas de deux* of the alligator and Susan the hipperina *[sic]*, is as satisfying as the Bluebird with Markova and Eglevsky, in a different tone, to be sure, but just as satisfying."[38]

Lounsbery distinguished the dashing Ben Ali Gator from the rest of the look-alike alligators by the way he moves; his very first entrance along a temple column bespeaks a dashing personality. In a few frames, the viewer can tell by the way he walks that a cocky, take-charge kind of guy has entered the

OPPOSITE, Fantasia *conductor Leopold Stokowski chats with Lounsbery who draws a dancing alligator in love with a hippo ballerina.* "Thanks to this assignment," *wrote John Culhane,* "Johnny Lounsbery became a star animator."

scene—a John Garfield type with Nureyev moves. Robert Feild wrote in 1942 that "Ben Ali needed little introduction. He crashed upon the stage and endeared himself not only to Hyacinth [Hippo] but also to every susceptible female in the audience. But the animator could not take his appeal for granted. Every flicker of an eyelid must be utilized to the utmost."[39]

Lounsbery strengthens our first impression of Ben Ali when the gator spies the lovely tutu-clad hippo below: he does an exaggerated take, flings off his cape—a grand gesture in synchronization with an equally grand musical thrust—and jumps off the balcony feet first, landing in a triumphant pose; his surprise appearance scatters the competition (hooded and caped alligators) like autumn leaves.

In a subsequent close-up, Ben Ali expresses desire and lust for the supine hippo before him, lying in all her corpulent voluptuousness. The lovesick lizard clutches his chest like an Aztec priest about to remove his own heart, flutters his eyelashes in violent ecstasy, and lets out a silent open-mouthed gasp. This is smoldering movie acting to rival Rudolph Valentino! "For Ben Ali to register his devotion took fifty drawings," notes Robert Feild. "But the animator considered neither facial expression nor general deportment sufficient to press the point home with finality. Notice the feathery contraption that Ben Ali sports for a hat. From a psychological point of view the quality of line assumed by these feathers is descriptive of all that he endured."[40]

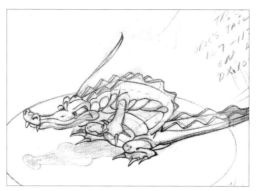

According to John Culhane, Norman Ferguson's "mastery of the staging of broad action is apparent in every scene" of "Dance of the Hours."

"Fergie was a great help when it came to looking at the pencil tests of the animation," said T. Hee. "Fergie would say to an animator, 'Why don't you exaggerate here? Why don't you pull that leg up a bit?' And he would know how to make a drawing to illustrate the broader action he was after."[41]

Be that as it may, John Lounsbery came into his own as an animator on *Fantasia*; as Fergie's heir apparent, he would soon take on broad and comic roles and sequences that might have gone to Ferguson. "His anatomy was correct," says Frank Thomas of Ben Ali Gator; as for Lounsbery's animation, Thomas comments that "He'd do it right. Do something flamboyant. It'd be strong, it'd be clear."[42]

It's worth noting that Lounsbery did not believe that Ferguson's drawing was inferior to his own, a marked difference of opinion from most of the other Nine Old Men. In 1971, Lounsbery told John Culhane he thought that animation had advanced "technically," but, he said, "I don't think that they display or stage the gags much better than *Snow White*. Milt's done a lot to change to this new style of highly skilled draftsmanship, like live action. Fergie didn't draw well. He really wasn't interested in drawing well. But he could sure tell a story—in the staging, timing, and the personality he got in there. And that's the difference between a fine artist and a damn fine animator."[43]

Unhappily, Norman Ferguson was moved farther away from his animation

Lounsbery caricatures natural actions in his animation; and his fine draftsmanship lends characters weight and believability.
OPPOSITE, *voice actor Ed Brophy (right) and Norman Ferguson (left) watch Lounsbery draw Timothy Mouse from* Dumbo,
BELOW, *Lounsbery ponders a plaster maquette of Dumbo.*

drawing board into important but encumbering and stressful supervisory positions; he became a sequence director on *Dumbo* (1941), the production supervisor on *Saludos Amigos* (1943), and both production supervisor *and* director on *The Three Caballeros* (1945). It may have been Walt's way of spreading Fergie's genius over a large group of animators; also a way to deal with an animator whose drawing technique was now considered inadequate and out of style. "Then somewhere along in there," Lounsbery told Culhane, "he struck a snag and wasn't so active in directing anymore."[44] The "snag" was Walt Disney.

"Ferguson's decline may have begun with a subtle friction with Disney that developed during the mid-1940s, which came to a head over the film *Saludos Amigos*," writes historian Steven Watts in *The Magic Kingdom*.[45] By the early 1950s, Ferguson was back working as a directing animator and having a tough time of it. He suffered from diabetes; he was also drinking heavily, mainly because (as Ward Kimball put it) he perceived he was "left by the wayside because he was not a trained artist." This was during *Peter Pan*'s production, when the Nine Old Men were ruling the roost. The studio fired Fergie in July 1953; four years later he was dead at age forty-five of a heart attack.

Ferguson's world had revolved around the Disney studio; he once said that when he became too old to animate "he'd take a job in the Disney parking lot."[46] It may therefore be more accurate to say that the great William Norman Ferguson died of a broken heart.

On *Dumbo*, Lounsbery became an animation director. Particularly hilarious is sequence 11, in which several ponderous, menopausal pachyderms create a gigantic pyramid atop a small ball; Dumbo is supposed to run out, spring from a trampoline, and land on top waving a tiny flag. Instead, he trips over his big ears, causing the elephants to tumble; they in turn collapse the entire circus tent. What is interesting is that though this is primarily an action sequence, Lounsbery animated all of the quieter, personality moments featuring Dumbo and Timothy—the crucial emotional glue for the whole shebang. Eight other animators took care of the elephants—struggling to maintain their balance, spinning out of control, collapsing on top of each other, falling, landing on a trapeze and a high wire, crashing into nets, and smashing wooden posts, which finally causes the big top to fold the hard way.

It was Lounsbery who handled Timothy instructing Dumbo in a "tough love" kind of way ("Don't forget to wave that flag! Okay, okay. Don't wave it no more. I saw ya."); panicking when the kid's ears intrude ("We gotta do something quick!"); Dumbo blinded by the spotlight, shyly trying to back up; tiny Timothy pushing Dumbo forward ("What's the matter with you, Dumbo? It's your cue! You're on, Dumbo!")

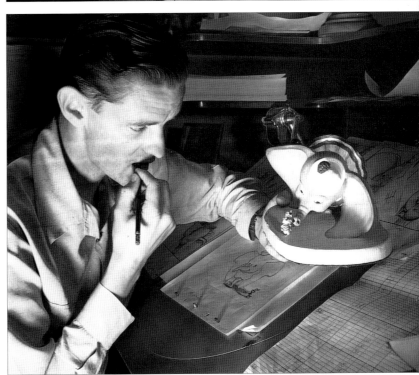

and pulling out a straight pin to provide the necessary "courage." Lounsbery animated Dumbo running determinedly as his ears slip from a knot above his head, and he did the crucial ear–foot fumble, which sends Dumbo catapulting over (not onto) the springboard. When all hell breaks loose, a few Lounsbery segments are interspersed, such as Timothy ducking behind a curtain and peeking out between his fingers, and *Dumbo*, scared to death, running and tripping again on those damnable ears. He also animated the final poignant scene in which Dumbo's trunk and eyes poke out of a hole in the

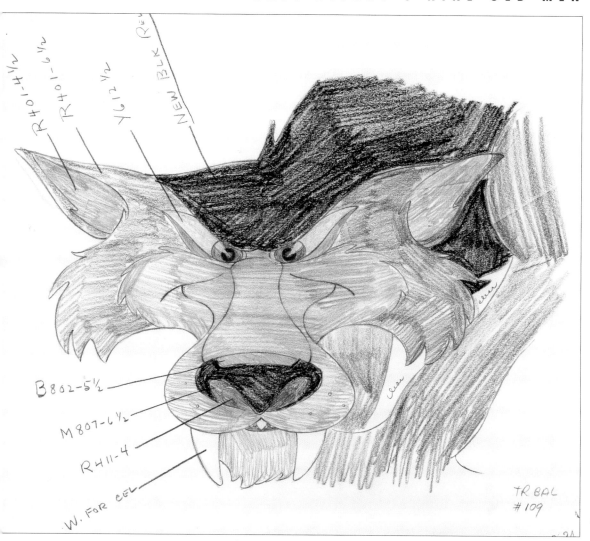

canvas of the destroyed tent; remembering Timothy's instructions, the baby elephant sadly waves his flag. The sequence is a fine example of Lounsbery's talent for mixing action with sensitive personality animation.

During the war years, Lounsbery was an animator on *Victory Through Air Power* (1943) and *The Three Caballeros* (1945), and various propaganda shorts (such as *Out of the Frying Pan into the Firing Line* (1942) and *Chicken Little* (1943); and he continued to bring Fergie's spirit to Pluto in shorts such as *Pluto's Playmate* (1941), *Pluto at the Zoo* (1942), *Pluto and the Armadillo* (1943), *Private Pluto* (1943), *Springtime for Pluto* (1944) and *Canine Patrol*

(1945). He signed a new contract with Disney in 1945 that within three years would raise his salary to $275 per week, not including the bonuses he steadily received.

After the war, Lounsbery returned to "directing animator" chores, which continued for nearly thirty years. In the Peter and the Wolf section of *Make Mine Music* (1946), he managed to create a wolf both ferocious and funny; he did the same for a bumptious, shape-shifting giant named Willie, who menaces Mickey Mouse atop a beanstalk in *Fun and Fancy Free* (1947).

Lounsbery inevitably became part of the Animation Board,

OPPOSITE, *Lounsbery's ferocious wolf in* Peter and the Wolf; THIS PAGE, *Lounsbery animating Willie the Giant from the "Mickey and the Beanstalk" in* Fun and Fancy Free *(1947).*

the pre–Nine Old Men group. Ollie Johnston found him "a quiet guy, very friendly, funny sense of humor, say funny little things."[47] "He wasn't pushy," recalls Frank Thomas. "He'd get mad and very disturbed about things, but he'd never push. In the studio he would laugh about things like [director Gerry] Geronomi. I'd be so mad I couldn't laugh." Thomas found Lounsbery introspective, but also "outgoing with people he knew real well." He was, like Eric Larson and Les Clark, "always careful not to offend," says Thomas. "In contrast to Woolie, [or] Milt, particularly. And Kimball."[48]

Because of his reticent personality, Lounsbery had to force himself to be assertive on key hiring and firing decisions. According to Frank Thomas, "He'd say, 'Well, this is all new to me. I never heard about this,' thereby letting himself off the hook. Or [he'd] say, 'I don't know. That's a big decision to make.' He wouldn't get any more involved than he had to. He was best working alone."[49]

Away from the studio, he was decidedly not alone; he and Florence were now raising three children: Kenneth, Andrea, and J. (John) K. The family lived far from "the glare of Hollywood," according to daughter Andrea Gessell, in "the farthest corner of the San Fernando Valley on a six-acre parcel they developed into a gentleman's ranch."[50]

The close-knit Lounsberys worked and played outdoors together in activities straight out of a Norman Rockwell painting. The kids belonged to 4-H and raised Herefords; the family even calved the heifers ("an unforgettable experience!"). They also raised chickens ("from the eggs to the dinner table"), and the family pets included two lambs, several ducks, two skunks, numerous dogs, two cats, and horses. Everyone in the family rode. "When I was only eight years old," recalls Mrs. Gessell, "Dad taught me how to properly tie a horse and then groom, and how to cinch a western saddle." He even knew how to trim horses' hooves. Lounsbery loved instructing his children; once he brought an old forge home to show son J. K. how to heat and bend steel, and he helped Kenneth set up a beehive.

Living in the foothills of a valley surrounded by woods and a lake, the family property was often invaded by four-legged predators (primarily attracted by the vulnerable, feathered 4-H projects). "It was Dad who would pick up and load his twenty-two rifle and go off into the black night in search of the furry bandit," says Andrea. Most were scared away by his flashlight or the hounds; others less fortunate met the taxidermist.

Lounsbery loved living close to the land and, as his

daughter put it, "could have been a pioneer settler." "For a man whose professional well-being was dependent upon his hands," observed his son Ken, "John Lounsbery had a curious disregard for the welfare of those hands. I've seen him lay brick; pound nails; shove medicine down throats of cows, horses, sheep; string barbed-wire fences with reckless abandon."

There was no television set in the Lounsbery home (a decision of both parents), for "TV just wouldn't allow us the time we needed to do all the work!" The deprivation of *The Mickey Mouse Club*, Dobie Gillis, and *Gunsmoke* resulted in "a houseful of children who loved to read. Even to the extent of sneaking a flashlight to bed so that a favorite book could be finished."

Up early every Saturday and Sunday and dressed in a plaid shirt and cowboy hat, Lounsbery went about the chores. He was a disciplinarian who expected his children "to keep busy and to help." They eagerly pitched in: weeding and maintaining the garden behind the pool cabana, and helping to lay bricks for the patio and walls. There were also fences to repair and stalls to clean, and sundry areas to sweep, trim, mow, and paint.

In his cozy den, Lounsbury sat at an old oak rolltop desk, his Navajo rug collection on the walls, surrounded by different sorts of saddles, including a Spanish antique with a wooden seat and heavy bridles. "He loved to collect old things from an interesting time in history," says his daughter. Such as the Revolutionary War rifle with bayonet that was handed down through his family; a Civil War cavalry flag (probably from grandfather General Heath); Indian arrowheads; an original map of the territories of the United States; a journal kept by a great uncle, a Methodist preacher in the 1800s who traveled from parish to parish on a mule.

John Lounsbery was not religious per se; "he just acted in a kind of religious way," says Florence. "I think he was Presbyterian. I was not anything in particular. We had a lot of friends we would travel with on ski trips and we'd go to Mass if they were Catholic or we'd go to the Presbyterian, if that's what they wanted to do."

At home he "never talked about what went on at the studio," according to Florence. "He never brought the work home with him. Loyal to his fellow workmen, fellow artists. And to Walt." Walt showed his appreciation for Lounsbery's loyalty and his work; knowing John, Florence, and the kids loved to ski, he allowed them to use his cabin at Mammoth "anytime we wanted," says Florence. "Sometimes he had Woolie Reitherman fly us up. Then we'd use [Walt's] car to get from the airport. He did give us those privileges."[51]

Monday through Friday, Lounsbery had breakfast with the family ("We were a three-meals-on-the-table-every-day family," says Andrea.), then left by 7:15 A.M. to drive to the studio through the valley, listening to newsradio in his snazzy little black '56 Ford Thunderbird. (Before the T-Bird, there had been a Volkswagen, an old green pickup truck, and a Ford station wagon.) In Burbank, the guard at the Disney studio gate would wave in the "regulars" who proceeded to their assigned covered parking. "There was a sense of pride and loyalty in the people who worked at Disney" in the 1950s, notes Andrea. "It was probably Disney's constant presence that created this sense of awe in his people. You never knew when he would show up around the studio."

Once, while visiting their father at work, Andrea and her brother J.K. were allowed to go on an errand to the "morgue," an underground area where the original drawings, cels, and backgrounds from most of the Disney films were stored. "Descending into the depths of this cool, strange, tunnel-like area," writes Andrea, "we were met by a man walking past us. Looking down at us, he asked, 'You're John's children, aren't you?' We both nodded our heads and then realized that this man, in this underground place, was Mr. Walt Disney! He shook our hands and wished us a good time and then left."

When Andrea visited the studio, her father made sure it was "a fun day." From time to time, he would interrupt his work to take his daughter for a walk to the commissary, or (better yet) through the live-action sets on the studio back lot. "He especially loved showing me where they were mechanically animating the monster squid in *20,000 Leagues Under the Sea* (1954) and later the Lincoln [Audio-Animatronics figure] for Disneyland. Dad was fascinated with the use of computers and anything else that was on the cutting edge of scientific discovery."

He would find a vacant desk in an office nearby for his daughter who would "sit in front of that big desk with the light that would illuminate the sheets of paper from below. Needing some encouragement, I would go in and watch him flip the pages from his stack of papers while penciling in his sketches as he worked. Dad could teach me many things, but his talent wasn't passed on so easily."

One of the projects Andrea observed her father developing was *Peter Pan* (1953), specifically the animation of George Darling, the film's stern but lovable patriarch. Lounsbery brought warmth and fun to the portly, veddy British Mr. Darling, a "practical man" until he glimpses Peter Pan's ghostly pirate ship passing the moon; then he gives in to the child part of himself (long buried) in a lovely, transitional moment (indeed, the film's final moment). "You know, I have the

THE LOUNSBERYS PRESENT A SHORT SHORT

Jon and Florence Lounsbery and their children: Kenneth, John K., and Andrea. BELOW, *a Lounsbery family Christmas card.*

strangest feeling," says he, as emotional memory slays rational thought, "that I've seen that ship before, a long time ago when I was very young."

Early in the narrative, Lounsbery animates him as a pompous, no-nonsense dad, the maker of unpopular decisions ("Wendy, this is your last night in the nursery.") Lord knows the poor man is made to suffer physically early on—there is plenty of slapstick trouncing as Mr. Darling trips over the kid's toys, bashes his head on bureau drawers, and falls down a lot. Lounsbery handles it all with wonderful verve. But Mr. Darling also suffers psychologically, particularly when the family dog receives more sympathy than he does. ("Aawwww! Poor Nana!") Throughout, the action is broad; Lounsbery's generous use of squash-and-stretch is always present in wild moments and quiet ones as well. At the end, for example, Wendy announces she is back in the nursery, which implies she has been absent without permission. Mr.

Darling, strict disciplinarian that he is, repeats the word "back." As he does, his face collapses into a squashed shape while he rises; when he pops open his mouth for the rest of the word, his head stretches into an aghast expression.

When Wendy mentions in passing she was kidnapped, Mr. D repeats that word, too. But the horror of that particular thought requires a very big reaction and Lounsbery goes all out. He cleverly starts the scene with Mr. Darling suppressing a yawn—a nice contrast for the concern he will soon express. When the implications of Wendy's word have sunk in, his head stretches with popped-open eyes, followed by a major squashing of the character's head within the body, combined with overlapping action as the worried father turns (in a wide arc) toward the source of his anxiety to ask in disbelief and anger, "Kidnapped?!" Lounsbery's control of line keeps the broadness from exploding into a rubbery feel; there is instead a disciplined plasticity.

Drawings of George Darling, the put-upon father in Peter Pan, *are examples of the dynamic elasticity Lounsbery put into his animation.*

"In doing human beings," observes animator John Pomeroy, Lounsbery "would take liberties that would reflect his shorts training. He could make something squash-and-stretch and be very elastic. And yet, because of his masterly draftsmanship, he could make it believable. So it didn't look too cartoon-y." Pomeroy, who animated the heroic Captain John Smith in *Pocahontas* (1995) and the male lead in *Atlantis* (2001), knew Lounsbery and emulates his style of animating. "His memory permeates so much of my career. I really enjoyed looking at his drawings and I enjoyed the man."

Lounsbery's animation in *Lady and the Tramp* of the Italian restaurant owner Tony and his cook Joe are particularly admired by numerous animators. Argumentative old friends, the pair whip up a special batch of garlic-filled pasta and meatballs for the two pooches, then add romance to the menu with an impromptu serenade ("Bella Notte"). Tony and Joe are cliché caricatures of Italian Americans, from their tempestuous temperaments to their broken-English accents. "Well, son'a ma'gun! Butcha, he's-a gotta cockerala Spanish's-a girl." (Translation: "Son of a gun! Butch, also known as Tramp, has a

cocker spaniel girlfriend.") But Lounsbery makes them real and warm-hearted. "Those were wonderful broad characters," says Pomeroy. "So great and Italian looking, you could smell them on the screen. I used to pull out and look at [Lounsbery's] rough drawings. All I could say was, gad, that's the way I want to draw!"[52] Andreas Deja considers Lounsbery's animation of the *Lady and the Tramp* pair to be "flawless."

Pomeroy noticed how Lounsbery's pencil drawings were "like brushwork. He would caress the paper, work in blues and reds and go over it in black. They had a particular type of feeling to them that nobody else had." Glen Keane was so impressed by Lounsbery's "passionate kind of drawing" that he started using the same type of pencil. "It's called the Blaisdell Layout Pencil," says Keane. "He used it on his animation and it gave him this really bold, powerful way of sculpting his drawings."[53]

"He had some of Ham [Luske]'s ability always to find the way to go further in strengthening his poses," write Frank Thomas and Ollie Johnston in their book *Disney Animation*.[54] Phil Mendez once observed Lounsbery doing so: "There, at an

In Lady and the Tramp, *Joe, the proprietor of an Italian restaurant, and Bull, an English bulldog, were both animated with warmth and verve by John Lounsbery.*

old Disney desk sat a thin figure, smoking a pipe and flipping four or five sheets of paper with one hand. The other hand would calmly reach in and scribble a few lines here and there to change an action or two."[55]

Like Luske, Lounsbery would also add an extra drawing to the action to make it stronger and more expressive. Thomas and Johnston cite a scene in *The Sword in the Stone*: a frustrated wolf, having chased and lost a meal, is exhausted and panting. Lounsbery gave him "a strong inhale and exhale with the head lifting and dropping and the tongue dragging, but it was not as funny" as it might be. So Lounsbery added one more extreme pose that went a bit further in widening the sides of the mouth and squeezing the eyes more. The result: "he was able to capture the pain and tension of the gasping wolf, which gave real meaning to the scene."[56]

"As a draftsman," write Thomas and Johnston, Lounsbery "was ideal for animation. His drawings were simple and loose and full of energy. They had volume and that elusive quality of life." In a recent interview, however, Thomas assessed his colleague's work more stringently: "It wouldn't have the oomph of Bill Tytla's animation when he was there, it wouldn't have the strength of somebody else's, or wouldn't have the quiet little innuendoes that Ollie was getting into his stuff. It would almost be like Milt's, except the drawing wouldn't hold up over the long haul." Very often, said Thomas, Lounsbery got stuck with a character because another animator "had to be pulled off 'cause he was needed someplace else. Have to get a guy to finish up what he started. That was happening to him all the time. The best thing about Johnny was that he could imitate anybody's style of drawing."

Often he had to take on scenes involving Milt Kahl's

characters. Among them: Prince Phillip in *Sleeping Beauty*; Shere Khan in *The Jungle Book*; the Sheriff of Nottingham in *Robin Hood*; Tramp in *Lady and the Tramp*; Pongo and Perdita in *101 Dalmatians*; Edgar the butler, elderly lawyer Georges Hautecourt, and grand dame Madame Bonfamille in *The Aristocats*—tough characters to draw, all of them, let alone animate. "John was a very good draftsman, the very best guy in following Milt's drawings," says Ollie Johnston. But anyone who backed up the egomaniacal, ill-tempered Mr. Kahl was like a praying mantis who mates knowing that afterward he may well become his partner's meal.

On the one hand, Kahl ignored Lounsbery contributions. "Milt never took the trouble to find out what John had done," claims Thomas. "But whenever he'd say, 'Now there's a good scene. Somebody had the sense to follow the design I made on the Indians [in *Peter Pan*] and he's done a good job of it.' I'd say, 'That's Lounsbery.' 'Well, uh, whoever it is, it's a good scene,'" Kahl would sputter. On the other hand, he often insulted or embarrassed Lounsbery publicly. "He could be destructive," recalls John Pomeroy. "He could intimidate someone like John Lounsbery. I remember Milt bragging about it to Frank and Ollie from across the hallway. It just seemed sort of crude to me. He was standing there, right after a screening, yelling to the other end of the hall that he

A model sheet for the bumbling wolf in Sword in the Stone; *Lounsbery at work on the character in 1963.* OPPOSITE, *Lounsbery (center) consulting with Wolfgang Reitherman (right) on* Winnie the Pooh and Tigger Too *(1974);* OPPOSITE, BELOW, *Lounsbery and Reitherman try out a routine for the elderly lawyer in* The Aristocats *(1970).*

wanted Johnny to change something. And he was bragging about how Johnny was looking like he was shaking in his boots and quaking at Milt's voice."[57]

"[Lounsbery] was the one who could tackle the change in styling in the Disney films Milt planned," explains Andreas Deja. "It was difficult for Frank and Ollie to take to certain abstract shapes. Lounsbery had an easier time with that because of the natural draftsman he was." One time, however, he turned down an assignment. "At the end of *The Aristocats*,"

relates Deja, "the scenes with the lawyer and Madame, Lounsbery was given those scenes. He said, 'There's no way I'm going to animate those Milt Kahl characters!' It was just too subtle for him, too straight."[58]

It was a classic Catch 22, observes Richard Williams. "He's got to follow Milt up. Milt does the butler [in *Aristocats*] and then inside the house Lounsbery has to take it on. And then Milt's going to savage John because it isn't as good as he would do. And Lounsbery knows that he's good enough to follow Milt. So he's stuck!"[59]

After years as a directing animator Lounsbery suddenly became the director of an entire short: *Winne the Pooh and Tigger Too*, released in 1974; at the time of his death in 1976, he was codirector with Reitherman of the compilation feature *The Many Adventures of Winnie the Pooh* (1977) and *The Rescuers* (with Reitherman and Art Stevens).

Mel Shaw remembered Lounsbery when he first saw him in 1934: "He walked with purpose and confidence. His natural and trained abilities must have given him this stride."[60] However, by the time Richard Williams met Lounsbery in the early seventies, he was "another one of these big guys—big shoulders [types who] sort of shrunk somehow. And he was

being bullied by Woolie." Adds Williams, "Somehow I got this bad impression." Animator Dale Baer once observed Lounsbery trying to leave a studio party early to go home and Woolie goading him with "Whatsa matter? You can't party on your own time?" The remark "bothered Louns for days after," says Baer.[61]

Williams, who became the Oscar-winning animation director for *Who Framed Roger Rabbit*, commiserated with Lounsbery about the pitfalls of directing. "Directing is kind of a pain in the ass," said Williams to Lounsbery, who replied, "Oh God. If I could just animate! If I could just close the door and have a scene and make it right, I'd get some satisfaction." While directing gives you power, continued Williams, "you can't really get what you want. It's administrative." Lounsbery sadly agreed: "Yeah. They pushed me into this thing."[62] He had no idea that he was being groomed: according to Mel Shaw, it was Ron Miller's intention to "place John Lounsbery as the new producer [of features]" after Woolie Reitherman retired.[63]

Out of loyalty to Walt and/or the studio, Lounsbery always did as he was told. "For the good of the picture," was his catchphrase, says John Ewing, his devoted assistant animator for ten years starting in 1958. Lounsbery's self-sacrificing once included screen credit; according to Ewing "the animators got together and worked out, according to footage, whose name appeared where in the credits. Johnny and one of the other 'Old Men' happened to have identical footage. There was some clearing of throats as they paused waiting for someone to volunteer a solution. Louns said that as far as he was concerned the other guy's name could go first. The other guy stared at his shoes, and his name appeared in front of Johnny's."[64] "John obediently did almost anything they asked him to do," says Don Bluth.[65]

To his assistants, Lounsbery was practically a god "who occupied a place in animation art as high as you could get."[66] He also had the reputation for "being an animator who could turn his assistants into *other* animators."[67] "His methods seemed to lead an artist more smoothly into animation,' explains Ewing. "His assistants were better prepared and equipped for the 'get on with it' style of animation. He certainly always allowed his assistant to try and do a scene. And he was never threatened by his assistant's success. Jealousy? Johnny never knew such a feeling."[68]

Lounsbery was also very protective toward those under his supervision. "He would do almost anything to keep from wounding me," says John Ewing, "even when I made the most stupid mistakes."

There was a ritual we had, repeated countless times, where I would bring my drawings in from the next room for him to have a look at. His words were almost always the same: "Hmmm. Pretty good," and he would reach for a fresh sheet of paper, place it over my drawing, and make the corrections. He talked me through the changes, always keeping his tone casual, seeming to suggest that what he was doing wasn't all that important. Then, when he was finished, he would say, "Well, that's just another way of doing it," and start to put his drawing in the wastebasket. I, of course, not being a complete fool, intercepted his drawing and took it back into my room and put it into the scene. Johnny knew it, and knew that that was what I should do, but he simply couldn't bring himself to insist that his way was best. I loved the guy.

"John was a very human kind of guy and very reachable," comments Don Bluth. "You could talk about anything. He was so helpful and encouraging. If you did the worst drawing in the world, he would just say, 'Well, here's the good part of it.' Build you up again, so your next drawing was better."

Early in his career John Pomeroy became upset when an assistant had "taken out all of the squash-and-stretch" in a scene of his in the *Winnie the Pooh* feature. He recalls Lounsbery "basically put his arm around my shoulder and said, 'Don't worry about it. I'll take care of it.' This man was acting as father confessor to me. He chewed out the cleanup artist and had the scene restored to where it originally was. He was one to ride to the rescue if you needed his help. In his own way."[69]

As is obvious in his animation, Lounsbery had a great sense of humor. It also carried over into his personal life, where it turned gently self-deprecating. "At home, Dad delighted in telling stories and jokes on himself," says his son Ken. Daughter Andrea recalled "he had the delightful ability to laugh when a story was told on him. Like the time he and Mom were dining at a fancy party and he ate the 'choke' part of the artichoke. Also, I wonder if the guys at the studio knew that Dad really enjoyed all the jokes that were passed around at lunchtime? Often he would repeat them at our dinner table that night. He would also share any new word game that he learned at the studio." Frank Thomas remembers Lounsbery joking about "always getting involved in something that he hadn't been able to think through." For example, pruning branches off trees in his backyard, falling off the ladder and knocking himself out. "He'd tell it with this sort of wistful look on his face."[70]

His sense of humor became essential in September 1970 when a freak fire destroyed the Lounsbery family's beloved home. "We lost everything," says Florence Shaw. "There was a fire in Newhall which was a refinery. In the meantime, a huge San Fernando Valley wind blew in and it went from there on down to the beach at Malibu." When John Culhane interviewed Lounsbery six months after the disaster, the animator joked that he was less busy with household chores. "We got a lull now," he said. "We were going to rebuild when an earthquake knocked down the remaining chimney. Somebody up there's trying to tell me something," he said, laughing.[71] In fact, Florence dusted off her architectural skills and the family eventually did rebuild a house on the property.

In the winter of 1976, John and Florence were skiing in Colorado when he first experienced chest pains. Back in Los Angeles his doctor prescribed nitroglycerin tablets for the continuing pain, which helped. A heart test was scheduled on February 13 at St. Joseph's Hospital across from the Disney studio; the night before, after working all day on *The Rescuers*, Lounsbery walked across the street and checked into the hospital, as planned. "He told us not to bother coming over because it was such a simple procedure," says his daughter Andrea. But that night she, her husband, and Florence visited him anyway. "Although Dad very seldom told us his feeling," said Andrea, "I could see that he was glad that we were there." He confided sheepishly to his daughter that he didn't like that the test was scheduled for Friday the thirteenth. "Knowing that Dad was not at all superstitious, I laughed at his little joke and loved him more for sharing it with me."

Lounsbery told his family to stay at home during the test the next day, so they were not present when the doctor and nurses struggled to revive him. "Dad's heart couldn't stand the pressure" says Andrea of the catheter that had been inserted in his veins. "The angiogram killed him," says Florence. The hospital finally performed a quadruple bypass, but he never regained consciousness.

"Our worst news is that our longtime friend and valued animator John Lounsbery died unexpectedly," wrote Frank Thomas to animator Larry Ruppel on March 11. "It left us not only shocked and grieved, but in something of a bind to carry on his work. It meant shifting veteran animator Art Stevens

Florence and John Lounsbery skiing in Colorado in 1976.

over to the director's spot, which leaves us shorthanded in finishing up *The Rescuers*, as well as starting various new productions. We will miss John, he is the first of the 'nine old men' to go."[72]

John Lounsbery's grave site at Forest Lawn overlooks the Disney studio. At his funeral service, "befitting a family man," only his sons and one son-in-law spoke. Instead of religious music, Andrea chose music from films her father had worked on, which was played by the chapel organist. "There was standing room only," says Andrea.

The other animators didn't give John much credit,

according to Don Bluth: "They figured he was a bread-and-butter animator. I think people who saw the pictures said John is really fabulous."

Indeed, John Lounsbery was a fabulous animator. There is something very satisfying merely about the way his cartoons looked and moved; looking a bit deeper, viewers can see a humanity and warmth he was always able to find and impart to audiences in even the most outrageous creatures. A few examples: his motherly rose vigorously conducting a blossom chorus in *Alice in Wonderland*; the clumsy dance of the owl and squirrels who stand in for the prince in *Sleeping Beauty*; in the

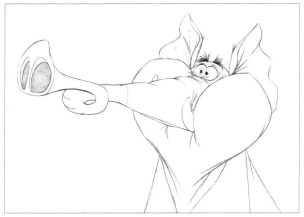

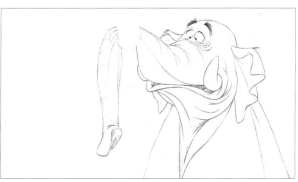
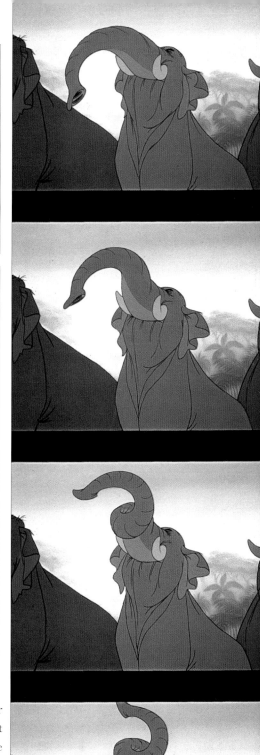

Some funny and touching characters brought to life by John Lounsbery: OPPOSITE, *a "princely" owl and a bumbling piglike henchman in* Sleeping Beauty; *Sergeant Tibs, a cat about to be imbibed by Horace Badun, a bad one in 101* Dalmatians; THIS PAGE, *the bugler elephant in* The Jungle Book, *whose musical aspirations are thwarted.*

same film, the piglike goon who desperately tries to please the evil fairy, Maleficent; the over-the-hill soldier-sheepdog and the bumbling dognappers Horace and Jasper in *101 Dalmatians*; in *The Jungle Book*, Colonel Hathi, a stern but warmhearted old elephant (another military veteran who has seen better days) inspecting a motley Dawn Patrol crew of misfits, slobs, and rebels.

"What I enjoy most," said Lounsbery, "is broader action. I like the heavies. I don't like the subtler things—the princes and the queens."[73] But his animation is full of subtleties; he brought a sensitivity to even the biggest heavies and the wildest action. He seemed not to be aware of the extent of his gift; or, if

he did, he took it for granted, or was perhaps embarrassed by it. It is hard to know, so tightly did he keep a lid on himself and his emotions.

Don Bluth recalls Lounsbery always saying, "'I dunno. Some days I just can't draw at all. I don't know what I'm doing. I should have done something else for a living.' He would always put himself down like that.

"John himself was so humble about his abilities."[74]

Two-year-old Marcus Fraser Davis in San Francisco, 1915. Master animator Davis specialized in female characters, such as Tinker Bell in Peter Pan; *he also added humor to Disney theme-park attractions, such as* Pirates of the Caribbean. OPPOSITE, *Marc Davis at his office at WED Enterprises (Walt Disney's initials), changed in 1986 to Walt Disney Imagineering.*

CHAPTER nine
Marc Davis

When Walt Disney approved of an artist's work, he rarely told him so directly. Usually he would express his delight to a third party and assume the good word would be passed along. A classic example of his oblique approach to praise occurred at an open house party in 1965 at WED Enterprises, the design and development organization Disney founded in the early fifties in Glendale, California.[1]

Walt and his wife, Lillian, were there, along with various company executives and artists and their families. On the walls were dozens of pen-and-ink and watercolor drawings made by Marc Davis for the "Pirates of the Caribbean" Disneyland attraction. When it opened two years later, it marked one of the most elaborate uses of Audio-Animatronics figures yet attempted.[2]

Davis's lively cartoons featured seventeenth-century pirates garbed in colorful tricorn hats, kerchiefs, and long coats, flashing their cutlasses and plundering villages; singing "Yo ho, yo ho!" and shooting muskets; discovering buried treas-

ure, chasing wenches, swigging from barrels, and other piratical activities—even riding a ghost ship. For all their grubby shenanigans, Davis's pirates are not bawdy or gruesome; they are, instead, bungling buccaneers whose slapstick gags garner chuckles from audiences rather than gasps. As in all of Davis's work, the draftsmanship is technically superb, and contains a warmth and humanity unique to this particular artist.

Walt was exceedingly pleased; but, of course, he didn't tell Davis. Instead, at the WED party he walked over to a group that included Marc and Alice Davis, Hazel George, the salty-tongued studio nurse, and the designer and colorist Mary Blair. "He took me by the arm," says Mrs. Davis, "and excused us from the group."

"Alice, I want to show you something," he said, gesturing to the wall containing Marc's drawings. "I want you to look at these!"

"I look at them every day, Walt. I'm making the costumes," said Mrs. Davis, who also constructed and tailored the costumes for the mechanical dolls in the "It's A Small World" attraction.

Walt always enjoyed a good give-and-take with Alice Davis, a no-nonsense Italian-Scotch American with strong opinions. "No! I don't mean it that way!" he said with irritation. "I want you to *look* at these. Aren't they magnificent?" he asked rhetorically. "These are the work of a genius! I'm having a book made of these. The public should see them. I have great plans. We're going to do some wonderful things.

"I haven't used Marc like I should have," continued Walt. "I have a whole building over there," he said gesturing toward Burbank, "filled with animators and that's all they can do. Marc can do story, he can do character, he can animate, he can design shows for me. All I have to do is tell him what I want and it's there. He's my Renaissance Man."[3]

During his forty-three years at the Disney studio, Marc Davis was essential to a dazzling variety of projects in both filmed and live entertainments. A master draftsman, he was assigned many of the toughest animation roles involving the human form, as was his good friend Milt Kahl, who often touted Davis as the superior draftsman. ("Marc is one hell of an artist, really damn good!")[4]

Davis specialized in female characters and brought to the screen an interesting assortment, such as Tinker Bell in *Peter Pan*, Maleficent and Briar Rose in *Sleeping Beauty*, and Cruella De Vil in *101 Dalmatians*; he also had a hand in designing several of the characters he animated. His gift for characterization and narrative involved him in story development for several features, most notably *Victory Through Air Power*, *Cinderella*, *Sleeping Beauty*, and *Bambi*. For the latter film, Davis's personality-filled story drawings and designs were "a breakthrough," according to Frank Thomas and Ollie Johnston, because "even the skeptics saw the possibility of a picture with deer as sympathetic main characters."[5]

Marc Davis is the only one of the Nine Old Men whom Walt asked to help plan attractions at Disneyland and the 1964 New York World's Fair; his creative contributions include the aforementioned "Pirates of the Caribbean" and "It's a Small World," as well as "The Jungle Cruise," "The Carousel of Progress," "The Enchanted Tiki Room," "The Haunted Mansion," and "Great Moments with Mr. Lincoln."

"If you can't draw it, you can't animate it," Davis once told an interviewer. The importance of knowing "how to draw, how to think in terms of drawing" was key to Davis's successful versatility. He was proud of his drawing ability and facility with a pencil. Basically self-taught during an essentially lonely childhood, he spent many an hour at local zoos sketching the animals, and observing and drawing human behavior everywhere else.

"To be an animator," he explained, "you have to have a sense of the dramatic, a feel for acting. You have to be a storyteller."[6]

Davis's gift for dramatic storytelling, plus the humanity, humor, and emotion he injected into his drawings, came from his life experiences and his keen observation. Thanks to a peripatetic, charismatic father, Davis attended twenty-three different schools before graduating from high school. Harry A. Davis, with his wife and son in tow, pursued the American Dream of getting rich quick in oil boomtowns from California to Florida, from Texas to Arkansas.

His idea of higher education was to find his teenaged son a job in a pool hall. "He wanted me to learn about life," says Davis of the father he affectionately described as a "rainbow chaser. And I did. You have to know about life, and you create out of what you know."[7]

Marc's father, a fascinating character who spoke ten languages fluently, was a magician and a musician as well as a master watchmaker—a man who "lived two hundred years in forty-eight."[8] The brief life of Harry A. Davis began in 1887 in Brooklyn, as one of ten children born to Russian and Polish Jews; his father was born in Odessa and his mother in Warsaw. Whatever the original family name may have been, it became Americanized at Ellis Island to "Dennis" and later "Davis."[9]

A pawnshop constituted the family business, but Harry's father was a wanderer. He took "a black magic act" on the road back to Russia accompanied by six-year-old Harry and an older sister. The trio traveled by sleigh across Siberia and other parts of Russia and eventually performed for the czar. Years later Harry recalled learning to swim in the Black Sea, and attending a school in Switzerland where he studied jewelry and watchmaking. Students were given a watch to repair with one piece missing, which they would have to manufacture themselves. "So literally you were a watch*maker*," said Marc of his father's craftsmanship. Harry looked down on America's so-called watchmakers because "these were guys who could take a piece out of a box" to replace a missing part.

Back in America, Harry briefly ran one of the first storefront "movie houses" in New York. When his father refused to help the business financially, Harry considered leaving home. A definite sign that he should move on came the morning his bull terrier (whom his father despised) defecated in one of the old man's shoes. Before he left Brooklyn for good, Harry's mother gave him a blood-red ruby ring for luck, which Marc inherited.

Harry was eager to go. His European journey had left him with permanently itchy feet; the hope of making a fortune in oil fueled (so to speak) his wanderlust. It led him (and subsequently Marc and his mother) to constant travel throughout the United States to mining towns and oil fields. Wherever he went, Harry supported himself as a jeweler-watchmaker and, occasionally, a mind-reading magician.

When footloose Harry was about twenty-five, he headed for Eureka at the northern tip of California; as there was no train from San Francisco, he had to go by ship. As Harry later

Looking like the Wizard of Oz is Harry A. Davis, Marc's father, who performed a "black magic" act and was, as Marc described him, "a rainbow chaser." RIGHT, *infant Marc with mother Mildred.*

told Marc, he had been all over the world in ships, but this turned out to be "the roughest trip in the whole world." As insurance against the seasickness he usually suffered, he bought a bottle of whiskey and tossed it into the bunk across from him. "When he woke up" from a nap, said Marc, laughing, "he was at sea and so sick he was never able to go over and get the bottle."

At a Eureka jewelry store Harry found work and also a pretty clerk (three years younger than he) named Mildred Fraser. Her Scottish father was a redwood and sugar pine lumberman who owned a large number of timber groves. "Her mother came out from the east in a covered wagon in the 1850s," said Marc. "The Civil War came and so they all got back in the wagon and went clear across the country again. Stayed there till the war was over. So my grandmother made three trips that way before she was eleven. Wonderful lady. In Eureka, she was the head of the Shakespeare club, of all things."

After Mildred and Harry wed, she accompanied him on his travels. "She adjusted to [the] traveling," said Marc. "I don't know how she did, 'cause she was sheltered in her background."[10] Harry occasionally booked himself into a vaudeville theater in whatever town they happened to be. Mildred assisted with his magic "mind-reading" act, apparently gathering written questions from the audience, which Harry held to his head and "read" (eyes closed) and answered. Meantime, his wife was busy offstage. "My mother would be downstairs, and this was before they had much in the way of radio," recalled Marc, who later also assisted his father. "My father had shoes that had metal plates on the bottom. He had a little rug with wires in it, so he could walk around on that and he would receive messages from my mother. It was a pretty good act."

On March 30, 1913, Marc Fraser Davis, Mildred and Harry's only child, was born in Bakersfield, California (another oil boomtown). He was named after Marcus Lichtenstein, owner of the jewelry shop where Harry was working, who served as the infant's godfather. "He gave me a five-dollar gold piece," said Marc, "which later during the Depression we ate."

Marc's earliest memory was of attending the 1915 San Francisco world's fair (the Pan-Pacific Exhibition), where his father "had something to do with the Chinese Pavilion." Now there were three rainbow chasers, two of whom—Marc and Mildred—became reluctant travelers as the years wore on. "I don't think my mother was crazy about it," said Marc recently. "We lived in places with oil fields along the road. He invested in some. I don't think he ever made much money in it. We went through all the places in the South." Marc remembered attending kindergarten in Reno, Nevada, in 1918 when he was five ("The Armistice took place."). There he had his "first creative experience": standing on a stage reciting "There was a crooked man who walked a crooked mile." "But I really got into being the crooked man, and everyone laughed," said he, recalling more than seventy-five years later the frisson he felt from the audience's reaction. "I was a hit!"[11]

The little family moved east to Tonopah, Nevada ("a mining town"), where Marc attended first grade. Then on to Wooster Falls, Texas. In Oklahoma, they moved diagonally up the state from Comanche to Seminole to Tulsa. In Tulsa, Marc took his first tentative art lessons from "a very nice lady [who] had an art club. She taught us how to fix up a canvas. And she had a very spicy technique, almost an Impressionist style."[12] It sparked Davis's lifelong interest in becoming a painter.

When Florida had it's first big land boom, the Davises were there in Little River, now part of Miami. "In a new town where I wasn't acquainted," said Marc, "I would amuse myself by drawing." It was a lonely existence for the boy. Sometimes his parents would leave him with a family of strangers and go off for two or three months at a time. "One family had a fantastic collection of books," said Alice Davis, "so Marc spent a whole summer reading them."

Perpetually the new kid on the block, Marc was always trying to make friends. "The first recess in school all these kids would gather round you," he recalled. "It was like, you and him fight." Often he would win them over with his drawing ability; sometimes he ended up with a black eye. Then there was the constant trauma of leaving behind whatever buddies he did manage to acquire. In any case, Marc always found himself contributing to school publications wherever he was. "His art is what saved him," says Alice Davis.

Harry "was just a restless man," Marc said, attempting to explain his father. "Had to have a lot of action." Sometimes he left Mildred and Marc for a month or more to establish himself in a new location, then he'd send for them. Their physical needs, if not their psychological ones, were somehow always taken care of. Except in Kansas City, Missouri, "a town we were in and out of a number of times." Marc remembered "being awfully cold as a youngster" there. "Snow and piling on

the top coat. My feet are still cold all the time." In 1928, before starting high school, he attended a summer class in painting and drawing at the Kansas City Art Institute.

Part of Harry's income came from gambling. It seems the part-time magician also had a magic touch with poker. Once, in Chicago, he beat the house by $50,000, then discovered the joint was owned by Al Capone. Frightened, he tried winning in reverse, as it were, which took quite a while. When the house was finally in the chips once again, Harry "was dined and wined" by the owners and returned to his family "very well dressed, spats, all the clothes, with walking stick, and a little bit of money. He was an extraordinary individual who lived a different kind of life," said Marc admiringly.

Marc retained vivid memories of his family's sojourn in 1923 (when he was ten) in a southwest Arkansas backwater named Smackover. It was yet another oil boomtown whose population exploded from 1,000 to 20,000 almost overnight. "It was a tent city and wooden shacks," said Marc, who arrived with his mother on a train from Kansas City. Harry, who had been in town for three months establishing his own jewelry store, met his son and wife at the train depot. Marc remembered they trudged through wet mud and his "poor mother had on high-heel shoes." Their temporary residence was "in the brothel area of town. The town was split in two by the railroad train and that was the wrong side of the tracks." Soon they moved into the back of the jewelry store in a two-story wooden building in which other families lived.

In wild and woolly Smackover "there was someone killed violently practically every day. We lived close to the little hospital and as a kid I was so curious I always had to go into the hospital every day to see somebody [who was wounded] wrapped up [in bandages], who died the following morning." The boy also witnessed a near-lynching. With a fiery cross burning in the middle of town, the Ku Klux Klan, with about a thousand townspeople, led a young African American man toward a wooden oil derrick festooned with a rope. "All of a sudden the chief of police with half a dozen of his men pulled out their guns and parted the crowd like Moses parting the Red Sea. God, it was the bravest thing I've even seen." He saved the young man, but three months later the police chief was dead of a drug overdose. "I figure that when he went into that crowd, those eyes dilated, he just scared the hell out of them," said Marc.

Liberal-minded Harry gave a job to an African American man named Vanderbilt ("Van") who ran errands and cleaned the jewelry store. "My father adored him," said Marc, who couldn't say the same regarding Van's wife. The poor woman terrified the young boy when he would see her on the street because "her whole nose had been cut off, so you just looked into this *thing*."

One pitch-black morning at 4 A.M., five shots were fired in the air, the signal that there was a fire in town. It was, in

High school graduate Marc Davis proudly displays a blood-red ruby ring, which Marc's grandmother gave for good luck to his father Harry, who passed it on to Marc.

fact, the Davis's building; flames eventually engulfed a quarter of a block. The fire was set "for insurance purposes" by "the Dane," a drugstore owner who lived upstairs. His arson tragically caused the death of the wife of a doctor: she ran back into the burning building to retrieve a memento and died in the flames. When Van arrived he helped the Davises to safety and bravely ran in and out of the conflagration retrieving items. "Finally my father just gave him a bear hug and held him so he wouldn't go back," recalled Marc. Soon after, the Davises left Smackover and Harry gave his friend Vanderbilt an old Model T Ford he had won in a card game.

The place where the Davis family lived longest (two years) was Galveston, Texas, on the Gulf of Mexico, where Harry "repaired all the chronometers that ran the ships." There, Marc spent his sophomore and junior high school years and his cartoons were published in yearbooks and a monthly paperback magazine titled *The Purple Quill*. He also studied one night a week with an art teacher. "My father didn't understand why I wanted to be an artist, instead of an architect. He thought, 'Architects make money, artists starve to death.' I can understand his point of view. But my father was an artist himself," said Marc, referring to Harry's watchmaking.[13]

During the Depression, Harry moved the family to California again; in Los Angeles for a year, Marc attended classes at Otis Art Institute and Harry worked again with a relocated Marcus Lichtenstein. They operated a jewelry store in the forecourt of Grauman's Chinese Theater, the Hollywood movie palace. Marc was fascinated with the American Indians and midgets who appeared in the theater's stage show and mingled and shopped in the forecourt. He remembered "running with the Indians" down Hollywood Boulevard and staring fascinated at the midgets who were "dressed to kill" in tuxedos and gowns. One little person, smaller than Marc but much older, took a cigar out of his mouth to curtly say (in a deep voice) "Get lost, kid!" to the gawking young man.

Marc graduated from high school in Klamath Falls in southern Oregon in 1931. "My father said he couldn't afford to send me to college, but he'd give me an education." So Harry got his son a job in the Waldorf pool hall racking balls. The joint was filled with men looking for work and bootleggers in "summer overcoats" selling fifths of whiskey to American Indians. The bootleggers insisted on cash payments and that the Indians drink the hootch on the spot. "So the pool hall was always full of sleeping or drunken Indians," said Marc. The pool hall owner's wife was a brothel madam, so Marc's duties included emptying the change in the whore-house slot machines. "Father was very good at psychology—he wanted me to learn about life. And I did."

The family next moved to an apartment in the Civic Center area of San Francisco near where Harry and a partner ran a novelty store on Market Street. "This was the bottom of the Depression," said Marc, "so they were not making a lot of money." Marc worked in a sign-painting shop and attended the California School of Fine Arts until he couldn't afford the tuition. So every morning he took a streetcar out to the Fleishacker Zoo to draw the animals on cheap butcher's paper. "I got to know the assistant director of the zoo," he told Paula Sigman-Lowery, "and they would let me in before they let the public in. They'd bring creatures out for me to draw. It was very exciting, and sometimes a little scary."

One of the huge, hairy orangutans took a liking to the young artist. "I put out my hand. He closed his hand around

charley – Orang-Utan –
3/22/33
MARC DAVIS

Jim – Orang-Utan
3/22/33
MARC DAVIS

mine. It was like sawed-off wood, no fleshy feeling at all. He didn't open his hand. My hand was like cemented in there. It took three [zoo]keepers five minutes to unwind his hand so mine could get out. I tell you this was an exciting experience!" In the evenings, Davis diligently studied anatomy diagrams and illustrations of skeletons in books in the public library across from his home. "Although I was drawing them in motion," he explained to Charles Solomon, "I wasn't thinking in terms of animating them. I was interested in capturing their movements in art, in the tradition of Frederick Remington's sculptures."[14]

For extra cash, Harry skillfully conducted "flat sales" of watches and jewelry in stores nearing bankruptcy throughout California. Marc made the show and price cards and accompanied his father as he sold Big Ben alarm clocks for thirty-five cents. "Every jewelry store in which he put on his sales," said Marc, "survived the Depression."

The Davis family moved upstate to Sacramento, where Marc drew occasional cartoons for the *Sacramento Bee* newspaper. One day Harry excitedly told Marc he must see a Walt Disney picture called *Three Little Pigs* at the local theater. "I was impressed," said Marc. "That song 'Who's Afraid of the Big Bad Wolf?' affected the whole world 'cause the wolf was at everybody's door."

The family's next relocation, fifty miles farther north to the town of Marysville, proved to be Harry's last move. Marc had a desk in a print shop, where he designed theater posters and also drew newspaper advertisements.[15] The "awfully nice man" who ran the movie theater in nearby Yuba City told Marc he had to see a new sensational Walt Disney short called *Who Killed Cock Robin?* (released June 1935). "Marvelous," said Marc of Jenny Wren, Disney's caricature of Mae West. "I think you ought to work for him," said the theater owner.

THIS PAGE AND OPPOSITE, *Davis became a self-taught expert in drawing animal anatomy from the hours he spent at the Fleishacker Zoo in San Francisco.*

Lions - From Life
March 29, 1933

Davis took the suggestion seriously. Having seen Disney's talent recruitment advertisements in magazines, he wrote a letter to the studio requesting an interview and signed it "M. Fraser Davis." A reply soon came from George Drake, the studio's trainee supervisor. "Dear Miss Davis," it began. "At the present time we are not hiring any women artists, but such time as we do we'll get in touch." Davis angrily threw the letter into a wastebasket.

Harry A. Davis's incessant wanderings came to an end when he suddenly died of a heart attack at age forty-eight. Nearly fifty people attended his funeral in Marysville, a silent testament to the innate charm of the man and the goodwill he inspired in his many travels. "We hadn't been living there very long, but everyone came to the funeral. It shows how much my father affected people—he had a tremendous personality."[16]

In 1960, Marc was conducting an art class at Chouinard on "Staging Humor and Comedy" and recalled two incidents with his father involving "disturbed dignity." He remembered becoming "hysterical with laughter" at age ten when Harry, wearing a white suit, stepped from a streetcar. It had started to rain and he "slipped in the mud and sat down hard." Young Marc began to laugh and his father merely sat there. "It must have been two or three minutes and he called me every four-letter word ever devised by man. I didn't want to laugh, but I was! He was shouting, 'I could be dying! I could be dead—and look at you!'"

Marc recalled another inappropriate reaction when he was in his late teens. He was watching Harry dressing the window of his jewelry store while balanced on a small stool and smoking a pipe. He lost his balance and fell. "He discov-

ers he has only half his pipe. He's looking for the other half. He thinks he's swallowed it. I think he's swallowed it. He thinks he's dying and I think it's funny! It's a strange and wondrous thing. Again I become hysterical."[17]

Now Harry *was* dead and Marc was his mother's sole support. "We had to figure out what to do. Finally we decided to get in my used car and go down to Los Angeles. I wanted to go someplace where I could work. I was offered work by a newspaper in Hollywood that no longer exists." People who viewed Davis's impressive art portfolio—particularly his animal anatomy sketches—urged him to apply at Disney, which finally he did. "I was hired on the spot," recalled Davis.

"The Depression was the greatest thing that could ever have happened to Walt," remarked Davis years later. "There was no employment for these young guys, including myself. And here was a man using artists."[18]

Davis started on December 2, 1935, and was immediately thrown into two weeks of intensive life-drawing classes under the supervision of Donald Graham, the studio's resident art instructor. Davis's drawing skill shone brightly in a sea of applicants who were, as he described them, mostly "unsuccessful newspaper cartoonists. They didn't know anatomy." Davis himself was a newspaper cartoonist with limited success, but, he said, "the experiences I had at the zoo and the library made a big difference."

George Drake, whom Davis has described as "a kind of creepy guy" instructed him (poorly) in the craft of making in-between animation drawings. One day Drake gave a brusque demonstration to Carl Barks, who was hired the same day as Davis. (Barks, who died in 2000 at the age of ninety-nine,

later became famous for illustrating Donald Duck comic books.) Cursing and sweating all the way, Drake banged out a dreadful drawing full of smudges, then left the room. Whereupon, Barks silently took an eraser and slowly eradicated all that Drake had wrought. "That was the most wonderful thing I ever saw," laughed Davis.

Davis quickly became close friends with Milt Kahl, who had joined the studio a year and a half earlier. At age twenty-six, Kahl was four years Davis's senior, but the two young men shared northern California backgrounds and both were formidable self-taught draftsmen. Though young, they were more worldly than most of the new arrivals at the studio, many of whom were dewy-fresh from colleges and art schools. Davis had experienced a great deal of the human condition thanks to his wandering dad; and Kahl had successfully navigated a freelance career in advertising in San Francisco. Neither was a college man. "I had great respect for him and his talent," said Davis recently. "He was full of hell, bombastic. I still feel the loss of him."

As far as Kahl was concerned, he and Marc had "a mutual admiration society for years. He's such a damn fine artist. He makes me look sick, as far as that's concerned. I mean being able to draw anything. Marc is really superb. We have mutual respect."[19]

In late spring 1936, Davis became an assistant animator on *Snow White*. Ironically, considering his expertise in drawing animal anatomy, he was not assigned to the film's many

animals, as Kahl was. "The very thing that I thought I had to offer the most wasn't available to me, because I worked on the human [Snow White]," he said.[20] He assisted Myron "Grim" Natwick (1890-1990), a pioneer animator renowned in the industry. Tall, athletic Natwick, friendly, with a folksy manner and Wisconsin twang, had put the moves into Krazy Kat and Felix the Cat and numerous Hearst comic-strip characters, such as Judge Rummy and Silk-Hat Harry. For the Fleischer Brothers, he animated Koko the Clown and, most famously, designed Betty Boop and animated the naughty flapper in her first six cartoons.[21]

It was a scene of Betty Boop climbing up a rapidly moving locomotive that caught Walt Disney's talent-searching eye. Natwick added details unusual for the period (1930)—such as Betty's hair and dress being whipped about her by the wind—and through it all she retained her feminine qualities. Natwick called it "the first serious animation I ever did."[22] Roy Disney went to New York to recruit Natwick, but he accepted a position at Ub Iwerks's new studio in Hollywood instead. "The rumor in the East was that the genius of the [Disney studio] was Iwerks," said Natwick, who learned otherwise after three years animating mediocre films starring forgettable characters such as Flip the Frog and Willy Whopper. In November 1934 he joined the Disney staff, "an event significant enough to be noted in Walt Disney's desk diary, as few such staff developments were."[23]

Natwick was an extraordinary animator because he had already done what Walt was trying to do with most of his raw recruits: master the drawing *and the animation* of the human figure. Natwick had studied art and drawing at the Chicago Art Institute and New York's National Academy of Design and, in 1925, had gone to Europe for three years of intensive art studies at the Vienna National Academy. "It was one of the most valuable decisions of my life," he said. The painters Egon Schiele and Gustav Klimt proved to be strong stylistic influences. When he earned his certificate, Natwick felt that his drawing had "bounded ahead."

The touch of feminine grace that Walt saw in Natwick's Betty Boop animation was something he hoped to attain in *Snow White*. The stilted movements of Persephone in *The Goddess of Spring* showed how daunting a task this was. But hope shone through when Natwick completed his first assignment: a *Cinderella* type of girl in the Silly Symphony *The Cookie Carnival* (released in 1935). "In the cookie girl, the Disney cartoons had for the first time an appealing heroine," writes animation historian Michael Barrier, "not a neuter to which a few crude symbols of femininity had been attached, as with

Minnie Mouse's skirt and eyelashes, but a character that was female at her core."[24]

After a year of animating only female characters (such as the girl viola in *Music Land* (1935) and the blind doll in *Broken Toys* (1935), Natwick was assigned to the heroine in *Snow White*. His "self-contained unit devoted to a single character" included three in-betweeners and three assistants, all strong drafts-men.[25] Marc Davis was Natwick's principal assistant and they proved a fine team. Natwick was "sloppy and disorganized" and his initial animation drawings were so rough they often resembled a ball of yarn.[26] Somehow Davis was able to pick out the right graphic lines to emphasize in his cleanups without killing Natwick's marvelous timing or the intention of an action; he was fastidious in adding the proper details to Snow White—a very difficult character to draw—so that her eyes didn't float about her face, and the little bow in her hair stayed a constant size, and the pleats in her dress moved like cloth, not cardboard. Having Davis as his assistant, said Natwick admiringly, "was like having two right arms."[27]

At forty-six years, Natwick was double Davis's age; his European life and art experiences and knowledge of fine food and wine made him a model of sophistication in his young assistant's eyes. "I've been asked many times what I learned from Grim Natwick," Davis once remarked. "One of the things was how to drink wine. At that time all I knew was that it was red and came in half-gallon bottles. Through Grim I found out that, gee, wine came in smaller bottles and [could be] white, [too]."[28]

The activities and creative atmosphere at the Hyperion Avenue studio during the late 1930s extended Davis's self-education. "We saw every ballet, we saw every film," he said. "If a film was good we would go and see it five times."

At one time, Walt rented a studio up in North Hollywood and every Wednesday night we would see a selection of films—anything from Chaplin to unusual subjects. Anything that might produce growth, that might be stimulating—the cutting of the scenes, the staging, how a group of scenes was put together. . . .

The comedies were always marvelous-Chaplin, Edgar Kennedy with his slow burn, Laurel and Hardy. Fred Astaire's dancing, from pose to pose—animation is pretty much like that; always with an attitude. We would all study the acting of Charles Laughton. We all read Stanislavsky. We didn't miss a trick, really. There was always someone around to bring something to your attention. We tried to understand Matisse and Picasso and others, even though our end result shows very little of that literally. . . . *The Cabinet of Dr. Caligari, Nosferatu* were things that we saw years and years back. There was no type of film done that we did not see. What you didn't get from one, you got from another . . .

Everybody here was studying constantly. We had models at the Studio and we'd go over and draw every night. We weren't making much, because the Studio didn't have much, but it was a perfect time of many things coming together into one orbit. Walt was that lodestone.

Davis recalled how "every day was an excitement."

Whatever we were doing had never been done before. It was such a great thrill to go in there. God, we'd hear music—like the great *Snow White* music—that had never been heard before. This was magic. There was excitement and there was competition; everyone was young and everyone was doing something.[29]

When conflict flared that summer of 1936 between Natwick and *Snow White*'s animation supervisor Ham Luske, young Davis learned to play the diplomat. Part of the problem was Luske's distrust of the "East Coast boys," animation studio veterans who came to Disney from New York with fixed ways and established work habits; men who were less pliable than the college kids being trained on the job. "Ham was kind of a stuffy guy," commented Davis.[30]

The main problem stemmed from differing interpretations of the live-action footage of dancer Marge Belcher shot to guide the animators. Natwick's redrawn images of Belcher as *Snow White* were more realistic and sexual than Luske (or Walt) wanted. (One might say Grim was more Grimm than Disney.) Luske, on the other hand, made Belcher's "figure conform to cartoon proportions" and gave her a presexual innocence that matched the story as it was then being developed. "They wanted her to look like a cute little girl who could be a princess," said Natwick. "We just tried not to clown her up."[31]

Davis did considerably more than that, according to Michael Barrier. "As Davis became aware of the hostility between Luske and Natwick," wrote Barrier in *Hollywood Cartoons*, "he gradually took it upon himself to make the necessary changes in Natwick's drawings.

Those changes went beyond the character's proportions to what Davis called a "kind of feeling of the character"; Natwick, he said, wanted the girl to have "a vitality," more than simple cuteness, and it was that vitality that Davis had to tame.[32]

"During the three and one-half years that Marc and I worked together at Disney's," wrote Natwick in 1979, "twenty months or nearly six hundred days were spent drawing Snow White herself in scene after scene for the picture that carries her name in the title." When the film was completed, Natwick left the studio, never to return; but he and Davis remained friends. "Marc was and is a superb artist," said Natwick. In 1990, Davis was a guest speaker at Grim Natwick's 100th birthday party in Los Angeles.[33]

Walt was barely aware of Davis during the production of *Snow White*, even though as Natwick's assistant he attended

ABOVE, *Davis in 1987;* OPPOSITE, *his first solo animation was the skunk Flower in* Bambi. *Davis's appealing story sketches showed animals expressing human thoughts yet retaining their animal qualities and anatomy.*

many sweatbox critique sessions. "It wasn't until I got to doing story sketches of *Bambi* that Walt was excited about my drawings," said he.[34] Joe Grant wanted Davis to join his Character Model Department, the studio's design and concept "think tank." But Davis opted for *Bambi*, the ambitious, poetic feature about life, love, and death among the animals of a great forest; eventually he spent a total of six years working on the project, "three on story, three on animation."

With *Bambi, Pinocchio,* and *Fantasia* in simultaneous production, as well as a full complement of shorts, the Hyperion Avenue studio was bursting at the seams. At first Davis and a small story crew worked in houses across the street where the art classes were held. Then they were moved miles away to rented space on Seward Street in Hollywood. "We wondered if it hadn't been a whorehouse," said Davis. "It had all these tiny rooms. Across the street there'd be a raid. They were shooting pornographic films and these girls in their silk kimonos [were] coming out and getting into police cars, as we were making *Bambi!*"[35] Walt rarely dropped by the Seward Street offices. "He would leave you alone for a long time if he

thought you were developing something that was all right or if he didn't have any ideas on it," Davis told Charles Solomon.

When the studio relocated in Burbank in late 1939, the *Bambi* story crew was among the first groups to move to the new quarters. "We finished the story in the 3-B wing and [Walt] was in and out of there regularly," said Davis.

"Whenever story director Perce Pearce would announce, 'Man is in the forest!' [a line from *Bambi* meaning "danger"] it meant Walt was down the hall."[36]

Walt wanted a high level of believability and reality in the characters, but many story sketches tended toward anatomically correct critters with no soul. The problem of humanizing deer and the other animals, while keeping them "real," was one of *Bambi*'s greatest challenges. And it seemed to be one that the artists would not meet until an early screening of the story reel revealed that "the most popular character was the broadly caricatured skunk." "There's the key to the thing," Walt exclaimed. The skunk sketches were by Marc Davis.[37] All of his animal story drawings shared qualities that were both human and animal. (Davis, in fact, used photos of human babies to model facial expressions for young *Bambi* and his friends.)[38] What Walt saw in Davis's story drawings of deer, skunks, and rabbits was an irresistible warmth, a humanity, and a communication of human attitudes and personality that shone through animal forms; all expertly drawn as a gentle caricature of animal anatomy.

"His deer looked like deer," write Johnston and Thomas in their book on the making of the film, "for they had lost

Davis, third from left, working in 1943 on Victory Through Air Power, *a wartime feature to which he contributed extensive story work, but received no screen credit.*

audience through animated drawings. It would happen many times in his long career, but (as another animator told him) that virgin experience would never happen again in quite the same way. It was like falling in love for the first time. "That's true," said Davis. "It happens only once."[41]

Davis experienced problems early on in his career regarding screen credit. On *Snow White*, he received none because he was only an assistant. (As unions became stronger through the years, assistants and even inkers and painters received screen recognition for their efforts.) On *Bambi* he asked to be listed as "M. Fraser Davis," but only "Fraser Davis" made it to the screen, which confuses many fans. ("Where's Marc Davis's name?" "Is Fraser Davis related to him?")

Davis's name is completely missing from the credits of *Victory Through Air Power*, even though he did extensive story work on the wartime feature. The climactic battle, for example, between a gigantic American eagle and an octopus representing Japanese armed forces was boldly defined by Davis's pastels in hot colors. "I did an awful lot of story work on [*Victory*]," said Davis. "And I was extremely upset because they forgot to give me screen credit. I did, personally, get an apology from Walt."[42]

In *Song of the South*, the name "Marc Davis" appears on the screen at last as one of the film's directing animators. He animated Brer Fox and Brer Bear constructing the tar baby; he also contributed story sketches to the live-action-animation combo sequences with Uncle Remus and Brer Rabbit. But he has always been quick to praise chief story architect Bill Peet for "a tremendous job" in developing the film's highly animatable cartoon situations and vivid personalities.

Davis next worked on *Wind in the Willows* when it was planned as a full feature. He animated mad Toad with his jolly horse Cyril, the evil weasels, and a tense sequence in which Mole is lowered on a rope to remove an important paper from a sleeping villain. The original story reels, created by James Bodrero, he recalled as witty and full of "brilliantly

none of their essential animal appearance or character, but they could be understood as having human thoughts and feelings."[39] "They had to have a plastic quality to be able to animate," Davis explained to writer Bob Thomas. "They had to express emotions. They're not animal but they're not human. They're somewhere in between. But they're also not a person in an animal suit. They're something unique all to themselves."[40] Walt was so taken by Davis's sketches that he said he wanted to see *them* on the screen. He turned to Milt Kahl and Frank Thomas and ordered them to teach Davis how to animate. "That's how I became an animator," said Davis.

However, Davis was not a complete novice when he was tutored by Kahl and Thomas. It might be said that he really learned animation from Grim Natwick on *Snow White*; as a master's assistant he gleaned pointers on timing and performance as well as animation's technical aspects. Natwick was also a specialist in animating female characters, which Davis later became. Therefore, Thomas and Kahl served as a deluxe finishing school for their gifted "pupil."

In any case, Davis learned quickly and well. Particularly memorable is his sequence of Flower the skunk falling in love. Davis recalled the once-in-a-lifetime thrill of sharing his own animation with a first-night audience. "When that thing came on the screen there," recalled Davis, "the theater almost burst with laughter." He, however, was crying tears of joy, so emotionally overwhelmed was he by the reaction to his work. For the first time, Marc Davis had personally connected with an

Marc and Alice Estes Davis, on their honeymoon in 1956.

illustrated" brief scenes, "faster cutting," and "more ideas thrown at you in a shorter space of time." But some animators complained "they didn't have [screen] time enough to do things." Eventually, the film was simplified, shortened in length and paired with a truncated version of *The Legend of Sleepy Hollow*.[43]

Davis enjoyed a lively social life and developed into a sophisticated bon vivant. He smoked using a cigarette holder and, according to Grim Natwick, "his gin martini has long been recognized as the finest martini west of the Mississippi River. Never to have tasted a Marc Davis martini is to have been denied an experience unparalleled in drinking tradition."[44] (High praise indeed from Davis's esteemed model of wine and liquor connoisseurship.) Davis also dated beautiful women. "I went out with a lot of girls before I married," Davis told Robin Allan, "and [Walt] used to joke and point out the women with big boobs."[45] At the beginning of the war, he married "an extremely attractive redhead" named Marion, who later worked for bandleader Bob Crosby.[46] Davis was also supporting both his mother and her sister, Myrtle Fraser, an elderly unmarried former schoolteacher whom he had moved to Los Angeles from Eureka. Davis bought a house on Brunswick Avenue in 1940, and he and Marion lived there until their three-year-old marriage foundered. "We just grew apart," he said. "That was that."[47]

In 1947, Donald Graham asked Davis to take over the advanced drawing class he was teaching at Chouinard Art Institute. For the next seventeen years he taught there one night a week and developed a loyal student following. One of his students was Alice Estes, an eighteen-year-old costume design major who had won a scholarship to Chouinard from the Long Beach Art Association. "My first duty," she says, "was to take two perfect pieces of white chalk to our new professor, Mr. Marc Davis, for his lectures." Dark-haired Ms. Estes resembled Audrey Hepburn, but with electric blue eyes; nine years later she and Marc married, but at first "we were strictly teacher and student," she says. "I graduated and then through a friend we met again." When Davis went on vacation to Europe "he was still going with a lot of different ladies," Alice recalls, but he wrote her a series of illustrated love letters, which she kept and framed. "He had quite a harem," commented Mrs. Davis recently with a smile.

What was Marc Davis like as a teacher? "He was the best," says Alice. "And he had huge classes ranging from ninety to a hundred students. They were practically hanging off the walls." After a model did a half-hour of quick poses, Davis would lecture for about forty-five minutes. After a break, she posed and then he spoke again. "In all the years I was in his classes," notes Alice, "he never repeated a single lecture. Which was truly amazing!" He drew rapidly on a blackboard and "nobody dared erase" his sketches, "because all the kids who couldn't take his class were in there next morning bright

and early taking notes. Then the night students would take notes." Often, when Davis returned to class on Tuesday evenings, his week-old sketches would still be on the board.

Davis was again a directing animator, this time for *Cinderella*, the studio's triumphant return to full-length animated features. It marked the beginning of a decade in which he was unhappily cast (often with Milt Kahl) on animating bland female human characters, such as Cinderella, Alice in *Alice in Wonderland*, Wendy in *Peter Pan*, and Briar Rose in *Sleeping Beauty*. For those straight characters, live-action photography was used as a reference, and Davis once told Thomas and Johnston with some heat that "he got a lot of crap characters" to animate. "Moving a girl around with rotoscope [tracings of live action] is a pretty rotten way to make a living."[48]

But Davis's angry comment short-changed his creative use of the reference material. His personal integrity as an artist did not allow him to merely trace over live action; his creativity and strong draftsmanship made him "stretch a thing further and move it around and get the essence of it," says Frank Thomas. "Just wonderful things he was able to do."[49] One lovely example is Davis's graceful animation of Briar Rose dancing while she sings. Live action must have provided basic information suggesting body and arm positions (the latter involved difficult foreshortening); but Davis gave each figure drawing an elegance, charm, and sculptural three-dimensionality. Rose exudes warmth and joy as she waltzes and spins with abandon.

A Grim Natwick-ish sophistication is present in Davis's Briar Rose, as it is in *Cinderella*; both young women could be innocent Snow White's older, more self-aware sisters. As noted, Eric Larson, who animated Cinderella as a sixteen-year-old "gal with braids" and a pug nose, considered Davis's version was "more the exotic dame." And, of course, it was Davis who animated the transformation of Cinderella from peasant girl into a Grace Kelly–like vision of refinement. The glamorous makeover involves much fairy dust as she raises her arms and her hair sweeps upward and her simple frock morphs into a silvery sheath worthy of Dior. Walt praised Davis (not to his face, of course) when he answered a visitor's query regarding his favorite piece of animation. "I guess it would have to be where Cinderella gets her ballroom gown," answered Walt. Much as he may have disliked the assignment, Davis "was very pleased" when Walt's comment got back to him.[50]

Davis also animated a couple of female characters of human form but supernatural origin, namely the fairies Tinker Bell (*Peter Pan*) and Maleficent (*Sleeping Beauty*). Formerly depicted on stage and screen as a mere spot of light,

the Disney version of Tinker Bell is a comely sprite dressed in a one-piece bathing suit with a blond 1950s "pixie" hairdo. Her shapely body was not based on Marilyn Monroe (as has often been said), but on the live-action reference model Margaret Kerry.

Disney's Tinker Bell, created mostly by men, packs into her tiny (but womanly) form just about every female behavioral cliché allowable in films in those prefeminist days. She is extremely possessive of Peter Pan (who offers her scant attention or encouragement) and so jealous of competition that she attempts to murder a rival for his affections (Wendy). She is vain and overly concerned about her looks; twice it is suggested that her buttocks pose a problem: their size prevents her from escaping through a keyhole; also, as she stands on a hand mirror preening and caressing herself, the reflection of her derrière gives her pause—she fails to realize that the foreshortening of her body in the mirror exaggerates her shape. Which would indicate that, despite her supernatural glow, she is not very bright intellectually. Her emotions rule; she is susceptible to the most transparent flattery and easily duped. Thanks to her gullibility, Captain Hook elicits Pan's secret hiding place from her with sugary words and false promises.

Davis's animation conveys all of the above and other, more positive qualities through pantomime, for Tinker Bell does not speak (she only jingles as she twinkles). She convincingly displays an array of emotions through how she moves, acts, and reacts. She has charm, spunk, willfullness, and a bold passion. She is not bland or passive; she reacts decisively and directly. Underneath her portrayal is Marc Davis's real-life love of women in general and women with strong personalities in particular, starting with his mother Mildred's endurance and strength, and ending with Davis's wife Alice, who is no shrinking violet. As Andreas Deja put it, Davis's animated women always "have a presence."

Maleficent, *Sleeping Beauty*'s evil fairy, is a regal presence, but Davis found her difficult to animate. "Maleficent was a problem," he said. "She basically stood there and talked directly to the audience. She had very little interaction with the other characters. That's extremely difficult to bring across."[51] The resourceful Davis sought opportunities for her to talk to and tease a pet raven, and he gave her a walking stick to wave about majestically. Her liveliest interaction with other characters occurs when she punishes her pig-faced goons by zapping them with her magic stick, a severe form of electric-shock therapy.

Davis also helped design the character; in his home library he found in a book on art of the Middle Ages "a religious painting of a character with a black robe on and there was this pattern of material that looked like flames. That intrigued me," he said, "so I used part of that [on Maleficent's long sleeves]." The bottom of her dress flares like coiling

Davis's masterful draftsmanship is apparent in this difficult scene of the Princess turning around in Sleeping Beauty. *Although basing it on live-action reference footage, Davis exaggerated the foreshortening and sweeping arcs of the arms, making the design more appealing.*

Marc Davis's love of women comes through in his animated portrayals, such as Tinker Bell.
Model Margaret Kerry provides reference footage to aid the animation.

OPPOSITE, *beautiful rough drawings by Davis of Maleficent,*
the evil fairy in Sleeping Beauty;
PHOTO THIS PAGE, *actress Eleanor Audley performs as*
Maleficent for the live-action reference film;
BOTTOM LEFT, *one of Davis's concept paintings of the character.*

Marvelously mean Cruella DeVil in 101 Dalmatians *was Marc's final work as an animator before he devoted his talents to designing characters and rides for Disney theme-park attractions.*
OPPOSITE, PHOTO, *actress Mary Wickes performing as Cruella for live-action reference footage.*

snakes. "Then the collar's points—I was trying to get a bat look to her. Of course the horns [of the headdress], just because it's a devil image. She had to be large and dominant because she frightened everybody half to death."[52]

Davis's swan song as an animator is the selfish, fur-loving, heavy-smoking, puppy-killing, too-much-money-for-her-own-good, fashion victim Cruella De Vil in *101 Dalmatians*. For the first time in a long while, Davis had a leading character he didn't share with any other animator, and he made the most of it. "I did every bit of her," he said proudly.[53] Unlike isolated Maleficent, Cruella is "pitted against the other characters eye to eye, mind to mind." In other words, she performs badly with others—and that's good. Whether slapping her stupid henchmen around or insulting a hostess by dousing a cigarette in a crumpet, Cruella puts on a great show.

Pencil-thin, like one of Tom Wolfe's "X-ray" society women, and swathed in a voluminous fur made from God knows what kind of luckless animal, Cruella dominates every

scene she appears in. During production of the film in 1960, Davis claimed she was partly based on Bette Davis (in *All About Eve*), Rosalind Russell (in *Auntie Mame*), and, of course, Tallulah Bankhead—as herself, dawww-ling! (Famed drag performer Lipsynka [John Epperson] also sees Kay (*Funny Face*) Thompson's flair as well.)

Cruella's two-tone (black-and-white) hair coloring came from the illustration in Dodie Smith's novel, but Davis found its disheveled style by looking "through old magazines for hairdos from 1940 till now." Her coat was exaggerated to match her outsized personality and, asked Davis, "what could we do to make a fur coat slightly ridiculous?" (He hung big tails on the back.) The lining is red because "there's a devil image involved."[54]

Davis's animation was supported by Bill Peet's brilliant adaptation of the story and the storyboards he drew by himself without a crew; Cruella's dialogue, basic look, and staging are all found in Peet's boards. Live-action reference

footage was shot of character actress Mary Wickes's edgy, angular movements.

But Davis claimed his greatest inspiration for defining Cruella was the "terrific" vocal performance of actress Betty Lou Gerson (1915–1999). A radio veteran since 1935, Gerson had been the narrator of Disney's *Cinderella* and later appeared in a cameo in *Mary Poppins*.[55] Cruella's Tallulah-esque tones and raucous laugh are redolent of countless cigarettes and an untold number of vodka martinis; her throaty voice evidences the wear and tear from years of decadence unspeakably divine. (And from screaming when she doesn't get her way.) Gerson's vocalization told Davis "this character was bigger than life, high in energy and, like a shark, always moving."[56]

In animating Cruella, said Davis, "what I really wanted to do was make her move like someone you wouldn't like."[57] But audiences love to hate Cruella. She's pure, one-hundred-percent bitch with no redeeming qualities. There's something funny and vicariously liberating in her total unawareness of how awful she really is.

Michael Barrier considers the design and the animation of Cruella De Vil to be "one last flowering of caricature" in "the increasingly literal quality of Disney animation."[58] Andreas Deja notes that "Marc likes to give his characters big hands. Cruella and Maleficent have really large hands, Aurora–Briar Rose as well. The other animators would not have gone as far."[59] Indeed, Davis's caricatured design of Cruella was critiqued by two of his Nine Old Men colleagues. Milt Kahl, looking over Davis's shoulder as he was animating, bluntly asked, "Damn it, do you have to make her feet so damn big? Do they have to be so clumsy? Why don't you make them thin, like this? And I told him the same thing went for the hands." (Davis claimed he was "only sore for a couple of hours" over Kahl's critique.)[60] Frank Thomas thought Davis "went overboard a little bit on the drawing of the face and it became more of a skull." It is true that in her over-the-top final scenes, as she madly wrecks her car, Cruella resembles the Phantom of the Opera. But in the original animation drawings from earlier sequences, Davis's love of women again comes through; her key poses and facial angles have a certain glamor.

Davis, by the way, did not approve of studying single drawings of his animation scenes. "These drawings are made to move and to create an illusion on the screen," he once stated emphatically. "They were never meant to hold still." He's right; whatever ravaged allure Cruella may have in one sketch is subsumed within the flurry of drawings that bring her to life on the screen. Each drawing may, in fact, reveal another aspect of her past life and present condition. But like all the greatest examples of character animation, Cruella's unique personality is expressed most vividly through movement.

Davis claimed Cruella was based partly on Bette Davis, Rosalind Russell, and Tallulah Bankhead.

After Davis completed his work on *101 Dalmatians*, he "took a stab" at doing concept sketches for *Chanticleer*, a feature that he, Woolie Reitherman, Milt Kahl, and Ken Anderson hoped to get off the ground. Davis's marvelous drawings of roosters, hens, owls, ducks, turkeys, and a fox are full of personality; unfortunately, management decided that "a bunch of chickens weren't very interesting."[61]

There being no imminent animation assignments for Davis in 1962, Walt asked him to go down to Disneyland and take a "good, hard, critical look" at the Mine Train Through Nature's Wonderland attraction. "See what you think about this thing,"[62] said Walt. Walt was so dissatisfied with the ride—a journey through a new wilderness into a painted desert populated with 204 lifelike critters—that he took the original designs home and redrew the entire thing himself.[63] "At this time," said Davis, "the people down at Disneyland were not very happy about the people that Walt sent from the studio. They seemed very jealous of us and it was like, 'Oh boy, here we go again.'" But "with great enthusiasm" Davis dutifully went to the theme park, "looked around and thought there was an awful lot of things wrong with some of the attractions." On the Mine Train, for example, each passenger "had two seats on each side of them, and when you sat down you [were] staring at three strangers opposite you. Well, people don't like to ride like that."

Davis redesigned the cars, then focused on the animation of the mechanized bears, foxes, gophers, and such. "They had no gags in it, no story at all," he discovered. "One kit fox's head is going up and down, then about a hundred feet away another kit fox's head is going left to right, so I took the two, put them nose to nose, so one is going up and down, the other moves side to side. So immediately you have humor!"

Several weeks later Walt asked Davis if he went to the park. "Oh yeah, I got a lot of ideas." Davis had made about forty drawings of "how I thought the whole thing ought to look." To which Walt replied, "Where are those damn drawings? I've just spent $50,000 on that ride!" It was 11 A.M. when Walt called a 1:30 P.M. meeting of the entire WED Enterprises crew. WED, the design and development organization formed to create Disneyland, was located in a room at the Burbank studio; in 1965 it moved to facilities in Glendale, where it became known as Walt Disney Imagineering.[64]

Walt ordered Davis to get his drawings into the WED room and pitch his ideas. "Everyone who was important was there, and here I am, a stranger from animation. So I stand up and I started explaining piece by piece." His knowledge of human and animal anatomy came to the fore in the impromptu lecture. Regarding the Mine Train cars, he noted that "sitting in an automobile we look out the front. Anything that is out here [on the side] we don't care about because there's no danger. We are always looking ahead because there can always be

something dangerous. That's why we look that way." Walt watched and listened avidly. "He was buying everything I had done," said Davis, "and was quite intrigued with it."

Walt gave Davis more and more theme-park assignments, although "there was a lot of guys there kind of hoping you would fall on your head." A WED executive once walked by Davis's desk to sneer, "And what are you doing with your little pencil now?"

Davis worked on the 1964–65 New York World's Fair presentations, including characterizations for G.E.'s Carousel of Progress, It's a Small World, and Great Moments with Mr. Lincoln. The latter was an extremely complex Audio-Animatronics figure of the sixteenth president of the United States that rose from its seat, gestured, and spoke. "Knowing that I was an animator," said Davis, "and knew a lot about anatomy [Walt] came to me and asked me to give it some thought." Davis studied reports on British prosthetics and created drawings for a movement reference booklet. "Putting down things that needed to be solved, really, more than anything else." After a spectacularly unsuccessful test of Mr. Lincoln's movements—during which Honest Abe had a spastic fit, blew fuses and a transformer—Davis turned to scriptwriter James Algar to joke, "Do you suppose that God is mad at Walt for creating man in his own image?"[65]

It's a Small World, a boat attraction using hundreds of Audio-Animatronics children and toys in settings representing over a hundred regions of the world, was designed by the gifted Mary Blair. Davis developed Mrs. Blair's stylized, colorful concepts into character sketches to "suggest which countries might be featured and how their children might be portrayed."[66] His quickly made, simple ink drawings with watercolor wash are very charming in their suggestions of motion and character relationships. In India, for example, a boy and girl dance with a friendly tiger; in Holland, a Dutch boy and girl loll in giant tulips; in Scotland, a kilted boy plays bagpipes as a girl dances a highland fling and a Scottie dog listens and watches appreciatively.

Davis created more elaborate idea drawings for other attractions. He worked, for example, on a redo of the Jungle Cruise "which was fun," he said. "I did the [Indian] elephant [bathing] pool and the whole [trapped] safari thing. I really did most of the ride posters as well. This was quite a change," he said happily of his 3-D assignments, "to get up from an animation desk and find out all of a sudden there were people with bulldozers and they wanted to know where you want this pile of dirt!"

As noted, he contributed scores of amusing concepts to the "Pirates of the Caribbean" attraction. His artwork suggested physical features and personalities of characters, possible settings, costumes, gags, situations, actions, reactions, even dialogue and sound effects. For example, in one of two

ABOVE, LEFT, *Davis sketches whimsical ideas for the* Pirates of the Caribbean *attraction;* ABOVE, RIGHT, *a maiden, in an elongated painting by Davis for* The Haunted Mansion, *is unaware that danger lurks;* OPPOSITE, *more* Haunted Mansion *concepts by Davis, seen* BELOW *consulting with Walt Disney and Blaine Gibson.*

adjoining drawings, a Magistrate's Lady dressed in a nightgown and cap opens window shutters to shout "Do not tell heem, Carlos!" The second drawings show the windows slammed shut as (says the caption) "a shot is fired. A puff of smoke comes from the window box. The flowerpots jump up. . . ."

Dozens of ideas were rejected, but not until Davis had staunchly "stood by his characters."[67] "If they want to cut something out of it, that's fine," he said. "It's somebody else's business. But I try to do the thing the best way I know how." He learned that lesson directly from Walt. Once, at a pitch session for a new attraction, Davis began by saying "I've got an expensive way and a cheap way of doing this." Walt got up from his seat, walked to the front of the room and put his hand on Davis's shoulder. "Marc, you and I do not worry whether anything is cheap or expensive," he said. "We only worry if it's good.

"I have a theory," continued Walt, "that if it's good enough, the public will pay you back for it. I've got a great big building out there full of all kinds of guys who worry about costs and money. You and I just worry about doing a good show!"[68]

Davis's animation in three dimensions seen from moving vehicles was, he said, "creating its own ground rules." He dis-

covered that "it certainly was not a storytelling medium. You could not tell a story and drive by it. But you can give an experience. And when you do it well, [it's] an experience you can't get any other place."[69]

Davis's sketches of ghostly characters and effects in The Haunted Mansion theme park attraction turned horror into fun. Particularly memorable were his stretching portraits—paintings that elongate as the audience rides an elevator to the mansion's basement. "Walt was delighted with those," Davis boasted proudly. In fact, Walt was extremely pleased with just about all that Davis created. Both men respected each other's talents and became quite fond of each other. "I think he liked his creative people tremendously," said Davis, "I think he had a lot of respect for them and still at the same time he had to keep this whole organization together."

Davis noticed a difference in Walt's attitude toward his employees over the years. "I think he became much more considerate. His relationship with people was a great deal easier in later days. But also, in the later days a lot of the struggle was not there either."[70]

Tears once came to Davis's eyes during an interview as he remembered his last meeting with Walt. In November 1966, a couple of weeks after surgery to remove a cancerous lung, Walt dropped by the WED offices in Glendale. For some reason," said Davis, "I like to think he wanted only to see me." He came into Davis's room and sat down. "God, he looked like hell," recalled Davis. "He was so God-damn thin." Shocked, Davis blurted out, "Well, one thing. They sure knocked a hell of a lot of weight off you." Immediately, he was "sorry [he] had said anything." A WED executive came by, but Walt told him, "Now I'm not working. I just want to sit here and talk to Marc."

There was an awkward pause as Davis thought, "Oh God, what do you say to him?" Finally, he showed Walt some drawings of bears for what became (five years later) a Walt Disney World attraction called Country Bear Jamboree. Singling out a bear with a tuba, Walt began to laugh hysterically. Between guffaws, he said that Davis "really had a winner here with these musical bears."[71]

Walt stayed for about twenty minutes looking at Davis's drawings. "He laughed and chuckled. Walt was like a child at Christmas," explained Davis. "As long as you had something to show him—as long as he had another 'present' to unwrap—he was happy."[72] Eventually, more WED executives arrived and took him to see a nearby mock-up for Flight to the Moon, a Tomorrowland attraction. He made a few comments, then turned to no one in particular. "I'm getting kind of tired," he said. "Do you want to take me back to the studio?" Since "there was no lack of offers to do that," said Davis, "I peeled off to go to my room." Walt walked about twenty feet, turned, then growled, "Good-bye, Marc."

Davis stopped in his tracks, overwhelmed with emotion. "He *never* said 'good-bye.' He'd say, 'Take it easy,' 'See you later.'" Three weeks later Walt Disney was dead.[73]

Marc Davis continued consulting and creating conceptual artworks for Walt Disney Imagineering (the renamed WED) for EPCOT at Walt Disney World and Tokyo Disneyland. His retirement in 1978 (after forty-three years at Disney) allowed him more time to travel and to draw. "You can never learn to draw too well. You must learn every day. I still draw everyday!" wrote Davis in 1980 to a fan in Sweden.[74]

In the early 1960s, Marc and Alice Davis became fascinated with the art and culture of Papua New Guinea and bought their first art from that island nation. In 1975 and 1978 the couple traveled to New Guinea and purchased numerous sculptures, paintings, costumes, and carved objets

d'art; more than 250 fierce and beautiful pieces fill their Los Angeles home. The Davises' love of Papuan art, Marc said, started with the "vitality of shape and form. It has an inventiveness of design like no other art in the world." He found it "more interesting" than African art, particularly the carved figures, which contain a vital quality "not far removed," he said, from film animation. "I tell my wife," said Davis, "sometimes at night, if we'll be real quiet, we can hear them dancing. They have a life of their own and many of these things were supposed to embed an ancestral spirit."

Although childless, the Davises developed an international surrogate family over the years made up of devoted friends. The couple's conviviality, sophistication, and good humor attracted people of all ages and life styles. Those lucky enough to have sampled Alice Davis's extraordinary culinary gifts and Marc's magic touch with a cocktail know how even a casual visit could quickly turn into a party. They were also fiercely loyal to their friends; for years their house was a second home to animator Vladimir Tytla and designer Mary Blair whenever they visited Los Angeles.

Marc Davis was always accessible to his fans and admirers, both young and old. For years he and Alice traveled around the globe participating in Disney events, and he was a longtime featured guest at the annual Disneyana Conventions. (He and Alice attended the Orlando convention for a final time together in September 1999.) Sculptures, serigraphs, and limited edition artworks based on characters Davis animated are eagerly snatched up, especially if autographed by the master. In 1992 he received a career salute from the Academy of Motion Picture Arts and Sciences.

But sometimes Marc Davis pondered the road not taken, particularly his early ambition to become a painter. "We studied and wanted to knock Michelangelo on his ass," he told this writer in 1994. Privately he never stopped painting through all his years at Disney. The general public glimpsed one of his works in a 1958 educational short film titled *4 Artists Paint 1 Tree*, taken from a Disneyland TV program. "Disney background artist Art Riley suggested that Marc, along with Eyvind Earle, Josh Meador, and Walt Peregoy go out and paint a magnificent old oak tree at Barham Blvd., near Forest Lawn Drive," wrote Paula Sigman-Lowery. "Art filmed them as they painted. The film, which demonstrated each artist's unique interpretation of the same subject . . . [has subsequently] been shown in art classes and schools around the world."[75]

In 1994, Marc Davis finally attained a longtime dream: he had his first one-man show of paintings at the Howard Lowery Gallery in Burbank, California. In December 1999, at age eighty-five, he enjoyed a second one-man exhibition and sale, this time at the Larry Smith Fine Art Gallery in Hollywood.[76]

Marc and Alice Davis, married for forty-four years, posed with their impressive collection of objets d'art from Papua New Guinea.

A week before Christmas 1999, Marc and Alice Davis joined Frank and Jeanette Thomas, Ollie and Marie Johnston, Joe Grant, and this writer for a dinner arranged by their close friends Howard E. and Amy Boothe Green, coauthors of *Remembering Walt.*[77] The get-together took place at Tam O'Shanter, a roomy steakhouse-bar built in the 1920s near the site of the old Hyperion Avenue studio. In the thirties it was a Disney hangout—a large, comfortable place of wood beams, thick rugs, toasty fireplaces, framed caricatures (by Disney artists), hearty food and drink.

Today's young, friendly staff is solicitous and patient with their mostly older clientele. Using canes and walkers to

ambulate, easing into and out of chairs, and requiring pillows to soften the wooden seats, the elders at the Tam make a slow parade in their entrances and exits.

Once settled, the Davises and the rest of the group enjoyed the holiday conviviality of the place and each other's company. All admired the Christmas decorations and a bauble-filled fir tree, the performers singing carols a cappella dressed in Dickensian costumes, and the tasty viands. Marc ordered a fine merlot and was in good spirits—his witty comments always accompanied by a characteristic short, deep chuckle.

The new year unfortunately brought a rapid downturn in Marc's health; during his hospitalization for a heart problem and excessive water retention, a large ulcer was discovered, as well as the reappearance of the cancer that years before he had battled successfully.

OPPOSITE, TOP, *Two grand old men of Disney: Marc Davis and Joe Grant, who, as of spring 2001, continues to work at Walt Disney Feature Animation as a creative director at age 93!* BOTTOM, 4 Artists Paint 1 Tree, *a short film made for the Disneyland TV program in 1958, showcased paintings by, left to right, Joshua Meador, Marc Davis, Eyvind Earle, and Walt Peregoy.*

While in the hospital, he suffered a stroke the morning of January 12, 2000; later that day he died peacefully, his beloved Alice by his side. He was three months short of his eighty-seventh birthday.

"With Davis's death," wrote his friend Neil Grauer in *The Baltimore Sun*, "the roster of the surviving artists who were animation's Leonardos, Michelangelos, and Raphaels grows even smaller—but his legacy, like that of the great Renaissance masters, endures."[78]

During his long life, Marc Davis, like his footloose father before him, explored many paths, only his were in the field of the arts. His absolute mastery of traditional drawing and painting led him to explore motion graphics and sequential storytelling, which he also mastered. This, in turn, brought him to create stories and characters for three-dimensional environments. Walt's Renaissance man had a profound impact on the many worlds of Disney in films, books, and real settings; his gentle, warm, humanist approach made his creations memorable and enduring.

"The whole thing with creativity," the enormously creative Marc Davis once said, "is [that] there's something new to do out there. Why not give it a try?"

The last group portrait of Walt Disney's Nine Old Men, July 1972:
(back row, left to right), Milt Kahl, Marc Davis, Frank Thomas, Eric Larson, Ollie Johnston;
(front row, left to right), Wolfgang Reitherman, Les Clark, Ward Kimball, John Lounsbery.

Legacy

N early fifteen years after appearing in Bob Thomas's book *The Art of Animation*, the Nine Old Men sat for a second group photograph in July 1972. They hadn't changed much. In their final color portrait before *Robin Hood* storyboards, the animators still look like bland midwestern businessmen posing for a corporate Christmas card.

One unused shot, however, shows a glimpse of their individual personalities and relationships. The photographer, no doubt desperate to inject life into the session, asked the men to assume the cliché position of a Hollywood cinematographer lining up a shot: making a frame with their hands, thumbtips touching. Each of the nine responded in his own way.

Wolfgang Reitherman, smiling broadly in short sleeves, thrusts his hands toward a nearby storyboard, the very picture of a dynamic director; next to him, Les Clark dutifully strikes a similar, more modest, pose; behind him, Ward Kimball, dressed in a pink shirt and electric-blue coat, mischievously aims his "camera" at the back of Clark's head. Milt Kahl sits watching Reitherman with a disgruntled expression, while Kahl's best buddy Marc Davis stands next to him, also staring at Reitherman with a forced smile; neither man gestures. Introspective Eric Larson turns away while wiping his eye, too embarrassed to strike the pose. John Lounsbery also pulls into himself and ignores the request, while smiling at the camera and lighting his pipe. Frank Thomas and Ollie Johnston, next to each other, laugh as both point their fingers in the same direction.

Hinted at in this candid photo are forty years of differences, similarities, antagonisms, loyalties, varying attitudes, and the personal characteristics of each of the Nine Old Men. "They brought a healthy variety of personalities, styles, and strengths to Disney films," writes Steven Watts in *The Magic Kingdom*.[1] "There was a rivalry, always a competition among

the animators that Walt called his Nine Old Men," Marc Davis once admitted. "But the genius of Walt in respect to this was that he kept all these varied personalities working together without killing each other!"[2]

With Walt as a guide, the Nine Old Men worked extremely well together during most of their lengthy tenure. Their collective work is impressive by any accounting, especially for the variety of roles they played and the sheer quality of their animation. As a whole, the animation is outstanding for its inventiveness, brilliant technique, immersion in new emotional territory, expressive intensity, humanity, and wit.

The films involving the Nine Old Men, according to Christopher Finch, provide "matchless examples of character animation. Artists like Milt Kahl, Ollie Johnston, Frank Thomas, and Marc Davis were to animation what Spencer Tracy or Charles Laughton were to screen acting. Ward Kimball was animation's Ernie Kovacs. Eric Larson was not only a superb animator but also as important a teaching figure, in his field, as Lee Strasberg was in his."[3]

The Nine carried forward the high standards of Disney animation forged in the 1930s; they maintained and enhanced them, offering inspiration to future generations. Their "secrets"—techniques, methods, and style—can be learned by studying the films, supplemented by the Thomas and Johnston books, which are so articulate and informative about the principles of Disney animation. These informational sources will always be there for the future.

Also working in today's animation industry are numerous animators and directors who benefited directly from the personal tutelage of the Nine Old Men. These "children" of the Nine have spread their mentors' influence widely. At the Disney studio, for example, there is Glen Keane, the animator who brought Tarzan brilliantly to life (in *Tarzan*, 1999); a quarter century ago he started as a trainee under Eric Larson and later assisted Ollie Johnston. He once wrote Johnston to thank him for "the many, many hours you poured into my life . . . standing behind you looking over your shoulder in our corner room [was] the greatest instruction and learning I have ever had in art. . . . Seeing your simple, clear solutions to my mindboggling drawing problems was revolutionary to me."[4]

To Keane, the Nine Old Men brought to the screen "a complexity of acting," garnered from an "intellectualism" and "a subtlety in the drawing, [which] their acting required. It was something that they were able to dig down deeper into themselves. It was something they got to by study. They really learned how to analyze and observe real life around them and put it into their animation."[5]

"This idea of getting better here at the studio now is so linked to their standards," says Andreas Deja, who began at Disney as a trainee animator in 1980. "I want to get back to these standards and surpass them. I really have those high goals." He believes they can be accomplished "by surrounding one self with all this beautiful work [drawings and scenes of the nine] and setting yourself as high a standard. Just aim there. That's my goal and I won't stop until I die. It's very important to me."[6]

Outside the Disney studio, director (and former Disney trainee) Brad Bird claims that the freshness he achieved in the animation of the acclaimed Warner Bros. feature cartoon *The Iron Giant* (1999) is due to taking "a cue from that Nine Old Men stuff where they each got to do multiple characters."[7]

A significant number of former Disney trainees, who worked with the Nine Old Men, have found success in all areas of animation; among them Dan Haskett and his character designs (for *The Simpsons* and other TV shows and features); Brenda Chapman, one of the directors of DreamWorks' first animated feature *The Prince of Egypt* (1998); Don Bluth, who trained scores of American and European animators for the features *An American Tail* and *The Land Before Time*, among other films; stop-motion director Henry Selick (*Tim Burton's The Nightmare Before Christmas*, 1994 and *James and the Giant Peach*, 1996); and Tim Burton, who has transferred his scary-toon sensibility to live-action features such as *Batman* (1989) and *Sleepy Hollow* (1999).

Richard Williams, director of the animation in *Who Framed Roger Rabbit*, began studying the work of the Nine Old Men in the late 1960s. For years, he brought veteran American animators (including Milt Kahl) to his London studio to lecture; some stayed to work as well, such as Grim Natwick and Art Babbitt. Today, Williams devotes a generous portion of the animation master classes he teaches around the world to the Nine's philosophy and techniques.

"I think their influence is overwhelming," he says. "They did it! They're the ones, who set the standards for everybody—for the medium, and to build on. As a unit they didn't 'invent' the medium. The 'invention' was from the earlier [group]—the Ham Luske, Babbitt, Tytla, Moore, Ferguson, Natwick, [Richard] Huemer [group]. The Nine Old Men were, of course, then the Nine Young Men, who sucked the goodies out of the old men. And took it to a higher level. They mastered the medium and were able to advance it. Generally speaking, they got it all in balance.

"Good art is everything in balance," continues Williams. "The technique is in balance [with] the personality, the drawing, the temporal aspects of it, the coloring, the emotion. And they got it together. So they could just hold you entranced by the scruff of the neck. And make you look. [They] were obviously extremely intelligent men. They're subtler. There's just more mastery of the medium, so they can transcend it. Because they had the medium at their fingertips, they could give the performance.

"Who's to say who's the best violinist?" asks Williams rhetorically. "I'm just grateful for them. I really am. I almost start to weep. What a wonderful thing to know people that good!"[8]

The legacy of the Nine Old Men embraces all techniques and styles, including computer animation. A current example of the adaptability and long-distance endurance of their methods and entertainment philosophy are the computer-generated films of John Lasseter, such as *Toy Story*, *Toy Story 2*, and *A Bug's Life*. "The greatest thing I learned from the Nine Old Men," said Lasseter recently, "is the importance of story and character. Especially from Eric, Frank, and Ollie. They instilled in me the clear knowledge that, above everything, [you have to] make a memorable character. Weave that character into a story that moves you."

Lasseter, a graduate of the animation program at California Institute of the Arts, started as a Disney trainee in 1979. "Frank and Ollie always talked about pathos as something to strive for," recalls Lasseter. "That elevates, you know. You can make something funny, but if you can move the audience with heartfelt emotions, pathos, sadness, that is where you bring it to another level. People really feel for those characters." As they feel sympathy for Buzz Lightyear in *Toy Story* when he discovers he is not an intergalactic superhero, but merely a toy.

"Frank and Ollie didn't want their animation to stand out as great animation. They wanted you to get caught up with the characters," he continued. "The character was alive to you, it just fit perfectly with what was happening in the story. It moved you. You don't remember the animation; you remember the moment in the movie with the character.

"At Cal Arts, we were the last generation to be [personally] nurtured by the Nine Old Men. They helped raise animation from a novelty to an art form. Through memorable characters. You never think of their work as pencil drawings on paper," concludes Lasseter. "You always think of their work as living characters.

"Who will live forever."[9]

NOTES

Introduction

1. Marc Davis, letter to Richard Williams, no date.

2. "Disney Animator Ward Kimball," *The Illustrator*, vol. 64, no. 1, Winter 1977, p. 8.

3. Frank Thomas and Ollie Johnston. *The Illusion of Life: Disney Animation* (New York: Hyperion, 1995), p. 159; Robert D. Graff and Robert Emmett Ginna. *FDR* (New York, Evanston, London: Harper & Row, 1963), p. 130.

4. Thomas and Johnston, *The Illusion of Life*, p. 159.

5. Ibid.

6. *New York Times*, film review of documentary film *Frank and Ollie*, June 20, 1997.

7. The animator was Bob Carlson. Michael Barrier to JC, December 2, 1999.

8. Charles Solomon, "The Last Laugh," *LA Weekly*, July 9–15, 1999, p. 42.

9. Walt said it to journalist–animation historian John Culhane on August 26, 1951; John Culhane to JC, October 6, 1998.

10. John Canemaker, "Sincerely Yours, Frank Thomas," *Millimeter*, January 1975.

Les Clark

1. Les Clark to JC, July 1973; LC to Michael Barrier, December 1, 1973; David R. Smith, "Disney Before Burbank: The Kingswell and Hyperion Studios," *Funnyworld* #20, 1979.

2. Les Clark to JC; Les Clark to Frank Thomas and Ollie Johnston, September 14, 1978.

3. Les Clark to Thomas and Johnston.

4. Les Clark to Michael Barrier.

5. Les Clark to JC.

6. Obituary, Disney Productions, September 14, 1979. Walt Disney Archives.

7. Mickey Clark to JC, December 16, 1998.

8. Ibid.; Miri Clark Weible to JC, January 13, 1999.

9. Mickey Clark to JC.

10. Miri Clark Weible to JC, December 3, 1998.

11. Marceil Clark Ferguson to JC.

12. Mickey Clark to JC.

13. Ibid.

14. Georgia Vester Clark to JC, July, 10, 1998; Miri Clark Weible to JC, January 13, 1999.

15. Mickey Clark to JC.

16. Les offered to pay for college for his brother Mickey, but Mickey refused the offer and got a job on his own at the Disney studio in 1941 in the shipping and receiving department. Mickey Clark worked his way up in the studio accounting department and in 1952 began handling the financial affairs of Walt's private company, Retlaw, Inc.; he retired as a vice president in 1984.

17. Georgia Vester Clark to JC.

18. Les Clark to JC, July 1973.

19. Russell Merritt, J. B. Kaufman. *Walt in Wonderland* (Baltimore: The Johns Hopkins Univerity Press, 1993), pp. 28, 81.

20. See: Michael Barrier. *Hollywood Cartoons* (New York and Oxford: Oxford University Press, 1999).

21. Les Clark to Michael Barrier, December 1, 1973.

22. Walt Disney Archives information sheet by David R. Smith, October 19, 1978.

23. Les Clark to Frank Thomas and Ollie Johnston.

24. Wilfred Jackson to Frank Thomas and Ollie Johnston, May 19, 1978.

25. Wilfred Jackson to Frank Thomas and Ollie Johnston.

26. Les Clark to Christopher Finch and Linda Rosenkrantz, April 24, 1972. Walt Disney Archives.

27. Ibid.

28. David R. Smith, "Ub Iwerks, 1901–1971," *Funnyworld* #14, Spring 1972, p. 35.

29. Les Clark to Christopher Finch and Linda Rosenkrantz.

30. *Variety*, November 21, 1928.

31. Les Clark to Frank Thomas and Ollie Johnston.

32. Les Clark to JC.

33. Les Clark to Frank Thomas and Ollie Johnston.

34. John Culhane to JC, October 6, 1998.

35. Les Clark to Frank Thomas and Ollie Johnston.

36. Les Clark to Christopher Finch and Linda Rosenkrantz.

37. Frank Thomas to JC, March 18, 1998.

38. Les Clark to Frank Thomas and Ollie Johnston.

39. Les Clark to Michael Barrier, December 1, 1973.

40. Les Clark to Frank Thomas and Ollie Johnston.

41. Les Clark to Michael Barrier, August 19, 1976.

42. Ibid.

43. Ibid.

44. Michael Barrier, *Hollywood Cartoons*. p. 88.

45. Les Clark to JC.

46. Les Clark to Michael Barrier.

47. Les Clark to Frank Thomas and Ollie Johnston.

48. Ken Peterson to Frank Thomas and Ollie Johnston, May 21, 1979.

49. Les Clark to Frank Thomas and Ollie Johnston.

50. Ibid.

51. Les Clark to Michael Barrier.

52. Les Clark to JC.

53. Les Clark to Michael Barrier, August 19, 1976.

54. Training Course Lecture, August 17, 1936. Walt Disney Archives.

55. Eugenio Barba and Nicola Savarese. *Dictionary of Theater Anthropology: The Secret Art of the Performer* (London and New York: Routledge, 1991), p. 226.

56. Les Clark to JC.

57. John Culhane to JC, October 6, 1998.

58. Les Clark to Frank Thomas and Ollie Johnston.

59. Les Clark to Michael Barrier, August 19, 1976.

60. Frank Thomas to JC.

61. Erna Englander to JC, July 10, 1998.

62. Frank Thomas to JC.

63. Ibid.

64. Richard became a Hughes Aircraft engineer, flew airplanes, worked on the technology involved in the 1969 moon walk, and invented a gyroscope with parts that do not wear out; he died of pancreatic cancer in 1994.

65. Miri Clark Weible is a fine-art watercolorist, who works out of her studio-gallery, The Miri Weible Fine Art Gallery, in Scottsdale, Arizona.

66. Miriam Lauritzen Clark died in 1989.

67. Les Clark to Michael Barrier, December 1, 1973.

68. Frank Thomas to JC.

69. Ollie Johnston, quoted in Thomas and Johnston, *The Illusion of Life*, p. 168.

70. Thomas and Johnston, *The Illusion of Life*, p. 329.

71. Ollie Johnston to JC, March 19, 1998.

72. John Canemaker, "Art Babbitt: The Animator as Firebrand," *Millimeter*, vol. 3, no. 9, September 1975, pp. 8–12.ff.

73. Richard Williams to JC, June 22, 1998.

74. Ken Peterson to Frank Thomas and Ollie Johnston.

75. Les Clark to Michael Barrier.

76. Frank Thomas to JC.

77. Ken Southworth to JC, August 19, 1998.

78. Frank Thomas to JC.

79. Ibid.

80. Georgia Vester Clark, phone interview with JC, January 29, 1999.

81. His last participation in a feature animation film was *The Rescuers*, released in 1977.

82. Georgia Vester Clark to JC, July 10, 1998.

83. Ibid.

84. Mickey Clark to JC.

85. Les Clark to Frank Thomas and Ollie Johnston.

Wolfgang Reitherman

1. John Culhane, "The Last of the Nine Old Men," *American Film*, June 1977, p. 15.

2. Chuck Champlin, Jr., "The Disney Days of Reitherman," *Los Angeles Times*, August 10, 1981.

3. Wolfgang Reitherman, Army of the United States Separation Qualification Record. I am grateful to Janie Reitherman for this document.

4. Janie Reitherman to JC, July 9, 1998.

5. John Pomeroy to JC, July 6, 1998.

6. Frank Thomas to JC, March 18, 1998.

7. Don Bluth to JC, December 2, 1998.

8. John Pomeroy to JC.

9. Wolfgang Reitherman to Christopher Finch and Linda Rosenkrantz, May 9, 1972.

10. Mica Productions, October 14, 1983. Walt Disney Archives.

11. Janie Reitherman to JC, March 19, 1999.

12. Ibid.

13. Ibid.

14. Ibid.

15. Ibid.

16. Mica Productions.

17. Ibid.

18. Ibid.

19. Personnel File March 21, 1942, Walt Disney Archives; Wolfgang Reitherman to Christopher Finch and Linda Rosenkrantz.

20. Janice Lovoos and Gordon T. McClelland. *Phil Dyke* (Beverly Hills, California: Hillcrest Press, Inc., 1988), p. 61.

21. Wolfgang Reitherman to Christopher Finch and Linda Rosenkrantz.

22. Mica Productions.

23. Notes on Disney—Chouinard Lecture Series, April 28, 1937. Walt Disney Archives.

24. Ibid.

25. Ibid.

26. WR interview by BBC, London 1970. Walt Disney Archives.

27. John Lasseter to JC, November 5, 1999.

28. Ibid.

29. Ollie Johnston to JC, March 19, 1998.

30. Ward Kimball to Steve Hulett, no date. Walt Disney Archives.

31. John Culhane. *Walt Disney's Fantasia* (New York: Harry N. Abrams, Inc., 1983), p. 121.

32. Culhane, *Walt Disney's Fantasia*, p. 123.

33. Ken Peterson to Frank Thomas and Ollie Johnston, May 21, 1979.

34. Mica Productions.

35. Ken Peterson to Frank Thomas and Ollie Johnston.

36. Ibid.

37. Don Bluth to JC, December 2, 1998.

38. Ward Kimball interview, March 20,1968. Walt Disney Archives.

39. Mica Productions, October 14, 1983.

40. Ibid.

41. Janie Reitherman to JC, March 19, 1999.

42. Janie Reitherman to JC, July 9, 1998.

43. Mica Productions.

44. Robert Reitherman was born in 1950 and Bruce in 1955; Bruce was the voice of Mowgli in *The Jungle Book* and Christopher Robin in *Winnie the Pooh and the Honey Tree*.

45. Thomas and Johnston, *The Illusion of Life*, p. 159.

46. WR to F and O January 17, 1979.

47. WR to Mica Prod.

48. Mica Productions.

49. Thomas and Johnston, *The Illusion of Life*, p. 330.

50. Barrier, *Hollywood Cartoons*, p. 550.

51. Ollie Johnston and Frank Thomas. *The Disney Villain* (New York: Hyperion, 1993), p. 112.

52. Andreas Deja to JC, December 18, 1998; see also Betsy Sharkey, "The Heart and Soul of a New Animator," *The New York Times*, May 19, 1996.

53. Charles Solomon, "A Salute to Wolfgang Reitherman," Academy of Motion Picture Arts and Sciences program notes, August 19, 1981.

54. Mica Productions, October 14, 1983.

55. Ibid.; Reitherman appeared in a behind-the-scenes reenactment of the *Lady and the Tramp* dogfight sequence on a Disneyland TV show titled "A Story of Dogs," which aired on December 1, 1954.

56. Mica Productions, October 14, 1983.

57. David R. Smith to JC, January 27, 2000.

58. Barrier, *The Hollywood Cartoon*, p. 567; September 1, 1939, meeting notes, Walt Disney Archives.

59. See "Bill Peet: Master Storyteller" chapter in *Paper Dreams: The Art and Artists of Disney Storyboards* by John Canemaker (New York: Hyperion, 1999), pp. 166–185.

60. Mica Productions.

61. Ibid.

62. Program notes, Los Angeles County Museum of Art—Disney Film Retrospective, July 11–September 27, 1986.

63. Ibid.

64. Christopher Finch. *The Art of Walt Disney* (Harry N. Abrams, 1995), p. 260.

65. James Thurber. *The Thurber Carnival* (New York and London: Harper Brothers, 1945), p. 47.

66. Ward Kimball to JC, March 17, 1998.

67. Janie Reitherman to JC, July 9, 1998.

68. *Burbank Ledger*, May 25, 1985.

69. Mica Productions.

Eric Larson

1. Glen Keane to JC, January 30, 1999.

2. Betsy Baytos to JC, September 14, 1998.

3. Dan Haskett to JC, September 30, 1998.

4. Andreas Deja to JC, December 18, 1998.

5. Mary E. Forgione, "Animated Animator," *The Leader Newspapers*, September 24, 1986; Eric Larson to Michael Barrier, October 27, 1976.

6. Eric Larson to Frank Thomas and Ollie Johnston, March 9, 1977.

7. Glen Keane to JC.

8. Roald O. Larson. "A Biography" [of Eric Larson, undated, unpublished]. Sent to JC, October 1, 1998.

9. Peter Larson to JC, May 20, 1998.

10. Burny Mattinson to JC, December 16, 1998.

11. Mica Productions, 1985.

12. Roald O. Larson, "A Biography."

13. Peter Larson to JC.

14. Ibid.

15. Peter Larson thinks the correspondence course was with the "Landen School of Art."

16. Roald O. Larson, "A Biography."

17. Mica Productions.

18. Roald Larson to JC, February 7, 1999.

19. Mica Productions.

20. Roald O. Larson, "A Biography"; articles and Disney press releases about Larson did not refer to his years at Commercial A&E, making it appear that he came to Los Angeles from Utah to sell a radio script, a notion Larson encouraged.

21. Undated, untitled Salt Lake City newspaper clipping © 1933. Courtesy Roald O. Larson.

22. Ibid.

23. Dorothy Hardy, "Eric Larson Retires from Disney Studios," *Denver Post*, August 1985.

24. Peter Larson to JC; Roald O. Larson to JC, Februry 7, 1999.

25. "A Biography."

26. Mica Productions.

27. Eric Larson to Michael Barrier, October 27, 1976.

28. Eric Larson to Frank Thomas and Ollie Johnston.

29. Eric Larson to Michael Barrier.

30. Eric Larson to Frank Thomas and Ollie Johnston.

31. Eric Larson to Michael Barrier.

32. Ibid.

33. Ward Kimball to JC, March 17, 1998.

34. Ibid.

35. Ibid. Some of the films Larson worked on as Luske's assistant include *Lullaby Land* (1933), *The Night Before Christmas* (1933), and *Funny Little Bunnies* (1934).

36. Eric Larson to Michael Barrier, October 27, 1976.

37. Thomas and Johnston, *The Illusion of Life*, p. 51.

38. Eric Larson to Michael Barrier.

39. Ibid.

40. Ibid.

41. Training Course Lecture, August 19, 1936. Walt Disney Archives.

42. Thomas and Johnston, *The Illusion of Life*, p. 110.

43. "Character Handling" by Ham Luske. October 6, 1938. Walt Disney Archives.

44. Eric Larson to Michael Barrier.

45. Ibid.

46. Ibid.

47. "Analysis and Handling of Animal Characters in *Snow White*," Walt Disney Archives, undated.

48. Eric Larson to Michael Barrier.

49. Ibid.

50. Mica Productions.

51. John Canemaker. *Felix: The Twisted Tale of the World's Most Famous Cat* (New York: Da Capo, 1996), pp. 53–54.

52. Mica Productions.

53. Eric Larson to Michael Barrier.

54. Dan Haskett to JC.

55. Eric Larson to Michael Barrier.

56. Ibid.

57. Ibid.

58. Thomas and Johnston, *The Illusion of Life*, p. 170.

59. Eric Larson to Michael Barrier.

60. Thomas and Johnston, *The Illusion of Life*, p.170.

61. Eric Larson to Michael Barrier.

62. The Aracuan appeared twice more: in the short *Clown of the Jungle* (1947), and in the "Blame It On the Samba," section of the feature-length *Melody Time* (1948).

63. Eric Larson to Thorkil Rasmussen, February 22, 1978. Walt Disney Archives.

64. Eric Larson to Michael Barrier.

65. Mica Productions.

66. Eric Larson to Michael Barrier.

67. Eric Larson to Thorkil Rasmussen.

68. Dale Oliver to JC, August 20, 1998.

69. Ibid.

70. Burny Mattinson to JC.

71. Mica Productions.

72. Burny Mattinson to JC.

73. Eric Larson to Michael Barrier.

74. Burny Mattinson to JC.

75. Eric Larson to Michael Barrier.

76. Ibid.

77. Don Bluth to JC, December 2, 1998.

78. Eric Larson to Howard Green, © 1985/86.

79. Burny Mattinson to JC.

80. Ken Peterson to Frank Thomas and Ollie Johnston, May 21, 1979.

81. John Ewing to JC, April 22, 1999.

82. Roland Crump to JC, April 22, 1999.

83. Dale Oliver to JC.

84. Eric Larson to Howard Green.

85. John Canemaker, "Disney Without Walt," *Print*, Nov./Dec. 1978, pp. 35–43.ff.

86. John Culhane to JC, October 6, 1998.

87. Burny Mattinson to JC.

88. Eric Larson to Thorkil Rasmussen.

89. Eric Larson to Michael Barrier.

90. Canemaker, "Disney Without Walt," p. 39.

91. Glen Keane to JC.

92. Ibid.

93. John Pomeroy to JC, July 6, 1998.

94. Ibid.

95. Eric Larson to Thorkil Rasmussen.

96. Jane Baer to JC, August 19, 1998.

97. Written by Eric Larson April 29, 1978. I am grateful to Roald Larson for making the poem available to me.

98. Betsy Baytos to JC, September 14, 1998.

99. Canemaker, *Disney Without Walt*, p. 37.

100. Jeffrey Varab to JC, July 9, 1998.

101. I am grateful to Roald Larson for Eric Larson's "Soliloquy."

102. John Ewing to JC, April 21, 1999.

103. Charles Solomon, *Enchanted Drawings— The History of Animation* (New York: Knopf), p. 270.

104. Smith, *Disney A to Z*, p. 57.

105. Finch, *The Art of Walt Disney*, p. 271.

106. *The Leader Newspapers*.

107. I am grateful to Roald Larson for "The Newness of Things" written by Eric Larson in November 1976.

Ward Kimball

1. Ward Kimball to JC, July 7, 1973.

2. Interview with Ward Kimball and Marc Davis, March 20, 1968. Walt Disney Archives.

3. John Culhane to JC, October 6, 1998.

4. Steven Watts, *The Magic Kingdom* (Boston, New York: Houghton Mifflin Company), p. 268.

5. Diane Disney Miller, *The Story of Walt Disney* (New York: Henry Holt and Company, 1956), p. 173.

6. Interview February 23, 1978. Walt Disney Archives.

7. Ward Kimball to JC.

8. Ward Kimball to JC, March 17, 1998.

9. A daughter, Irene, was also born to Charles and Helen Kimball, but she died after one year.

10. Ward Kimball to JC.

11. Kelly Kimball to JC, December 16, 1998.

12. Ibid.

13. Ward Kimball to JC.

14. Ibid.

15. Kelly Kimball to JC.

16. Ward Kimball to JC, September 7, 1999.

17. Ward Kimball to JC, March 17, 1998.

18. Ibid.

19. "Disney Animator Ward Kimball," *The Illustrator*, vol. 64, no. 1, Winter 1977, p. 4.

20. Ward Kimball to JC.

21. Ibid.

22. Ibid.

23. *The Illustrator*, pp. 4–5.

24. Ward Kimball to JC.

25. Ward Kimball to Thorkil Rasmussen, February 23, 1978. Walt Disney Archives.

26. Kelly Kimball to JC.

27. *The Illustrator*, p. 5.

28. "Ward Kimball who for the last two years has been the outstanding cartoonist and freehand artist in the high school, won the community scholarship in art, annually awarded to the outstanding art students in the high school graduating class. The scholarship is full-time tuition in the Santa Barbara School of the Arts for one year. He plans to accept the scholarship and attend the school during the next year." Untitled Santa Barbara newspaper, June 1932.

29. *The Illustrator*, p. 6.

30. Ibid.

31. Ward Kimball to JC, January 14, 1999.

32. Ibid.

33. Ward Kimball to Christopher Finch and Linda Rosenkrantz, May 10, 1972.

34. Ward Kimball to JC.

35. Ward Kimball to Christopher Finch and Linda Rosenkrantz.

36. Ward Kimball to JC.

37. Ward Kimball to Christopher Finch and Linda Rosenkrantz.

38. Ibid.

39. Ibid.

40. Ibid.

41. Ibid.

42. Ibid.

43. Ibid.; Ward Kimball to JC.

44. Ward Kimball to Christopher Finch and Linda Rosenkrantz.

45. Ibid.

46. Ward Kimball to JC, March 17, 1998.

47. Ibid.

48. Ward Kimball to Thorkil Rasmussen, February 23, 1978.

49. Ibid.

50. Ken Peterson to Frank Thomas and Ollie Johnston, May 21, 1979.

51. Ibid.

52. Ward Kimball to Christopher Finch and Linda Rosenkrantz.

53. Letter from George Drake to Ward Kimball, June 19, 1935. I am grateful to Pete Docter for bringing this document to my attention.

54. *The Illustrator*, p. 8.

55. Ken Peterson to Frank Thomas and Ollie Johnston.

56. Michael Broggie. *Walt Disney's Railroad Story* (Pasadena: Pentrex, 1997), p. 56.

57. *Walt Disney's Railroad Story*, p. 56.

58. Ward Kimball to JC, July 7, 1973.

59. "Comments on The Cricket" by Ward Kimball, June 17, 1939. Walt Disney Archives.

60. Frank Thomas to JC, March 18, 1998.

61. Ward Kimball to JC, July 7, 1973.

62. Barrier, Michael. *Hollywood Cartoons*, p. 312.

63. Ward Kimball, February 23, 1998. Walt Disney Archives.

64. Ward Kimball transcript, May 25, 1964. Walt Disney Archives.

65. Ward Kimball to Rick Shale, January 29, 1976.

66. Ward Kimball to Steve Hulett, no date.

67. Frank Thomas to JC, March 18, 1998.

68. Ward Kimball to Charles Solomon, August 28, 1986.

69. Ward Kimball to Richard Shale, January 29, 1976.

70. Richard Williams to JC, June 22, 1998.

71. Diane Disney Miller. *The Story of Walt Disney* (New York: Henry Holt and Company, 1957), p. 175.

72. Ibid.

73. Ibid.

74. Leonard Mosley, *Disney's World* (New York: Stein and Day, 1985), p. 216.

75. Steven Watts, *The Magic Kingdom*, p. 266.

76. Ward Kimball to Richard Hubler, May 21, 1968.

77. *Walt Disney's Railroad Story*, p. 77.

78. Mica Productions, July 1, 1984. Walt Disney Archives.

79. Ward Kimball to Richard Hubler.

80. Details on Walt and Ward's trip to the Chicago Railroad Fair can be found in Steven Watts, *The Magic Kingdom*, pp. 266–273; Leonard Mosley, *Disney's World* (New York: Stein and Day, 1985), pp. 216–219; Michael Broggie, *Walt Disney's Railroad Story*, pp.72–79.

81. Leonard Mosley, *Disney's World*, p. 218.

82. Michael Barrier, *Hollywood Cartoons*, p. 396.

83. Kelly Kimball to JC, December 16, 1998.

84. *The Illustrator*, pp. 4–8, 28–30.

85. Milt Kahl to Michael Barrier, November 4, 1976.

86. Richard Williams to JC, June 22, 1998.

87. Ibid.

88. WK to Richard Shale, January 29, 1976. Walt Disney Archives director David R. Smith notes that "Ward really had a very close attachment to Mickey. . . . He was one of the first people to collect Mickey Mouse memorabilia, and he helped bring about a resurgence in interest in the old-style Mickey with the fortieth birthday TV show he produced." David R. Smith, undated note to JC, January 2000.

89. Milt Kahl to Richard Williams, January 2, 1987.

90. John Kimball to JC, December 18, 1998.

91. Ward Kimball to JC, March, 17, 1998.

92. Ward Kimball to JC, July 7, 1973.

93. Ward Kimball, March 20, 1968. Walt Disney Archives.

94. Ward Kimball to JC, July 7, 1973.

95. Ward Kimball to Richard Shale, January 29, 1976.

96. Gregory Solman, "From Mouseketeer to Metro Light," *Millimeter*, October 1996, p. 53.

97. Ward Kimball to JC, January 14, 1997.

98. *The Illustrator*, p. 29.

99. John Kimball to JC.

100. Ward Kimball to JC.

101. Inter-Office Communication from Eric Larson, October 2, 1978. Walt Disney Archives.

102. Ward Kimball to Richard Shale.

103. Ollie Johnston to JC.

104. Don Bluth to JC, December 2, 1998.

105. Sybil Kahl Byrnes to JC, August 26, 1998.

106. Kelly Kimball to JC.

107. John Kimball to JC.

108. Kelly Kimball to JC.

109. Ward Kimball to JC, March 17, 1998.

110. Ward Kimball to Richard Hubler, May 21, 1968.

111. Ward Kimball to Richard Shale.

112. Ward Kimball to Thorkil Rasmussen, February 23, 1978.

113. David R. Smith to JC, July 7, 1973.

114. Ward Kimball to JC.

115. Ward Kimball to Thorkil Rasmussen, February 23, 1978.

116. Marc Davis to Robin Allan, June 11, 1985.

117. Leonard Maltin, *The Disney Films* (New York: Crown Publishers, 1984), p. 195.

118. Ward Kimball to JC.

119. John Kimball to JC.

120. Ward Kimball to JC, July 7, 1973.

121. Ward Kimball to Richard Hubler, May 21, 1968.

122. Ward Kimball to JC, July 7, 1973.

123. Included was the twenty-ton locomotive Emma Nevada, plus an 1881 passenger coach, a 1905 caboose, and an 1890 boxcar, among other items. Kimball may eventually donate the entire railroad, which includes another locomotive, 900 feet of track, a depot filled with antique railroad memorabilia, and a building housing three vintage firefighting vehicles. *Burbank Leader*, November 18, 1992, p. A-5.

124. *The Illustrator*, p. 30.

Milt Kahl

1. Dave Michener, "The Mighty Milt." Undated remembrances. I am grateful to Richard Williams for this material.

2. John Pomeroy to JC, July 6, 1998.

3. John Ewing to JC, April 21, 1999.

4. Don Bluth to JC, December 2, 1998.

5. Mica Productions, November 3, 1983.

6. Milt Kahl to Michael Barrier and Milt Gray, November 4, 1976.

7. Ibid.

8. Julie Kahl to JC, August 1, 1998.

9. Milt Kahl to Michael Barrier and Milt Gray.

10. Richard Williams to JC, June 22, 1998.

11. Ollie Johnston to JC, March 19, 1998.

12. Richard Williams to JC, June 22, 1998

13. Discussion with Milt Kahl, Cal Arts, April 2, 1976. Walt Disney Archives.

14. Ward Kimball to JC, March 17, 1998.

15. Ibid.

16. Frank Thomas to JC, March 18, 1998.

17. Thomas and Johnston, *The Illusion of Life*, p. 173.

18. Iwao Takamoto to JC, November 21, 1998.

19. Richard Williams to JC, June 22, 1998.

20. Stan Green letter to Richard Williams, no date.

21. Andreas Deja to JC, December 18, 1998.

22. John Culhane, "The Last of the Nine Old Men." *American Film*, June 1977, p. 14.

23. Marc Davis, Character Design and Development Lecture, June 29, 1960. Walt Disney Archives.

24. Iwao Takamoto to JC, November 21, 1998.

25. Richard Williams to JC.

26. Andreas Deja to JC.

27. Ollie Johnston to JC, March 19, 1998.

28. Milt Kahl to Robin Allan, June 9, 1985.

29. Richard Williams to JC.

30. Mica Productions. Walt Disney Archives.

31. Julie Kahl to JC, August 1, 1998.

32. Sybil Kahl Byrnes to JC, August 26, 1998; Peter Kahl to JC, September 10, 1998.

33. Sybil Kahl Byrnes to JC.

34. Milt Kahl to Robin Allen, June 9, 1985.

35. Mica Productions.

36. Ibid.

37. Richard Williams to JC.

38. Frank Thomas to JC, March 18, 1998.

39. Milt Kahl to Chistopher Finch and Linda Rosenkrantz, May 18, 1972.

40. Sybil Kahl Byrnes to JC.

41. Milt Kahl to Michael Barrier and Milt Gray.

42. Ibid.

43. Milt Kahl to Richard Williams, January 2, 1987.

44. Milt Kahl, Hollywood Cartoonist Union lectures, no date. Walt Disney Archives.

45. Milt Kahl to Michael Barrier and Milt Gray.

46. Ken Anderson letter to Richard Williams, undated.

47. Ibid.

48. Marc Davis letter to Richard Williams, no date.

49. In the final film, Jiminy Cricket plays the scene; the cricket was not yet a part of Disney's film when Kahl did his test.

50. Ollie Johnston to JC, March 19, 1998.

51. Milt Kahl to Michael Barrier and Milt Gray.

52. Charles Solomon, "An Afternoon with Ollie Johnston, Frank Thomas, and Pinocchio," *Animation World Magazine*, issue 3.4, July 1998.

53. Milt Kahl to Richard Williams, January 2, 1987.

54. Julie Kahl to JC.

55. Character Design and Development lecture, June 29, 1960. Walt Disney Archives.

56. Ibid.

57. "The Mighty Milt."

58. Talent Development Discussion Group on Animal Action, December 20, 1973.

59. Mica Productions.

60. Ollie Johnston to Andreas Deja, September 15, 1987.

61. Ken Anderson letter to Richard Williams.

62. Discussion with Milt Kahl, April 2, 1976.

63. Thomas & Johnston, *The Illusion of Life*, p. 363.

64. Richard Williams to JC.

65. Mica Productions.

66. Frank Thomas to JC.

67. Ibid.

68. Stan Green letter to Richard Williams.

69. Discussion with Milt Kahl, April 2, 1976. Walt Disney Archives.

70. "Mighty Milt."

71. Milt Kahl, Hollywood Cartoonist Union lectures, no date. Walt Disney Archives.

72. Ollie Johnston to Christopher Finch and Linda Rosenkrantz, June 2, 1972.

73. Richard Williams to JC.

74. Don Bluth to JC.

75. Dale Oliver to JC, August 20, 1998.

76. Don Bluth to JC.

77. John Ewing to JC, July 17, 1998.

78. Richard Williams to JC.

79. Ibid.

80. John Ewing to JC.

81. Dale Oliver to JC.

82. Jane Baer to JC, August 19, 1998.

83. John Ewing to JC.

84. Iwao Takamoto to JC, November 21, 1998.

85. Stan Green letter to Richard Williams.

86. Milt Kahl to Richard Williams, January 2, 1987.

87. Mica Productions, November 3, 1983.

88. Milt Kahl to Christopher Finch and Linda Rosenkrantz, May 18, 1972.

89. Frank Thomas to JC

90. Richard Williams to JC.

91. Stan Green letter to Richard Williams, undated.

92. Alice Davis to JC, March 16, 1998.

93. Marc Davis to Richard Williams, undated letter.

94. Andreas Deja to JC.

95. Ward Kimball, however, is the only animator Walt called a genius in print.

96. Richard Williams to JC.

97. Iwao Takamoto to JC.

98. He wasn't.

99. Milt Kahl to Michael Barrier and Milt Gray.

100. Milt Kahl to Bob Thomas, May 14, 1973. Walt's idea was used for the ending of *The Jungle Book*.

101. Milt Kahl to Christopher Finch and Linda Rosenkrantz.

102. John Kimball to JC. John Kimball attributes this story to his father, Ward.

103. Sybil Kahl Byrnes to JC.

104. Peter Kahl to JC, September 10, 1998.

105. Sybil Kahl Byrnes to JC, August 26, 1998.

106. Peter Kahl to JC.

107. Julie Kahl to JC.

108. Ibid.

109. Ken Peterson to Frank Thomas and Ollie Johnston, May 21, 1979.

110. Peter Kahl to JC.

111. Mica Productions, November 3, 1983.

112. Alice Davis to JC, March 16, 1998.

113. Peter Kahl to JC.

114. Phyllis Bounds, born December 22, 1919, was the daughter of Lillian Bounds Disney's brother Wade.

115. The ink and print unit, headed by Phyllis Bounds Detiege, used Xerox "in a much different way than I thought we should use it for a feature," art director Ken Anderson told Milton Gray. "They were making nice, definite, finished, heavy lines and it worked out very well, eliminating the cost of ink and paint." Ken Anderson to Milton Gray December 14, 1976; as Phyllis Bounds, she was a Disney Studio TV commercial coordinator from 1954 to 1957 and a talent scout from 1963 to 1966. She died June 21, 1983, of emphysema. George Hurrell once called her one of the three most beautiful women he ever photographed; the others were Joan Crawford and fashion model Lily Carlson.

116. Peter Kahl to JC.

117. Ibid.

118. Sybil Kahl Byrnes to JC.

119. Ibid.

120. Ibid.

121. Richard Williams to JC.

122. Jane Baer to JC, August 19, 1998.

123. Peter Kahl to JC.

124. Ibid.

125. Don Bluth to JC, December 2, 1998.

126. Ollie Johnston to JC, March 19, 1998.

127. Andreas Deja to JC.

128. Ollie Johnston to Andreas Deja, September 15, 1987.

129. Brad Bird to JC, May 21, 1999.

130. Discussion with Milt Kahl, April 2, 1976. Walt Disney Archives.

131. Frank Thomas to JC.

132. Milt Kahl to Michael Barrier and Milt Gray.

133. Ibid.

134. Frank Thomas to JC.

135. Eric Cleworth phone conversation with Richard Williams, 1990.

136. Milt Kahl to Michael Barrier and Milt Gray.

137. "Milt Kahl of Greenbrae animated classic Disney films," *San Rafael Independent*, June 17, 1979.

138. Julie Kahl to JC, August 1, 1998.

139. Sybil Kahl Byrnes to JC, August 26, 1998.

140. Richard Williams to JC.

141. Ken Anderson to Richard Williams.

142. Milt Kahl to Richard Williams, January 2, 1987.

143. Milt Kahl. Hollywood Union AFL-CIO/IATSE Local 839 Lecture #3. March 16, 1977. Text courtesy of Richard Williams.

Frank Thomas

1. Olivier, Laurence. *Laurence Olivier On Acting*. (New York: Simon and Schuster, 1986), p. 29.

2. *Frank and Ollie* documentary film transcript, March 1993. I am grateful to Theodore Thomas and Kuniko Okubo for access to unedited material from their fine documentary film and allowing me to publish it.

3. Andreas Deja to JC, December 12, 1998.

4. Interview with Frank Thomas, Zagreb Animation Festival, June 1974. Walt Disney Archives.

5. Dale Oliver to JC, December 19, 1998.

6. Thomas and Johnston, *The Illusion of Life*, p. 174.

7. Dale Oliver to JC, December 19, 1998.

8. Ibid. August 20, 1998. Dale Oliver attributes the comment to Blaine Gibson.

9. John Pomeroy to JC, July 6, 1998.

10. Theodore Thomas to JC, June 29, 1999.

11. Don Bluth to JC, December 2, 1998.

12. Frank Thomas to JC, March 18, 1998. All biographical information is from this interview unless otherwise noted.

13. Theodore Thomas to JC, June 29, 1999.

14. Mica Productions, April 3, 1985.

15. Theodore Thomas to JC.

16. Frank Thomas to JC.

17. Theodore Thomas to JC.

18. Ollie Johnston to JC, March 19, 1998.

19. *Frank and Ollie* film transcript, August 7, 1992.

20. *Frank and Ollie* film transcript, March 1993.

21. Thor Putnam to JC, November 4, 1998.

22. *Frank and Ollie* film transcript, March 1993.

23. Thor Putnam to JC.

24. James Algar to Robin Allan and William Moritz, June 8, 1985.

25. Thor Putnam eventually became a top layout man. His work includes "A Night on Bald Mountain" section in *Fantasia*.

26. *Frank and Ollie* film transcript, August 5, 1992.

27. "Complete History of Frank Thomas," April 5, 1981. Walt Disney Archives.

28. Frank Thomas to JC.

29. Mica Productions, April 25, 1985.

30. Frank Thomas to Bob Thomas, May 10, 1973.

31. Frank Thomas animation lecture #1. AFL-CIO/IATSE Local 839, Summer 1978. Walt Disney Archives.

32. Frank Thomas to JC.

33. Frank Thomas to Christopher Finch, May 17, 1972.

34. Thomas and Johnston, *The Illusion of Life*, pp. 475–477.

35. Frank Thomas to JC, July 1973.

36. Frank Thomas to Christopher Finch.

37. Glen Keane to JC, January 30, 1999.

38. Ollie Johnston to JC, March 19, 1998.

39. Frank Thomas to Christopher Finch.

40. Ollie Johnston and Frank Thomas. *Walt Disney's* Bambi. *The Story and the Film* (New York: Stewart, Tabori & Chang), p. 143.

41. Ibid, p. 161.

42. Frank Thomas to Göran Broling, May 8, 1996. I am grateful to Mr. Broling for allowing me to quote from this letter.

43. Ibid.

44. Frank Thomas to JC, March 18, 1998.

45. Ibid.

46. *Frank and Ollie* film transcript, March 30, 1993.

47. Mica Productions, April 3, 1985.

48. Johnston and Thomas, *Walt Disney's Bambi*, pp. 182–183.

49. Ibid, p. 183.

50. Frank Thomas to Bob Thomas, May 10, 1973.

51. *Frank and Ollie* film transcript, August 5, 1992.

52. Frank Thomas to JC, March 18, 1998.

53. Mica productions, April 3, 1985.

54. Frank Thomas to Christopher Finch and Linda Rosenkrantz, May 17, 1972.

55. Ibid.

56. Mica Productions, April 5, 1985.

57. Frank Thomas to JC, July 1973.

58. Ibid.

59. Mica Productions.

60. *Thoughts & Memories #1*, by Frank Thomas. December 6, 1976. Walt Disney Archives.

61. *Frank and Ollie* film transcript, August 5, 1992.

62. Ibid.

63. John Pomeroy to JC, July 6, 1998.

64. Mica Productions.

65. Glen Keane to JC, January 30, 1999.

66. LG interview with Frank Thomas: Zagreb Animation Festival, June 1974.

67. Ibid.

68. Theodore Thomas to JC.

69. John Culhane to JC, October 6, 1998.

70. Marc Davis to JC, March 16, 1998.

71. Milt Kahl to Michael Barrier and Milt Gray, November 4, 1976.

72. *Frank and Ollie* film transcript, August 7, 1992.

73. Bob Thomas, *The Art of Animation* (New York: Simon and Schuster, 1958), p. 37.

74. Mica Productions.

75. Dale Oliver to JC, August 20, 1998.

76. Eyvind Earle, *Horizon Bound on a Bicycle* (Los Angeles: Earle and Bane, 1990), p. 239.

77. Dan Haskett to JC, September 30, 1998.

78. Ibid.

79. Frank Thomas to Bob Thomas, May 10, 1973.

80. Theodore Thomas to JC.

81. Frank Thomas to Christopher Finch.

82. Theodore Thomas to JC.

83. Jeanette Thomas, *Frank and Ollie* film transcript, March 1993.

84. Frank Thomas, *Frank and Ollie* film transcript, March 1993.

85. Mica Productions.

86. *Frank and Ollie* film transcript, August 6, 1992.

87. Ibid.

88. *Frank and Ollie* film transcript, March 28, 1993.

89. Frank Thomas to JC, November 3, 1988.

90. Frank Thomas letter to Larry Ruppel, November 27, 1973. I am grateful to Mr. Ruppel for allowing me to quote from these letters.

91. Ibid, August 2, 1981.

92. Christopher Finch, *The Art of Walt Disney* (New York: Harry N. Abrams, 1995), p. 264.

93. "The Men Who Made Pinocchio Come Alive," by Stephen Holden. *The New York Times*, June 20, 1997.

94. *Frank and Ollie* film transcript, March 28, 1993.

Ollie Johnston

1. Mica Productions transcript, 1985. Walt Disney Archives.

2. John Culhane, "The Last of the Nine Old Men," *American Film*, June 1977, p. 15.

3. Andreas Deja to JC, December 18, 1998.

4. Glen Keane to JC, January 30, 1999.

5. Ollie Johnston to JC, March 19, 1998; notes by Ollie Johnston given to JC, July 24, 1998. All biographical information is from these sources unless otherwise noted.

6. Frank Thomas to JC, March 18, 1998.

7. Ibid.

8. Ibid.

9. *Frank and Ollie* film transcript, March 1993.

10. Ollie Johnston and Frank Thomas. *Walt Disney's* Bambi, p. 144.

11. A Discussion with Ollie Johnston, February 1978, California School of the Arts.

12. John Canemaker. "Vladimir Tytla: Master Animator." Katonah Museum of Art, Katonah, N.Y. exhibit and brochure, September 18–December 31, 1994.

13. Ollie Johnston to Christopher Finch/Linda Rosenkrantz, June 2, 1972.

14. *Frank and Ollie* film transcript, August 5, 1992.

15. Richard (Rick) O. Johnston, a musician, wrote (with Stan Fidel) the song "Best of Friends" in *The Fox and the Hound*.

16. Johnston and Thomas, *Walt Disney's* Bambi, p. 144.

17. Ollie Johnston to Christopher Finch.

18. Richard Shale. *Donald Duck Joins Up* (Ann Arbor: UMI Research Press, 1982), p. 64.

19. Ollie Johnston to Mike Lyons, November 18, 1994.

20. *Frank and Ollie* film transcript, August 4, 1992.

21. Mica Productions, August 4, 1985.

22. Ibid.

23. *Frank and Ollie* film transcript, March 1993.

24. Ollie Johnston to Bob Thomas, May 17, 1973.

25. Broggie, *Walt Disney's Railroad Story*, p. 100.

26. Jake Grubb, "Ollie Johnston—Man With a Dream," *Senior Life*, June/July 1978, pp. 30, 35, 62.

27. John Lasseter to JC, November 5, 1999.

28. A Discussion with Ollie Johnston, February 1978. Walt Disney Archives.

29. Mica Productions.

30. Andreas Deja to JC.

31. *Storyboard/The Art of Laughter*, vol. 4, #1, February/March 1993, p. 9.

32. Ollie Johnston to Christopher Finch and Linda Rosenkrantz, June 2, 1972.

33. Certificate of Death, Registration District #1917, Registrar's #465. I am grateful to Albert Miller for obtaining this document. Ollie Johnston claims that, according to a rumor, Moore, who always "had to get home," left the hospital without permission and died at his own house.

34. Frank Thomas phone interview with JC, February 19, 1999.

35. Ollie Johnston to JC, October 19, 1999.

36. Fred Moore file, Walt Disney Archives.

37. Mica Productions.

38. Ibid.

39. *Frank and Ollie* film transcript, August 5, 1992.

40. Ollie Johnston to Chrisopher Finch.

41. Frank Thomas, letter to Larry Ruppel, July 26, 1976.

42. Ollie Johnston to Bob Thomas, September 27, 1976.

43. Dale Oliver to JC, August 20, 1998.

44. John Lasseter to JC, November 5, 1999.

45. Ken Johnston to JC, September 21, 1999.

46. Ollie Johnston to JC, March 19, 1998.

John Lounsbery

1. Ed Hansen to JC, March 1, 1999.

2. Don Bluth to JC, December 2, 1998.

3. Ken Peterson to Frank Thomas and Ollie Johnston, May 21, 1979; Frank Thomas to JC, March 18, 1998.

4. John Ewing to JC, July 17, 1998.

5. Glen Keane to JC, January 30, 1999.

6. "Thoughts on John Lounsbery by Some of His Friends at Disney," February 1976. I am grateful to Andrea H. (Lounsbery) Gessell, daughter of John Lounsbery, for this document.

7. John Ewing to JC.

8. Richard Williams to JC, June 22, 1998.

9. Dale Baer to JC, October 13, 1999.

10. John Pomeroy to JC, July 6, 1998.

11. Florence (Lounsbery) Shaw letter to JC, November 15, 1999.

12. Florence (Lounsbery) Shaw interview with JC, June 1, 1998.

13. Paul Van Name, "A Tribute to Walt Disney Productions," USC—Delta Kappa Alpha's 39th Annual Award Banquet brochure, April 9, 1978.

14. Notes from Ken Lounsbery's eulogy for his father, February 1976. Collection of Andrea H. (Lounsbery) Gessell.

15. "John Lounsbery Biography." Walt Disney

Productions, May 9, 1974. Both Mary Lounsbery and her son Art would also die of heart attacks; Charles was killed as a young man in a hiking accident climbing Pike's Peak.

16. Notes from Ken Lounsbery's eulogy.

17. Ken Lounsbery thinks his father may have worked his way west as a railroad pole setter. Florence (Lounsbery) Shaw to JC, November 15, 1999.

18. "Thoughts on John Lounsbery by Some of His Friends at Disney, February 1976. Collection of Andrea H. (Lounsbery) Gessell.

19. Florence (Lounsbery) Shaw to JC.

20. Mel Shaw to JC, January 31, 1999.

21. John Lounsbery Biography, Walt Disney Archives; John Lounsbery to John Culhane, April 22, 1971.

22. John Lounsbery to John Culhane.

23. Thomas and Johnston, *The Illusion of Life*, p. 105.

24. Don Graham, "Animation—Art Acquires a New Dimension," *American Artist*, December 1940, pp. 10–12.

25. Thomas & Johnston, *The Illusion of Life*, p. 99.

26. John Lounsbery to John Culhane, April 22, 1971.

27. Andreas Deja to JC, December 18, 1998.

28. Ken Peterson to Frank Thomas and Ollie Johnston, May 21, 1979.

29. Ollie Johnston and Frank Thomas. *The Disney Villain* (New York: Hyperion, 1993), p. 56.

30. Moroni Olsen was also the voice of the Magic Mirror in *Snow White*.

31. List dated June 15, 1938, "scenes under Ferguson's supervision." Walt Disney Archives.

32. John Culhane to JC, October 7, 1999.

33. WDP Inter-Office Communication May 3, 1938. Walt Disney Archives.

34. *The Disney Villain*, p. 62.

35. Ibid, pp. 62–62.

36. Culhane, John. Walt Disney's *Fantasia* (New York: Harry N. Abrams, 1983), p. 178.

37. Robert Baral, "Baronova as Mlle. Upanova," *The American Dancer*, January 1941.

38. Lincoln Kirstein, "Mickey Mouse Joins the Ballet," *Dance*, vol. 8, #5, December 1940, pp. 15, 32.

39. Robert D. Feild. *The Art of Walt Disney* (New York: The Macmillan Company, 1942), pp. 246–247.

40. Feild, *The Art of Walt Disney*, p. 247.

41. Culhane, *Walt Disney's Fantasia*, p. 170.

42. Frank Thomas to JC, March 18, 1998.

43. John Lounsbery to John Culhane, April 22, 1971.

44. Ibid.

45. Steven Watts, *The Magic Kingdom* (Boston/New York: Houghton Mifflin Company, 1997), p. 139.

46. Shamus Culhane, *Talking Animals and Other People* (New York: St. Martin's Press, 1986), p. 351.

47. Ollie Johnston to JC, March 19, 1998.

48. Frank Thomas to JC.

49. Frank Thomas to JC, March 18, 1998.

50. "John M. Lounsbery—Thoughts from his daughter, Andrea" by Andrea (Lounsbery) Gessell to JC, June 11, 1998. All personal information is from this document unless otherwise noted.

51. Florence Shaw to JC.

52. John Pomeroy to JC, July 6, 1998.

53. Glen Keane to JC, January 30, 1999.

54. *Disney Animation*, p. 176.

55. Phil Mendez letter to *The Pegboard*, Local 839 IATSE newsletter, undated copy, 1976.

56. *Disney Animation*, p. 109.

57. John Pomeroy to JC.

58. Andreas Deja to JC.

59. Richard Williams to JC, June 22, 1998.

60. Mel Shaw to JC, November 15, 1999.

61. Dale Baer to JC, October 13, 1999.

62. Richard Williams to JC.

63. Mel Shaw to JC, November 15, 1999.

64. John Ewing to JC, July 17, 1998.

65. Don Bluth to JC, December 2, 1998.

66. John Ewing.

67. Ibid.

68. Ibid.

69. John Pomeroy to JC.

70. Frank Thomas to JC.

71. John Lounsbery to John Culhane.

72. Frank Thomas to Larry Ruppel, March 11, 1976.

73. John Lounsbery to John Culhane.

74. Don Bluth to JC.

Marc Davis

1. WED is now Walt Disney Imagineering.

2. Dave Smith. *Disney A to Z* (New York: Hyperion, 1996), p. 389.

3. Alice Davis to JC, March 16, 1998; January 7, 1995.

4. Milt Kahl to Robin Allan, June 9, 1985.

5. Ollie Johnston and Frank Thomas. *Bambi: The Story and the Film*, p. 125.

6. "Two Disney Artists." *Crimmer's: The Harvard Journal of Pictorial Fiction*, p. 40.

7. Paula Sigman-Lowery. "Portrait of an Artist. The Life and Art of Marc Davis." Exhibition catalogue. Howard Lowery Gallery 1993, p. 3.

8. Alice Davis to JC, March 16, 1998.

9. Marc Davis to John Canemaker, March 16, 1998; phone interview October 22, 1999. All biographical information is from these two interviews unless otherwise noted.

10. Marc Davis to JC, January 7, 1997.

11. Marc Davis to Paula Sigman-Lowery, p. 3.

12. Ibid, p. 4.

13. Marc Davis to Paula Sigman-Lowery.

14. "Historical Perspective" by Charles Solomon. *Animation Magazine*, Summer 1992, pp. 31–33.

15. Marc Davis to Robin Allan, July 27, 1990.

16. Marc Davis to Paula Sigman-Lowery.

17. "Staging Humor and Comedy," Chouniard Art School Animation Class, May 27, 1960.

18. Marc Davis to Richard Hubler, May 21, 1968.

19. Mica Productions, November 3, 1983.

20. Marc Davis to Paula Sigman-Lowery.

21. "Grim Natwick" by John Canemaker. *Film Comment*, January/February 1975, pp. 57–61.

22. Ibid, p. 59.

23. Michael Barrier, *Hollywood Cartoons* (New York, Oxford: Oxford University Press, 1999), p. 193.

24. Ibid, pp. 193–194.

25. Ibid, p. 194.

26. Ibid.

27. Ibid. p. 199.

28. Marc Davis to JC.

29. "Two Disney Artists." *Crimmer's: The Harvard Journal of Pictorial* , pp. 40–41.

30. Marc Davis to JC.

31. *Film Comment*, p. 59.

32. *Hollywood Cartoons*, p. 198.

33. "Animation by Grim Natwick." *Cartoonist Profiles*, #43, September 1979, pp. 26–31.

34. Marc Davis to JC.

35. Marc Davis to JC, January 7, 1995.

36. Charles Solomon, "Historical Perspective."

37. *Walt Disney's* Bambi, p. 125.

38. Marc Davis to Mica Productions, October 4, 1985

39. Johnston and Thomas, Walt Disney's *Bambi*, p. 125.

40. Marc Davis to Bob Thomas, May 25, 1973.

41. *Storyboard/The Art of Laughter*, December/January 1991–91, pp. 16-20ff.

42. Marc Davis to Bob Thomas.

43. Ibid.

44. "Animation" by Grim Natwick.

45. Marc Davis to Robin Allan, June 11, 1985.

46. Alice Davis to JC.

47. Marc Davis to JC.

48. Marc Davis to Frank Thomas and Ollie Johnston, January 18, 1979.

49. Frank Thomas to JC.

50. *Storyboard/The Art of Laughter*.

51. "Historical Perspective" by Charles Solomon.

52. Marc Davis to Mica Productions.

53. "Two Disney Artists," p. 38.

54. "Character Design and Development" lecture, June 29, 1960.

55. Obituary, *Boston Herald*, January 16, 1999.

56. "That Old Black Magic" by Jamie Simons. *The Disney Channel Magazine*, April/May 1993.

57. Historical Perspective" by Charles Solomon.

58. Barrier, *Hollywood Cartoons*, p. 567.

59. Andreas Deja to JC.

60. "Character Design & Development."

61. Some of Marc Davis's drawings were published in *Chanticleer and the Fox*, a 1991 children's book by Disney Press.

62. Marc Davis to Bob Thomas, May 25, 1973; *Storyboard/The Art of Laughter*.

63. Smith, *Disney A to Z*, pp. 332–333.

64. Ibid, p. 535.

65. Thomas, *Walt Disney—An American Original*, p. 312.

66. *Walt Disney Imagineering* (New York: Hyperion, 1996), p. 52.

67. Ibid, p. 91.

68. Marc Davis to Bob Thomas.

69. Ibid.

70. Marc Davis to Richard Hubler.

71. *Walt Disney Imagineering*, p. 48.

72. Marc Davis to Mike Lyons, March 27, 1998.

73. Ibid. Marc Davis to Richard Hubler, May 21, 1968.

74. Marc Davis to Göran Broling, September 17, 1980.

75. "The Art of Marc Davis," an exhibition at Howard Lowery Gallery, Burbank, California, December 15, 1993–98 January 1994, "Portrait of an Artist." Catalog notes by Paula Sigman-Lowery.

76. Opening reception December 2, 1999.

77. Amy Boothe Green and Howard E. Green. *Remembering Walt* (New York: Hyperion, 1999); Howard E. Green is also a key figure of the Disney motion-picture publicity and marketing team and vice president of studio communications. Amy Boothe Green is a freelance writer for publications such as *Los Angeles Magazine*, *Disney Magazine*, and *The Disney Channel* magazine.

78. Neil Grauer, "Disney artist drew map for modern animators," *The Baltimore Sun*, January 26, 2000.

Legacy

1. Steven Watts, *The Magic Kingdom* (Boston, New York: Houghton Mifflin Company, 1997), p. 267.

2. Marc Davis to John Culhane, no date.

3. Finch, *The Art of Walt Disney*, p. 265.

4. Glen Keane to Ollie Johnston, April 2, 1985.

5. Glen Keane to JC, January 30, 1999.

6. Andreas Deja to JC, December 18, 1998.

7. Brad Bird to JC, May 21, 1999.

8. Richard Williams to JC, June 22, 1998; Richard Williams' Animation Masterclass, P. O. Box 15, Tenby, Pembrokeshire, UK SA70 7WH, United Kingdom.

9. John Lasseter to JC, November 5, 1999.

Page numbers in italics refer to illustrations

ACKNOWLEDGMENTS

When this project began early in 1998, I flew to Los Angeles to meet with master animators Marc Davis, Ward Kimball, Ollie Johnston, and Frank Thomas, the four surviving members of Walt Disney's Nine Old Men. I had known and interviewed them many times over the years; but now I was privileged to spend an entire day with each gentleman and ask probing questions about their childhoods and family backgrounds, earliest work experiences, relationships with colleagues and Walt Disney, and their personal philosophies regarding the art of animation. Each artist patiently and candidly provided me with new and detailed information. I owe a great debt of gratitude to Marc (who has since passed away), Ward, Ollie, and Frank, and to their wives: Alice Davis, Betty Kimball, Marie Johnston, and Jeanette Thomas. Their confidence in me was very reassuring and gave the whole venture a positive liftoff. I thank them, and also family members Theodore Thomas, Kuniko Okubo Thomas, and Ken Johnston, for their enthusiastic support and for the interviews, letters, family photographs, drawings, and remembrances they so generously shared. In my subsequent research into the lives and work of the other five of the Nine Old Men—Les Clark, Milt Kahl, Eric Larson, John Lounsbery, Wolfgang Reitherman—I received equally solid and generous help from their families. I am sincerely thankful to Janie Reitherman, Kelly Kimball, John Kimball, Julie Kahl, Sybil Kahl Byrnes, Peter Kahl, Mickey Clark, Georgia Clark, Marceil Clark Ferguson, Miriam Clark Wible, Roald Larson, Peter Larson, Bland Larson, Andrea H. Lounsbery Gessell, Ken Lounsbery, and Florence and Mel Shaw.

At the Walt Disney Studios, I was allowed full access to data and artwork thanks to Roy Disney, Chairman, Feature Animation; Peter Schneider, Chairman, Walt Disney Studios; Thomas Schumacher, President, Walt Disney Feature Animation; and Martin A. Sklar, Vice Chairman and Principal Creative Executive, Walt Disney Imagineering.

For nearly thirty years I have relied on the Walt Disney Archives, a unique informational resource for all things Disney. Once again, Archives founder David R. Smith and manager Robert Tieman proved to be extraordinarily knowledgeable and helpful; they, along with Becky Cline and Collette Espino, tirelessly supported my insatiable research needs. Dave and Robert also generously volunteered to comb the manuscript for factual errors and made numerous helpful suggestions.

I consider everyone at the Archives a friend, as I do the team at the Walt Disney Animation Research Library, a treasure trove of original artwork from the films. None of my endless requests to view scores of folders of original animation drawings from dozens of films proved daunting to Lella Smith, director of the ARL, or to senior researcher Laurence Ishino, who knows the fabulous ARL collection like no one else. Even the most obscure items were cheerfully searched for—and found. In addition, Lella arranged for high-quality reproductions of the selected artworks by Vivian Procopio, Fox Carney, Doug Engalla, Tamara N. Khalaf, and Ann Hansen, as well as computer scanning by Patrick White of family photographs of the Nine Old Men. This is my third book project working with the fine crew at the ARL, and once again they turned what could have been an overwhelming task into an exceedingly pleasant experience. As did Ed Squair at the Walt Disney Photo Library, who again enthusiastically found the rare, the unusual, and the never-before- or rarely published photograph, negative, film frame, and still; his tireless diligence and imagination contributed greatly to this book. I am deeply grateful for the support of several colleagues who are renowned animation historians and distinguished authors. Charles Solomon, Michael Barrier, Robin Allan, Michael Lyons, William Moritz, Howard and Amy Green, Jeff Kurtti, and John Culhane allowed me to mine their vast knowledge of the subject through formal interviews or conversations, and all generously delved into their private files to unearth rare transcripts and audiotapes of interviews with the Nine Old Men and several of their peers.

For numerous personal kindnesses as well as for sharing of a variety of animation materials, I am thankful to Howard and Paula Lowery, Albert Miller, Pierre Lambert, Göran Broling, Neil A. Grauer, and Les V. Perkins. I wish to thank three fine contemporary animators who went to great lengths to aid me, including Richard Williams, who sent me extensive material for a book he is planning on Milt Kahl and also gave me a candid interview; Larry Ruppel, who allowed me access to his extensive correspondence with Frank Thomas; and Andreas Deja, who cogently discussed the art of each of the Nine Old Men and selected and reproduced in color numerous sequential drawings from his spectacular personal collection.

A number of people who worked with the Nine Old Men and/or were personally close to them gladly took the time to correspond or sit for an interview (or two), including Thor Putnam, Bernie Mattinson, Joe Grant, Dale Oliver, John Pomeroy, Roland Crump, Dale Baer, Jane Baer, Carl Bell, Ron Husband, Volus Jones, Ken Southworth, Don Bluth, Mary Bosocca, Betsy Baytos, Ed Hansen, Dan Haskett, Iwao Takamoto, Glen Keane, Neil Richmond, Tiger West, Joe Ranft, John Ewing, Mark Mitchell, Pete Docter, and John Lasseter.

For various courtesies and kindnesses, I wish to thank Ed Oboza, Sylvia Fitzpatrick, Tim O'Day, Mike Guerino, Grace Simpson, Julia Keydel, Eugene Salandra, Jeffrey Lane, Eleanor Kolchin, Peter Weishar, Mark Mitchell, Sam Ewing, Peter Staller, Jonathan Annand, Charles Kimbrough, Beth Howland, and Holly Howland. Disney publisher Ken Shue came up with the idea for this book, and I appreciate his support. At Disney Editions, I was fortunate to work with the following top professionals: Jody Revenson, Duryan Bhagat, Janet Castiglione, Sara Baysinger, Cindy Tamasi, Christopher Caines, and Richard Thomas. Robert Cornfield, my literary agent, continues to be an enthusiastic guide and friend.

This is my third book designed by the brilliant and essential Holly McNeely; her artistic sensibilities and instinct for making animation live on the page are extraordinary.

It was a great pleasure to work again with Wendy Lefkon, my warm and supportive editor. A total pro, Wendy always goes the extra mile to make sure everything backing me up is solid. I trust her completely and rely on her unfailing ability to make me laugh. She makes the most daunting project fun.

Last but never least, this book is the better for my partner Joe Kennedy's constant companionship, loving support, and advice.

John Canemaker is an internationally recognized animator and animation historian. He designed and directed animation sequences in the Peabody Award–winning CBS documentary *Break the Silence: Kids Against Child Abuse*, and the Academy Award–winning HBO documentary *You Don't Have to Die*. His award-winning short animated films, which include *Bridgehampton, Confessions of a Stardreamer, Confessions of a Stand-Up, Bottom's Dream*, and *John Lennon Sketchbook*, are part of the permanent film collection of the Museum of Modern Art.

He is the author of seven acclaimed books on animation history, including *Paper Dreams: The Art and Artists of Disney Storyboards* (Hyperion); *Before the Animation Begins: The Art and Lives of Disney Inspirational Sketch Artists* (Hyperion); *Felix: The Twisted Tale of the World's Most Famous Cat* (Da Capo); *Winsor McCay: His Life and Art* (Abbeville); *The Animated Raggedy Ann & Andy* (Bobbs-Merrill); and *Treasures of Disney Animation Art* (Abbeville). He has written more than a hundred essays, reviews, and articles on animation for periodicals, such as *The New York Times, The Los Angeles Times*, and *Time* and *Print* magazines. His cartoons illustrate the children's book *Lucy Goes to the Country* (Alyson Wonderland).

Canemaker is a tenured professor and director of the animation program at New York University's Tisch School of the Arts. The John Canemaker Animation Collection, part of the Fales Collection in Bobst Library at New York University, is an archival resource on animation history that opened to scholars and students in 1989. Canemaker has lectured on the art and artists of animation throughout the United States and in Brazil, Canada, England, France, Italy, Japan, Slovakia, Spain, Switzerland, and Wales. He divides his time between Manhattan and Bridgehampton, Long Island.

3.02